THE FEDERAL COURTS AS A POLITICAL SYSTEM

Third Edition

SHELDON GOLDMAN
University of Massachusetts

THOMAS P. JAHNIGE
Late, Smith College

HARPER & ROW, PUBLISHERS, New York
Cambridge, Philadelphia, San Francisco,
London, Mexico City, São Paulo, Singapore, Sydney

1817

For Gertrude and Harry Liebeskind

Sponsoring Editor: *Marianne J. Russell*
Project Editor: *Susan Goldfarb*
Cover Design: *Wanda Lubelska*
Text Art: *Vantage Art, Inc.*
Production: *Marion Palen / Delia Tedoff*
Compositor: *ComCom Division of Haddon Craftsmen, Inc.*
Printer and Binder: *R. R. Donnelley & Sons Company*

The Federal Courts as a Political System, Third Edition
Copyright © 1985 by Sheldon Goldman and the Estate of Thomas P. Jahnige.

All rights reserved. Printed in the United States of America. No part of this book may be used or reproduced in any manner whatsoever without written permission, except in the case of brief quotations embodied in critical articles and reviews. For information address Harper & Row, Publishers, Inc., 10 East 53d Street, New York, NY 10022.

Library of Congress Cataloging in Publication Data

Goldman, Sheldon.
   The federal courts as a political system.

   Includes bibliographies and index.
   1. Courts—United States. 2. Law and politics.
I. Jahnige, Thomas P. II. Title.
KF8700.Z9G63   1985   347.73′202   84-25271
ISBN 0-06-042376-6   347.30712

84 85 86 87 9 8 7 6 5 4 3 2 1

KF
8700
.29
.G64
1985

Contents

Preface

The objective of the third edition has been to bring this book up to date in terms of the workings of the federal judicial system and to integrate within its framework much of the important research in the field appearing in the nine years since the second edition was published. It is a testament to the intellectual vigor of the field of politics and the judicial process that there has been so much literature to review, and I must apologize in advance and assume full responsibility, not only for any errors of fact or interpretation that may be found but also for any omissions in citations of significant work.

This edition would not have been possible without the help of those acknowledged in the prefaces to the first and second editions. Additionally, I would like to thank Professors Milton Heumann, Jeffrey Morris, and Elliot Slotnick for having read the manuscript and for their valuable suggestions. James McCafferty of the Administrative Office of the United States Courts once again provided maps, charts, and the latest indispensable statistics and reports from the Administrative Office. Finally, I wish to acknowledge the intellectual stimulation, friendship, and overall support of my departmental brothers-in-law Dean Alfange, Jr., and John Brigham.

Although Tom Jahnige died before the second and third editions were written, there is hardly a page in this book where his contributions are not felt. This was truly a collaboration, and I hope that this edition will serve as an ongoing memorial.

SHELDON GOLDMAN

Preface to the Second Edition

Planning for this edition began shortly before Tom Jahnige's untimely death from Hodgkin's disease. Tom was enthused about undertaking a second edition, because we were both gratified with the response of colleagues and students alike concerning the usefulness of the first edition. I have sought to carry through the general points Tom and I agreed would provide the basis for this edition. In particular, the systems framework as we originally utilized it has been retained, but of course many new materials have been incorporated that have been published or became available since the first edition. Original empirical analyses have also been brought up to date. New sections (such as the one on legal services lawyers and the one on criminal sentencing) have been added where appropriate, to take into account the latest developments concerning the federal judicial system, as well as the research topics that have been the focus of increased scholarly attention since the first edition.

There are many people to thank. First and foremost, David Danelski has been a constant source of encouragement and excellent suggestions. He was for Tom and remains for me a treasured friend and colleague. There are numerous scholars in the field without whose research contributions this book could not have been written. A glance at the index should indicate some measure of my indebtedness to them. In particular, I would like to thank Professor Jerry Goldman for providing most helpful data, comments, and suggestions concerning Chapter Four and for leading me to some of the excellent studies published by the Federal Judicial Center. James McCafferty of the Administrative Office of the U.S. Courts was specially helpful in providing the immensely useful maps and reports prepared by the Administrative Office. Professor Jonathan Casper read the entire manuscript and offered valuable advice. . . . Molly Jahnige did a superb job of typing the manuscript, and her help in meeting manuscript deadlines and in proofreading was in the spirit of collaborator rather than typist.

SHELDON GOLDMAN

Preface to the First Edition

In this text we seek to demonstrate the workings of the federal courts as a political system within the context of the larger American political system. Systems analysis as developed by David Easton and adapted for our concerns provides the conceptual framework.

To write a relatively brief introductory work imposes severe limits. The subject matter is so vast that sins of omission (and perhaps commission) will be evident in the pages ahead and for that we must assume full responsibility. Nevertheless, we have attempted to integrate a large body of material concerning the federal judicial process and its political context so that an otherwise unrelated torrent of data and analysis will hopefully make some sense to the beginning student. It is our hope that, rather than provide obscure jargon, systems concepts as developed here can help to sharpen the student's analytical abilities.

We would be less than candid if we did not acknowledge that systems analysis has recently been subjected to severe scrutiny by some in the discipline. Although the major issues raised are discussed in the final chapter, it is perhaps useful at the outset to emphasize that we believe the principal virtues of the framework are its organizing and heuristic qualities. *At best,* judicial systems analysis is one step toward the development of an empirical theory of courts and judicial behavior.

We have a special debt to Professor David J. Danelski for his encouragement and advice. His constructive suggestions were invariably pertinent and surely whatever merit this book possesses must be attributed in large measure to him. Numerous other scholars contributed more indirectly to this enterprise. We hope their invaluable contributions are recognized by the footnote citations. . . . Some of the original empirical analyses were undertaken with the aid of grants from the University of Massachusetts (faculty research, growth, and computer time grants) and the Social Science Research Council to Sheldon Goldman. Smith College generously provided Thomas Jahnige with a semester's leave in which to work on this book. The *Rutgers-Camden Law Journal, Jurimetrics Journal,* and

Polity have allowed us to draw upon our articles which have appeared in their publications.

Once again, our wives patiently endured our affair with textbook writing and to them we affectionately dedicate this book.

THOMAS P. JAHNIGE
SHELDON GOLDMAN

chapter *1*

Introduction

The Chief Justice bemoans the work load of the Supreme Court. Students of courts dutifully note that all levels of federal courts have had burgeoning caseloads over the past two decades. Some newspaper commentators suggest that justice in America is not working as it should; others suggest that there is a crisis of legitimacy concerning our courts. Decisions of the federal courts are praised and attacked, evoking deep emotions in those on both sides of a wide variety of civil liberty issues, such as abortion, or the busing of schoolchildren as part of a school desegregation plan, or prayer in the public schools, or various "rights" of those accused of crimes. There have been moves in Congress to remove certain types of cases from the federal courts. Constitutional amendments have been proposed to overturn Supreme Court decisions. As the 1984 presidential election campaign accelerated, there was talk of what the consequences of another four years of Republican rule would mean for the membership of the Supreme Court. The argument went that surely, with a majority of the justices aged 75 and over, whomever was elected would have the opportunity to name several justices, thus shaping the Supreme Court for at least a generation. A Republican victory, it was asserted, would mean a shift from a moderate conservative court to a court on the far right ideologically. Would such a court command the respect and obedience of those whose rights were no longer protected? These and other considerations, events, and questions concerning the federal courts have made it clear in recent years that what happens to and in the federal courts matters and that students of politics are well advised to pay attention to the courts.

But how should the courts be studied? What general theory, model, or framework can best aid the student of politics to come to grips with the full range of court-related phenomena? One such general framework that has been widely used by political scientists to study other aspects of politics is *political systems analysis.*[1] In this book systems analysis as developed by David Easton[2] is used to study the federal judicial process.[3]

A system, according to Easton, is "any set of variables regardless of the degree of interrelationship among them."[4] In practice, political scientists are interested in political systems in which the basic unit interactions are highly dependent upon and interrelated with one another and which as a set exhibit *boundary-maintaining* characteristics. This means that those involved in the interactions behave in such a manner as to strive to maintain the system's integrity and cohesion.[5]

Every political system exists within and is affected by the physical, biological, social, economic, and cultural environments (all of which may also be analyzed from a systems approach). What distinguishes a political system from these environments is that its interactions deal with the authoritative allocation of values for a society;[6] that is, a political system is concerned with deciding in the name of society who within that society gets what, when, where, and how.[7]

Those who do the interacting are considered to be the *politically relevant members* of the system. They are, in Easton's words, "those members of a system who count, . . . who share in the effective power of the system."[8] Some of them are considered in systems terminology to be the *authorities,* that is, those occupants of systemic roles who exercise discretion and influence in making decisions for allocating such valued things as wealth, power, prestige, and ideals. The system's *regime rules* specify the manner by which the authorities may allocate those values.

Political systems are *open systems.* They are thus constantly subject to stresses or disturbances that emanate from the environment. If the system is to persist, these disintegrative forces must be defused. In other words, these disturbances must be confronted and processed if the system's authorities are to maintain their ability to allocate values for the society and to induce most members of the system to accept those allocations as binding. How the system handles such disturbances shapes the nature of that particular political system. To understand how a system persists means discovering how it deals with and reduces stress.

Constantly entering the system are *demands* for particular authoritative allocations of values. At the same time, the system's politically relevant members hold certain views reflecting their satisfaction or dissatisfaction with the system. These attitudes can be specific in relation to past allocations (in systems terminology this is called *specific* support) or more general or diffuse views of the system (called *diffuse* support). The demands and the two types of support are a major *input* to the system.

The authorities in their institutional roles confront, evaluate, reshape, and process this input. This decision-making stage is called *conversion* (or the conversion of inputs into systemic responses). The decisions that are made are *output* of the system. The output's subsequent impact generates behavioral responses that are communicated or fed back *(feedback)* to the system as new input.

These are Easton's basic political systems concepts. They provide the organizational framework for examining the structure, process, and behavior of the federal courts.

THE FEDERAL COURTS AS A POLITICAL SYSTEM

The federal judicial system[9] can be conceptualized as encompassing all interactions in American society concerning the authoritative allocation of values involving the judicial authorities of the federal courts. Courts primarily allocate values by deciding cases and issuing rules of procedure and other court orders. The authorities of the system include judges, jurors, administrative and supporting court personnel, and private attorneys as well as attorneys for the federal government whose practice takes them before the federal courts. Litigants and witnesses are not considered authorities because their behavior is not governed by any unique role considerations other than such general cultural injunctions as "tell the truth," nor do they make authoritative decisions for the system. Rather, they are considered politically relevant sources and carriers of demands and information. Members of the general public are also considered politically relevant when they are aware of the operation of the system and act (or can be expected to act) in response to its output. The same is true of interest groups and the mass media. The federal judicial system's regime rules include the formal laws, rules, and procedures followed and applied by the authorities in processing demands and various legal and judicial cultural concepts such as judicial neutrality, adherence to precedent, and lawyer advocacy. Figure 1.1 illustrates the interrelationship of the principal systems concepts in the federal judicial system.[10]

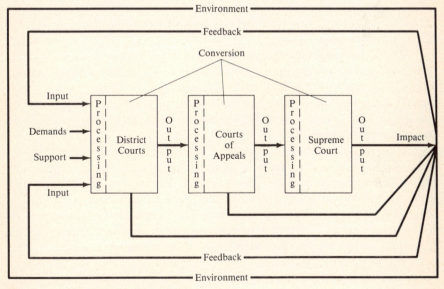

Figure 1.1   The federal judicial system

Input

The federal judicial system is embedded in an environment that includes the various physical, biological, social, economic, cultural, and, of course, political systems. The political environment contains all other political systems within the United States including Congress, the 50 state judicial systems, the 50 state legislative systems, and the federal and state executive-bureaucratic systems. These systems are constantly subjected to the changing material and psychic conditions of the members populating them. Such conditions generate needs, wants, resentments, and expectations to which the federal judicial system as an open system is subject. They are transmitted to the courts as demands principally through litigation. As with all political systems, both the form and content of acceptable demands may be limited by two types of mechanisms that regulate the flow of demands: regime rules and gatekeeping.

Regime rules control the flow of demands by inhibiting many wants from being converted into demands in the first place. Within the federal judicial system such regime rules are subsumed in concepts such as *jurisdiction* (whether the court has the legal authority to adjudicate the matter), *standing to sue* (a variety of rules to determine whether the court will recognize the litigant and the matter brought to court; for example, is there a genuine case or controversy in which the litigant is personally involved?), and *justiciability* (whether the matter is suitable for resolution by the judicial branch; for example, is there a remedy that is appropriate for the court to administer or is the matter better resolved by the political branches of government). Regime rules not only regulate demand flow at the point of introduction of litigation into the system, but they may limit the extent to which a demand will be treated by the system. Certain formal and informal rules and processes result in settlement without trial of most litigation in the federal system. Other rules and processes operate to regulate demand input at the appellate stage.

The second major mechanism limiting demand flow is what Easton calls "gatekeeping."[11] Gatekeepers are those situated at the boundary of the system and at various points within it who reduce the number of demands or modify their content. Judges and particularly attorneys (both public and private) perform this function for the federal system by, for example, encouraging guilty pleas and out-of-court settlements.

Support (both specific and diffuse) is another key input for the federal judicial system. A major source of stress on the system can be a decline of favorable attitudes on the part of the politically relevant members of the system concerning particular policy outputs and/or the general functioning of the system. High levels of unfavorable specific or diffuse attitudes are thought to be related to difficulties in obtaining compliance with the system's output. Because the federal courts have no independent enforcement machinery to compel compliance, coercion, when it is needed, must be supplied by executive officials. At the very least, therefore, the federal judicial system requires a minimum level of positive support among these officials to be able to function.

By definition, demands and support as inputs link the system to the different kinds of disturbances that originate in the environment. Disturbances that stem exclusively from *within* the system, however, can be separately considered as "withinputs." According to Easton, withinputs are "those demands formed through experiences and activities [of those in the system when acting] in strictly political roles."[12] Demands and other inputs of positive or negative support on the part of the lower federal courts toward the Supreme Court, as well as the reverse, can be considered a type of judicial system withinput. Various intrasystemic structures, such as judicial councils and conferences, can also generate withinput as well as process it.

Conversion

Conversion, it will be recalled, is the decision-making-by-the-authorities stage. A complete portrait of conversion in the federal judicial system would include an analysis of jury decision making as well as decision making by all other authorities in the system (including private and government attorneys, the Federal Bureau of Investigation [FBI], law clerks, and administrative court personnel) as they exercise discretion and influence judicial output by virtue of the decisions they make within the system. Since judges, however, are the primary authorities of the federal judicial system, our focus will be on them and judicial conversion.

Output

Judicial outputs involve both the workings of the federal judicial system, such as the rules concerning the processing of criminal and civil cases, and the transactions between the judicial system and its political and other environments (the latter being responsible for most of the business of the federal courts). *Authoritative outputs* are the binding rulings resolving particular cases, judicially articulated rules of procedure, and court orders. *Associated outputs* include the written justification for the rulings as well as public and private activity related in any way to the judge's official position.

Feedback

The outputs return "to haunt the system"[13] by stimulating behavioral responses by members of the political system. These responses are fed back to the authorities (this is called "information feedback") through various formal and informal channels. A major form of feedback for the federal judicial system consists of the new demands (cases) fed into the system in response to past decisions. Another obvious form of feedback is in the appointment of new judges to the Supreme Court and the lower federal courts. Easton assumes that the authorities are responsive to feedback in order to minimize discontent or satisfy grievances that arose over the initial outputs. Indeed, Easton categorically states that "without feedback and the capacity to respond to it, no system could survive for long, except by accident."[14]

These and other systems concepts will be examined more thoroughly in subsequent chapters, and their utility for understanding the federal judicial process will be demonstrated. However, at this point it is helpful for purposes of illustration to use the basic systems approach for an interpretation of two key events concerning the Supreme Court. The first event involves the federal judiciary's handling of federal and state economic regulation cases during the 1930s. The second concerns the transformation of the Warren Court into the Nixon Court.

THE HUGHES COURT AND THE SWITCH OF 1937

From the 1880s well into the 1930s, the Supreme Court developed and applied legal doctrines that permitted it to question the constitutionality of certain kinds of state and federal economic regulation.[15] By maintaining the old conservative doctrines promoting economic laissez-faire during the years of national trauma and widespread hardship of the Great Depression, the Court was clearly out of step with the times, needs, and wants of the country. Finally after the 1936 presidential election, President Roosevelt presented a court reform plan to Congress that would have potentially increased the membership of the Supreme Court to a maximum of 15 members (the plan was popularly referred to as Roosevelt's "court-packing" plan).

Several months later an unusual judicial event occurred. The Supreme Court suddenly began sustaining the constitutionality of state and federal economic regulation. This switch was most dramatically signaled by a change in the voting behavior of Justice Owen Roberts. Early in 1936 Roberts had voted with Justices Van Devanter, McReynolds, Sutherland, and Butler to form a 5–4 majority striking down New York State's minimum wage law (*Morehead* v. *New York ex rel. Tipaldo*[16]). However, after the election of 1936, Roberts joined Chief Justice Hughes and Justices Cardozo, Brandeis, and Stone to uphold a Washington State minimum wage law indistinguishable from the New York law (the case was *West Coast Hotel* v. *Parrish*[17]). This was the turning point. The Court's new permissive attitude toward government economic regulation found expression in case after case thereafter. This profound change on the part of Justice Roberts became known, in light of the Roosevelt court-packing plan, as the switch-in-time-that-saved-nine.[18] How can the systems framework interpret these momentous events?

At the outset we can consider the judicial authorities on the Hughes Court. The justices differed markedly in their political, economic, social, and jurisprudential attitudes. Four justices (Van Devanter, McReynolds, Sutherland, and Butler) can perhaps be best described as political reactionaries in that they were simply not attuned to the political, economic, and social realities of twentieth-century America. Three justices (Cardozo, Brandeis, and Stone) were political liberals in that they recognized the need of government to be able to confront the grave economic crisis and to be able to manage the economy of the nation. Justice Roberts was somewhat more moderate than the reactionaries, and Chief Justice Hughes was somewhat to the left of him. As Chief Justice, Hughes was entitled (when he voted with the majority) to make the assignment as to who would write the Court's opinion. Hughes was vitally concerned with who spoke for the Court on what issue, and this meant that he liked to be on the winning side so that he could exercise his opinion-assignment power.[19] Apparently he tried to make antigovernment decisions less provocative by assigning the opinion either to Justice Roberts, one of the more diplomatic nonliberals, or to a liberal if one happened to be voting with the majority.[20] We can interpret Hughes's behavior as Chief Justice as attempting to favorably influence diffuse if not specific support.

The political and nonpolitical environments must also be considered. The country was in the midst of the most devastating economic depression in our history. A frighteningly large proportion of the nation was unemployed and destitute. The economic and social environments were the source of profound disturbances that were translated into demands presented to all levels of government for immediate relief measures and programs that would reverse the Depression. The political, social, and economic environments ultimately were the source of demands on the Hughes Court to sustain the constitutionality of New Deal legislation.

The Court's antipathy toward economic and social welfare legislation to ameliorate the harsh effects of the Depression produced a great variety of activity within the environment as the economy continued to falter, as social and political unrest increased, and as unemployment continued high and wages remained low. Within the law schools and the universities, criticism of Court policies was severe. Politicians gained office and popularity by supporting views of economic regulation that the Court had ruled unconstitutional. There was talk about amending the Constitution. Congress and the state legislatures passed new economic regulations after the old ones had been declared invalid. Finally the presidential court-packing plan was introduced, which public opinion polls initially showed to be favorably received by a majority in the country.

As an open system these facts were fed back to the Court. The widespread denunciation of the Court by politicians and the press, the Gallup polls that indicated that a large majority of Americans opposed the Court's policies, Roosevelt's landslide victory in 1936 and his subsequent court reform plan were negative feedback of the most profound sort. More formally, new litigation was the principal conveyor of feedback from the political branches of government.

The loss of both specific and diffuse support, the demands from the President and Congress, the fact that its decisions produced more stress on the Court rather than less, the fact that the ability of the Court to allocate values authoritatively and to have those allocations accepted as binding was seriously threatened, all meant that the Court *had* to adjust its output if it was to retain its integrity as a system. *Something had to give if the federal judicial system as then constituted was to persist.* And it did. Output changed and the Court abandoned its restrictive economic policies. That it was Roberts and, to a lesser extent, Hughes who were vehicles of the change is largely irrelevant from a systems viewpoint. The change in output could even have been brought about through the more "normal" mechanism of appointment (as will be seen shortly with our second example). The point is that the federal judiciary as an open system is subjected to this feedback. Its future policy outputs are ultimately influenced by the impact of previous outputs and subsequent feedback.

FROM THE WARREN COURT TO THE NIXON COURT

Just as the pre-1937 Court was generally committed to laissez-faire economic values and was activist in promoting them, the Warren Court was committed to civil libertarian values and was activist on their behalf. The pre-1937 Court generally had the backing of the political right and the opposition of the political left, while the Warren Court generally derived its backing and opposition from exactly the opposite sources. The output of the Court in the 1930s before 1937 did not adequately respond to negative feedback, but rather served to increase stress on the system. The ability of the system to persist was so threatened that a change in output was inevitable. It would seem that there also are parallels with the Warren Court.

Over the years the Warren Court accumulated a host of vigorous opponents. The landmark desegregation decisions, the reapportionment decisions, those concerning prayers in the public schools as well as obscenity, the rights of alleged subversives, and most importantly the rights of criminal defendants stimulated an opposition that substantially reduced positive support for the Court among the general public and government officials.[21] Feedback was increasingly negative and for the most part output was unresponsive. A high point for the opponents of Warren Court policies occurred in June, 1968, with the fight over the nomination of Associate Justice Abe Fortas to succeed Chief Justice Earl Warren (who had previously announced his intention to retire). Fortas became the scapegoat for the liberal Court, and both were subjected to fierce verbal attacks during the Senate filibuster over the nomination. When the Senate failed to invoke cloture to end debate, Justice Fortas asked President Johnson to withdraw his nomination because of his desire to put a stop to (in his words) "destructive and extreme assaults upon the Court."[22]

Concurrently, in the 1968 presidential campaign the Supreme Court became a major issue (just as its rulings were in the 1936 campaign). Two presidential candidates, Richard M. Nixon and George C. Wallace, attacked the Court for its civil libertarian policies, in particular those relating to the rights of criminal defendants. Both anti-Court candidates received a combined total of 57 percent of the popular vote, and one became President. Then, in a move somewhat analogous to Roosevelt's court-packing stratagem, the Nixon Administration moved against Justice Fortas, who, because of the earlier controversy, was one of the more vulnerable Warren Court liberals. The end result was the creation of a vacancy on the Court that, along with the vacancy of the Chief Justice slot, permitted President Nixon to appoint two justices who would (and did) bring about a turnaround on the Court particularly concerning the issue of the rights of criminal defendants.[23] How the Nixon Administration brought about the Fortas resignation is of interest.[24]

In the May 5, 1969, issue of *Life* magazine, an article appeared containing serious allegations and insinuations of improper behavior on the part of Justice Fortas.[25] These same charges had been dismissed six months earlier by the previous Democratic Administration's attorney general (Ramsey Clark) as being without merit.[26] However, within a two-week period, the Republican Nixon Administration successfully exerted pressure on liberal Democrat Justice Fortas to resign from the Court. During that period the Justice Department initiated a federal grand jury investigation into charges against Fortas's old law firm (a move that questioned the integrity of the firm and, by implication, Fortas);[27] the Justice Department vigorously investigated the allegations and subpoenaed personal letters and papers of financier Louis Wolfson, with whom Fortas allegedly was improperly involved;[28] Attorney General John Mitchell hinted to the press that the Justice Department had uncovered "far more serious" (but unspecified) wrongdoings that would become public unless Fortas resigned;[29] conservative Republican members of Congress announced their intention of instituting impeachment proceedings against Fortas if he did not resign immediately;[30] and Attorney General Mitchell met with Chief Justice Warren, reportedly to brief him on the matter and to enlist his aid in persuading Fortas to resign.[31]

The low level of support for the Court seems in part responsible for the fact that few came to Fortas's defense. Although the public record contained no shred of evidence that Justice Fortas ever interceded on behalf of or took part in any legal, administrative, or judicial matter concerning Wolfson or his associates, the pressure was too great and Fortas resigned, well aware that impeachment proceedings would further damage the Court's prestige as well as his own.[32] Shortly thereafter another liberal, Justice Douglas, accused the Administration of also trying to force him off the bench. At the time nothing came of Douglas's charges or his fears,[33] but some months later he was subjected to such a renewed attempt —an attempt led by then–Republican House Leader Gerald R. Ford.[34]

The most successful form of feedback calculated to change output is the appointment of new justices. Within the first six months of holding office, President Nixon not only had an opportunity to appoint a new associate justice, but also had the chief justiceship position to fill. To the latter post he appointed Warren Burger, a strong opponent of the Court's civil libertarian views concerning various rights of criminal defendants. As associate justice, Nixon first nominated an economic and political conservative from South Carolina, Chief Judge (of the U.S. Court of Appeals for the Fourth Circuit) Clement Haynsworth. Haynsworth's nomination was opposed by labor and civil rights groups as well as by those who accused Haynsworth of judicial insensitivities perhaps even more serious than those that forced Fortas's resignation because they involved allegations concerning Haynsworth's voting behavior as an appeals court judge.[35] President Nixon nevertheless strongly supported Haynsworth and frankly admitted to newspaper reporters that "the Court needs balance, . . . a man who is conservative."[36] The Senate defeated the Haynsworth nomination and also the subsequent nomination of another southern conservative, G. Harrold Carswell. However, the President eventually succeeded in placing on the Court Judge Harry Blackmun, a conservative midwestern federal court of appeals judge.[37] In early autumn, 1971, Justices Black and Harlan, both in ill health, retired, and President Nixon filled the vacancies with two more conservatives, a southerner and former American Bar Association president, Lewis Powell, and a Justice Department official, William Rehnquist.

The transformation of the liberal Warren Court to the more conservative

Nixon Court, although not as dramatic as the switch-in-time of 1937, nevertheless is what could be expected from adopting the systems approach. Something *had* to give. Support for the Court was at a low ebb among the general public and among key government officials. Instead of reducing stress, output was contributing to it. Although systems analysis could not predict the form that change would take or precisely when it would occur, the approach nevertheless alerted us to the variables that inevitably precede change.

WHY USE THE SYSTEMS APPROACH?

The previous examples briefly considered two well-known judicial events from a broad systems perspective. At the very minimum, systems analysis extends our view. It allows us to consider interactions and processes that otherwise might be ignored. The systems framework imposes a logic on political institutions, actors, and events. It provides concepts with which to organize large and diverse accumulations of data. Systems analysis is simple enough for the beginning student to comprehend despite lack of familiarity with the statistical and mathematical techniques of the social sciences, yet at the same time studies using such techniques can be placed and discussed within the systems framework. Systems analysis, then, can provide useful organizing concepts and can serve as a helpful heuristic device. Despite several limitations of the framework,[38] it undoubtedly helps to illuminate the intricate workings and interrelations of the federal judicial system.

NOTES

1. See William C. Mitchell, "Political Systems," *International Encyclopedia of the Social Sciences,* 15 (1968), 473–479.
2. Easton first developed political systems analysis in "An Approach to the Analysis of Political Systems," *World Politics,* 9 (1957), 383–400. His most extensive formulations upon which this book is based were contained in *A Framework for Political Analysis* (Englewood Cliffs, N.J.: Prentice-Hall, 1965) and *A Systems Analysis of Political Life* (New York: Wiley, 1965). Easton responded to his critics in "Systems Analysis and Its Classical Critics," *Political Science Reviewer,* 3 (1973), 269–301, and in "Systems Analysis in Politics and Its Critics," in H. J. Johnson (ed.), *Political Theory* (Dordrecht, The Netherlands: Reidel, 1973).
3. Alternative political systems analyses of the state and/or federal judiciaries (some of which borrow in part from Eastonian analysis) include: S. Sidney Ulmer, "Homeostatic Tendencies in the United States Supreme Court," in S. Sidney Ulmer (ed.), *Introductory Readings in Political Behavior* (Skokie, Ill.: Rand McNally, 1961), pp. 167–188; James Herndon, "The Role of the Judiciary in State Political Systems: Some Explorations," in Glendon Schubert (ed.), *Judicial Behavior: A Reader in Theory and Research* (Skokie, Ill.: Rand McNally, 1964), pp. 153–161; Walter Murphy, *Elements of Judicial Strategy* (Chicago: University of Chicago Press, 1964), pp. 31–36; Glendon Schubert, *Judicial Policy-Making* (Glenview, Ill.: Scott, Foresman, 1965; revised edition, 1974); Jay Sigler, *An Introduction to the Legal System* (Homewood, Ill.: Dorsey Press, 1968); Joel B. Grossman, "A Model for Judicial Policy Analysis: The Supreme

Court and the Sit-In Cases," in Joel B. Grossman and Joseph Tanenhaus (eds.), *Frontiers of Judicial Research* (New York: Wiley, 1969), pp. 405–460; Joel B. Grossman and Austin Sarat, "Political Culture and Judicial Research," *Washington University Law Quarterly* (1971), 177–207; Daryl R. Fair, "A Framework for Analyzing the Elements of Stability in Judicial Policy-Making," *Rutgers-Camden Law Journal*, 3 (1972), 395–409; Henry R. Glick and Kenneth N. Vines, *State Court Systems* (Englewood Cliffs, N.J.: Prentice-Hall, 1973); Charles H. Sheldon, *The American Judicial Process: Models and Approaches* (New York: Dodd, Mead, 1974); Lawrence Baum, "Policy Goals in Judicial Gatekeeping: A Proximity Model of Discretionary Jurisdiction," *American Journal of Political Science*, 21 (1977), 13–35. Also see Sheldon Goldman and Austin Sarat (eds.), *American Court Systems: Readings in Judicial Process and Behavior* (San Francisco: Freeman, 1978). See Thomas P. Jahnige and Sheldon Goldman (eds.), *The Federal Judicial System: Readings in Process and Behavior* (New York: Holt, Rinehart and Winston, 1968), for an earlier and less complete adaptation of Eastonian analysis than now presented. A discussion of the major analyses published during the 1960s and how they differ from Eastonian analysis as used here can be found in Sheldon Goldman and Thomas P. Jahnige, "Systems Analysis and Judicial Systems: Potential and Limitations," *Polity*, 3 (1971), 334–359. It should be noted that in this book the subject of military justice is not treated. Rather the focus is exclusively on the principal federal civilian courts. Various aspects of military justice, however, are investigated in S. Sidney Ulmer, *Military Justice and the Right to Counsel* (Lexington: University Press of Kentucky, 1970); Paul Lermack, "Summary and Special Courts-Martial," Ph.D. dissertation, University of Minnesota, 1972; Joseph W. Bishop, Jr., *Justice under Fire: A Study of Military Law* (New York: Charterhouse, 1974); and Harold F. Nufer, *American Servicemembers' Supreme Court* (Washington, D.C.: University Press of America, 1982).

4. Easton, *A Systems Analysis of Political Life*, p. 21.
5. Easton discusses this in *A Framework for Political Analysis*, pp. 25, 36.
6. *Ibid.*, p. 50.
7. This is a paraphrase of Harold Lasswell's famous definition. See his *Politics: Who Gets What, When, How* (Cleveland: Meridian Books, World, 1958). For an alternative and broader view of politics see Harry Eckstein, "Authority Patterns: A Structural Basis for Political Inquiry," *American Political Science Review*, 67 (1973), 1142–1161. Cf. Fred M. Frohock, "Notes on the Concept of Politics: Weber, Easton, Strauss," *Journal of Politics*, 36 (1974), 379–408.
8. Easton, *A Systems Analysis of Political Life*, p. 22.
9. It should be recognized that the federal judicial (or court) system can also be conceptualized as a subsystem of the larger American political system, and for certain purposes it is more useful to so treat it.
10. The diagram is a simplification of reality. It is applicable to cases that begin in the district courts and are appealed to the appeals courts and then to the Supreme Court. Certain demands in the form of litigation can take other routes not illustrated by the diagram. For example, a limited type of case, such as a challenge to the constitutionality of the apportionment of congressional or state legislative districts or a Voting Rights Act suit, is authorized to be heard by three-judge district courts and then can be appealed to the Supreme Court, thus bypassing the appeals courts. Most federal agency appeals bypass the district courts and go directly to the appeals courts. Appeals from the highest state courts are demands made exclusively on the Supreme Court.
11. Easton, *A Systems Analysis of Political Life*, pp. 87–96, 133–137.
12. *Ibid.*, p. 55.

13. *Ibid.,* p. 29.

14. *Ibid.,* p. 32.

15. This is recounted in Robert G. McCloskey, *The American Supreme Court* (Chicago: University of Chicago Press, 1960) and Sheldon Goldman, *Constitutional Law and Supreme Court Decision-Making: Cases and Essays* (New York: Harper & Row, 1982), chaps. 4 and 5. Also see the description of the 1937 "revolution" in Loren P. Beth, *Politics, the Constitution and the Supreme Court* (New York: Harper & Row, 1962), pp. 111–130. But cf. Martin Shapiro and Douglas S. Hobbs, *American Constitutional Law: Cases and Analyses* (Cambridge, Mass.: Winthrop, 1978), pp. 153–161.

16. 298 U.S. 587 (1936).

17. 300 U.S. 379 (1937).

18. But cf. Roberts's explanation of his behavior in Felix Frankfurter, "Mr. Justice Roberts," *University of Pennsylvania Law Review,* 104 (1955), 313–316.

19. David J. Danelski, "The Assignment of the Court's Opinion by the Chief Justice," paper read at the Midwest Conference of Political Scientists, Annual Meeting, 1960, pp. 18–22. Perhaps the classic example of a Chief Justice dominating opinion assignment was John Marshall's voting with the majority even when he disagreed with it so that he could write the Court's opinion. See John R. Schmidhauser, *Judges and Justices: The Federal Appellate Judiciary* (Boston: Little, Brown, 1979), pp. 110–116. In general, see David W. Rohde, "Policy Goals, Strategic Choice and Majority Opinion Assignments in the United States Supreme Court," *Midwest Journal of Political Science,* 16 (1972), 652–682; Gregory James Rathjen, "Policy Goals, Strategic Choice, and Majority Opinion Assignment in the U.S. Supreme Court: A Replication," *American Journal of Political Science,* 18 (1974), 713–724; Elliot E. Slotnick, "Who Speaks for the Court? Majority Opinion Assignment from Taft to Burger," *American Journal of Political Science,* 23 (1979), 60–77.

20. David J. Danelski, "The Influence of the Chief Justice in the Decisional Process of the Supreme Court," in Goldman and Sarat (eds.), *American Court Systems,* pp. 514–515. It should also be noted that there was probably another motive for Hughes's voting with the majority. If Hughes would have been a fourth member of a minority, he could avoid a 5–4 decision by going along with the majority and thereby give greater weight to the majority's decision and opinion.

21. Supporting data and citations are presented in Chapters 4 and 7. Also see Fred P. Graham, *The Self-Inflicted Wound* (New York: Macmillan, 1970).

22. *New York Times,* October 3, 1968, p. 42.

23. These points are explored in later chapters. Also see James F. Simon, *In His Own Image: The Supreme Court in Richard Nixon's America* (New York: McKay, 1973); and Leonard W. Levy, *Against the Law: The Nixon Court and Criminal Justice* (New York: Harper & Row, 1974).

24. Although there is much behind-the-scenes detail of which we know little, in light of the sordid, illegal, and unethical modus operandi of the Nixonians that is now a matter of public record (see, e.g., the 1973 Senate Watergate Committee Hearings and the 1974 Impeachment Proceedings of the House Judiciary Committee), it is now plausible to interpret the actions of the Nixonians described in the text as having their genesis in what would later be known as a political enemies strategy. For a different view of these events see Robert Shogan, *A Question of Judgement: The Fortas Case and the Struggle for the Supreme Court* (Indianapolis: Bobbs-Merrill, 1972).

25. William Lambert, "The Justice . . . and the Stock Manipulator," *Life,* May 5, 1969, pp. 32–37. One of Lambert's sources in the White House was the later-to-be-convicted Watergate conspirator E. Howard Hunt, who let Lambert see and copy forged State

Department cables that, if published, would have damaged the reputation of the Kennedy Administration. Lambert did not use this particular material. See J. Anthony Lukas, "Watergate: The Story So Far," *New York Times Magazine,* July 22, 1973, p. 14.

26. *New York Times,* May 15, 1969, p. 28.
27. *Congressional Quarterly,* May 9, 1969, p. 674. Also see *New York Times,* May 8, 1969, p. 34.
28. *New York Times,* May 18, 1969, p. 1.
29. *New York Times,* May 12, 1969, p. 35.
30. *New York Times,* May 8, 1969, p. 34. Also see *New York Times,* May 12, 1969, p. 1.
31. *New York Times,* May 13, 1969, p. 23; *Congressional Quarterly,* May 16, 1969, pp. 705–709.
32. *New York Times,* May 16, 1969, p. 1. Fortas conceded that he had entered into an agreement with Wolfson to head the Wolfson Family Foundation for a $20,000 annual lifetime retainer. However, after Wolfson was indicted for illegal stock manipulation Fortas canceled the agreement and returned the $20,000 payment he had already received. This occurred in late 1966, more than two years before the *Life* magazine story was published.
33. *New York Times,* May 27, 1969, p. 34. According to John Ehrlichman, who was a senior White House aide to President Nixon, it was months later that the President decided to go after Douglas in an effort to remove him from the Court once it became clear that the liberals in the Senate would be successful in blocking Nixon's choice of Clement Haynsworth to succeed Fortas. See John Ehrlichman, *Witness to Power: The Nixon Years* (New York: Simon & Schuster, 1982), p. 122.
34. See *New York Times,* November 8, 1969, p. 1; *Congressional Quarterly,* April 17, 1970, p. 1045; William O. Douglas, *The Court Years: 1939–1975* (New York: Random House, 1980), pp. 359–377.
35. *New York Times,* October 21, 1969, p. 35. See Edward N. Beiser, "The Haynsworth Affair Reconsidered: The Significance of Conflicting Perceptions of the Judicial Role," *Vanderbilt Law Review,* 23 (1970), 263–291.
36. *Congressional Quarterly,* October 24, 1969, p. 2103.
37. *Congressional Quarterly,* April 17, 1970, p. 1044. The preceding account, of course, is an oversimplification of the events that occurred in the Senate. A full appreciation of the dramatic events of the doomed Haynsworth-Carswell nominations would have to take into account the Senate as a system including its relationship to the President. See Joel B. Grossman and Stephen Wasby, "Haynsworth and Parker: History Does Live Again," *South Carolina Law Review,* 23 (1971), 345–359.
38. A discussion of some limitations of the framework can be found in Goldman and Jahnige, "Systems Analysis and Judicial Systems: Potential and Limitations." Also see chap. 8.

2

Regime Rules: Systemic Organization, Procedures, and Norms

The federal judicial system, like every political system, is characterized by a complex of rules and concepts prescribing the process by which decisions are made by the authorities. These rules and concepts are the system's *regime rules.* Many are formally stated in statutes and judicial rules or are written in the U.S. Constitution. Others exist as commonly held beliefs as to "how things should be done" and how the authorities should behave. Together they go far in determining the roles and powers of the system's various authorities, its organization, and its procedures.

Regime rules give the system much of its surface stability and continuity. Individual lawyers, jurors, and judges continuously enter and leave the system. Yet most of the rules and norms relating to structure, procedure, and roles remain beyond even a complete change of personnel. Although regime rules do change over time, the changes—such as with criminal or civil procedure—have tended to be slow and moderate. Major rules concerning judicial and legal roles have changed very little in the last century and a half.

Here we are concerned with the system's formal structure, in particular, its links to the state judicial systems, its internal structures, and how the system formally processes demand input. This is followed by a consideration of the roles systemic authorities are expected to play in processing cases, with attention to such legal cultural norms as judicial impartiality, lawyer advocacy, and *stare decisis* (the rule of adherence to precedent). The chapter concludes with a view of the federal judicial system as a bureaucratic organization. Using Max Weber's ideal type of bureaucracy, we look at the extent to which the structure of the federal judiciary approximates this model. This is of interest because Weber and later students of bureaucracy have suggested that inherent in bureaucratic organization are certain limits on how authorities behave and make decisions as well as on the kind of decisions made.

THE FEDERAL AND STATE JUDICIAL SYSTEMS: DIFFERENCES, OVERLAP, AND LINKS

In addition to the federal judicial system, each state and the Commonwealth of Puerto Rico has its own system. The total number of state and local courts in the United States in 1980 was 18,252.[1] In these courts in fiscal 1982 more than 25 million civil and criminal cases (excluding juvenile and traffic charges) were filed. In contrast, in fiscal 1982 there were only about 206,000 criminal and civil cases commenced within the federal district courts.[2] Not only is the federal system small in comparison to the full range of judicial activity, but it is also small in comparison with many individual state systems. For example, there are over 100 more full-time judges in the New York state judicial system as there are in the entire federal system. Each year large state court systems such as New York's dispose of a vastly greater number of civil and criminal cases (and are much more expensive to run) than the federal system. Most common crimes and most private wrongs leading to civil suits fall under the jurisdiction of state courts alone. State law and judicial proceedings generally affect the day-to-day life of the average citizen more directly than do their federal counterparts.

The courts of each state judicial system are totally independent of the courts of every other state system. Although Article IV, Section I of the Constitution declares that "Full Faith and Credit shall be given in each State to the public acts, Records, and judicial Proceedings of every other State," this is a very minimal demand that means in practice, for example, that a business incorporated in one state is recognized as a valid corporation by all other states. Normally the courts of different nations follow much this same procedure in litigation. A commercial contract made in England, for example, will generally be viewed as valid by the courts of France.

The relationship of state courts and law to federal courts and law is much more complex. For some purposes state courts serve as an alternative to the federal courts. By congressional statute state courts have exclusive jurisdiction over civil suits between citizens of different states (these are called "diversity" cases) where the amount sued for is less than $10,000 and concurrent jurisdiction with the federal courts in diversity cases involving larger amounts (that is, the suit may be tried in either a state or a federal court, the option resting with the litigants). In many other cases, even of the most local variety, questions of federal law must be taken into account. In civil suits, when state courts try cases that raise federal questions, the substantive law is federal although the procedural law is state. In criminal cases, procedure is also affected by federal constitutional interpretations. State judges are bound by oath to follow federally announced constitutional rights concerning, for example, interrogation, right to counsel, use of tainted evidence, voluntariness of confession, jury selection, and right of appeal, regardless of what state statutes, previous state judicial interpretations, or state constitutional provisions may say. Failure on the part of a state's courts to interpret properly and to comply with any question of federal law may eventually result in having the judgment overturned by a federal court.

Since 1938 federal courts are similarly called upon to interpret and enforce state law in diversity cases.[3] They are supposed to follow state judicial interpretations of state law. The relationship between the federal courts and the state courts is not symmetrical, however. While state court proceedings can be reviewed by the federal judiciary to oversee proper implementation of federal law, federal court proceedings cannot be reviewed by the state judiciaries. Thus, the state courts have no way of supervising how the federal courts deal with state law.

Once the site of trial is established and the case has been tried, all appeals must remain within the same court system. A case can never be appealed from the courts of one state to those of another. Under some circumstances (to be discussed in a moment), a state case can be appealed to the federal system, but never, no matter what the substantive law involved, can a case be appealed from a federal to a state court.

In a criminal case a defendant can only be brought to trial in a court of the government whose law was broken.[4] Thus, a New Jersey court cannot try a person for committing a crime in New York even if that person is apprehended in New Jersey. If the crime was a state crime, the accused can only be tried in a court of the State of New York. Therefore, New York authorities must request extradition from New Jersey. If the crime was a federal offense, the accused can only be tried in a federal court. Although the courts of each government have exclusive original jurisdiction over their own criminal cases, the federal courts have exercised a supervisory role over state criminal procedures.

Compliance of state judges to federal law is encouraged by procedures for review by state and federal courts. Failure by a trial judge to give proper weight and interpretation to a validly raised federal question normally opens the case to appellate review within the state's own court system, where the claim may be aired. Failure of the state appellate courts, out of either ignorance or defiance, to demand compliance with the federal law can result in one of two different forms of federal judicial intervention.

The oldest, most obvious, and best-known of these is appellate review by the United States Supreme Court. This is available for both state civil and criminal cases. The Supreme Court's rulings are binding both for the jurisdictional (Is the claim pressed truly federal?) and for the substantive (What does federal law require?) questions. The Supreme Court reviews relatively few state cases and does not extensively supervise state court proceedings. Indeed, with civil cases there are still large areas of state judicial activity and substantive law beyond the reaches of federal judicial power.

The second method by which a state court proceeding may be reviewed by the federal judiciary has much broader implications for obtaining compliance. It concerns only criminal cases in which the defendant is found guilty and placed in jail. Such a prisoner may institute a *habeas corpus* action before a U.S. district court on the ground that the conviction was characterized by a violation of the Constitution. Extensive use of this federal *habeas corpus* relief stems from a 1963

Supreme Court decision.[5] Traditionally it was used only for challenging the unlawful detention of a prisoner by executive officials—as when military authorities arrest and hold civilians when civil courts are in operation or law enforcement officials hold a captive without pressing charges or proceeding to trial. Technically in its use involving state prisoners, a federal *habeas corpus* action is a proceeding ordering the jailer to bring the prisoner to court and to indicate the basis for detention. Its effect, however, is to allow a federal district judge to review state court proceedings to make sure that federal constitutional norms have been followed. Failure by a state to make such a showing results in release of the prisoner or a new trial. In contrast to the difficulties encountered in obtaining Supreme Court review, having a district court consider a state prisoner's *habeas corpus* case is relatively easy. The very status of the petitioner as a prisoner is the chief consideration, although the federal district judge is given the option of refusing to grant the petition if it is shown that the petitioner has deliberately bypassed state remedies. Furthermore, since there are 89 district courts (in the states) and only one Supreme Court, we can readily see why modern federal *habeas corpus* allows for much more extensive surveillance of state criminal proceedings than was traditionally available by Supreme Court review. In the 1960s, when the number and impact of federal norms relating to state criminal procedures grew rapidly, the federal judiciary thus devised a way for greatly increasing its ability to gain compliance.

Although there are overlaps and links, it is nevertheless useful to conceptualize the federal judicial system as distinct from the state judicial systems. One state judiciary has no direct relationships with any other state judiciary. Different states recruit judges by different methods. Interactions of the state judiciaries with the federal judiciary are relatively infrequent. In contrast, the federal courts constitute integrated sets of relationships.

THE INTERNAL STRUCTURE OF THE FEDERAL JUDICIAL SYSTEM

The federal judicial system consists of courts and administrative bodies. The most important courts are the three principal constitutional courts: the U.S. Supreme Court, the 12 U.S. courts of appeals,[6] and 90 of the 94 U.S. district courts.[7] They are called constitutional courts because they are authorized by Article III, the judicial article, of the Constitution. This article protects these judges from diminution in pay and provides for lifetime appointment.

Congress has also created from time to time various other administrative agencies and specialized courts that also perform a judicial or quasi-judicial function. Most of these (e.g., the National Labor Relations Board, the Federal Trade Commission, and the Interstate Commerce Commission) are not considered a part of the judicial branch. Others, such as the U.S. Claims Court, the U.S. Court of Appeals for the Federal Circuit (handling claims, customs, and patent appeals), and the U.S. Court of International Trade, are part of the federal judicial system and are considered constitutional courts. Such courts and agencies together handle many more cases than do the principal constitutional courts. In practically all cases their decisions can be appealed or reviewed by the regular federal courts. The formal structure of the United States court system is presented in Figure 2.1.

Another part of the judicial branch that has rather unique characteristics of jurisdiction and status are the federal district courts and local courts operating in the territories of Guam, the Northern Mariana Islands, and the Virgin Islands. Until April, 1982, there was also a territorial court in the Panama Canal Zone. However, under the provisions of the Panama Canal Act of 1979, American presence and courts in the Canal Zone came to an end. In the territorial courts, the U.S. district courts exercise jurisdiction over local as well as regular federal cases. These three territorial courts are also unique in other ways. Foremost among them is that the judges of the district courts of the Northern Mariana Islands, Guam, and the Virgin Islands are appointed for a set number of years and their salaries are not protected from diminution by Congress. Before 1966 this was also true of another territorial court, the federal District Court of Puerto Rico, but since a 1966 statute its judges have had lifetime tenure. Like the regular district courts it only exercises federal jurisdiction (this was true even before 1966). The territorial courts outside the continental United States, along with the Court of Military Appeals and the Tax Court, are considered legislative rather than constitutional courts because they are seen as implementing one of the enumerated powers of Congress as stated in Article I of the Constitution. The U.S. District Court for the District of Columbia is the only territorial district court within the continental United States. Before the District of Columbia Court Reorganization Act became law in 1970, the U.S. District Court had both federal and local jurisdiction. Now the District Court handles federal cases, leaving the local cases (involving laws applicable only to the District of Columbia) to the local municipal-type lower courts. In 1933, the Supreme Court ruled that both the District Court and the U.S. Court of Appeals for the District of Columbia—both of whose judges can be involuntarily removed only by impeachment and whose judicial salaries cannot be diminished by Congress—are both legislative and constitutional courts.[8] The other lower courts in the District of Columbia, on the other hand, are strictly legislative courts. As can be seen, the distinction between a constitutional and a legislative court is of the type that would have delighted those meticulous medieval scholastics who argued about how many angels would fit on the head of a pin.

Responsibility for administrative matters is diffused among each circuit's judicial council and to a much lesser extent judicial conference, the Judicial Conference of the United States, the Administrative Office of the United States Courts, and the Federal Judicial Center.[9] Each circuit's judicial council consists of judges of that circuit's court of appeals and at least two or three district court judges. Each council monitors caseloads and district judge assignments, and in general supervises its district courts. The councils are authorized by the Administrative Office Act of 1939 to order federal judges within their respective circuits to comply with council policies, or the policies set by the national judicial conference, or indeed those set by Congress. Since the enactment of the Judicial Councils Reform and Judicial Conduct and Disability Act of 1980 they have had special disciplinary authority over judges within the circuit.

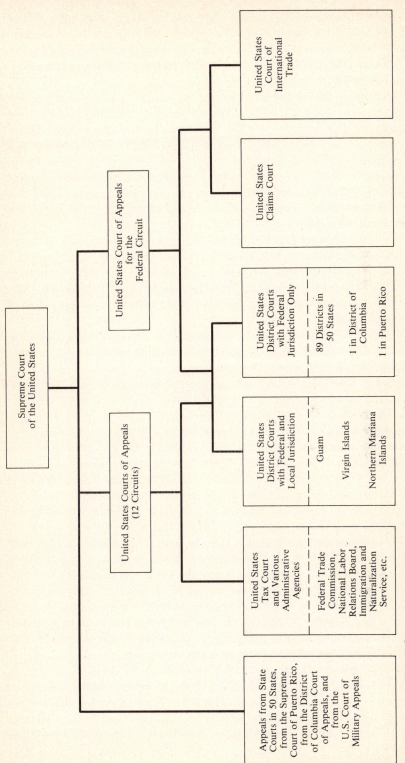

Figure 2.1 The United States court system

The circuit conferences consist of the district and appeals judges of each circuit and selected members of the federal bar. These annual conferences are primarily social gatherings, but they also provide communication links within the circuit, between the circuit and the national judicial conference, and between the circuit and the bar.

The Judicial Conference of the United States consists of the chief judges of the appeals courts and one district judge from each circuit. The Chief Justice of the Supreme Court presides over the conference, which serves as the central administrative policy-making organization for the federal judicial system. The Judicial Conference and its committees consider and formulate proposed legislation concerning the federal courts, raising such matters as additional judgeships and court personnel, salaries, budgets, and revised rules of criminal and civil procedure. The conference's recommendations are transmitted to the appropriate congressional committees.

The Administrative Office of the U.S. Courts assumes responsibility for the more routine administrative matters such as preparation of the budget, supervision of clerical and secretarial personnel as well as probation officers, staff work for the Judicial Conference, and congressional liaison. The Administrative Office also compiles detailed statistics on the work of the system which are published in its annual reports.

The Federal Judicial Center is responsible for coordinating and planning educational and training programs (such as sentencing institutes, seminars for new district judges[10] and bankruptcy judges, institutes for probation officers, and the training of the United States magistrates and circuit executives), for undertaking research into the workings of the system, and for developing new technology to assist the courts.

Because of the administrative responsibilities exercised as chairman of the Judicial Conference of the United States, in addition to the position as Chairman of the Board of the Federal Judicial Center and the responsibility for selecting the director of the Administrative Office of the United States Courts, the Chief Justice of the United States Supreme Court can be considered the titular head of the federal judicial system. In 1983 over 16,000 people were employed within the system.[11]

The district courts are the basic points of input. They are the system's main trial courts (the U.S. Court of International Trade previously known as the Customs Court, the U.S. Claims Court, and the Tax Court handle trials in their respective spheres; U.S. magistrates located within the districts try minor offenses). In 1983 there were 94 district courts with 515 district judge positions authorized by Congress. In addition, a large number of senior (retired) district judges helped out by sitting as trial judges.[12] Under legislation enacted in 1984, in 1985 an additional 61 district judge positions were created thereby bringing the total number of district judgeships to 576. Supporting personnel within the districts include law clerks, secretaries, court clerks, probation officers, bankruptcy judges, and U.S. magistrates. In fiscal 1983, 241,842 civil cases and 35,872 criminal cases were commenced in them. In the same year they tried 14,601 civil cases and 6656 criminal cases.[13] The large discrepancy between cases commenced and cases that go to trial is only partly a manifestation of "delay in court." More importantly, it is indicative of how many civil cases are settled out of court and how many criminal cases are disposed of by guilty pleas, usually achieved by a "bargain" between the defendant and the prosecution, or by dismissal.

Each state, the Commonwealth of Puerto Rico, the District of Columbia, Guam, the Virgin Islands, and the Northern Mariana Islands has, as is shown in Figure 2.1, at least one district. Texas, California, and New York State have four. The number of judges assigned to each district varies from 1 to 27.[14]

The jurisdiction of the district courts is original only. It includes all federal crimes, federal civil and diversity cases where the amount in controversy exceeds $10,000,[15] admiralty and maritime cases, review and enforcement of actions by certain federal agencies, and various other cases assigned by Congress. (As noted earlier, three territorial district courts also exercise local jurisdiction.) The district courts also perform various administrative and supervisory tasks. These include naturalization of aliens, approval of passport applications, supervision of bankruptcy proceedings, and parole of federal prisoners.

Cases in the district courts are generally tried before a single judge. However, special three-judge district courts whose membership includes at least one circuit court judge may be convened to consider certain special cases such as those concerning apportionment of congressional or state legislative districts and those involving rights protected by the Voting Rights Act of 1965 and the Civil Rights Act of 1964. In fiscal 1983, 27 such courts were convened. Sixteen concerned civil rights (primarily voting rights) issues, 9 concerned reapportionment, and 2 involved review of other laws or regulations.[16]

The losing party in a case tried before a district court has the right to an appeal. Generally these appeals are heard by the court of appeals in whose circuit the district court lies. Under special circumstances, however, appeal may be direct to the Supreme Court. This primarily occurs (1) with cases heard by three-judge district courts; (2) when a federal statute has been declared unconstitutional and the United States appeals the case; and (3) when a case is of great public importance and requires immediate settlement such as the famous Nixon tapes case, which when decided by the Court hastened the collapse of the Nixon presidency.[17]

The 12 U.S. courts of appeals with general jurisdiction (the circuit boundaries are shown in Figure 2.2) are directly above the district courts in the formal judicial hierarchy. In 1983 there were 132 authorized appeals court judgeships. There were also 50 senior (retired) judges performing substantial judicial service on circuit panels.[18] In 1985 the number of authorized appeals court judgeships was raised to 156 (or 168 if judgeships on the specialized U.S. Court of Appeals for the Federal Circuit are counted). Appeals court jurisdiction includes all cases tried by the district courts except for those few where appeal is direct to the Supreme Court. These courts also consider cases calling for review or enforcement of actions and orders of many federal independent regulatory agencies, administrative agencies, and departments. The courts of appeals do consider a few original proceedings all of which concern the behavior of district court judges. Supporting personnel include law clerks, secretaries, and court clerks. Each circuit has authorized for it a circuit executive to handle administrative matters

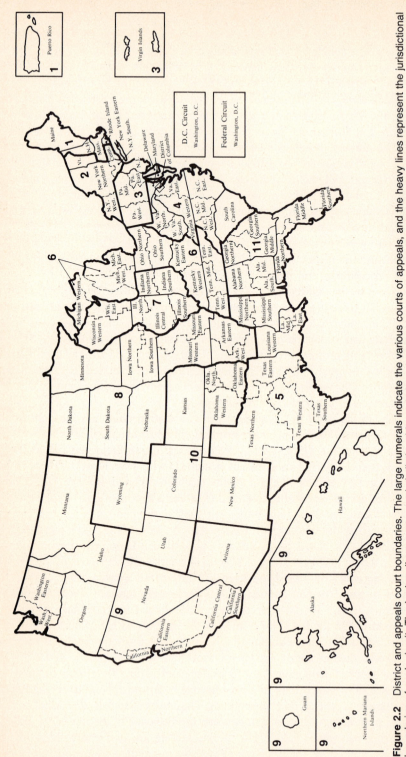

Figure 2.2 District and appeals court boundaries. The large numerals indicate the various courts of appeals, and the heavy lines represent the jurisdictional boundaries of each circuit. The broken lines represent jurisdictional boundaries of district courts in states having more than one district.

within the circuit, thereby providing the chief judge of each circuit with considerable managerial assistance and expertise.[19] In fiscal 1983, there were 29,630 cases filed in these courts, about six times as many filings as there were only 20 years earlier. Included were 25,039 appeals from the district courts, 3069 petitions to review or enforce administrative orders, and 834 original proceedings.[20]

The courts of appeals have from 6 to 28 judges. The number is determined by Congress and is supposed to reflect the work load of the circuit.[21] In considering cases, judges normally sit in ad hoc panels of three. Ordinarily, the chief judge of the circuit makes the assignments. In controversial cases, all the judges may hear the case *en banc,*[22] but in practice this is exceedingly rare. In fiscal 1980 out of the 7563 cases in which hearings were held, only 45 were heard *en banc.*[23]

Besides its regular judges, each circuit has designated to it a member of the Supreme Court. The two most senior associate Supreme Court justices are each assigned to two circuits, the Chief Justice is assigned to two (and in addition the specialized Federal Circuit), and the other justices are each assigned to one. This is a link to an earlier era, before the appeals courts were established as separate intermediate-level courts. Then, during recesses of the Court, Supreme Court justices would literally "ride the circuit" and sit as circuit judges (although their duties consisted of presiding over trials). Today, on occasion, justices are called upon to act on petitions from their respective circuits for emergency relief when the Supreme Court is not in session. This may include, for example, a stay of execution in a capital case. The justices usually attend the circuit conferences of the circuits to which they are assigned, thus maintaining personal links to the judges of the circuit much as their predecessors had done during the circuit-riding era.

At the apex of the formal judicial hierarchy is the Supreme Court. The Court is only one court in a system of over 100, and it has only 9 judges out of about 900 in the federal judiciary. It delivers full opinions in relatively few cases. For example, during the 1983–1984 term only 164 full opinions of the Court were written. Yet not only is it the most visible court in the system, it is undoubtedly the most visible court in the nation and perhaps the world. The Court exercises *judicial review* over the acts and actions of government and governmental officials at all levels of government. Many of the policies announced by the Court can be formally changed only by constitutional amendment or by the Court itself.

The Court has both original and appellate jurisdiction. Article III of the Constitution, as modified by the Eleventh Amendment, suggests that the Court's original jurisdiction is extensive. It includes cases between two or more states or between the United States and a state; cases involving foreign ambassadors ministers, consuls, and their staffs; and cases commenced by a state against the citizens of other states or nations. With cases between two or more states and those commenced against foreign diplomatic personnel, the Court has exclusive original jurisdiction. With all of the other cases mentioned, it has concurrent original jurisdiction with the district courts.[24] Thus the Supreme Court takes relatively few cases under its original jurisdiction. In fact, from its establishment through the end of its 1983–1984 term, the Court had adjudicated under its original jurisdiction and issued full opinions in only 164 cases.[25] The Court is, in other words, primarily a forum for appellate review.

There are presently four methods by which a case under the Court's appellate jurisdiction is brought before the Court for review. These are *certiorari,* appeal, certification, and extraordinary writ. Only the first two methods are of any quantitative significance.

After one's case has been considered by a state court of last resort, a U.S. court of appeals or the U.S. court of appeals for the federal circuit, any disappointed litigant may petition the Supreme Court for a writ of *certiorari,* which is technically an order to the court whose decision is being challenged to send up the records of the case so that the Supreme Court can make certain that the lower court's decision correctly applied the law. Congress has given the Court complete discretion as to whether or not it will grant the certiorari petition. The writ is issued if at least four justices so vote. In practice, it is granted in only a small proportion of cases brought to the Court. In the 1978–1981 period, about 11 percent of lawyer-drafted petitions and under 3 percent of self-drafted petitions (mostly drawn by impoverished prisoners in state and federal prisons) were granted.[26] This, it should be mentioned, was a decline from the early 1960s, when about 13 percent of lawyer-drafted petitions and about 4 percent of pauper petitions were granted.

Under the terms of the Judiciary Act of 1925, certain types of cases are entitled to review by the Supreme Court. This technical right to an appeal exists (1) in cases coming from a state court of last resort when either a federal law or treaty has been held unconstitutional or a state law or provision of a state constitution has been upheld against the challenge that it conflicts with a federal law, treaty, or the U.S. Constitution; (2) in cases from a U.S. court of appeals when either a state law or provision of a state constitution has been ruled unconstitutional; and (3) in cases from a court of appeals, a U.S. district court, and the U.S. court of appeals for the federal circuit when a federal law has been held unconstitutional and the United States or one of its agencies, officers, or employees is a party. Appeals can also be made from a three-judge district court. In practice, most appeals come from state courts.

Although disappointed litigants in the cases just mentioned technically have a right to an appeal, in fact, a "rule of four" similar to that used for certiorari exists. In the 1967–1970 terms, the Court dismissed over 40 percent of appeals filed for "lack of a substantial federal question" or "want of jurisdiction." In the 1976 term, the figure was about 55 percent dismissed. Just as with certiorari petitions, appeals can be divided into two groups: lawyer-drafted appeals and appeals *in forma pauperis* (literally "in the form of a pauper," that is, those appeals by poor litigants, usually prisoners). In the 1969–1972 terms, lawyer-drafted appeals accounted for about three out of four appeals heard on the merits, with the balance accounted for by pauper appeals.[27] Even getting an appeal accepted, however, may not do the appellant much good. Often the Court disposes of it without any oral argument by "affirming" the decision of the "court below."[28] In sum, the members of the Court, in deciding whether to take an appeal for an extended consideration of the case, appear to treat such appeals much as they do petitions for certiorari. Although there are historical and surface technical differences between the writs, the Court in practice exercises discretion with each.

Certification cases arise when the judges of a court of appeals or a district court ask the Supreme Court to rule on questions of law in cases pending in their respective courts for which there is considerable uncertainty. Such cases rarely occur. Even more rare is the taking of a case on an extraordinary writ. Acting on such a writ the Supreme Court can directly intervene into the activities of a trial judge, either directing the judge to perform some act *(mandamus)* or forbidding him or her from some other act (prohibition). It is not unusual each term for only one or not even any such cases to be accepted.

Less than half of the approximately 300 cases decided each year by the Court on the merits have been subjected to a full hearing, including oral argument (whereby lawyers for both sides have a limited time to argue their case in person before the Court and to be questioned by the justices). About 85 percent of these cases are then disposed of by a detailed opinion of the Court written and signed by one of the majority justices. The remainder of these cases and those for which no oral argument was conducted are typically disposed of by a *per curiam* opinion (a short, unsigned opinion literally "by the Court") or a brief memorandum order such as "dismissed," "affirmed," "vacated," or "reversed and remanded" (i.e., overruled and sent back to the "court below" for final disposition).

As can be seen, the Supreme Court exercises great flexibility in allocating its time and deciding which questions it will treat. In practice, the contemporary Court will consider any case that at least four justices, for whatever their reasons, decide they want to hear.

THE JUDICIAL ROLE AND THE JUDICIAL PROCESS

The United States has a regime in which the legitimacy of its policies supposedly rests upon those policies being an expression of popular will. In conflict with this democratic ideal are the federal courts whose primary authorities are appointed for life and are legally held accountable to no one. Individually and collectively these judicial authorities can make national policies that are authoritatively superior to those made by the regime's popularly elected legislative and executive officials.

The presence of a nondemocratic, independent, policy-making judiciary exercising judicial review in an otherwise popularly based government becomes even more difficult to rationalize when it is realized that such an institution is not a necessity of modern government. Other democratic political systems, Great Britain's, for example, manage quite well without a court system that makes constitutional policies. Nor is a constitutional court system a prerequisite for the maintenance of federalism. The Swiss seem to do nicely without one.

Why our judicial system has developed as it has is in part explained by the recognition that historically most Americans, besides advocating popular sovereignty (i.e., "government of the people, by the people, and for the people"), have also wanted a "government of laws, not men." The basic law, traditionally the very symbol of law in America, is the United States Constitution. In the quest for a government bounded by the basic law, the judiciary—an institution whose function is the application of law in the resolution of disputes—became a major institution for making national policies.[29]

In making policy the judiciary's legitimacy rests, at least traditionally, upon its acting judicially. In other words, the historic rationale for allowing judges to pronounce national policies based on constitutional law was that judges were expected to be judgelike. This implies certain standards of fidelity to law, impartiality, objectivity, and professionalism. Yet, as any student of American history knows, this is only half the story. The basic ideological ethos, perhaps since the election of Jefferson and definitely since the election of Jackson, is profoundly democratic. When over the long run the flow of judicial policy-making has systematically run counter to popular needs or popular constitutional interpretations, the legitimacy of those policies has been seriously questioned. A fascinating tension, therefore, surrounds judicial policy-making, and this tension is reflected in regime rules related to judicial role playing.

Role[30] conceptions provide the normative framework through which members of a system determine how they should behave when performing systemic duties or functions. They serve as reference points for members in two ways. First, a member's expectations concerning the role he or she occupies indicates how he or she should and should not act in various situations. Second, in a similar manner, this same person feels secure in performing those aspects of his or her role that are based on widely acknowledged regime rules because of the expectation that other members of the system will likewise adhere to the regime rules relating to their roles. This is important since most roles are complementary rather than redundant; for example, the adversary process at trial is conceived of as two opposing advocates and a neutral and impartial judge and jury.

The social and psychological pressures (to say nothing of potential disciplinary actions) involved in directing authorities in a professionally staffed system such as the federal judiciary to follow the regime rules related to their roles are numerous. Members of the legal profession typically have been immersed in an environment of legalism from about the age of 22 on. This legal-cultural environment is created and maintained in law school, through membership in various professional organizations, by intraprofessional contacts, and, of course, for most, through a constant workday world as judge or lawyer. Much of the intent and effect of this process is to indicate to the lawyer and potential lawyer how to think and act when confronted with a legal situation. Generally, the rewards of higher professional attainment and respect are reserved for those who have demonstrated at least surface conformity to such regime rules.

To examine these regime rules as they define the roles played by the major authorities in the processing of litigation, one could turn to the literature of traditional jurisprudence.[31] There are, however, problems with this literature and it must be used with care. First, despite the multitude of efforts to articulate, rationalize, and formulate judicial system roles into codes of ethics, rarely does full agreement exist as to just what constitutes proper behavior under all circumstances for such authorities as trial and appellate judges, defense lawyers, and prosecutors. Second, this literature has typically been denigrated by many behavioral scientists as camouflaging a reality of personal values, biases, convenient informal relations, and even unethical behavior. Although it is now clear that traditional jurisprudence provides neither an accurate nor a complete description of empirical reality, it is also apparent that it does suggest certain regime rules, certain norms that provide the basis for much role playing.

The idealized case of traditional jurisprudence goes through three stages: pretrial, trial, and appeal. Traditional jurisprudence focuses upon trial and appeal as the most important parts of this process. In so doing, it betrays a bias toward the adversary method. There is strong evidence, however, against the primacy of the adversary method in the empirical world of civil litigation and criminal case processing. Typically, in the federal district courts over 90 percent of civil cases are settled out of court prior to trial or before its conclusion, and for over 60 percent of criminal defendants a trial judgment is avoided by a plea of guilty or *nolo contendere,* usually arrived at through bargaining between the prosecution and the defense. With somewhat more than half the remaining criminal defendants, the prosecution drops the charges. Thus, for only about one in six or seven defendants does trial occur.[32] These figures indicate that most cases are not resolved by an adversary process but rather by pretrial negotiations.

Bargaining before trial requires a very different set of roles than does an adversary proceeding. Lawyers familiar with the existing world of settling cases adjust their behavior to meet the functional needs of the system.[33] Making the situation more complex, however, is the fact that if negotiation does not lead to an out-of-court settlement or a guilty plea, a trial will result and the lawyers will then assume adversary roles. In civil cases even the judge is affected by this role switch. At pretrial the judge was probably an aggressive arbitrator trying to pressure the litigants to settle;[34] at the trial the judge becomes a more passive referee.

In the Anglo-American legal tradition, trial is highly formalized combat between two parties. Both the high level of formalization—typified by extremely technical rules concerning, for example, framing of the complaint and the presentation of evidence—and the emphasis on winning gives a trial a sporting atmosphere. This no doubt explains the popularity of courtroom fiction where the trials are more gamelike than is typical.

In the model trial one typically finds the following participants: a judge, two parties or litigants (plaintiff and respondent in a civil suit, prosecutor and defendant in a criminal case), their lawyers, witnesses, and a jury. Traditional theory presumes that the trial will resolve two types of questions: questions of fact and questions of law. It further presumes that these two questions can be both analytically and empirically distinguished.

It is the jury's task to decide on the questions of fact, that is, what happened. In many civil suits, the jury also sets damages by deciding how much the case is worth to the plaintiff. The jurors are not supposed to decide until all the evidence has been presented. In a civil case, the jury decides which side "a preponderance of the evidence" favors. In a criminal case, it decides whether the defendant is guilty "beyond a reasonable doubt." Civil and criminal proceedings are kept separate from each other. This is true even if the same action, for example an assault, leads to both types of trial, a criminal proceeding to bring the perpetrator of the assault to justice and a civil action by the victim to collect damages. A court's verdict of guilty in the criminal case cannot be used as evidence in the civil trial; an award of damages in the civil case cannot be used as proof of guilt in the criminal proceeding.

Often when there are no contested facts and the amount of damages is not an issue, the trial is held before a judge only without a jury. This is called a "bench trial." Parenthetically, it should be noted that a jury trial is not mandatory. If both parties agree, the right to a jury trial can be waived and a bench trial held. For various historical reasons, cases in equity, in contrast to cases in law, are always tried before a judge only.

In a bench trial the judge tends to be rather active. Since there are no jurors and often no witnesses, the main participants (judge and counsel for each side) are all professional lawyers. The exchange between bench and bar tends to be spirited and framed in the highly technical language of the law.

In a jury trial the judge is more passive. This is true not only in comparison to a bench trial but also in comparison with trial judges in other Western nations such as Great Britain.[35] In the model jury trial the judge instructs the jury as to the substantive law of the case and also maintains proper procedure and decorum. In the course of the trial the judge is mainly concerned with ruling on matters of procedure. Uncorrected procedural errors may lead to a higher court's reversing or vacating the trial court's judgment.

The law concerning procedure is mainly concerned with what types of physical evidence, testimony, and questioning of witnesses are permissible for establishing the facts of the case. The courtroom professionals, judge and lawyers, are expected to be alert and allow only permissible evidence, since jurors cannot be expected to know what is permissible and what is not. There are tight restrictions on what evidence may be introduced, particularly in criminal trials. For example, coerced confessions, illegally seized evidence, hearsay evidence, and testimony concerning a defendant's past or prior criminal record are generally forbidden.

The tools available to the judge for maintaining proper procedure and preserving courtroom decorum are many. For example, the judge: (1) may forbid the submission of various forms of evidence or instruct the jurors to disregard it; (2) may call a mistrial, thus causing a new trial to be held; (3) can give a directed verdict to the jury if he or she finds the evidence in no way can be held to constitute the alleged wrongdoing; and (4) may discipline counsel or witnesses by citing them for contempt of court.[36] After both sides have completed their presentations, the judge states the law of the case to the jury and spells out the consequences of various findings of fact. The jury makes a collective decision, which in the federal judicial system must be unanimous, unless in civil suits both parties agree to abide by the verdict or finding of a majority of the jurors. A "hung" jury, that is, one where an unanimous decision is not reached, results in a mistrial (but note that under contemporary Supreme Court rulings unanimous juries in the states are not required, thus allowing the states, if they wish, to permit less than unanimous jury verdicts).[37]

After the verdict of the jury is delivered, the judge states it as the judgment of the court and specifies the remedy or sentence, if any. In a civil case in law, the typical remedy that the plaintiff asks for and receives is damages paid in money. In a case in equity a much greater range of remedies is possible. These include the *injunction* (a court order instructing the respondent not to do or continue to do some action that would cause irreparable harm to the plaintiff) and the writ of *specific performance* (an order obliging the respondent to abide by the terms of the contract or agreement to specifically do or not to do something). In criminal cases many types of sentences are presently given. They are still centered, however, on the traditional ones of fine, probation, and imprisonment.

Although they are the court's formal decision makers, judge and jury themselves do not unearth evidence. Evidence is presented to them by the opposing lawyers, whose function it is to gather documents, physical exhibits, and witnesses for establishing the facts of the case. Similarly, control of errors in both procedure and substantive law, even though requiring rulings from the bench, rests upon objection and argument by the lawyers. Rarely will a judge stop the submission of forbidden evidence unless called to do so from the bar. Nor, in actuality, does an error in procedure or interpretation of substantive law including judicial precedent generally provide grounds for appeal unless it is objected to within time limits set by the system's procedural rules. Just as courts are not self-starting (that is, they do not go out searching for cases, but depend upon cases being brought to them by a plaintiff or prosecutor), neither are they automatically self-correcting.

Most of the content of the lawyer's role as partisan advocate has already been suggested. However, there are limits to lawyer advocacy. These stem from the lawyer's collateral role as "officer of the court." According to the Canons of Legal Ethics,[38] a lawyer is liable to possible punishment in the form of censure, suspension, disbarment, or contempt if, for example, the lawyer promotes a case that he or she knows is patently spurious or knowingly allows presentation of perjured or deliberately misleading testimony or falsified documents or physical evidence. The canons also require the lawyer to present evidence and precedents even though they may be detrimental to the client's cause, and lawyers are supposed to behave so as to preserve the decorum of the court and the integrity of the judicial process. In practice, however, sanctions are rarely applied to enforce the canons.[39]

Thus far we have outlined almost the full structure of the model trial with hardly mentioning either witnesses or, seemingly the most important participants of all, the private litigants. This is because their parts are very small and the standards of behavior expected from them are minimal. A litigant, for example, once the lawyer has been hired and once the case goes to trial (a decision that can always be averted by an out-of-court settlement in a civil case or a guilty plea in a criminal case) has little else to do. At most the litigant takes the stand to testify (and in criminal cases the defendant has the constitutional right not to do so). There, the only normative demand upon the litigant, as with all witnesses, is to tell the truth. Failure to do so may lead to a charge of perjury and subsequent judicial proceedings.

After judgment is entered, the disappointed party (except for the prosecution in a criminal case when there is an acquittal) has to decide whether to appeal. Appellate proceedings are only supposed to be used for correcting legal errors from the trial. The only questions, therefore, are questions of law: substantive, procedural, or both. Despite this conceptualization of appeal, one sometimes finds in the opinions of appellate courts the most surprising "facts" as compared to those ostensibly established during the trial. These "facts," moreover, may be social or economic facts and not necessarily the narrowly construed facts of the dispute.

Since at appeal there are no facts to determine, there are no witnesses, rarely are there displays of physical evidence, and, of course, there is no jury. The only active participants are the judges and the lawyers. The litigants are usually not even present. Similar to a bench trial, the exchange between bench and bar can be spirited. As at trial, it is the lawyer's role to be a partisan advocate in preparing the brief and during oral argument. In Supreme Court cases, when there are larger implications of the policy at issue, other interested parties are often allowed to join the formal parties through the presentation of *amicus curiae* (friend of the court) briefs.

Like trial judges, appellate judges are expected to be objective articulators of the law. They are expected to adhere to precedent (the rule of *stare decisis*). Since, however, the ostensible reason for appeal is that the trial courts can err, or the precedents are conflicting or ambiguous, the questions considered in the model appeal are those in which there supposedly is some professional doubt as to what is the law. Thus, the typical appellate judge has a greater opportunity than the typical trial judge to be a creative policymaker.

There is no general agreement as to how creative and how broad judicial policy-making should be. Those who most feel the tensions of having a nondemocratic policy-making judiciary in a democratic system have generally urged judicial restraint. This means avoiding, when possible, cases that force policy-making or, if avoidance is impossible, deciding them narrowly. Others, who welcome the opportunity to use the legal tools developed by the judiciary to correct what they perceive as injustice, are called judicial activists. They show less reluctance to exercise judicial power and to consider politically controversial issues and make broad constitutional policies.

Interestingly, there seems to be no consistent ideological orientation associated with either one of these two role conceptions. In the late nineteenth and early twentieth centuries, conservatives were activist on economic and social welfare policy while liberals urged judicial restraint. Since the late 1930s liberals have generally been activist on civil liberties policy while conservatives espouse restraint. A simplified chart (Figure 2.3) suggests the cross-cuttings of ideology and role on the Supreme Court. Of course in reality ideology and role concept are more complex phenomena, with each better represented by a continuum rather than a dichotomy.

Appellate court decisions that the judges consider important are usually announced with a full opinion. The Opinion of the Court, among other things, is an appellate court's attempt to show to both members of the legal profession and the general public that the judicial criteria of objectivity, professionalism, and

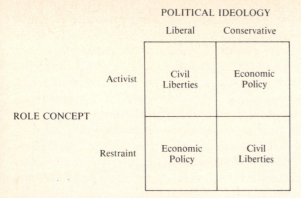

Figure 2.3 Ideology and role concept

fidelity to the law have been met. If there is a dissenting opinion, its main purpose is to show that the court has erred while attempting to meet these judicial criteria. A concurring opinion falls somewhat in between and seeks to demonstrate alternate paths to the same result reached by the majority or to highlight certain points glossed over in the main opinion. Typically, all types of opinions contain citations of appropriate precedents, statutes or constitutional provisions, historical materials on legislative intent, and treatises by recognized legal scholars. In recent years the courts have more frequently turned to commentaries and analyses published in law reviews. Even various social science writings have been cited. The purpose of all these citations is to legitimize the decision, to show that the court acted professionally.

THE FEDERAL JUDICIAL SYSTEM AS A BUREAUCRACY

The federal judicial system displays most of the attributes of Max Weber's ideal type of *bureaucracy*.[40] In fact, much of Weber's original description is concerned with governmental organizations exercising judicial or quasi-judicial functions even though he conceived of bureaucracy as a form of organization found in private as well as governmental institutions.

In brief, Weber states that the function of a bureaucratic organization is the administration of law. This consists of the application of technical rules and norms to particular cases. The rules and norms are typically given, or at least not disapproved, by institutions that lie outside and formally above the bureaucratic unit. The authority of the organization's officials is binding only to the extent to which these externally given rules and norms are faithfully and objectively applied. This model in large part is consistent with traditional notions of the federal judiciary's constitutional relationships with the states, Congress, and the President.[41]

This organizational model, however, appears to provide little explanation for the large degree of discretion shown by the federal courts, particularly the Supreme Court, in articulating judicial norms. This is both a function of various aspects of the model which are thus far unstated and a reflection of some unique characteristics of American constitutionalism and the federal judiciary.

No bureaucracy can resolve particular disputes without articulating rules and norms on its own unless the system of law being applied meets the following criteria: (1) Each rule or norm is unambiguous; (2) the entire set of rules and norms is detailed and complete; and (3) all the rules and norms are consistent with one another. Obviously the set of rules and norms that the federal courts use for resolving cases does not and, to some degree, cannot meet all these criteria.

No law, no matter how detailed and complete, is unambiguous for all cases. This is especially true in a world of rapid technological and social innovation. The Constitution and many federal statutes such as the Sherman Antitrust Act primarily contain general principles. General principles, however, cannot be used for resolving concrete cases without the presence of interstitial norms and rules. According to Weber, it is some outside institution, Congress, for example, whose task it is to supply these rules through legislation. In fact, neither Congress nor any other institution has done so for all areas.

For example, in *Bibb* v. *Navajo Freight Lines*[42] one finds a situation in which a lack of interstitial rules, though not surprising, proved important. The case concerned truck mudflaps. In the absence of action by either Congress or the Interstate Commerce Commission, two states had passed directly conflicting regulations. Full enforcement of both regulations was seriously hampering the flow of interstate truck transport, a situation inconsistent with the principle of freely flowing domestic trade implicit in the commerce clause of the Constitution. The Supreme Court created a national mudflap regulation in order to resolve the dispute. In similar cases the Court has decided the permissible length of railroad trains[43] and the maximum width of motor trucks.[44]

Like all bureaucracies, the federal judiciary enforces norms and rules given it by institutions exterior to it *acting in their legal capacities*. But unlike most bureaucracies, the federal judiciary has allocated to itself the function of determining when these institutions (e.g., Congress, the President, administrative agencies, the states) are so acting. This means that the federal courts, in articulating rules and norms, are involved in more than just interstitial interpretation.

Even though the federal judiciary demonstrates a broader discretion in making the rules and norms that it applies in adjudicating cases than do most bureaucratic organizations, this discretion is exercised in a bureaucratic manner. It is based on the interstitial interpretation of written law in the adjudication of particular concrete cases. The broader and more creative policy-making aspects of this process are carried on most visibly by the highest court in the system, the Supreme Court. But even the Supreme Court operates under limits resulting from its bureaucratic nature. It is not, as both its attackers and apologists have sought to maintain, either a legislature or an ongoing constitutional convention.

Not only does the federal judicial system exhibit the functional attributes of a bureaucratic organization, it also exhibits structural attributes. This should not be surprising since the central core of Weberian analysis is that function and structure are irrevocably bound to each other. Let us compare, therefore, the basic attributes of bureaucratic structure with the structure of the federal judicial system.

Bureaucratic organization is characterized by a rigidly prescribed division of labor based upon geography and function. This division of labor concerns both the subunits of the organization and the offices making up each unit. The actions taken by each official and subunit have authority only insofar as their actions lie within the official's or subunit's sphere of competence. Subunits are arranged hierarchically with a right to appeal the decisions of a lower subunit to a higher one. This serves to maintain uniformity in decision making. The main mechanism for achieving uniform decision making, however, is through the technical training of the officials. This is accomplished by selecting officials by appointment only from among those who have demonstrated the proper technical qualifications as certified by education and/or examination. Officials, once appointed, are bound to their office by a salary. In general, officials regard their salary as their primary means of support and treat their offices as life-long careers. The private and official lives of the officials are radically separated. Officials are not to appropriate either the funds or resources of their offices for private use. All official acts and decisions are put formally in writing. These constitute the "files" of the organization.

Note how easily Weber's analysis of bureaucracy accounts for the essentials of judicial organization, selection, tenure, formal behavior, and procedure. The organization's basic subunits are its courts. Each has a unique geographical and/or functional jurisdiction. Lower courts are linked to higher courts through appellate review. Judges in particular, but other court officials as well (including lawyers), must meet certain technical qualifications. Selection of permanent court officials is by appointment. Remuneration for the most important of these officials —the judges—is by set income that cannot be diminished. It is of such a scale that it is their primary or sole source of income.[45] Judicial authority extends only to official acts. All official acts are set down as written transcripts, orders, rules, and opinions. The whole system is permeated by rigid rules relating to such matters as jurisdiction, procedure, admissibility of evidence, remedies, and appellate review.

To Weber, the structural characteristics of bureaucracy account for the ability of this mode of organization to rationally carry out its function of administration. This rationality is manifested in consistency, efficiency, and impersonality in decision making. To Weber, bureaucracy was a laudable term. But as we know both from popular lore and from works of later sociologists, bureaucracy has some not so laudable, *dysfunctional*[46] aspects. The rigid rules and impersonality of the system exact large temporal, monetary, and psychic costs upon the bureaucracy's clients. Organizational and procedural maintenance become of greater importance to officials than the accomplishment of such formal goals as efficient administration of the law. Rigid adherence to precedent may lead to decisions that are irrelevant or even counterproductive in a society characterized by rapidly changing social mores and a developing technology. For example, judicial economic conservatism in the early 1930s—a conservatism that largely ignored changes in economic patterns and relationships—can in one sense be considered to have been a bureaucratic problem.

Weber's model of bureaucracy also obscures many informal patterns of behavior prevalent in organizational life. This obscurity in itself decreases the suitability of the Weberian ideal type as an explanatory model. Systems analysis, in contrast, suggests the investigation of all systemic interactions, both formal and informal. It is these more informal interactional and behavior patterns that will receive the greatest emphasis in the following chapters.

NOTES

1. *State Court Organization 1980* (Washington, D.C.: U.S. Department of Justice, Bureau of Justice Statistics, May, 1982), pp. 6–7, 10–11, 54–66.
2. *Annual Report of the Director, Administrative Office of the United States Courts, 1982.* The Report is hereafter cited as *Report, U.S. Courts.* Note that the fiscal year refers to the 12-month period and year ending June 30. Fiscal 1982 thus began July 1, 1981, and ended June 30, 1982. For a broad cross-cultural consideration of litigation and the role of courts, see Austin Sarat and Joel B. Grossman, "Courts and Conflict Resolution: Problems in the Mobilization of Adjudication," *American Political Science Review,* 69 (1975), 1200–1217. Also see Wolf V. Heydebrand, "The Context of Public Bureaucracies: An Organizational Analysis of Federal District Courts," *Law and Society Review,* 11 (1977), 759–821. The fiscal 1982 figures for the entire nation were derived from *Bureau of Justice Statistics, Special Report,* February 1983, Table 1, p. 2.
3. Between 1842 and 1938, federal courts disregarded state law and instead developed and applied national norms. See Swift v. Tyson, 16 Pet. 1 (1842). For a likely explanation of why this happened see Sheldon Goldman, *Constitutional Law and Supreme Court Decision-Making* (New York: Harper & Row, 1982), pp. 115–116. Erie R. Co. v. Tompkins, 304 U.S. 64 (1938), reverted to the pre-1842 practice of using state law.
4. There is an exception to this usually categorically stated rule. Under a civil rights law passed in 1866, two grounds were given for removal of state criminal cases to the federal courts prior to trial. These are (1) cases involving federal officials charged with crimes when performing their duties (this is to prevent state harassment of federal officials involved in investigations or law enforcement), and (2) cases where the defendant can point to a specific state law, constitutional provision, or judicial interpretation that would "predictably" deprive him or her of equal civil rights. Particularly in the mid-1960s, petitions for removal to the federal district courts increased dramatically. See Georgia v. Rachel, 384 U.S. 780 and City of Greenwood v. Peacock, 384 U.S. 808 (1966), for Supreme Court interpretation of the second ground particularly. Also see Johnson v. Mississippi, 421 U.S. 213 (1975).
5. Fay v. Noia, 372 U.S. 391 (1963), removed technical barriers that previously had made it difficult for state prisoners to institute *habeas corpus* actions in federal district courts. In 1976, however, the Burger Court cut back such federal supervision in state cases raising illegal search and seizure issues as long as the matter was litigated in the state courts. See Stone v. Powell, 428 U.S. 465 (1976).
6. These are the appeals courts of general jurisdiction. The Eleventh Circuit Court of Appeals came into being in 1980 when Congress divided the old Fifth Circuit. The twelfth appeals court is the court of appeals for the District of Columbia Circuit. Note that there are also appeals courts with limited specialized jurisdiction. Congress in

1971 created the Temporary Emergency Court of Appeals to have exclusive jurisdiction over certain appeals from the district courts involving challenges to the Economic Stabilization Act of 1970. In subsequent years, appeals were authorized for district court decisions concerning controversies arising under the Emergency Petroleum Allocation Act of 1973, the Energy Policy and Conservation Act of 1975, and the Emergency Natural Gas Act of 1977. The statute creating the court provided that its judgments are reviewable by the Supreme Court. Personnel of the court are drawn from the ranks of active federal judges. Contrary to initial expectations, the court was not flooded with litigation. In fiscal 1981 it decided 57 cases. See *Report, U.S. Courts, 1981,* p. 54. In 1982 Congress created the U.S. Court of Appeals for the Federal Circuit to handle claims, customs, and patent appeals. This new court replaces the old U.S. Court of Customs and Patent Appeals as well as the appellate division of the U.S. Court of Claims. This appeals court has its own separate judgeships and is considered on the same footing as the 12 appeals courts with general jurisdiction.

7. Eighty-nine U.S. district courts are located within the 50 states. The ninetieth is the U.S. District Court for the District of Columbia (Washington, D.C.). The remaining four courts are territorial and legislative courts.

8. O'Donoghue v. United States, 289 U.S. 516 (1933).

9. A detailed analysis of the structure and functions of these administrative bodies can be found in Peter G. Fish, *The Politics of Federal Judicial Administration* (Princeton, N.J.: Princeton University Press, 1973). Note also that for the Supreme Court as well as in each circuit and district, there is a clerk's office that administers the day-to-day operations of their courts. At the circuit level there are also the circuit executive offices and at the Supreme Court level the office of the Administrative Assistant to the Chief Justice of the United States, offices concerned with administrative practices and managerial policies. Also see, in general, Russell Wheeler and Howard R. Whitcomb, *Perspectives on Judicial Administration: Readings in Court Management and the Administration of Justice* (Englewood Cliffs, N.J.: Prentice-Hall, 1977).

10. See Beverly B. Cook, "The Socialization of New Federal Judges: Impact on District Court Business," *Washington University Law Quarterly* (1971), 253–279.

11. *Report, U.S. Courts, 1983,* p. 38.

12. In fiscal 1983, 175 senior judges sat and many of them handled the normal caseloads assumed by judges in active service. *Report, U.S. Courts, 1983,* p. 3.

13. *Report, U.S. Courts, 1983,* pp. 4, 7, 290.

14. A detailed discussion of the concept of district as well as appeals court "constituencies" can be found in Richard Richardson and Kenneth Vines, *The Politics of Federal Courts* (Boston: Little, Brown, 1970), Chap. 3.

15. The $10,000 minimum amount also applies to every member of a class in a class action suit (brought on behalf of all those similarly situated). See Zahn v. International Paper Co., 414 U.S. 291 (1973).

16. *Report, U.S. Courts, 1983,* p. 186.

17. United States v. Nixon, 418 U.S. 683 (1974). Another such expedited case was Youngstown Sheet and Tube Co. v. Sawyer, 343 U.S. 579 (1952), the famous "steel seizure" case that arose when President Truman ordered the Secretary of Commerce to take over the steel mills in order to prevent a union strike that would impair the Korean War effort. In 1981 the Court expedited the case of Dames & Moore v. Regan, 453 U.S. 654 (1981), which concerned the transfer of Iranian assets held by American banks under the terms of the agreement that ended the hostage crisis (American embassy personnel were held hostage in Iran by the revolutionary government). It should be understood that expedited cases are rare.

18. *Federal Court Management Statistics, 1983* (Washington, D.C.: Administrative Office of the U.S. Courts, 1983), p. 15.

19. According to the 1971 legislation that created the positions, each circuit executive is appointed by the Judicial Council and serves at its pleasure. See Robert J. Martineau, "The Federal Circuit Executives: An Initial Report," *Judicature,* 57 (1974), 438–445.

20. *Report, U.S. Courts, 1983,* Tables B-1, B-3. There were also 688 bankruptcy appeals.

21. *Report, U.S. Courts, 1968,* pp. 49–51, 100. See also *Congressional Record—Senate,* August 25, 1967, pp. 12218–12237. But cf. Richardson and Vines, *Politics of Federal Courts,* pp. 41–45; and Glendon Schubert, *Judicial Policy Making,* rev. ed. (Glenview, Ill.: Scott, Foresman, 1974), pp. 16–23.

22. See Paul D. Carrington, "Crowded Dockets and the Courts of Appeals: The Threat to the Function of Review and the National Law," *Harvard Law Review,* 82 (1969), 580–585.

23. *Report, U.S. Courts, 1980,* p. 49.

24. Diplomatic personnel can bring suits in the state courts as well as in the federal courts.

25. Henry J. Abraham, *The Judicial Process,* 4th ed. (New York: Oxford University Press, 1980), p. 181; "The Supreme Court, 1978 Term," *Harvard Law Review,* 93 (1979), 279; "The Supreme Court, 1979 Term," *Harvard Law Review,* 94 (1980), 293; "The Supreme Court, 1980 Term," *Harvard Law Review,* 95 (1981), 343; "The Supreme Court, 1981 Term," *Harvard Law Review,* 96 (1982), 309; "The Supreme Court, 1982 Term," *Harvard Law Review,* 97 (1983), 300.

26. The percentages were calculated from data presented in *Harvard Law Review,* 93 (1979), 278; 94 (1980), 292; 95 (1981), 342.

27. Statistics on appeals were calculated from data from the *Harvard Law Review* and *Statistical Abstract of the United States, 1973* (Washington, D.C.: U.S. Department of Commerce, 1973), p. 159, Table 259. At this point, a note of caution is in order. We found that, with almost all the court statistics examined where there was more than one source reporting, there were usually minor and sometimes major discrepancies in the figures. In general, for Supreme Court statistics reliance was placed on the *Harvard Law Review's* annual summary; for the lower federal courts the publications of the Administrative Office of the U.S. Courts provided the data. When data were lacking from these two sources other sources were used, in particular the *Statistical Abstract,* whose data are supplied by the Administrative Office. Beginning with the 1970 term, there have been major changes in the statistics gathered for the Supreme Court which make it impossible to conduct certain types of analyses. The *Harvard Law Review* explained, "The elimination or consolidation of certain categories was mandated by reductions in the statistics prepared by the Office of the Clerk of the Supreme Court" (*Harvard Law Review,* 87 (1973), 310). Thus, statistics concerning appeals for more recent terms along the lines presented in the text are not available.

28. For example, in the 1976 term, 289 appeals were acted on with 157 dismissed and 90 disposed of summarily. Only 42 cases (about 15 percent) were either scheduled for full hearing or the Court postponed a decision on jurisdiction. See Robert L. Stern and Eugene Gressman, *Supreme Court Practice,* 5th ed. (Washington, D.C.: Bureau of National Affairs, 1978), p. 256, note 4. It should be noted that unlike a denial of certiorari, which supposedly implies no approval or disapproval of lower court behavior, both the decisions to affirm and to dismiss are decisions on the merits of the case. Every year the Court dismisses a number of appeals as improperly brought, but then treats them as petitions for certiorari that are denied. This process makes it clear that the Court is not necessarily giving approval to the lower court decision.

29. For an explanation of how this process occurred and some of its ramifications, see

Alexander Bickel, *The Least Dangerous Branch* (Indianapolis: Bobbs-Merrill, 1962), especially pp. 1–33.

30. Talcott Parsons, one of the leading social system theorists, saw role at the heart of a social system. See, in particular, Parsons and Edward A. Shils (eds.), *Toward a General Theory of Action* (Cambridge, Mass.: Harvard University Press, 1951); and Parsons, *The Social System* (New York: Free Press, 1951). Perhaps more comprehensible to the student is William C. Mitchell, *Sociological Analysis and Politics: The Theories of Talcott Parsons* (Englewood Cliffs, N.J.: Prentice-Hall, 1967). Note that role is discussed from the perspective of judicial conversion in Chapter 5.

31. This literature is immense and has a vast range as to quality, approach, and subject matter. Traditional views of legal and judicial roles and norms are discussed, for example, in Lewis Mayers, *The American Legal System,* rev. ed. (New York: Harper & Row, 1964); Edward H. Levi, *An Introduction to Legal Reasoning* (Chicago: Phoenix Books, 1948); Henry S. Drinker, *Legal Ethics* (New York: Columbia University Press, 1953); Geoffrey C. Hazard, Jr., *Ethics in the Practice of Law* (New Haven, Conn.: Yale University Press, 1978).

32. These figures are for recent fiscal years. See, for example, *Report, U.S. Courts, 1983,* Tables C-4, D-7.

33. See Arthur L. Wood, "Professional Ethics among Criminal Lawyers," *Social Problems,* 7 (1959), 70–83; Jerome E. Carlin, *Lawyers' Ethics* (New York: Russell Sage Foundation, 1966). In general, see the articles and bibliography in *Law and Society Review,* 13 (1979), 189–687, devoted to various aspects of plea bargaining and the behavior of lawyers.

34. See, for example, the account of one federal district judge in J. Skelly Wright, "The Pretrial Conference," *Federal Rules Decisions,* 18 (1962), 141–158, reprinted in Sheldon Goldman and Austin Sarat (eds.), *American Court Systems* (San Francisco: Freeman, 1978), pp. 119–121.

35. Delmar Karlen, *Anglo-American Criminal Justice* (New York: Oxford University Press, 1967), Chap. 8; Fred L. Morrison, *Courts and the Political Process in England* (Beverly Hills, Calif.: Sage, 1973), Chap. 7.

36. Litigants, too, can be disciplined. See Illinois v. Allen, 397 U.S. 337 (1970).

37. The Supreme Court upheld a Louisiana state law that enabled a 9-out-of-12-person majority to render a jury verdict. See Johnson v. Louisiana, 406 U.S. 356 (1972). However, nonunanimous six-person juries were forbidden in Burch v. Louisiana, 441 U.S. 130 (1979).

38. The Canons of Legal Ethics and the Canons of Judicial Ethics have been formulated and published by the American Bar Association. Courts have occasionally given them the force of law in disciplining those who violate them. See Drinker, *Legal Ethics.*

39. See Carlin, *Lawyers' Ethics,* especially Chaps. 6 and 9; F. Raymond Marks and Darlene Cathcart, "Discipline within the Legal Profession: Is It Self-Regulation?" *Illinois Law Forum* (1974), 193–236. The code of ethics for lawyers is subject to severe scrutiny by Jethro K. Lieberman in his *Crisis at the Bar: Lawyers' Unethical Ethics and What to Do About It* (New York: Norton, 1978).

40. *The Theory of Social and Economic Organization,* trans. by A. M. Henderson and Talcott Parsons (New York: Free Press, 1947), pp. 329–341. See also Martin Shapiro, *The Supreme Court and Administrative Agencies* (New York: Free Press, 1968), for an extensive use of "bureaucratic theory" applied to the Supreme Court; and Wolf V. Heydebrand, "The Context of Public Bureaucracies: An Organizational Analysis of Federal District Courts," *Law and Society Review,* 11 (1977), 759–821.

41. See, for example, Hamilton's view of the Supreme Court in Jacob E. Cooke (ed.), *The Federalist* (New York: World, 1961), *Federalist* No. 78, pp. 521–530.
42. 359 U.S. 520 (1959).
43. Southern Pacific Co. v. Arizona, 325 U.S. 761 (1945).
44. South Carolina State Highway Department v. Barnwell Bros., 303 U.S. 177 (1938). Regarding the length of trucks, see Raymond Motor Transport v. Rice, 434 U.S. 429 (1978), and Kassel v. Consolidated Freightways Corp., 450 U.S. 662 (1981).
45. In 1984, judicial salaries were the following: district judge, $76,000; appeals judge, $80,400; associate justice of the Supreme Court, $100,600; Chief Justice of the Supreme Court, $104,700.
46. "Dysfunctional" refers to aspects of systemic processes and structures that by their operation tend to defeat the achievement of systemic goals. See Robert K. Merton, *Social Theory and Social Structure,* rev. ed. (New York: Free Press, 1957), for a development of the concepts of functional and dysfunctional.

chapter 3

The Authorities: Recruitment, Backgrounds, and Some Interaction Patterns

In order to appreciate how a political system functions—what values it allocates and why it allocates those values the way it does—some knowledge is needed about the authorities of that system. The previous discussion of regime rules suggested the framework within which the authorities behave. Now we examine the authorities themselves more closely in terms of recruitment, backgrounds, and some patterns of interaction. Because judges of the three principal constitutional courts are the primary authorities for the federal judicial system, we devote much of our attention to them. But we also briefly examine some other authorities within the system, particularly government and private lawyers and jurors.[1]

JUDICIAL RECRUITMENT

A number of questions that deserve answering are raised by the subject of judicial recruitment. How are judges chosen? What kind of people does the selection process favor? What socialization experiences do they have in common, and what are the implications of the current recruitment process for the administration of justice?

Judicial selection in the United States is unlike the selection processes of most Western democracies, where many of the fictions associated with traditional jurisprudence are more strongly maintained and being a judge is treated as a distinct profession requiring specialized judicial training. Here, judicial recruitment is a political process with few formal requirements. Nowhere in the Constitution is there a requirement that one must be a lawyer in order to be appointed to the Supreme Court although, of course, in practice only lawyers have served on the Court. To become a federal judge requires (1) nomination by the President; (2) senatorial confirmation by a simple majority vote; and (3) presidential appointment (i.e., the signing and delivery of the Commission, a routine and presumably nondiscretionary act of the President). Behind stages one and two lie a complex of activities.

The appointment of any one judge is the culmination of a unique series of interrelated events that propel one person and not another toward the nomination. Understanding any one particular nomination requires obtaining access to a myriad of often confidential materials. No one appointment can be adequately explained without study of the unique transactions involved.[2] The discussion of recruitment that follows, however, is a general examination of participants and considerations that are thought to be relevant for at least some of the appointees some of the time. First, the focus is on lower court appointments, then on Supreme Court nominations.

Selection of a lower federal court judge typically involves a number of different participants. They include: (1) the President; (2) officials in the Justice Department, especially the Attorney General, the Deputy Attorney General, and their assistants; (3) the U.S. senators of the President's party from the state where the potential nominee resides; (4) various other political leaders of the President's party, such as members of Congress, state party chairpersons, governors, national committeemen and committeewomen, and mayors of large cities from the state "receiving" the nomination; (5) those who aspire to federal judgeships (and their supporters among the bar and bench) who campaign for a position by contacting those just mentioned; (6) the members and particularly the chairperson of the American Bar Association's Standing Committee on Federal Judiciary; and (7) the members of the Senate, in particular those serving on the Senate Judiciary Committee. President Carter was responsible for adding an eighth set of participants, the members of specially created judicial nominating commissions; however, Carter's successor, President Reagan, abandoned the commission concept.

The Process

Traditionally, the Justice Department has maintained files on likely candidates for newly created judgeships and vacant or soon-to-become-vacant lower court judicial positions. In filling a judgeship, Justice officials usually start by considering names proposed by senators and other important party leaders, or they might have their own candidate to promote. The candidates are then informally investigated by an aide to the deputy attorney general (such as the executive assistant) who typically contacts a wide variety of persons both in and out of government.[3] The names of the leading candidates are given to the American Bar Association Standing Committee on Federal Judiciary, which since the Eisenhower Administration has investigated and rated those candidates. The ratings currently used are "Exceptionally Well Qualified," "Well Qualified," "Qualified," and "Not Qualified." At the early stages, the committee gives Justice officials an informal tentative-but-probable rating of the leading contenders. Poor tentative ratings can be used by Justice officials as the basis for dropping candidates from consideration.

The process changed somewhat when President Carter was elected President. Carter adopted what on the surface was a merit-type procedure for selecting appeals court judges and he encouraged Democratic party senators to adopt analogous commissions for recruiting district court judges. By executive order, Carter created the United States Circuit Judge Nominating Commission with at least one panel for each circuit. For each vacancy, the nominating commission was to recommend five qualified persons and the Carter Administration was to select its nominee from among those recommended. Similarly, senators were asked to establish nominating commissions to help fill district court judgeships. The Administration preferred that several names be forwarded to the Justice Department; however, the Carter officials acquiesced to the practice of senators screening the list of those recommended by the senators' commissions. In a number of instances, Democratic party senators did not establish nominating commissions and instead relied on the traditional practice of senators of the president's party making their recommendations to the Justice Department. The Carter Administration emphasized its desire to throw open the nominating process so that women, blacks, and Hispanics in particular would be actively recruited. In this, as will be discussed later in this chapter, the Carter Administration was successful. In terms of establishing a so-called merit process, the Carter Administration was successful only to the extent that well-qualified Democrats were for the most part recommended by the commissions (which themselves consisted predominantly of those affiliated with the Democratic party).[4] President Reagan, however, returned to the more traditional process of selection.

A candidate who has strong senatorial backing and support of the party leaders from the candidate's state is assured of nomination and confirmation if he or she also meets the standards of the Justice Department and the ABA committee. However, when there is no consensus as to the nominee, Justice officials must engage in extensive negotiations with the senators and/or other party leaders of the President's party. The extent to which Justice officials will defer, in particular, to the wishes of senators depends upon instructions from the President. Presidents Eisenhower, Kennedy, and Carter let it be known that their Justice Department officials were authorized to negotiate for the best possible nominees, and with the Carter Administration that also meant women and minorities. President Johnson, on the other hand, although sympathetic—even at times deferential—to the wishes of Democratic party senators, took a personal interest in the nominees and instituted greater White House involvement than probably has occurred previously or subsequently.[5] Presidents Nixon and Ford put their confidence in their Attorney Generals to handle matters as they saw fit on a case-by-case, senator-by-senator basis.[6] The Reagan Administration followed this practice.

Prior to the Nixon Administration, the Justice officials would, on the basis of their own and the ABA committee's investigations, be ready to decide whom to recommend for a post. The Justice officials typically would informally check with members of the Senate Judiciary Committee to make sure no unexpected difficulties with a nomination would arise. Then, as a virtual last step in the process, the FBI would be instructed to conduct a routine investigation of the candidate. Assuming no unexpectedly adverse information was uncovered, the attorney general would formally make the recommendation in a letter to the President. The White House would then announce the nomination and send the appropriate nomination papers to the Senate.

This process, particularly the use of the FBI investigation, changed during the Nixon Administration, although the beginnings of the expanded use of the FBI can be traced to the Morrissey nomination fiasco in 1965 (discussed in greater detail shortly) in which some crucial facts about Morrissey's past were discovered by newspaper reporters rather than the FBI. The Morrissey episode convinced Justice officials that the FBI investigation would have to be more thorough to further prevent such embarrassments. But it was not until the Nixon Administration took office that the major changes occurred.

In the early days of the Nixon Administration, Justice officials and the ABA committee agreed that, in order to be seriously considered, each candidate for a judicial slot would be required to complete an extensive questionnaire that would provide a wide variety of personal and professional information about the candidate. Candidates would also be required to sign waivers permitting inspection of all their medical records. Among other matters the questionnaire contains items asking each candidate to list the ten most important cases handled and the names of opposing counsel and the judges before whom the cases came. In the hands of the FBI the completed questionnaire and the medical records waiver have provided the basis for a thorough, more wide-ranging investigation than the routine FBI investigations of the past.

During the Senate's consideration of the ill-fated Carswell nomination to the Supreme Court, newspaper reporters dug from the clipping files of a local newspaper an account of a racist speech that Carswell had once made as a young candidate for public office, and this caught the Justice Department and the FBI by surprise. After Carswell, the FBI would go through the clipping files of the local newspapers in the areas where the candidate had lived as part of the investigation. During the Nixon years the FBI became a major tool for discovering the racial, social, economic, and political views of the candidates. Thus, the information contained in the FBI dossier in the hands of the Justice officials is a powerful resource in the negotiations with senators.

Once a nomination is sent to the Senate, it is given to the Senate Judiciary Committee. Then, as a matter of routine, the chairman of the Senate Judiciary Committee sends out what are known as the "blue slips." These are forms that officially notify the senators from the nominee's home state that the nomination has been received by the committee. The form also has space for the senator's reply and, in addition, contains this caveat: "Under a rule of the Committee, unless a reply is received from you within a week from this date, it will be assumed that you have no objection to this nomination."[7] In practice, before 1979, a senator, especially a member of the President's party, who opposed the nominee would quietly inform the chairman of the Senate Judiciary Committee and withhold the blue slip. That nomination would then never be acted upon by the committee. When Senator Edward Kennedy became chairman in 1979, he announced that under his chairmanship no longer would a nomination die by failure to return the blue slip. Instead, Kennedy declared that *all* nominations would be acted upon by the full committee and the committee would determine whether or not to proceed with the nomination.[8] In general, it is during closed sessions that the committee determines when and if it will hold public hearings. In 1981, when the Republicans took control of the Senate, Kennedy lost his chairmanship and Republican Senator Strom Thurmond took command. He let it be known that he would be more sympathetic to his senatorial colleagues when they objected to a nominee from their state. However, Thurmond also made it clear that the traditional formula of opposition must be invoked—that is, the senator must assert that the nominee is "personally obnoxious." This in fact came into play with a nominee from Wisconsin who was opposed by Democratic Senator William Proxmire (Wisconsin). Because Senator Proxmire was not of the President's party, Senator Thurmond proceeded with the nomination and held a hearing, but he carefully established in questioning Proxmire that the nominee was *not* "personally obnoxious" to Proxmire.[9]

When Senator Kennedy became chairman of the Senate Judiciary Committee, he established an investigatory staff for the committee to examine the backgrounds of the nominees so that the committee would be in an independent position to make its own evaluation and not have to rely on the Justice Department. Kennedy's successor, Senator Thurmond, retained the committee's investigatory apparatus but installed his own investigatory team. Assuming that the senators of the President's party from whose state the nominee comes approve the nomination and the committee's investigation turns up nothing negative, the committee typically votes to recommend confirmation and sends the nomination to the floor of the Senate. On occasion, opposition is voiced on the Senate floor against a nomination. It is customary, however, for the Senate to vote to confirm a nominee favorably recommended by the committee. Once the nomination is confirmed, it is sent to the President, and he signs the appointment documents. The judge takes the judicial oath and begins serving on the federal bench.

Selection Variable: "Qualified" Appointments

Perhaps the most important constraint on all principal participants in the recruitment process is the now widespread expectation that judicial nominees should be "qualified." Obviously the federal bench is no place for party hacks and incompetents. The problem, however, is how to evaluate a candidate for a judicial post. What makes one person "qualified" and another not? Ostensibly the ABA committee makes distinctions in its ratings, for example, between "Exceptionally Well Qualified" and "Well Qualified" or between "Qualified" and "Not Qualified" on the basis of age, professional (particularly trial court) experience, reputation, scholarly qualities, and "judicial temperament." But how objective are these criteria and, more important, how objective is the ABA committee in applying them?

One study of the ABA committee during the Kennedy Administration revealed that assessments of candidates were primarily made by Wall Street and Bar Association–establishment types.[10] In the past, the organized bar was known to oppose candidates with liberal views. A prominent example of this occurred when the organized bar almost en masse opposed the nomination of liberal Louis Brandeis to the Supreme Court in 1916.[11] By the mid-1960s, however, the American Bar Association seemed to have become somewhat less conservative,[12] and, in fact, the ABA committee in 1968 supported liberal Abe Fortas's nomination to the chief justiceship at a time when conservative criticism of the Supreme Court was at a peak (although the ABA was of no help to Fortas less than a year later when he was, in effect, forced to resign from the bench[13]). Even if the ABA is no longer biased against liberal views and those who hold them[14] and may now be able to more objectively evaluate judicial candidates of different ideological leanings, the question nevertheless remains whether a private group should play such a role in recruitment of such important authorities.

In 1965, the ABA committee's role and political clout in the recruitment process came into prominent view when the Johnson Administration decided to nominate a man considered unqualified by the members of the ABA committee. In late September, 1965, President Johnson sent to the Senate the nomination of Boston Municipal Court Judge Francis X. Morrissey for a position on the District Court of Massachusetts. Morrissey, an old friend of the Kennedy family, was sponsored by Senator Edward Kennedy. The ABA committee could barely contain its outrage. A parade of ABA dignitaries testified against Morrissey before the Senate Judiciary Committee.[15] Editorial writers throughout the country, stimulated by ABA opposition, decried the nomination.[16]

The chairman of the ABA committee questioned Morrissey's integrity by testifying that Morrissey, in gaining admission to the Georgia bar, claimed he was a resident of Georgia only to leave shortly thereafter for Boston. Morrissey, in his defense, testified that he had remained in Georgia for about six months after receiving his law degree from an unaccredited Georgia law school and during that time tried to establish a law practice. He had thus considered himself a Georgia resident. A few days after Morrissey's testimony, however, a Boston newspaper revealed that during the time that Morrissey claimed he was a Georgia resident, he was a candidate for a seat in the Massachusetts legislature, a fact the FBI investigation on Morrissey failed to reveal!

Although the Massachusetts Bar Association endorsed Morrissey and Senator Edward Kennedy pressed hard for the nomination, the nomination appeared doomed. On October 21, 1965, Kennedy dramatically asked the Senate to send the nomination back to committee, and his colleagues complied. Two weeks later the President withdrew the nomination at Morrissey's request.

Aside from illustrating the activity of the ABA committee, this episode also demonstrates how difficult it has been for a judgeship to be obtained for a person considered by the ABA to be unqualified.[17] However, it should be noted that because of the very extensive FBI investigation, in instances where a candidate was given a marginal rating, the Justice officials could suggest to the ABA committee chair that the information upon which the relatively poor rating was based was inadequate and that the committee should go back and recheck the candidate, this time contacting different sources. Apparently this was done in a few instances and resulted in better ratings.[18]

Early in his Administration, President Nixon pledged that he would not nominate any person rated "Not Qualified" by the ABA committee.[19] Thus, the ABA committee was given a veto in the judicial recruitment process that lasted up to the last days of the Administration. But, during Nixon's last full day in office, bowing to pressure from Republican Senator Lowell Weicker (Connecticut), he sent to the Senate the nomination of Thomas Meskill, governor of Connecticut (and former congressman), to fill a vacancy on the prestigious U.S. Court of Appeals for the Second Circuit. Meskill was unanimously rated "Not Qualified" by the ABA committee.[20] Meskill's nomination brought out the opposition of leading law professors from the Yale and University of Connecticut law schools,[21] as well as the ire of the editorial writers of the *New York Times.*[22] Yet the ABA was on less firm ground than with the Morrissey nomination because, after all, they were dealing with a former congressman and an incumbent governor. The unwillingness of the ABA committee to fight as they did in the Morrissey case and their inability to clearly face the issue of whether Meskill had the competence and judicial temperament for a seat on the prestigious Second Circuit was the major reason why the ABA lost the fight.[23] Despite the Meskill episode, it is clear that those who aspire to be serious judicial candidates can be expected to be attuned to the ABA's values and norms of behavior (such as can be identified).

A recently introduced element in the selection process that has a bearing on the selection of "qualified" judges is the use of the investigatory apparatus by the Senate Judiciary Committee since 1979. The committee's investigation became of critical importance for two southern Carter Administration nominations. The most dramatic instance concerned Charles B. Winberry, Jr., who was nominated for the federal district bench in North Carolina. Winberry, who was once campaign manager for Democratic Senator Robert Morgan, was rated "Qualified" by the ABA. But on the basis of the investigatory staff's work, which seriously questioned whether Winberry was qualified, the Senate Judiciary Committee voted not to approve him. The ABA committee, apprised of the new charges, conducted its own investigation and then changed its rating to "Not Qualified."[24] This was the first instance in modern senatorial history of the Senate Judiciary Committee going against the wishes of a fellow senator of the President's party and from the state where the vacancy was to be filled and rejecting a nomination that had been found by the ABA (at least initially) to be qualified for appointment.

The Senate Judiciary Committee's investigatory staff also turned up information that delayed and in effect buried the nomination of the first black to a federal district judgeship in Virginia. Virginia state court judge James Sheffield, rated "Qualified" by the ABA, informed of the allegations at his confirmation hearing then asked for a postponement so that he could prepare a response to them.[25] The nomination, however, was in reality killed.[26]

Even with a Justice Department and FBI investigation, the ABA evaluation, and the Senate committee's own investigation, someone with questionable qualifications can slip by. One such instance in 1979 was particularly embarrassing for both the Carter Administration and Senator Kennedy. A Texas nominee for a district court position, David O. Belew, Jr., survived the screening process and was confirmed by the Senate. Then, in an interview with a local newspaper, he used a racial epithet and seemed to suggest that he had put one over on the Senate Judiciary Committee.[27]

Selection Variable: Party Considerations

As far back as statistics have been gathered, judicial appointments have primarily gone to members of the President's party. In recent administrations at least 90 percent of those appointed have had partisan credentials.[28] By maintaining the importance of partisan considerations, the administration strengthens the President's party and his position as party leader. Reward of the party faithful who have the other necessary qualifications for judicial office encourages lawyers with judicial ambitions to become politically involved. To depart from the tradition of partisan consideration would invite conflict with senators and other party leaders who expect that partisans will be given first preference.

At the very least, senators and major state and local leaders of the President's party expect to be able to "clear," that is, to approve, all appointments of people from their states or localities. Without such influence a party leader's political standing would be severely undermined. At times the appointment situation can become quite complex and drawn out when the senators and other major party leaders support different candidates. Similarly, intraparty politics in which a powerful senator is up against the Administration can also result in a long extended process. This was evident, for example, in the events concerning a vacancy on the First Circuit.

The First Circuit was given a new judgeship as part of the Omnibus Judgeship Act of 1978, which created 117 new federal district judge and 35 new appeals court judge positions. Massachusetts is the largest state within the First Circuit, and Massachusetts Senator Edward Kennedy let it be known that his choice to fill the vacancy was Archibald Cox, the former Watergate special prosecutor, Harvard Law School professor and noted legal scholar, and close associate of the Kennedy family.[29] This was the beginning of an impasse that lasted close to two years. Apparently the Carter Administration did not appreciate this leak to the press that appeared to undermine the integrity of the circuit judge nominating commission created by Carter. The Administration no doubt was not eager to provide a precedent for other senators of shortcircuiting (by announcing in advance who will be chosen) the commission process and denying the Administration the right to make its own choices for the circuits. The Carter Administration warmly praised Kennedy's choices for four federal district court positions in Massachusetts,[30] but when Kennedy began pushing for Cox's appointment (after the list from the commission with Cox's name on it was sent to the President), the Administration said no, citing Cox's age as the reason. Kennedy's anticipated and then actual challenge to Carter for the Democratic presidential nomination resulted in a stalemate—and the continued vacancy on the First Circuit.

After Carter won renomination, negotiations were conducted with Senator Kennedy in order for Carter to obtain Kennedy's active support in the general election campaign. One of Kennedy's conditions—which Carter agreed to—was Carter's promise to nominate Kennedy associate and Chief Counsel to the Senate

Judiciary Committee (and Harvard Law School Professor) Stephen Breyer to the vacancy on the First Circuit.[31] On the home front in the committee, Senator Kennedy won support for Breyer from the ranking Republican member of the committee, Senator Strom Thurmond. Thus, after the election, Carter nominated Breyer, whose name was one of three on a list forwarded to Carter from the nominating commission for the First Circuit. With Thurmond the incoming chairman of the Senate Judiciary Committee keeping the Republicans in line, Breyer was confirmed, becoming the last Carter appointee to the federal courts.

In this example it is clear that the nominating commission was used in such a way as to approximate the traditional selection process. Furthermore, the example shows the importance of party politics, particularly the expectation of leading politicians of the President's party that they will be able to "clear" if not actually pick the appointees from their states.

Selection Variable: Ideological and Policy Position Considerations

It is difficult to pinpoint with precision the extent to which an administration will take into consideration the ideological or policy views of a candidate. There is evidence, however, that such considerations do play a role. A Democratic administration will rarely appoint a Reagan conservative and a Republican administration will not go out of its way to appoint a Kennedy liberal.

Nixon, prior to his election in 1968, made it perfectly clear that he would appoint judicial conservatives to the Supreme Court, and he implied that they would be appointed to the lower courts as well.[32] When running for reelection in 1972, Nixon boasted that his appointments to the federal courts made the Constitution "more secure," and he promised to continue to appoint more "strict constructionists."[33] Examination of Senate Judiciary hearings on Nixon nominees revealed several instances when ideology was explicitly recognized as an important selection consideration. For example, one nominee was introduced by his senator as "a strict constructionist."[34] Another nominee was lauded as one who will practice "judicial restraint."[35] Another, an incumbent state judge, was praised for being "a conservative but perceptive thinker."[36] One observer gave this assessment of the Nixon appointees in an interview with journalist Donald Dale Jackson:

> You can't be a federal judge today unless you believe the whole hardnosed line. It's like getting ahead in the FBI—you have to be for the death penalty, you have to regard all the criminal decisions of the Warren Court as wrong. I've never seen such stereotypes. Any background of liberalism or orientation towards the Bill of Rights is a disqualifier. . . . There are some exceptions, where you have liberal Republican senators like Percy or Javits. But if there's no liberal senator, then you get one-hundred-percent law and order.[37]

It should be emphasized, as suggested in this quote, that the involvement of moderate and liberal senators in the appointment process in a number of instances blunted the sharp edge of the Nixon Administration's professed right-wing goals.

Presidents Ford and Carter were not as openly concerned with the ideological and policy positions of their appointees, but there is evidence to suggest that this consideration was nevertheless present.[38] President Reagan has been more avowedly ideological, and his Administration's right-wing policy preferences were manifested in numerous judicial appointments to known conservatives such as Sandra Day O'Connor (to the Supreme Court) and Robert Bork, Ralph Winter, Richard Posner, and Antonin Scalia (to the appeals courts). In one publicized instance a Republican woman lawyer, rated "Well Qualified" by the ABA and about to be named to the U.S. Court of Appeals for the Eighth Circuit, was abandoned by the Reagan Administration after right-wing critics protested that she was "a strong feminist" and liberal.[39]

A study of behind-the-scenes activity concerning appeals court appointments during the Eisenhower and Kennedy Administrations revealed examples of ideological considerations prominently at work.[40] One instance during the Kennedy Administration occurred when the two Democratic senators from Montana, from where the appointee would be chosen, narrowed their list to two men (James Browning and Russell Smith) and decided to leave the final selection to the Justice officials. A Washington, D.C., attorney, James Rowe, himself once a member of the Justice Department, wrote a letter to Attorney General Robert Kennedy and succinctly articulated the alternatives faced by the Justice officials. The letter began by noting that the choice of candidates involved Browning and Smith.

> Assuming that I exaggerate and that these men are actually comparable in competence and judicial temperament, there are I think the intangibles which weigh more heavily in favor of Browning than of Smith. I must tread softly here for, by definition, intangibles are hard to weigh. Nonetheless, I submit the trend as toward Browning and against Smith.

> First, not only is the Ninth Circuit a weak bench, it is a conservative bench quite out of step with the premises of the New Frontier as almost all of us understand those premises. In the great run of cases it does not matter whether a judge is liberal or conservative if he is a good judge. There are a handful of cases, however,—and, Heaven knows, they always seem to be the important ones!— where the judicial mind can go either way, with probity, with honor, self-discipline and even with precedent. This is where the "liberal" cast of mind (we all know it, few of us can define it) can move this nation forward, just as the conservative mind can and does hold it back. This is intangible truth, but every lawyer knows it as reality! Browning would go forward, Smith would hold back.

> Second, the political point of view of a candidate deserves weight when other things are equal, or almost equal. . . . I know of Browning's devotion to the Democratic Party. . . . I personally know that over the years he has contributed vast amounts of time and money to good Democrats. On this point, both of his Senators will strongly attest. . . .

> Smith is entitled, as aren't we all, to his convictions and if his convictions in the 1950s happened to be Eisenhower that was not only his privilege, it was his duty. But I also think privilege and duty carry with them the consequences of their acts. I do not think it is unduly partisan of me if I feel a good man cannot and should not live in both worlds![41]

Browning received the appointment. Five years later the Montana senators backed Russell Smith for a district judgeship and President Johnson made that appointment.

Supreme Court Appointments

The three considerations of competence, party, and ideology are all relevant for Supreme Court appointments. Supreme Court nominations in this century have typically gone to respected lawyers and judges of the President's party who share the President's ideological proclivities. Moreover, unlike lower court appointments, Supreme Court appointments have tended to be the personal choice and occasionally a personal friend of the President. Early examples suggesting the interplay of ideology along with party and friendship to the President in Supreme Court appointments include President John Adams's appointment of staunch Federalist John Marshall to the chief justiceship in 1801; Jackson's appointment in 1836 of strong supporter and close cabinet member Roger B. Taney to succeed Marshall; and Grant's appointments in 1871 of William Strong and Joseph Bradley, both supporters of Grant's legal tender policy (significantly, with the votes of these two justices a new Court majority, much to the relief of the Grant Administration, overturned the previous Court's restrictive legal tender policy).

Ideology   President Theodore Roosevelt's correspondence with Massachusetts Senator Henry Cabot Lodge concerning the Supreme Court nomination of Massachusetts Supreme Judicial Court Justice Oliver Wendell Holmes further illustrates the importance of ideology. Before nominating Holmes, Roosevelt wrote to Lodge: "I should like to know that Judge Holmes was in entire sympathy with our views, that is, with your views and mine . . . before I would feel justified in supporting him."[42] Years later President Franklin D. Roosevelt took care to appoint economic liberals to the courts.

Another description of the saliency of ideology in the appointment of Supreme Court justices is found in a report by journalist James Clayton of a 1963 interview with Attorney General Robert Kennedy about President Kennedy's two appointments to the Supreme Court.

> Thinking back on the process months later, the Attorney General tilted back in his chair and said: "You wanted someone who generally agreed with you on what role government should play in American life, what role the individual in society should have. You didn't think about how he would vote in a reapportionment case or a criminal case. You wanted someone who, in the long run, you could believe would be doing what you thought was best. You wanted someone who agreed generally with your views of the country." Both he and the President believed that [Byron] White and [Arthur] Goldberg met that test.[43]

President Nixon frankly admitted on several occasions that he was deeply concerned with the policy views of those he appointed to the Supreme Court.[44] His intention to appoint conservatives was apparent with the nominations of Warren Burger, Clement Haynsworth, G. Harrold Carswell, Harry Blackmun,

Lewis Powell, and William Rehnquist. President Reagan likewise made it clear that he would appoint conservatives.[45]

Geographic Representation   State or geographic representation is also a consideration for federal court appointments. Under federal law, federal district judges must reside in the districts to which they are appointed. With the courts of appeals, the custom is to appoint an individual from one of the states within the circuit. Since 1978 there have been enough positions so that now each state is "represented." Geographic representation on the Supreme Court stems from the nineteenth-century practice of Supreme Court justices riding the circuit and sitting as circuit judges. It was then a matter of convenience to appoint a judge who would ride the circuit of the region in which he resided. Today the general practice appears to be that every major section of the country is "represented" on the Supreme Court. In fact, after the Haynsworth and Carswell defeats, President Nixon attempted to make Southern representation on the Court an issue. In so doing, he frankly admitted the saliency of geographic representation as a consideration in the appointment process.[46] Nixon eventually made good his promise to put a Southerner on the bench with the appointment of Lewis F. Powell of Virginia.

Religious-Ethnic-Sexual Considerations   There seems to be an expectation of religious representation held by some of the nation's principal minority groups. However, the extent to which religion is actually considered by an administration cannot be conclusively determined. The first Roman Catholic to sit on the Court was Roger B. Taney, a Jackson appointee. However, there is no evidence that Taney's religion was relevant for his appointment. Since 1894, however, with the exception of a seven-year period (1949–1956), there has been at least one member of the Catholic faith on the Court.

The first member of the Jewish religion to serve on the Court was Louis Brandeis, a Wilson appointee. Judging from some of the opposition to Brandeis's nomination, he probably was nominated and confirmed despite his religious affiliation.[47] From Brandeis's appointment in 1916 until mid-1969 there was at least one member of the Jewish faith sitting on the Court. These justices included Cardozo, Frankfurter, Goldberg, and Fortas. Starting with Cardozo, who replaced Holmes, these four justices occupied the same seat; that is, they succeeded one another. However, after Fortas resigned from the bench in May, 1969, President Nixon's nominees for Fortas's seat were all Protestant (two Southerners and one Midwesterner). There has not been a member of the Jewish religion on the Court since 1969.

President Johnson's appointment of Thurgood Marshall in 1967 is probably the beginning of Afro-American representation on the Court. Johnson was well aware of the historic nature of the appointment. In announcing it he stated, "I believe it is the right thing to do, the right time to do it, the right man and the right place."[48]

This seems to suggest that as long as religion and ethnicity remain important to Americans, and there is little evidence that the "melting pot" has substantially lowered their importance thus far,[49] there will be an expectation that each important minority group will have "a seat" on the Court.

As for women on the Supreme Court, the stark fact is that no president from Washington through Ford nominated a woman (it was not until the late nineteenth century that women were even allowed to practice law before the Supreme Court). President Carter, had he the opportunity, would likely have placed a woman on the Court. During his successful campaign for the presidency, Ronald Reagan pledged that he would appoint a woman, and on July 7, 1981, President Reagan kept his word by nominating Sandra Day O'Connor. It seems probable that O'Connor will be joined or succeeded by other women and that sexual representation has now been established on the Court.

Nominations and the Senate In the nineteenth century, close to one out of three nominations to the Supreme Court met fatal resistance in the Senate.[50] In the twentieth century, the rate has been about one out of nine (with three of the four rejections occurring in the 1968–1970 period). Apparently, with the conspicuous exception of President Nixon, twentieth-century presidents have taken into account probable senatorial reaction when considering candidates for the Supreme Court. At least until the Nixon presidency, it was a common practice for presidents to informally check with members of the Senate Judiciary Committee as well as the leadership of both parties in the Senate. In all likelihood this increased sensitivity to the probable reactions of the Senate and the efforts made by presidents to smooth the way for nominees was responsible for the low rejection rate. Only four nominees in the twentieth century failed to achieve senatorial confirmation: President Hoover's nomination in 1930 of Fourth Circuit Judge John J. Parker; President Johnson's nomination in 1968 of Justice Abe Fortas for the position of Chief Justice;[51] and President Nixon's first two nominations for Fortas's vacated seat, Appeals Judges Clement Haynsworth (Fourth Circuit) and G. Harrold Carswell (Fifth Circuit). The first two nominations aroused *unexpectedly* fierce ideological and partisan opposition with severe anti-Court overtones when they were submitted to the Senate.[52]

In conclusion, it is prudent to remember that the considerations discussed serve only to narrow the population from which the appointee will be chosen. Through the operation of one or another of these considerations, many potential candidates are eliminated. Still there may be a number of possible candidates. Understanding why one person is selected and not another requires intensive study of the entire complex of events surrounding that particular appointment. The careful student of recruitment will keep this in mind.

JUDICIAL BACKGROUNDS

Who are the people recruited for judicial office? What are their backgrounds? Have they shared the same socialization experiences and if so what are they? These are some of the questions that have interested political scientists, particularly because of the evidence suggesting that the values of decision makers influence their decisions and the survey evidence suggesting that certain attitudes and values are associated with backgrounds and experiences.[53] Examined in this section is the extent to which certain backgrounds (which have presumably facilitated the development of certain values) are overrepresented or underrepresented as compared to the population at large.

Family Backgrounds

Studies of the family backgrounds of federal judges have revealed that historically high social status and wealth have been greatly overrepresented on the federal bench. The leading study of the backgrounds of Supreme Court justices reveals that close to 90 percent of the justices came from economically comfortable families and the remainder from humble backgrounds.[54] In the period before the Civil War, the justices came primarily from the landed gentry. After the Civil War until recently, the justices came predominantly from the upper middle class (where the fathers tended to be in one of the professions). This pattern, however, appeared in the late 1960s to have at least temporarily ended. The Supreme Court of 1968–1969 contained the largest number of justices from humble beginnings ever to sit on the Court at one time. On the Court then were the great-grandson of a slave (and son of a country club steward), the son of a railroad worker, the son of poor Irish immigrants, the son of an impoverished minister who died when the boy was five, and the son of a poor merchant. This perhaps reflected the progress the country made over the preceding four decades toward achieving equal opportunity for all.[55]

With the exception of James Wilson (a Federalist) and Samuel Miller, Earl Warren, and Warren Burger (Republicans), all of the Supreme Court justices through 1984 with humble backgrounds were Democrats. In all, 25 percent of the justices appointed by Democratic presidents (9 out of 36) were from humble backgrounds, while only about eleven percent of the justices appointed by Republicans (5 out of 47, 2 of whom were Democrats) were from such backgrounds.[56] This no doubt reflects the difference in the groups to which each party has appealed, a difference that has persisted for almost as long as our parties have been in existence. Further examination of the data lends support to this. The three Democratic appointees with humble backgrounds appointed in the nineteenth century were Jackson or Van Buren appointees. The remaining six were appointed during or since Franklin D. Roosevelt's Administration. All these administrations had vigorously sought support from low-status voters.

The available data concerning lower court judges indicate much the same pattern. At least three-fourths of the Eisenhower appointees to the courts of appeals and at least one-half of the Kennedy appointees came from the middle or upper classes. However, close study suggests that the high-status Eisenhower appointees were a cut above the Kennedy appointees (as determined by father's education and occupation). Of a sample of 11 Kennedy appointees personally interviewed, only one reported that his father had completed higher education. Of a sample of 16 Eisenhower appointees, 9 reported that their fathers graduated from either college or a professional school.[57]

Study of other aspects of family background reveals that historically about two-thirds of all Supreme Court justices came from politically active families and about one-third of the justices were related to prominent judges.[58] The 1983–1984 Supreme Court, however, contained no justice who fit into these categories.

Education

Close to 85 percent of those appointed to the Supreme Court have attended the "best" law schools or (as was typical of legal education in the nineteenth century) had served apprenticeships with prominent lawyers and judges.[59] Findings for the lower court appointments of the Eisenhower and Kennedy Administrations were that about one-third of the judges went to state-supported law schools and the remainder went to private schools.[60] A larger proportion of Eisenhower than Kennedy appointees attended Ivy League law schools.[61] This appeared to reinforce other findings that the Republican Eisenhower appointees tended to come from a higher social class than did the Democratic Kennedy appointees, the assumption being that one had to be fairly well heeled to be able to attend an Ivy League law school in the 1920s. Democratic President Johnson, however, appointed about the same proportion of Ivy League law school graduates as President Eisenhower did, and Democratic President Carter's proportion was comparable to his Republican predecessors and successor.[62]

At first blush this would seem to undermine the class-party argument. However, a plausible explanation for the more recent findings is as follows. As the applicants to Ivy League schools (including their professional schools) have increased since the mid-1930s, these schools have increasingly considered ability and not just family background or financial status as the basis for admission. Since the average age of the Johnson appointees was 51, this would place their legal education precisely during the period when the Ivy League law schools were undergoing their transformation from aristocracy to meritocracy.[63] Starting with the Johnson Administration, we would then expect there to be negligible differences in the proportion of Democratic and Republican appointees with an Ivy League legal education. This is precisely what has happened as findings for the Nixon, Ford, Carter, and Reagan appointees show. Thus an Ivy League law school education does not, as it would have in the past, necessarily suggest that the appointee comes from the upper middle class or upper class.

Religious and Ethnic Background

Close to nine out of ten Supreme Court justices have been affiliated with a Protestant religion, and of these about eight out of ten have been identified with what sociologists consider high-status Protestant religions.[64] Low-status Protestants as well as the Catholic and Jewish appointees have typically been Democrats. Tables 3.1 and 3.2 report similar findings for lower court judges. Again it is possible to conclude that differing ethnic and class support given to the major parties is reflected in the appointments. The figures also reveal that there is an "overrepresentation" of "higher-status" religions on the bench today. It should be kept in mind, however, that it is not uncommon to convert from a low-status

Table 3.1 RELIGIOUS ORIGINS OR AFFILIATIONS OF LOWER FEDERAL COURT JUDGES BY THE APPOINTING ADMINISTRATIONS

Administration	Protestant		Catholic		Jewish	
	Number	Percent	Number	Percent	Number	Percent
Combined Harding, Coolidge, and Hoover[a]	170	82.1	8	3.8	8	3.8
Roosevelt[b]	132	67.0	52	26.4	7	3.6
Truman[c]	75	59.1	38	29.9	12	9.4
Eisenhower[d]	133	78.2	27	15.8	10	5.8
Kennedy[e]	73	58.9	38	30.7	13	10.4
Johnson[f]	94	58.0	49	30.2	19	11.7
Nixon[g]	163	72.8	41	18.3	20	8.9
Ford[h]	45	70.3	13	20.3	6	9.4
Carter[i]	153	59.3	69	26.7	36	14.0
Reagan[j]	90	62.5	42	29.2	12	8.3

Sources: For appointees from Harding through Truman, Samuel Lubell, *The Future of American Politics* (Garden City, N.Y.: Doubleday, 1956), p. 83. For the Eisenhower and Kennedy appointees, Sheldon Goldman, "Characteristics of Eisenhower and Kennedy Appointees to the Lower Federal Courts," *Western Political Quarterly,* 18 (1965), p. 759. For the Johnson through Reagan appointees, Sheldon Goldman, "Reagan's Judicial Appointments at Mid-term: Shaping the Bench in His Own Image," *Judicature,* 66 (1983), 339, 345.
[a]Out of 207 appointments for which religious background of 21 judges was unknown.
[b]Out of 197 appointments of which 6 judges were unrecorded.
[c]Out of 127 appointments of which 2 judges were unrecorded.
[d]Out of 170 appointments to the district and appeals courts. Some estimates of religion made.
[e]Out of 124 appointments to the district and appeals courts. Some estimates of religion made.
[f]Out of 162 appointments to the district and appeals courts. Some estimates of religion made.
[g]Out of 224 appointments to the district and appeals courts through August 8, 1974. Some estimates of religion made.
[h]Out of 64 appointments to the district and appeals courts. Some estimates of religion made.
[i]Out of 258 appointments to the district and appeals courts. Some estimates of religion made.
[j]Out of 144 appointments to the district and appeals courts through Sept. 1, 1984. Some estimates of religion made.

Table 3.2 THE RELIGIOUS ORIGINS OR AFFILIATIONS OF ALL DEMOCRATIC AND REPUBLICAN APPOINTEES TO THE FEDERAL COURTS OF APPEALS, 1953–1984

Religion[a]	Republican administration appointees[b]		Democratic administration appointees[c]		1979 U.S. populace[d]
	Number	Percent	Number	Percent	Percent
Higher social status, Protestant religion	54	41.9	26	22.2	8
Roman Catholic	23	17.8	29	24.8	29
Jewish	12	9.3	16	13.7	2
Lower social status, Protestant religion	16	12.4	28	23.9	39
Other Protestant (unspecified)	23	17.8	18	15.4	12
Unknown or other	1	0.8	—	—	10
Total	129	100.0	117	100.0	100

[a]Religious origins if known, or religious affiliation.
[b]Includes all appeals court appointees of the Eisenhower, Nixon, Ford, and Reagan (through Sept. 1, 1984) Administrations.
[c]Includes all appeals court appointees of the Kennedy, Johnson, and Carter Administrations.
[d]Source: *Religion in America,* The Gallup Index, 1981, Report No. 184, January 1981, pp. 11, 18.

Protestant sect to a high-status sect. Undoubtedly this has occurred and is in part responsible for the overrepresentation.

The relatively few black Americans on the federal bench have been primarily appointed by Democratic presidents. President Eisenhower did not name any black Americans to a federal district court or a court of appeals. President Kennedy named four to district courts and one to an appeals court. President Johnson named five to district courts, two to appeals courts, and was responsible for the first appointment of a black American to the Supreme Court. The Republican Nixon and Ford Administrations returned to the appointment tendencies of past Republican Administrations in that white, middle- or upper-class, high-status Protestants received the bulk of appointments, and the only appointments to blacks on the three principal courts were the nine named to the district courts.

The major breakthrough came with the Democratic Carter Administration. President Carter made a commitment to appoint black Americans to the federal courts, and he followed through. Carter appointed 28 blacks to the federal district courts and 9 to the appeals courts. Had Carter the opportunity, he would have appointed Wade McCree, his solicitor general and a distinguished black jurist, to the Supreme Court.[65] Republican Reagan, through mid-1984, returned to the pre-Carter pattern and appointed only two blacks to lifetime positions (one to a district court and one to an appeals court).

Gender

Until recently women have been virtually nonexistent in the American judiciary. President Reagan was, of course, responsible for the appointment of the first woman to the Supreme Court. Until the Carter Administration, very few women received appointments to the lower federal courts. The first woman on a court of appeals was appointed by President Franklin D. Roosevelt.[66] It was not until the Administration of Lyndon Johnson, over three decades later, that another woman was named to an appeals court. President Carter, however, placed 11 women on the courts of appeals and 29 women on the federal district courts. Although President Reagan broke the sex bar on the Supreme Court, the number of women placed by his Administration on the lower federal courts has been considerably less than the Carter Administration (through mid-1984 he named eleven women to lifetime federal district court positions and two to the appeals courts). Overall, women account for about 7 percent of the federal judiciary.

Political Activism

The political nature of the recruitment process results in many, if not most, federal judges having been politically active before starting their judicial careers. On the 1983–1984 Supreme Court we find that Chief Justice Warren Burger played a key role in the Republican Convention of 1952,[67] Byron White was a campaign strategist and political associate of John F. Kennedy, Sandra O'Connor was an Arizona Republican state senator and served as majority leader, and William Rehnquist was an active supporter of Barry Goldwater during the 1964 presidential campaign. About 75 percent of all appeals judges serving in 1963 had been politically active in the party that ultimately was responsible for their appointments.[68] In subsequent years similar figures have been found concerning the backgrounds of partisan activism of lower court appointees.[69]

Career Experiences

When we turn to major career experiences we find that a substantial portion of Supreme Court justices held high political or legal office or were prominent lawyers or law professors.[70] About 25 percent of all appeals judges serving in 1963 had at some time served with the U.S. Attorney's office, in the Justice Department, or in another legal capacity for the federal government. Since 1963, through five administrations (Johnson, Nixon, Ford, Carter, and Reagan through 1982), less than one-third of the district judge appointees had neither judicial nor prosecutorial experience (federal, state, or local) in their career profiles. At the appeals court level, only about one-fourth of the appointees had neither judicial nor prosecutorial experience. By contrast, about 60 percent had judicial experience and close to 40 percent (including some with judicial experience) had prosecutorial experience.[71]

At the time of appointment to the district courts, about half the Eisenhower and Kennedy appointees were in private practice. Significantly, a larger proportion of Democratic Kennedy appointees than Republican Eisenhower appointees were with small law firms.[72] About 44 percent of the Johnson district court appointees as compared to about 58 percent of the Nixon district court appointees were in private practice. Once again, a considerably larger proportion of Democratic than Republican district court appointees were from small firms, while close to twice the proportion of Nixon than Johnson appointees were from large law firms. The figures for the Ford Administration show about 44 percent in private practice, for the Carter Administration about 48 percent, for the Reagan Administration about 51 percent. However, the proportion of Carter appointees from large law firms was about the same as that of the Ford appointees, and close to that of previous and subsequent Republican Administrations.[73] The remainder of all seven administrations' appointees were for the most part in either governmental or judicial positions. At the time of appointment to the appeals courts, about 25 percent of the Eisenhower and Kennedy appointees, approximately 30 percent of the Johnson, about 33 percent of the Nixon and Carter, but only about 16 percent of the Ford and Reagan appointees were in private practice. About half or more of the appeals courts appointees of all seven administrations held judicial positions (mostly federal district court positions), and the balance were primarily in governmental positions. Some 14 percent of the Carter appointees and 16 percent of the Reagan appointees were law professors at the time of their appointment.

CONSEQUENCES OF THE RECRUITMENT PROCESS

It is appropriate to consider what difference it makes that we recruit our judicial authorities the way we do, the consequences this has for the larger American political system, and the implications of the recruitment process for the administration of justice.

Consequences for the Larger Political System

No doubt, as most political scientists argue, the nature of the recruitment process has very important consequences for the American political system. Presidents can and do use their power of judicial appointment to further Administration policy. President Franklin Roosevelt, for example, learned early that the federal judiciary could block important Administration programs. Consequently, he took care to offer judicial appointments to supporters of his New Deal programs. Other presidents have similarly been concerned with the ideological or policy views of their nominees. The recruitment process thus permits party responsibility.

The judiciary, a branch of government not directly responsible to the electorate, can be kept in touch with popular sentiment through the process of political recruitment. Judges chosen by a democratically elected administration can be expected to be in harmony, in a general sense, with the goals and commitments of the administration and to some extent the sentiments of the current majority. It should be apparent, then, that judicial appointments represent an output of the executive and legislative systems. The inputs that are processed to produce the appointment outputs are similar to other inputs produced by the democratically elected branches of government. Feedback from judicial policies becomes part of that input. New demands concerning the direction that judicial policies should take are part of that input. Demands as to the type of judges who should sit on the bench are input to the appointment process. Thus, it is apparent that the political recruitment process not only permits but encourages party responsibility and by so doing provides a potential link between court output and the current political climate.

The recruitment process, by virtue of its responsiveness to partisan considerations, has resulted over the long run in a diversity of social, economic, and political outlooks being represented on the federal bench. One wonders whether a recruitment process less politically sensitive would have or could have resulted when it did in the appointments of a black and a woman to the Supreme Court or could have produced the current mix on the lower courts of labor lawyers, corporation lawyers, solo practitioners, Wall Street-type lawyers, members of minority ethnic groups, women, and old-stock Americans. Political recruitment tends to make the judiciary a career with openings for at least some members of all groups and classes within American society.[74]

Women and black Americans are, of course, the most seriously underrepresented on the federal courts. Women and black Americans have, over the past decade, found the barriers lowered, attitudes changing, and new opportunities to pursue legal careers. They are also much more politically important than ever before. Political recruitment can be credited with resulting in the appointment of a woman to the Supreme Court (Reagan Administration) and a significant increase in the number of black Americans and women on the lower federal bench (Carter Administration).

A recruitment process rooted in politics also encourages talented people who aspire to federal judgeships to participate in politics. It is doubtful whether a democratic political system can be viable without providing inducements to encourage capable minds and talents to participate. Whether or not a judgeship is a proper inducement is, of course, a matter of dispute.

There are, however, less attractive consequences of political recruitment. Spokespersons for the organized bar have argued that, at times, the process is incompatible with the objective of placing the *best* qualified people available on the bench. Although there are difficulties in assessing the qualifications of candidates for judicial positions and certainly in determining who is the *best* available, there are certain standards that one could argue are objectively necessary for the successful functioning of the judicial system as well as for the larger American political system.[75] For example, the appointment of dishonest persons, incompetents, segregationists, or proponents of the views of extreme right- or left-wing groups would clearly be dysfunctional for the judicial system and larger political system. In practice, a few dishonest people, some incompetents, and dozens of segregationists have received appointments in the not-too-distant past.[76]

It is also noted that the selection process puts the chief litigant (i.e., the Department of Justice) into the position of recruiting the judges before whom its cases will be tried. This may add a pro-government bias to recruitment and give the public the impression that federal judges tend to be more sympathetic to the claims of the government than to those of the citizenry. Furthermore, it is claimed that the public is dissatisfied with the nexus of politics and judicial selection and that *political* selection lessens public confidence in the judicial process. In addition, it has been argued that inevitably a few occasions have arisen under the current process when a nominee has been subjected to public abuse and harassment by senators (e.g., the 1968 hearings and Senate floor debate on the nomination of Justice Fortas to the chief justiceship; the 1969–1970 controversies over the nominations of Judges Haynsworth and Carswell). This could well undermine the public's confidence in and support for the courts.

There have been various proposals for altering the recruitment process. Essentially these proposals[77] seek to eliminate partisan considerations and to intensify the influence of the organized bar. They would deemphasize the political participation and party responsibility advantages of the present process and stress bar association participation and responsibility to the norms and values of the highest strata of the legal profession. Some cynics claim that efforts to reform the recruitment process reach a peak during Democratic administrations and a nadir during Republican administrations. The Nixon, Ford, and Reagan Administrations demonstrated little inclination to suggest basic reform of the recruitment process. Indeed, the Reagan Administration specifically rejected the commission concept as utilized by the Carter Administration.

Consequences for the Administration of Justice

Available data suggest that federal judges, whatever their party or appointing administration, share much in common. Regardless of their economic and reli-

gious origins, those appointed to the federal courts have had a good legal education, have been socialized into the legal profession, and have tended to have
governmental legal experience. They tend to be solidly grounded in the middle
or upper middle class at the time they become federal judges, and it is not
unreasonable to assume that they share the predominant middle-class social,
economic, and political values of American society.[78]

Yet there are differences in degree in the results of the recruitment process
so that recruitment patterns of Democratic administrations differ from those of
Republican administrations. Democratic presidents tend to appoint more judges
from lower-status backgrounds as defined in economic, religious, and ethnic
terms. The questions that come to mind are: Do these differences produce a
distinction (subtle or otherwise) in the decisional patterns of Democratic and
Republican judges? Is the administration of justice influenced by the backgrounds
of the judges who decide the cases? Are some background characteristics and
experiences more important than others?

Although the answers to these questions will be considered when we examine judicial conversion, it is appropriate to note here a line of thinking that has
won wide acceptance among political scientists:[79] Judges have opportunities to use
judicial discretion. As a result they may disagree as to how a case should be
decided. They differ because they have different hierarchies of political values and
different ways of perceiving and evaluating reality as well as different concepts
of their role as judge. The differences in backgrounds and experiences may yield
the key to why a judge behaves in certain ways. Thus it has been widely accepted
during the last several decades that the administration of justice—that is, the type
of "justice" that is dispensed—is intimately connected with the judges who do
the dispensing. It is believed, therefore, that judicial recruitment has profound
consequences for the administration of justice and thus the operation of the
federal judicial system.[80]

GOVERNMENT LAWYERS

Of the more than 600,000 American lawyers in practice, over 20,000 work for
the federal government.[81] Many are involved in activities relating to federal
litigation. In particular these are lawyers employed by the regulatory agencies and
the Department of Justice. The bulk of federal litigation is handled by the Justice
Department principally through the Office of Solicitor General, the six legal
subject area divisions of the Justice Department,[82] and the offices of the United
States attorneys.

The solicitor general and staff decide what cases the federal government will
take to the Supreme Court. Cases that raise matters of major importance for the
government are personally argued before the Supreme Court by the solicitor
general. Staff members represent the federal government in other cases brought
before the Supreme Court in which the government is either a litigant or *amicus
curiae.* Typically the solicitor general's office participates in over half the cases
the Supreme Court hears on the merits.

Each of the six Justice Department divisions is led by an assistant attorney general and staff lawyers with competence in the specialized legal areas. The divisions supervise the handling of litigation by the U.S. attorneys, or in some major cases may send a staff lawyer to prepare a case before the district court. The divisions handle the appeals to the appeals courts and also assist the solicitor general's office with cases taken to the Supreme Court.

The 94 U.S. attorneys' offices are responsible for most of the prosecutions and much of the other litigation involving the government before the district courts.

It should be apparent that these government lawyers influence to a significant extent the rate of demand input as well as the kind of demands that go into the system. This is a gatekeeping task similar to that performed by judges and private lawyers (more about gatekeeping in the next chapter). Government lawyers are clearly authorities of the federal judicial system in that they occupy decision-making roles that affect the allocation of values. It is therefore appropriate to study them by asking the sort of questions political scientists ask about other authorities: What are their backgrounds and how are they recruited? How do they perceive their roles? What are their relationships with one another and with the other politically relevant members of the system? Why do they make decisions to prosecute or to appeal? How is their behavior related to their attitudes and values? What are their relationships with the politically relevant members of the larger political system?

United States Attorneys

The position of U.S. Attorney was created by the Judiciary Act of 1789. Today there is one such lawyer in each of the 94 federal judicial districts. Their offices vary in size, with some U.S. attorneys having only one assistant U.S. attorney and others, such as those in the large metropolitan areas, having considerably more. (For example, the Southern District of New York in New York City has over 100 assistant U.S. attorneys.) The attorney general has formal supervision over the U.S. attorneys and can, for example, instruct them to try or not to try a case or relieve a U.S. attorney from handling a case, substituting a Justice Department lawyer, or fire any assistant U.S. attorney at any time. The President appoints U.S. attorneys to four-year terms after their nominations have been confirmed by the Senate. They can be reappointed indefinitely or removed by the President at his discretion. Typically, U.S. attorneys are members of the President's party, and this is facilitated by the custom of U.S. attorneys resigning their posts when the opposition party wins the presidency.

The recruitment of U.S. attorneys has many similarities to judicial recruitment.[83] Screening of candidates is done in the Justice Department (by the director of the Executive Office for U.S. Attorneys). Senators of the President's party and state and local party leaders recommend people, and senators in particular expect to "clear" all nominations. Federal district judges can influence the selection process by their power to make a court appointment to fill a vacancy on a temporary basis (until the Senate confirms the new U.S. attorney). The most pronounced difference between recruitment of U.S. attorneys and recruitment of federal judges is the absence of any institutionalized participation on the part of the organized bar. Again, similar to judicial recruitment, administrations tend to be interested in the policy views of the candidates. Those appointed tend to have a history of party activism and to be in essential sympathy with the administration.[84] Of course, no particular appointment can be understood without knowledge of the transactions that preceded it.

Study of the backgrounds of U.S. attorneys suggests that a marked pattern of localism underlies recruitment. Most U.S. attorneys are born in the state in which they serve. A majority have attended college or law school in their home state (but about one-third have received all their schooling without leaving the confines of their state[85]). The recruitment process suggests that those with a local background and extensive local ties have the greatest opportunities for appointment. It is likely that they are more parochial and less "cosmopolitan" in attitudes, values, and life-style. This can be expected to affect decisions to prosecute, the conduct of pretrial negotiations, and relationships with others in the system.[86]

United States attorneys are disproportionately drawn from the high-status Protestant denominations,[87] with the South having the largest proportion of those affiliated with Protestant denominations and Republican administrations appointing proportionately more Protestants than Democratic administrations (findings similar to those for judicial appointees). Most U.S. attorneys have been active in party politics before their appointments, and most have had prior governmental experience including public prosecutorial positions. In recent administrations about one-fifth of the U.S. attorneys have had governmental experience as an assistant U.S. attorney. At the time of appointment, however, about half were in private practice.

Many U.S. attorneys regard their position as a stepping stone to a federal judgeship. Political scientist James Eisenstein surveyed contemporary U.S. attorneys and found that close to six out of ten indicated that they aspired to a federal judgeship. Many U.S. attorneys and assistant U.S. attorneys saw their position as one that enabled them in the course of their work to make contacts with leading members of the bar. Such contact was thought to be able to enhance their professional opportunities when they returned to private practice.[88]

In attempting to understand the relationship between United States attorneys *(USA)*, assistant United States attorneys *(AUSA)*, and United States district court judges *(USDCJ)*, it is necessary to recognize the powers of the judge.[89] The judge decides when cases will be heard and when briefs, motions, and answers must be submitted. The judge is ruler of the courtroom and can reprimand or punish lawyers, make rulings on the admissibility of evidence, comment to and charge the jury, and, of course, decide the case. The judge's determination of who wins has the most direct effect on the careers of USAs and AUSAs because their reputations rest on their ability to win criminal and civil cases.

The larger districts contain larger numbers of USDCJs and larger numbers of AUSAs. The proportion of time any given member of the USA's office spends before each judge is less than in a one- or two-judge district. Procedures for scheduling cases and the atmosphere surrounding trials tend to be more formal in the larger districts. In contrast, the small districts, especially those containing only one USDCJ, place the USA at the mercy of the judge. Interaction is frequent and procedures are less formal. The USA frequently becomes intimately acquainted with the judge, thereby acquiring a knowledge of the judge's idiosyncracies that affects decisions to prosecute and courtroom strategy.[90]

Interaction is also facilitated by the close physical location of both the judges' offices and the USA's office. Typically both offices are housed in the same building and opportunities for interchange may arise. It is to the advantage of the USA to establish as close a working relationship with the judges as possible. As one AUSA has stated it: "If you have a good relationship, the judge is willing to listen to you present your arguments. He may [eventually rule against you] . . . but at least he's willing to listen to you."[91] Furthermore, a cooperative and sympathetic judge will be lenient with the USA's office concerning scheduling of motions, answers, and so forth. During the trial the judge who is on good terms with the USA's office is likely to be considerate in the treatment of government lawyers. A USA also benefits from the frequent informal talks that characterize a close relationship. The judge then tends to be more understanding of the USA's problems and the USA gains insight into the judge's thinking. These talks, of course, provide a USA with an opportunity not ordinarily shared by private attorneys to influence judges. One USA gave an example: "For instance, the judge might say, 'I don't quite get what you were driving at in court the other day.' This gives you an opportunity to explain again in congenial surroundings. This is an opportunity to persuade."[92]

The nature of the relationship between the judge and the USA's office depends also on the judge's conception of his or her role. Judges have different views as to the propriety of their suggesting that a particular case or type of case be prosecuted or not prosecuted or suggesting the form in which cases should be brought to court. Judges have different views as to how they should behave in conducting a trial. For example, personal values can motivate a prosecution-minded judge to intervene when it appears that a defendant the judge thinks is guilty is about to go free. On the other hand, a judge who feels strongly that it is one's duty to see that justice is done will interject questions to witnesses or elucidate matters for the jury. Some judges are aloof because they believe it is not their job to tell the USA what cases to prosecute or how to prosecute them, to give critique sessions to AUSAs, or to show favoritism to government lawyers. At the other extreme are judges who feel it is their duty to carefully supervise the behavior of the USAs. An example of this latter relationship is suggested by the following observation of an AUSA.

> The judges go beyond themselves in overseeing the office. They don't say we shouldn't bring certain categories of cases anymore. But they are concerned with whether specific cases should be prosecuted. The Chief Judge will be in the U.S. Attorney's office all the time. They'll talk about the status of different cases and the different investigations pending. That's where [the Chief Judge] plays quite an important role. The judges feel like we are working for them to some extent. And we are, but this can go too far.[93]

James Eisenstein, however, believes that most judges fall between these two extremes.

In some smaller districts, judges sometimes work closely with the USA. One former USA recalled that:

> After the judge had made up his mind, he would tell me how he was going to decide the case. We'd write an opinion for him. We'd do all the work, and he'd just sign it. All our dealings were straight across the board. We handled more damn stuff when we were in there. . . .[94]

Legal Services Lawyers

By 1983, close to 5000 lawyers were employed by more than 300 federally funded local legal services programs. These legal services lawyers are engaged in an enterprise vastly different than that engaged in by U.S. attorneys, assistant U.S. attorneys, and other Justice Department and federal agency lawyers. Instead of handling litigation on behalf of the federal government, legal services lawyers handle litigation on behalf of individuals too poor to hire their own attorney. The program originated as part of the Economic Opportunity Act of 1964 (the original "war on poverty" legislation sponsored by the Johnson Administration), and the Legal Services Division was housed in the Office of Economic Opportunity (OEO). Neighborhood law offices were not initiated by OEO. People in the local community (typically, young reform-minded activist lawyers) prepared proposals for the Legal Services Division, and those proposals that met certain stated specifications were funded. By 1973 over $70 million was being spent to operate the over-900 legal services offices (of varying sizes) around the country. About a million cases a year were being handled on behalf of poor people who otherwise would be denied access to the state and federal court systems.

The program was controversial from the start. At first legal services lawyers took on criminal cases as well as civil matters, but that aroused the opposition of, among others, the local law enforcement establishment and the local criminal bar. As a result, in 1967 Congress passed an amendment to the Economic Opportunity Act that forbade neighborhood law offices from handling criminal cases unless there was no other public means to assist the poor criminal defendant. What this has meant in practice is that legal services lawyers have almost exclusively been engaged in civil suits.

But here, too, there has been continuing controversy because legal services lawyers have been assisting the poor not only with grievances concerning private individuals or businesses but also with grievances involving public officials and agencies. This has meant that the federal government has financed lawsuits against state and local governmental agencies and in some instances against itself as well. Some of these lawsuits have been successful, and as a consequence in some cases governmental agencies have been ordered by courts to spend millions of additional dollars for aid to the poor.[95] Some public officials actively opposed the legal services program, and they were encouraged in 1972 by Vice-President Spiro

Agnew, who seemed to be speaking for the Nixon Administration when he attacked legal services lawyers for becoming "ideological vigilantes" on behalf of political and social reform.[96]

The legal services program in 1973 appeared to be in trouble as the Nixon Administration was in the process of dismantling OEO. However, the American Bar Association went on record in support of the program as well as in favor of higher funding for legal services.[97] For several years, backers of the program had advocated a separate Government Legal Services Corporation, and the Administration publicly favored that device, although it had found fault with some of the provisions of a 1971 bill to establish such a corporation, and Mr. Nixon had vetoed it. When the director of the program was fired in February, 1973, he charged that the Nixon Administration was really trying to kill the program.[98] It took almost a year and a half, but finally in 1974 an independent Legal Services Corporation passed Congress and was signed into law by President Nixon on July 25, just two weeks before he left office. The legislation attempted to meet some of the objections of the opponents of legal services in that it contained numerous restrictions on the political and reform activities of the legal services lawyers and the types of cases the program could handle. (For example, legal services lawyers cannot handle lawsuits aimed at desegregating public schools or facilitating the obtaining of abortions.[99])

The legal services program was less controversial during the Ford and Carter presidencies, and, particularly under Carter, had its largest budget to date from the federal government. In addition, President Carter publicly lauded the Legal Services Corporation and its mission.[100] In contrast, President Reagan tried to kill legal services but was met with considerable opposition not only in Congress but by the American Bar Association.[101] The legal services budget was slashed and the message was unmistakably clear that a conservative Republican Administration and the legal services corporation are politically incompatible.

Clearly the neighborhood law offices have had an impact on the poor as well as on the various court systems, including the federal judicial system (pumping about one million cases into the state and federal judicial systems each year surely has had profound effects on the demand input processes of these court systems[102]).

Other Government Lawyers

Brief mention should be made of some other government lawyers directly involved in the federal judicial system. For example, in fiscal 1983 there were 152 federal public defenders working in 34 of the 89 districts in the states.[103] (Each district court has the option of instituting a public defender's office or staying with the traditional method of assigning private counsel to represent indigents; under the Criminal Justice Act funds are available to finance either option.) In eight other districts, community defender organizations operated on sustaining grants approved by the Judicial Conference of the United States. In the District of Columbia, a Public Defender Service is the institution used.

Each lower federal court judge is entitled under federal law to "appoint necessary law clerks and secretaries." Typically, lower court judges have two or three law clerks. Justices of the Supreme Court are entitled to hire four (although some hire fewer), and the Chief Justice has the additional aid of the office of the Administrative Assistant to the Chief Justice. The law clerks to lower court judges are selected by the judges from law school graduates. Appointments are typically for one year, thereby producing a constant turnover of clerks. At the Supreme Court level, law clerks are now chosen from among the law clerks to lower court judges. In 1983–1984, 18 of the 33 clerks had previous experience as clerks for judges on the District of Columbia circuit and the remainder had served with other lower courts.[104] There has been some speculation that the law clerks, presumably by bringing with them the latest thinking in the law schools and the fresh perspective of the young, are in a position to influence the judge and the course of the judge's decision making. There is no hard evidence to definitively support or refute this, although a survey of judges revealed a preference for high turnover among law clerks and a tendency to use them in the course of substantive decision making.[105] At the Supreme Court level, the clerks who brief the petitions for certiorari may have the opportunity to influence the threshold certiorari decisions, but here, too, our evidence is largely anecdotal and unsystematic.[106] After he retired from the Supreme Court, Justice Potter Stewart observed in an interview that "opinions tended to be longer at the time I left and perhaps more the product at least preliminarily, of the law clerks than when I first came."[107] During fiscal 1974 the judges on the U.S. Court of Appeals for the Fourth Circuit experimented with the use of staff attorneys not assigned to any one judge. These attorneys had what would seem to be great potential for influencing the course of decision making by the court in that they would initially review appeals and make recommendations to the judges. However, an extensive study of staff attorneys came to the conclusion that they mirrored the policy views of the judges of the circuit and exercised little independent authority.[108] Today, staff attorneys are used in all the circuits in addition to the law clerks who work for the individual judges. In sum, it appears that law clerks and possibly staff attorneys meet the systems definition of authorities in that they occupy systemic roles and have at least some (if only perhaps minor) influence on the course of the system's policy output. However, it is hard to demonstrate with precision the extent of their influence.

PRIVATE LAWYERS

It is difficult to determine how many nongovernmental lawyers practice before or participate in the preparation of cases tried in the federal courts. Of greater importance, however, is the kind of private lawyer who practices before the federal courts, in particular the nature and style of practice. It would be useful to be able to present evidence that would indicate what differences (if any) there are in the backgrounds, attitudes, and values of lawyers whose practice takes them primarily before the federal courts as opposed to those whose practice is largely in the local courts. Although such data are unavailable, there are several studies by sociologists of law that have focused on the legal profession. Their findings shed some light on these questions.

Two principal approaches have been used to study the legal profession: the client-group approach and the style-of-practice approach.[109] The client-group approach leads the researcher to examine the segment of the bar that serves a specialized group of clients, for example, business enterprise, interest groups, or criminal defendants. Historically, lawyers for business and property interests have been the principal nongovernment lawyers practicing in the federal courts. This was particularly true during the 70-year period following the Civil War, when the relationship of government to private enterprise was the subject of constitutional policy-making.[110] Today the federal courts are heavily involved in litigation involving government regulation of industry, in particular statutory interpretation and the rulings of regulatory agencies. It is likely that a significant proportion of private lawyers who come before the federal courts represent business and financial concerns and are either "house counsel" (employed by the business) or associated with a large law firm.[111] Lawyers representing particular labor unions are also, of course, before the courts in connection with labor litigation.

Another group of lawyers that comes before the federal courts represents interest groups. Included are the staff lawyers and volunteer lawyers of the civil rights, civil liberties, and public interest group organizations[112] and the staff lawyers of business associations and the AFL-CIO. One might speculate that there are differences in the backgrounds and values of lawyers who work, for example, for organized labor, the NAACP, and the Chamber of Commerce.

A segment of the bar that has wide contact with the federal judicial system is the criminal bar. There is some evidence that suggests that criminal lawyers differ from lawyers primarily engaged in civil suits. One study[113] reported that, in contrast to civil lawyers, criminal lawyers tended to be divorced from the business community. They were also found, when compared to civil lawyers, to be more active in political party work, to have more liberal voting preferences, and generally to have a lower status among members of the profession and the community at large. The criminal bar has been described as containing a few high-priced, well-known practitioners who cater to the select few who can afford them, and the private practitioners, legal aid lawyers, and public defenders who handle the bulk of criminal cases. Most private criminal law practitioners earn their living by handling a large volume of business. Many of these private practitioners do little in the way of preparing cases and are more concerned with their own niche in the social structure of the courthouse than with their clients.[114] Typically, eight out of ten convictions in the federal district courts involve a guilty plea.[115] This suggests that the routine relationships that have been found to exist in local courthouses between criminal lawyers and public prosecutors may also exist in the federal courthouses between defense attorneys and the U.S. attorney. Other criminal lawyers may simply be taking advantage of the widely publicized backlogs in the federal courts[116] and the intricacies and uncertainties of federal criminal procedural policies to negotiate the best possible deal for their clients.

Studies using the style-of-practice approach for the analysis of the legal profession have revealed similar findings. Lawyers who practice the "institutional style" tend to be corporation lawyers whose clients are from the highest economic strata and whose cases frequently take them before the appeals courts and the U.S. Supreme Court. These lawyers handle antitrust, securities, credit financing, tax, and regulatory agency matters. The corporation lawyer is typically drawn from a high-status, white Protestant background and has graduated from a private liberal arts college and a prestigious law school.[117] In contrast, the lawyers who practice solo or "metropolitan style" are frequently of new American stock, come from low-status families, and are graduates of the less prestigious law schools. Their clients are both individuals and small businesses, and the cases they handle are primarily personal injury, criminal cases, workmen's compensation, divorce, and real estate. There is little contact between the two types of lawyers.[118] The solo practitioners appear primarily in the city courts, although some handle criminal cases in the federal courts. The institutional lawyers generally handle the economic cases of large business and financial institutions, and this means that they typically practice before the federal courts.[119]

JURY SELECTION AND BEHAVIOR

Juries are the principal nonprofessional authorities in the judicial process, and they share decision making with trial judges. Under the Sixth Amendment to the Constitution, jury trials in federal criminal cases are guaranteed to all who want them. Typically, over half the criminal defendants who plead not guilty choose to exercise this right (rather than have their cases tried by the judge alone).[120] The Seventh Amendment guarantees jury trials for most federal civil cases, but only about one-third of the litigants whose cases come to trial exercise their jury trial option, while the balance have their cases heard and decided only by the judge.

Several studies of both federal and state juries have suggested that there have been wide disparities in the selection of jurors.[121] In the South, blacks were grossly underrepresented.[122] In the North as well as the South, juries have consisted disproportionately of white-collar, middle- to upper-class, middle-aged (or older) males.[123] Before 1969 potential federal jurors were chosen individually by a court clerk or jury commissioner at his discretion. The selection procedure in widespread practice was the "key-man" procedure, whereby the person responsible for jury selection solicited names of prospective jurors from "important" people in the community.

The Federal Jury Selection and Service Act of 1968 eliminated the key-man procedure and required that jurors be randomly selected from voter registration lists. The law requires each jury clerk or commissioner to include on the list the names of at least one-half of one percent of the total names on the voter registration lists in that federal district. Each county within the district court must be represented by at least one-half of one percent of the registered voters in that county. All names are randomly picked and potential jurors fill out questionnaires to determine their eligibility. Each federal district has its own jury selection procedure in accord with the broad guidelines of the act. There is evidence that these procedures for jury selection have changed the makeup of federal juries. For example, it was reported that within a month after the law went into effect in the

Southern District of New York, more women, laborers, and nonwhites were serving on federal juries than had served previously.[124]

The behavior of juries is another matter.[125] One major research project was conducted by the lawyers and sociologists associated with the University of Chicago Jury Project.[126] The principal research was reported in *The American Jury,* whose data base consisted of a sample of both federal and state jury trials (the researchers did not distinguish between federal and state juries, nor apparently did they believe such a distinction was relevant for their purposes). The findings were manifold. Perhaps of greatest general interest was the finding that in only about 20 percent of criminal or civil trials did the jury come to a conclusion different from that reached by the judge. In other words, in about four out of five cases both jury and judge were in agreement.[127] Where they differed, the jury in criminal cases tended to be "non-rule minded" and thus more lenient than the judge in their willingness to "move where the equities are."[128] However, no marked directionality in judge-jury disagreements in civil cases was found.[129] The judge-jury disagreements were seldom found to be over the facts alone, but rather to be over values alone or as they are inextricably involved with the determination and evaluation of facts.[130]

The Chicago researchers were unable to discern a relationship between the backgrounds of the jurors and their decision making, but the possibility of such relationships was not ruled out.[131] Earlier work by a member of the project had suggested that jurors of German and British ancestry have a greater tendency to favor criminal convictions than those of African and Slavic ancestry.[132]

The deliberations of juries have also been of interest and have been studied by simulation[133] and by attempts to reconstruct the deliberations through interviews of jurors.[134] The Chicago researchers interviewed jurors who decided 225 criminal cases in Chicago and Brooklyn and collected other data on jury first ballot voting. They found that unanimity prevailed on the first ballot vote in 31 percent of the cases.[135] Where the vote was evenly split, the final verdict was guilty as often as it was not guilty. In nine out of ten of all other cases, the jury eventually decided in accord with majority sentiment evidenced on the first ballot. Kalven and Zeisel, senior authors of *The American Jury,* emphasized that "with very few exceptions the first ballot decides the outcome of the verdict" and that "the real decision is often made before the deliberation begins."[136] How do juries manage to achieve consensus? Kalven and Zeisel suggest that the consensus-building process is a combination of "rational persuasion, sheer social pressure, and the psychological mechanism by which individual perceptions undergo change when exposed to group discussion."[137]

NOTES

1. This chapter does not contain a consideration of the police authorities of the federal system. It should be mentioned that while the principal police work is done by the Federal Bureau of Investigation (FBI), there are other federal agencies engaged in such work. In addition to the FBI, within the Department of Justice there is the Immigration Border Patrol. Within the Department of the Treasury, there are the

Bureau of Narcotics, the Secret Service, and units concerned with violations of federal income and other taxes and customs laws. Within the Postal Service, there is the inspector's office, with responsibility for investigating postal offenses. On the FBI see John T. Elliff, *Crime, Dissent, and the Attorney General: The Justice Department in the 1960's* (Beverly Hills, Calif.: Sage, 1971). Also see Victor S. Navasky, *Kennedy Justice* (New York: Atheneum, 1971), Chaps. 1–3.

Note also that other federal judicial system authorities not discussed in this chapter include federal magistrates (who perform minor judicial duties), probation officers (whose presentence reports on convicted criminals may heavily influence the sentence handed down by the judge), bankruptcy judges, and parole board members (who exercise discretion in the granting, denial, or revocation of parole).

2. For a theoretical discussion of appointment transactions, see David J. Danelski, *A Supreme Court Justice Is Appointed* (New York: Random House, 1964), pp. 145–153.

3. The judicial selection process is examined in some detail by Joel B. Grossman, *Lawyers and Judges* (New York: Wiley, 1965); Sheldon Goldman, "Judicial Appointments to the United States Courts of Appeals," *Wisconsin Law Review* (1967), 186–214; Harold W. Chase, *Federal Judges: The Appointing Process* (Minneapolis: University of Minnesota Press, 1972); Donald D. Jackson, *Judges* (New York: Atheneum, 1974), Chap. 12; Sheldon Goldman, "Carter's Judicial Appointments: A Lasting Legacy," *Judicature,* 64 (1981), 344–355; Sheldon Goldman, "Reagan's Judicial Appointments at Mid-Term: Shaping the Bench in His Own Image," *Judicature,* 66 (1983), 334–347; Elliot E. Slotnick, "The A.B.A. Standing Committee on Federal Judiciary: A Contemporary Assessment," *Judicature,* 66 (1983), 348–362, 385–393; W. Gary Fowler, "A Comparison of Initial Recommendation Procedures: Judicial Selection Under Reagan and Carter," *Yale Law & Policy Review,* 1 (1983), 299–356.

4. For an analysis of the commission created by President Carter, see Larry C. Berkson and Susan B. Carbon, *The United States Circuit Judge Nominating Commission: Its Members, Procedures and Candidates* (Chicago: American Judicature Society, 1980). Nominating commissions were created by senators to fill federal district court judgeships in 30 states. For an extensive study of the workings of these commissions and their impact on judicial selection, see Alan Neff, *The United States District Judge Nominating Commissions: Their Members, Procedures and Candidates* (Chicago: American Judicature Society, 1981). Also see Elliot E. Slotnick, "The U.S. Circuit Judge Nominating Commission," *Law & Policy Quarterly,* 1 (1979), 465–496; and Elliot E. Slotnick, "Federal Appellate Judge Selection During the Carter Administration: Recruitment Changes and Unanswered Questions," *The Justice System Journal,* 6 (1981), 283–304. During the first two years of Ronald Reagan's presidency, district court positions were filled in 30 states. In 15 states the senators used selection panels and offered the panels' choices to the Justice Department. See Fowler, "A Comparison of Initial Recommendation Procedures," pp. 314–316.

5. Chase, *Federal Judges,* p. 184; Neil D. McFeeley, "The Judicial Selection Process in the Johnson Administration," paper presented at the 1982 Annual Meeting of the Western Political Science Association.

6. Interview with John Duffner, Executive Assistant to the Deputy Attorney General, August 28, 1974. Interview with Philip Modlin, Office of the Deputy Attorney General, United States Department of Justice, December 19, 1980.

7. A copy of such a blue slip is contained in the *Hearings on the Nomination of Phillip W. Tone to Fill a Vacancy on the United States Court of Appeals for the Seventh Circuit, Subcommittee on Nominations, Senate Judiciary Committee, May 1,*

1974 (unpublished hearing). Judge Tone, an Illinois resident and at the time of his nomination a federal district court judge, was sponsored by Charles Percy, the Republican senator from Illinois. Percy sent back his blue slip with the handwritten reply "Fully approve—rating especially well qualified by ABA" followed by his signature. The other Illinois senator, Democrat Adlai Stevenson, handwrote "No objections" and signed his name.

8. *Boston Globe,* January 26, 1979, p. 2. Also see Neff, *op. cit.,* 42–44.

9. *Hearings, Senate Judiciary Committee, Confirmation of Federal Judges, Part 2,* Serial No. J-97-52 (Washington, D.C.: Government Printing Office, 1982), p. 157.

10. Grossman, *Lawyers and Judges,* pp. 250–251.

11. A. L. Todd, *Justice on Trial: The Case of Louis D. Brandeis* (New York: McGraw-Hill, 1964).

12. For example, the president of the American Bar Association during 1969–1970 was Bernard G. Segal. The *New York Times* published an article about Segal at the time he assumed office that contained the observation that Segal "represents the small group of comparatively liberal and highly successful corporate lawyers who have dominated the organization for the last dozen years, shepherding its philosophy from conservatism to progressivism." The article also noted that Segal "has campaigned arduously in behalf of civil rights." See *New York Times,* August 15, 1969, p. 36. During the controversy over the legal services program, the ABA came down firmly in favor of the program, which at that time was under attack by conservatives. See *New York Times,* February 13, 1973, p. 11. The ABA at that same meeting voted to support the "exclusionary rule" and to oppose legislation that would permit the introduction in a criminal trial of illegally obtained evidence. In 1981, the ABA committee on federal judiciary was chaired by a woman, and included among its membership was one black male and one Hispanic male. See Neff, *op. cit.,* p. 44. The ABA leadership assailed moves made by conservative Republicans to take away federal court jurisdiction in some controversial areas of social policy. See *New York Times,* April 29, 1982, p. B12. In recent years the ABA's leadership body, the House of Delegates, has passed resolutions in favor of providing free legal aid for Haitian refugees, asking Congress to apologize to Japanese-Americans for their forced internment during World War II, supporting curbs on the nuclear arms race, advocating the elimination of tax deductions for business meals taken at private clubs that practice racial or sexual discrimination, and favoring better legal representation for those facing the death penalty. These are among a number of liberal resolutions that have originated with the ABA's Section on Individual Rights and Responsibilities. See "Rights Unit's Ideas Gain in Bar Group," by David Margolick, *The New York Times,* August 12, 1984, p. 16.

13. At the request of Republican Senator Williams of Delaware, an ABA committee examined Fortas's relationship with financier Louis Wolfson and expressed the opinion that eight canons of judicial ethics appeared to have been violated. See *New York Times,* May 21, 1969, p. 1.

14. Cf. John R. Schmidhauser, *Judges and Justices: The Federal Appellate Judiciary* (Boston: Little, Brown, 1979), pp. 23–37; Albert P. Melone, *Lawyers, Public Policy and Interest Group Politics* (Washington: University Press of America, 1979); Chase, *Federal Judges,* pp. 157–164.

15. This account of the Morrissey affair is drawn from Chase, *Federal Judges,* pp. 173–177.

16. Chase, *Federal Judges,* p. 174.

17. Concerning the Carter Administration, see Neff, *op. cit.,* p. 44.

18. Interview with John Duffner, August 28, 1974. There is obvious subjectivity and imprecision involved in the ratings process despite the ABA committee's efforts to articulate and apply certain criteria. On occasion the committee is divided over what rating to give a candidate. For example, in 1963, a Kennedy nominee for a post on the Sixth Circuit, George C. Edwards, Jr., received a "Qualified" rating from a majority of the committee, with a minority voting "Not Qualified." See Chase, *Federal Judges,* pp. 167–168. Another example, in 1973, is that of the committee rating of Joseph T. Sneed for a seat on the Ninth Circuit. The ABA committee chairman, as is the procedure, sent the committee report to the Senate Judiciary Committee. The report on Sneed was as follows: "A substantial majority of our Committee is of the opinion that Joseph T. Sneed is *well qualified* for appointment as Judge. . . . A small minority found him *qualified.* However, some of those who voted *well qualified* indicated that they would have found Mr. Sneed *exceptionally well qualified* except for his lack of trial experience." (Italics added.) *Hearings on the Nomination of Joseph T. Sneed to Fill a Vacancy on the United States Court of Appeals for the Ninth Circuit, Senate Judiciary Committee, August 2, 1973* (unpublished hearing). In 1980, for example, the ABA committee was not unanimous in the ratings of about 40 percent of those appointed to the federal courts that year. In general see Chase, *Federal Judges,* Chap. 4; Jackson, *Judges,* pp. 257–269; and Grossman, *Lawyers and Judges.*

19. *Congressional Quarterly,* August 15, 1969, p. 1484. Note that after the Haynsworth-Carswell defeats, the Administration, in an unprecedented move, agreed to submit the names of the leading candidates for Supreme Court vacancies to the ABA committee. Although it was not explicitly stated, the implication was clear that the Administration would not nominate a person to the Supreme Court who received the "Not Qualified" rating. See *New York Times,* July 28, 1970, p. 1. This new procedure had its first test in the early fall of 1971 when two vacancies caused by the retirements of Justices Black and Harlan were to be filled. The Administration first submitted to the ABA committee the name of conservative Virginia Congressman Richard H. Poff. At the outset it had been leaked to the press that Poff was under serious consideration, and immediately civil rights groups and organized labor mounted a campaign against him. (Poff's voting record in the House over a period of 19 years included total opposition to civil rights legislation and marked unfriendliness to the position of organized labor.) Before the ABA committee had an opportunity to conclude their deliberations concerning Poff's candidacy, Poff decided to take himself out of the running. See *Congressional Quarterly,* October 16, 1971, p. 2129. Within two weeks, the Nixon Administration submitted to the ABA committee a list of six persons. The White House requested that the committee focus on two names, the presumed front-runners for the two nominations, Herschel H. Friday (a Little Rock, Arkansas, lawyer and specialist in municipal bond law) and Mildred L. Lillie (a California state appeals court judge). The names of the six surfaced and opposition mounted. The committee found Lillie unqualified by a vote of 11 to 1, and it split down the middle on a rating for Friday, with half the committee voting Friday not qualified and the other half voting "not opposed." The upshot was that Friday and Lillie were dropped along with the arrangement with the committee concerning candidates for Supreme Court positions. When President Nixon announced the nominations of Lewis Powell and William Rehnquist for the vacancies on October 21, 1971, it came as a surprise to the ABA committee as well as to the rest of the nation. See Jackson, *Judges,* pp. 352–353.

20. Senator Weicker was clearly not on good terms with the ABA committee. The *New*

York Times (October 12, 1973, p. 37) suggested that the ABA committee had found Weicker's candidates for the Second Circuit to be not qualified, while Weicker in turn viewed the committee and the Second Circuit as "snooty." The impasse between Weicker and the committee over the Second Circuit vacancy had existed since Judge Joseph Smith's retirement in November, 1971. Judge Smith occupied one of the two "Connecticut" seats (in fact, those positions from the time of their creation had been filled only by Connecticut residents). When Senator Weicker sponsored Governor Meskill to replace Smith, it was no doubt difficult for the Justice officials to dismiss a candidate with such impressive surface credentials. We can speculate that by the spring of 1974 Justice officials felt they had no choice but to yield to Weicker. Weicker's prestige with Connecticut Republicans and, of course, Governor Meskill's career were directly on the line. When he agreed to be Weicker's choice, Governor Meskill had taken himself out of running for reelection. In any event, the Meskill nomination was announced and sent to the Senate (the White House evidently had hesitated) on Nixon's last working day in office. Finally, in April, 1975, Thomas Meskill was confirmed and sworn into office.

21. *Congressional Quarterly,* September 21, 1974, pp. 2570–2571; *New York Times,* September 15, 1974, p. 22.
22. *New York Times,* September 18, 1974, p. 40.
23. The committee had based its "Not Qualified" rating ostensibly on Meskill's lack of trial experience. A decade later, another candidate for an appeals court position, J. Harvie Wilkinson III, with a total lack of trial experience, nevertheless received a "qualified" rating from the committee and as a result of what appeared to be a departure of its policy of not approving those without *any* trial experience, the committee and its standards were subject to sharp attack. See the hearings of the special session of the Senate Judiciary Committee on the ABA's rating procedures and the Wilkinson nomination held on August 7, 1984, *Hearings Before the Committee on the Judiciary, United States Senate, Ninety-Eighth Congress, Second Session* (Washington, D.C.: U.S. Govenment Printing Office, 1985).
24. See the account in *Congressional Quarterly Weekly Report,* 38, No. 10 (March 8, 1980), 674.
25. *New York Times,* October 10, 1980, p. A18.
26. During the time of the fall 1980 presidential campaign a total of 16 pending nominations, including Sheffield's, faced Republican opposition because the Republicans anticipated a presidential election victory in November and they wanted a Republican president to fill those positions. With Ronald Reagan's election in November 1980, those 16 nominations were doomed.
27. *New York Times,* July 14, 1979, p. 5; *Houston Post,* May 11, 1979, p. B1.
28. See, for example, Sheldon Goldman, "Carter's Judicial Appointments: A Lasting Legacy," *Judicature,* 64 (1981), 348, 350; and *Legislative History of the United States Circuit Courts of Appeals and the Judges Who Served during the Period 1801 through May 1972* (Washington, D.C.: U.S. Senate, Committee on the Judiciary, 92nd Congress, Second Session, 1972), p. 2.
29. *New York Times,* November 28, 1978, p. A16.
30. *Boston Globe,* January 26, 1979, p. 2.
31. *Boston Globe,* November 12, 1980, p. 3.
32. See, for example, *New York Times,* November 3, 1968, p. 1, and January 4, 1970, p. 46. During the 1970 congressional campaign, Nixon made it obvious that this was precisely what he was doing and intended to continue doing. See *New York Times,* October 25, 1970, p. 1.

33. *New York Times,* October 16, 1972, p. 1.
34. *Hearings on the Nomination of Thomas G. Gee to Fill a Vacancy on the United States Court of Appeals for the Fifth Circuit, Subcommittee on Nominations, Senate Judiciary Committee, July 10, 1973* (unpublished hearing), p. 5.
35. *Hearings on the Nomination of D. Dortch Warriner to Fill a Vacancy on the United States District Court, Eastern District of the State of Virginia, Subcommittee on Nominations, Senate Judiciary Committee, May 15, 1974* (unpublished hearing), p. 2.
36. *Hearings on the Nomination of John A. Reed, Jr., to Fill a Vacancy on the United States District Court, Middle District of the State of Florida, Subcommittee on Nominations, Senate Judiciary Committee, July 26, 1973* (unpublished hearing), p. 5.
37. Jackson, *Judges,* p. 270.
38. With respect to the Carter Administration, see, for example, Neff, *op. cit.,* p. 119; and Berkson and Carbon, *op. cit.,* p. 137.
39. *New York Times,* December 24, 1981, p. B4, and January 7, 1982, p. A26.
40. Goldman, "Judicial Appointments," pp. 203–212.
41. Letter dated June 17, 1961, from James Rowe to Robert Kennedy, in Justice Department "A" file of James Browning. That Browning received the nomination is even more noteworthy because the ABA committee rated him "Not Qualified." The Kennedy people in the Justice Department, however, viewed the rating as a manifestation of antiliberal bias on the part of those Montana lawyers contacted by the ABA whose views provided the basis for the rating. Interestingly, Judge Browning has served well on the bench (this evaluation is based on highly favorable references to Browning in personal interviews with appeals judges and others as well as a reading of a number of his opinions). For another account of Judge Browning's nomination see Grossman, *Lawyers and Judges,* pp. 144–145.
42. As quoted in John Schmidhauser, *Judges and Justices: The Federal Appellate Judiciary* (Boston: Little, Brown, 1979), p. 90. In general, see Henry J. Abraham, *Justices and Presidents* (New York: Oxford University Press, second ed. 1985).
43. James E. Clayton, *The Making of Justice: The Supreme Court in Action* (New York: Dutton, 1964), p. 52, as cited in Henry J. Abraham, *The Judicial Process,* 2nd ed. (New York: Oxford University Press, 1968), p. 66. It is of interest to note that White and Goldberg's voting behavior on the Supreme Court diverged. See Joel B. Grossman, "Dissenting Blocs on the Warren Court: A Study in Judicial Role Behavior," *Journal of Politics,* 30 (1968), 1068–1090; Glendon Schubert, *The Judicial Mind Revisited: Psychometric Analysis of Supreme Court Ideology* (New York: Oxford University Press, 1974).
44. See, for example, *New York Times,* November 3, 1968, p. 1, November 22, 1969, p. 1; *Congressional Quarterly,* October 24, 1969, p. 2103.
45. See, for example, *Congressional Quarterly,* October 25, 1980, p. 3200.
46. See President Nixon's statement in the *New York Times,* April 10, 1970, p. 14. Note that during the 1970 congressional campaign, Vice-President Agnew pledged that the Administration would place a Southern conservative on the Supreme Court. See *New York Times,* October 27, 1970, p. 1. In general, see William J. Daniels, "The Geographic Factor in Appointments to the United States Supreme Court: 1789–1976," *Western Political Quarterly,* 31 (1978), 226–237.
47. See Todd, *Justice on Trial.*
48. As quoted in *CQ Guide to Current American Government, Fall 1967* (Washington, D.C.: Congressional Quarterly, 1967), p. 85.
49. See, for example, Michael Parenti, "Ethnic Politics and the Persistence of Ethnic Identification," *American Political Science Review,* 61 (1967), 717–727; and Nathan

Glazer and Daniel P. Moynihan, *Beyond the Melting Pot* (Cambridge, Mass.: M.I.T. and Harvard University Press, 1963).

50. *Congressional Quarterly,* November 21, 1969, pp. 2312–2313.

51. When Justice Fortas was nominated for elevation to the chief justiceship, President Johnson also nominated Fifth Circuit Judge Homer Thornberry to fill the vacancy that would exist upon Fortas's elevation. Since Fortas's nomination was not approved, no vacancy existed and Thornberry's nomination also died.

52. President Johnson was particularly disturbed about Republican opposition to the Fortas nomination because he had gone to the trouble of clearing the nomination with Republican Senate Minority Leader Everett Dirksen. See the transcript of the Johnson press conference in the *New York Times,* August 1, 1968, p. 16. The Parker and Fortas nomination fights were won by opponents of the Court. The Haynsworth and Carswell battles were won largely by supporters of the Court. A journalistic account of the Carswell fight can be found in Richard Harris, *Decision* (New York: Dutton, 1971). Also see Joel B. Grossman and Stephen Wasby, "Haynsworth and Parker: History Does Live Again," *South Carolina Law Review,* 23 (1971), 345.

53. The major public opinion polls regularly break down their surveys by demographic variables such as age, sex, region, religion, income, education level, occupation, and party affiliation.

54. Schmidhauser, *Judges and Justices,* pp. 49–55.

55. The Supreme Court of 1983–1984 contained two justices from humble backgrounds. For an analysis of social mobility and opportunity throughout American history, see P. M. G. Harris, "The Social Origins of American Leaders: The Demographic Foundations," *Perspectives in American History,* 3 (1969), 159–344.

56. This analysis adds the following to Schmidhauser's list of justices from humble backgrounds: Justices Douglas, Brennan, and Fortas.

57. Sheldon Goldman, "Politics, Judges, and the Administration of Justice: The Backgrounds, Recruitment, and Decisional Tendencies of the Judges on the United States Courts of Appeals, 1961–1964," Ph.D. dissertation, Harvard University, 1965, pp. 64–67.

58. Schmidhauser, *Judges and Justices,* p. 57.

59. John R. Schmidhauser, "The Justices of the Supreme Court: A Collective Portrait," *Midwest Journal of Political Science,* 3 (1959), Table 8, reprinted in Glendon Schubert (ed.), *Judicial Behavior* (Skokie, Ill.: Rand McNally, 1964), p. 222.

60. Sheldon Goldman, "Characteristics of Eisenhower and Kennedy Appointees to the Lower Federal Courts," *Western Political Quarterly,* 18 (1965), p. 757. Note that Richardson and Vines reported that about six out of ten district judges serving in 1963 had attended law school in the same state in which their district was located. A similar pattern of localism or regionalism was found for appeals judges. They suggested that state and sectional values and viewpoints may thereby be absorbed and represented on the bench. See Richard J. Richardson and Kenneth N. Vines, *The Politics of Federal Courts* (Boston: Little, Brown, 1970), pp. 70–73.

61. The figures are 21.5 percent of the Eisenhower district court appointees as compared to 18.4 percent of the Kennedy district court appointees; 28.8 percent of the Eisenhower appeals court appointees as compared to 19.1 percent of the Kennedy appeals court appointees. From Goldman, "Characteristics of Eisenhower and Kennedy Appointees to the Lower Federal Courts."

62. See Sheldon Goldman, "Reagan's Judicial Appointments at Mid-Term," *Judicature,* 66 (1983), pp. 338, 344.

63. A suggestive article is by Christopher Jencks, "Social Stratification and Higher

Education," *Harvard Educational Review,* 38 (1968), 277–316, especially the argument on pp. 289–290.

64. Schmidhauser, *Judges and Justices,* pp. 62–68. Also see Nicholas Jay Demerath, III, *Social Class in American Protestantism* (Skokie, Ill.: Rand McNally, 1965); Garlen Gockel, "Income and Religious Affiliation: A Regression Analysis," *American Journal of Sociology,* 74 (1969), 632–647; Bruce L. Warren, "Socioeconomic Achievement and Religion: The American Case," *Sociological Inquiry,* 40 (1970), 130–155; David Knoke, "Religion, Stratification and Politics: America in the 1960s," *American Journal of Political Science,* 18 (1974), 331–345.

65. Conversation with former Attorney General Griffin Bell, June 1, 1981.

66. See Beverly B. Cook, "The First Woman Candidate for the Supreme Court—Florence E. Allen," *Yearbook, Supreme Court Historical Society* (Washington, D.C.: Supreme Court Historical Society, 1981), pp. 19–35. In general, see Elaine Martin, "Women on the Federal Bench: A Comparative Profile," *Judicature,* 65 (1982), 306–313.

67. Julius Duscha, "Chief Justice Burger Asks: 'If It Doesn't Make Good Sense, How Can It Make Good Law?' " *New York Times Magazine,* October 5, 1969, p. 149.

68. Goldman, "Politics, Judges, and the Administration of Justice," p. 93.

69. See Goldman, "Reagan's Judicial Appointments," pp. 339, 345.

70. Schmidhauser, *Judges and Justices,* pp. 79–99.

71. It is reasonable to speculate that Justice officials prefer considering candidates with judicial or prosecutorial experience because such experience means that the candidate has a public track record that can be evaluated. In addition, a prosecutorial background may be favored by Justice officials because such a background is likely to have sensitized one to the problems a prosecutor's office faces and one might be more understanding if not sympathetic to the government's side in criminal prosecutions.

72. Goldman, "Characteristics of Eisenhower and Kennedy Appointees to the Lower Federal Courts," p. 758. This too suggested that there were class differences in the appointments of both administrations.

73. Goldman, "Reagan's Judicial Appointments," p. 338.

74. This does not necessarily mean that all groups will take the same advantage of these opportunities. Members of certain groups and classes in society have been at a disadvantage not only in acquiring financial resources necessary for an undergraduate and legal education but also in acquiring the cultural values and attitudes that encourage such an education and the deprivations required in the process of obtaining it. Historically, lower-class Catholics, low-status Protestants particularly of rural background, lower-class black Americans, and women (to some extent) have been least likely to acquire the necessary resources or to have the appropriate supportive values. Of course, women and racial minorities have also historically faced outright discrimination denying them equal opportunity with others to pursue legal and judicial careers. Thus, political judicial recruitment has not resulted in creating a judiciary that mirrors American society. It should also be noted that discriminatory barriers within the legal profession have resulted in different legal career paths taken by women and racial minorities. See Elliot E. Slotnick, "The Paths to the Federal Bench: Gender, Race and Judicial Recruitment Variation," *Judicature,* 67 (1984), 370–388.

75. See, for example, the argument in Sheldon Goldman, "Judicial Selection and the Qualities that Make a 'Good' Judge," in *The Annals of the American Academy of Political and Social Science,* 462 (July, 1982), 112–124.

76. See, for example, Navasky, *Kennedy Justice,* Chap. 5.

77. Note that the commissions used by the Carter Administration were not nonpartisan. See Neff, *op. cit.,* Berkson and Carbon, *op. cit.,* and Slotnick, "The U.S. Circuit Judge Nominating Commission."

78. See, for example, Stuart S. Nagel, *The Legal Process from a Behavioral Perspective* (Homewood, Ill.: Dorsey, 1969), pp. 199–218; J. Woodford Howard, Jr., *Courts of Appeals in the Federal Judicial System* (Princeton, New Jersey: Princeton University Press, 1981), Chap. 4.

79. Perhaps the earliest and best statement of this position is that by Charles G. Haines, "General Observations on the Effects of Personal, Political, and Economic Influences in the Decisions of Judges," *Illinois Law Review,* 17 (1922), 96–116, reprinted in Schubert (ed.), *Judicial Behavior,* pp. 40–49.

80. The empirical testing of the hypotheses suggested by this argument has produced some support for the propositions as they have been tested with aggregates of judges in terms of broad backgrounds categories. Studies of individual judges (judicial biographies and single-judge analyses), however, have more persuasively documented the development of attitudes, values, and role concepts in the context of specific background experiences. Chapter 5 contains a discussion of these points along with some of the relevant evidence. Note that the evidence does show a link between appointing administration and judicial decisional tendencies. See Robert A. Carp and C. K. Rowland, *Policymaking and Politics in the Federal District Courts* (Knoxville, Tenn.: University of Tennessee Press, 1983); and Jon Gottschall, "Carter's Judicial Appointments: The Influence of Affirmative Action and Merit Selection on Voting on the U.S. Courts of Appeals," *Judicature,* 67 (1983), 164–173.

81. Barbara A. Curran, "The Legal Profession in the 1980's: Selected Statistics from the 1984 Lawyer Statistical Report," paper presented before the Law and Society Association, annual meeting, 1984. Also see *The 1984 Lawyer Statistical Report: A Profile of the Legal Profession in the United States* (Chicago: American Bar Foundation, in press).

82. The divisions are Antitrust, Civil, Civil Rights, Criminal, Land and Natural Resources, and Tax.

83. See the discussion in James Eisenstein, *Counsel for the United States: U.S. Attorneys in the Political and Legal Systems* (Baltimore: Johns Hopkins University Press, 1978), pp. 35–48.

84. For example, a Nixon appointee to a U.S. attorney post revealed in an interview: "Obviously this Administration was elected on the basis of certain pledges it made that fell in the legal area. And I believe that it would be incumbent on a U.S. Attorney to attempt—within the limits of the law—to carry out these policies. . . . Other things being equal, since the office has somewhat of a policy-making role which ought to reflect the Administration's policy, those who are appointed [should be] in sympathy with the policies and work to carry them out." *New York Times,* October 12, 1969, p. 62. Also see Eisenstein, *Counsel for the United States,* p. 37.

85. Eisenstein, *Counsel for the United States,* p. 49.

86. Eisenstein, *Counsel for the United States,* pp. 197–206. For an examination of state prosecuting attorneys, see George F. Cole, *Politics and the Administration of Justice* (Beverly Hills, Calif.: Sage, 1973), Chap. 4.

87. Eisenstein, *Counsel for the United States,* pp. 51, 241.

88. *Ibid.,* pp. 174–176.

89. The analysis in this section is drawn from Eisenstein's study, *Counsel for the United States,* in particular Chap. 7, and its earlier version, his doctoral dissertation (Yale, 1968), Chap. 3. References are to the published version.

90. *Ibid.,* pp. 133, 146–149.
91. *Ibid.,* p. 135.
92. *Ibid.,* pp. 135–136.
93. *Ibid.,* p. 140.
94. *Ibid.,* p. 139.
95. *New York Times,* July 6, 1972, p. 17. For an overall view of the "war on poverty" legislation and legal services, see Mark R. Arnold, "The Good War That Might Have Been," *New York Times Magazine,* September 29, 1974, pp. 56ff.
96. *New York Times,* February 11, 1973, p. 24. For a more scholarly appraisal of these lawyers see Howard S. Erlanger, "Lawyers and Neighborhood Legal Services: Social Background and the Impetus for Reform," *Law and Society Review,* 12 (1978), 253–274.
97. *New York Times,* February 13, 1973, p. 11.
98. *New York Times,* February 13, 1973, p. 13.
99. For details of the legislation see *Congressional Quarterly,* July 27, 1974, pp. 1981–1982.
100. *Congressional Quarterly,* May 13, 1978, p. 1204.
101. *Congressional Quarterly,* March 14, 1981, p. 466; March 21, 1981, p. 529; February 13, 1982, p. 275.
102. In general, see Harry P. Stumpf, *Community Politics and Legal Services: The Other Side of the Law* (Beverly Hills, Calif.: Sage, 1975); Earl Johnson, Jr., *Justice and Reform: The Formative Years of the OEO Legal Services Program* (New York: Basic Books, 1974); Joel F. Handler, Ellen Jane Hollingsworth, and Howard S. Erlanger, *Lawyers and the Pursuit of Legal Rights* (New York: Academic Press, 1978).
103. *Annual Report, Administrative Office of the U.S. Courts, 1983,* pp. 38, 192, 440–441.
104. See *The National Law Journal,* August 15, 1983, p. 7. For 1984–1985, all but one of the 38 law clerks had previous lower court clerkships including eight from clerkships on the Court of Appeals for the District of Columbia and seven from the Second Curucit. *National Law Journal,* July 30, 1984, p.4. In general, see John Bilyeu Oakley and Robert S. Thompson, *Law Clerks and the Judicial Process* (Berkeley: University of California Press, 1980).
105. Oakley and Thompson, pp. 86–105, 142–145.
106. See "The Decision to Decide" and Nathan Lewin, "Helping the Court with Its Work," in Walter Murphy and C. Herman Pritchett (eds.), *Courts, Judges and Politics,* 2nd ed. (New York: Random House, 1974), pp. 87–94, 497–501. Also see "Judicial Clerkships: A Symposium on the Institution," *Vanderbilt Law Review,* 26 (1973), 1123–1257; J. Harvie Wilkinson, III, *Serving Justice: A Supreme Court Clerk's View* (New York: Charterhouse, 1974). David N. Atkinson, in his study of Justice Sherman Minton, sent questionnaires to the Justice's former law clerks and he also personally interviewed some of them. Atkinson concluded that Justice Minton considered the law clerks "valuable contributors to the decision-making process" and that the law clerks at times did influence Minton's judicial behavior. David N. Atkinson, "Mr. Justice Minton and the Supreme Court," Ph.D. dissertation, University of Iowa, 1969, p. 127, and pp. 121–124, 162–164. Also note the description of law clerks in Nina Totenberg, "Behind the Marble, Beneath the Robes," *New York Times Magazine,* March 16, 1975, 15, 58–67; and Bob Woodward and Scott Armstrong, *The Brethren* (New York: Simon & Schuster, 1979). Justice Stevens in 1982 acknowledged "They [his law clerks] examine them [certiorari petitions] all and select a small minority that they believe I should read myself. As a result I do not even look at the papers in over 80 per cent of the cases that are filed." John Paul Stevens, "Some Thoughts on Judicial Restraint," *Judicature,* 66 (1982), 179.

107. As quoted in *The Third Branch* (publication of the Federal Judicial Center), January 1982, p. 3.

108. Steven Flanders and Jerry Goldman, "Screening Practices and the Use of Para-Judicial Personnel in a U.S. Court of Appeals," *Justice System Journal,* 1 (1975), 1–16.

109. See the discussion in Richard S. Wells, "The Legal Profession and Politics," *Midwest Journal of Political Science,* 8 (1964), 166–190.

110. See Robert G. McCloskey, *The American Supreme Court* (Chicago: University of Chicago Press, 1960), pp. 101–179.

111. See the data reported in the two studies by Nathan Hakman: "Lobbying the Supreme Court—An Appraisal of 'Political Science Folklore,' " *Fordham Law Review,* 35 (1966), 15–50; "The Supreme Court's Political Environment: The Processing of Noncommercial Litigation," in Joel B. Grossman and Joseph Tanenhaus (eds.), *Frontiers of Judicial Research* (New York: Wiley, 1969), pp. 199–253. Cf. Karen O'Connor and Lee Epstein, "Amicus Curiae Participation in U.S. Supreme Court Litigation: An Appraisal of Hakman's 'Folklore,' " *Law and Society Review,* 16 (1981–1982), 311–320.

112. See Jonathan D. Casper, *Lawyers before the Warren Court* (Urbana: University of Illinois Press, 1972) and *The Politics of Civil Liberties* (New York: Harper & Row, 1972). Also see Ann Fagan Ginger (ed.), *The Relevant Lawyers* (New York: Simon & Schuster, 1973); Stuart A. Scheingold, *The Politics of Rights: Lawyers, Public Policy, and Political Change* (New Haven, Conn.: Yale University Press, 1974). The latter two works focus on the new breed of activist lawyers committed to social change and working on their own or with the newer activist groups. Also see Karen O'Connor, *Women's Organizations' Use of the Courts* (Lexington, Mass.: Lexington Books, 1980).

113. Arthur Lewis Wood, "Informal Relations in the Practice of Criminal Law," *American Journal of Sociology,* 62 (1956), 48–55. Also see Delmar Karlen, *Anglo-American Criminal Justice* (New York: Oxford University Press, 1967), pp. 34–35.

114. Abraham S. Blumberg, "The Practice of Law as a Confidence Game: Organizational Cooptation of a Profession," *Law and Society Review,* 1 (1967), 15–39. Also see Jonathan D. Casper, *American Criminal Justice: The Defendant's Perspective* (Englewood Cliffs, N.J.: Prentice-Hall, 1972), Chaps. 3, 4; Cole, *Politics,* Chap. 5.

115. See the discussion of plea bargaining in Chapter 4.

116. See Paul D. Carrington, "Crowded Dockets and the Courts of Appeals: The Threat to the Function of Review and the National Law," *Harvard Law Review,* 82 (1969), 543–549.

117. See Erwin O. Smigel, *The Wall Street Lawyer* (New York: Free Press, 1964). The second edition of Smigel's book (Bloomington: Indiana University Press, 1970), however, reports that New York City's largest law firms are undergoing greater "democratization" in that there are increasing openings for Jews and blacks as well as increasing interest in aiding the poor with their legal problems. In spite of these developments, there is fragmentary evidence that some graduates from the prestige law schools were bypassing a corporation law career, at least temporarily during the late 1960s and early 1970s. For example, it was reported that none of the 39 editors of the Harvard Law Review graduating in 1970 planned to enter private practice immediately. They preferred instead to clerk for judges or to work with public or private poverty, social reform, or civil liberties groups (*New York Times,* November 19, 1969, p. 37). A systematic survey of University of Chicago law school graduates revealed no widespread changes in career choices, but did note that the top-ranking

graduates were more likely than were earlier top graduates to go into legal reform and assistance-type jobs. See Rita J. Simon, Frank Koziol, and Nancy Joslyn, "Have There Been Significant Changes in the Career Aspirations and Occupational Choices of Law School Graduates in the 1960s?" *Law and Society Review,* 8 (1973), 95–108. Also see, Frances Kahn Zemans and Victor G. Rosenblum, *The Making of a Public Profession* (Chicago: American Bar Foundation, 1981).

118. Jack Ladinsky, "Careers of Lawyers, Law Practice, and Legal Institutions," *American Sociological Review,* 28 (1963), 47–54. Also see Jerome E. Carlin, *Lawyer's Ethics* (New York: Russell Sage Foundation, 1966), pp. 11–40; and John P. Heinz and Edward O. Laumann, *Chicago Lawyers: The Social Structure of the Bar* (New York: Russell Sage, 1983).

119. A third style of practice (the rural style) is suggested by Wells, "The Legal Profession and Politics."

120. *Statistical Abstract of the United States, 1968* (Washington, D.C.: Government Printing Office, 1968), Table 224, p. 152; *Annual Report, U.S. Courts, 1983,* Table C-7, p. 290.

121. See, for example, Edward N. Beiser, "Are Juries Representative?" *Judicature,* 57 (1973), 194–199; Hayward Alker, Jr., Carl Hosticka, and Michael Mitchell, "Jury Selection as a Biased Social Process," *Law and Society Review,* 11 (1976), 9–41; C. K. Rowland, W. A. Macauley, and Robert A. Carp, "The Effects of Selection System on Jury Composition," *Law & Policy Quarterly,* 4 (1982), 235–251.

122. See S. Sidney Ulmer, "Supreme Court Behavior in Racial Exclusion Cases: 1935–1960," *American Political Science Review,* 56 (1962), 325–330; Dale W. Broeder, "The Negro in Court," *Duke Law Journal* (1965), 19–31.

123. See Hans Zeisel, "Dr. Spock and the Case of the Vanishing Woman Juror," *University of Chicago Law Review,* 37 (1969), 1–18; Edwin S. Mills, "A Statistical Profile of Jurors in a United States District Court," *Law and the Social Order,* 1 (1969), 329–339; and the studies cited in note 121.

124. *New York Times,* January 13, 1969, p. 26.

125. Technically jury behavior should be studied as the conversion process for this set of authorities within the system. However, since the focus of this book will be on judicial conversion, it is convenient to discuss jury behavior here.

126. See the bibliography of publications based on that project in Harry S. Kalven and Hans Zeisel, *The American Jury* (Boston: Little, Brown, 1966), pp. 541–545. Cf. Michael H. Walsh, "The American Jury: A Reassessment," *Yale Law Journal,* 79 (1969), 142. For an overview of jury research by others as well as the Chicago researchers, see Howard S. Erlanger, "Jury Research in America: Its Past and Future," *Law and Society Review,* 4 (1970), 345–370. Also see Stuart Nagel and Lenore Weitzman, "Sex and the Unbiased Jury," *Judicature,* 56 (1972), 108–111; Edward N. Beiser and Rene Varrin, "Six-Member Juries in the Federal Courts," *Judicature,* 58 (1975), 424–433; Michael J. Saks, *Jury Verdicts: The Role of Group Size and Social Decision Rule* (Lexington, Mass.: Heath, 1977); Reid Hastie, Steven D. Penrod, and Nancy Pennington, *Inside the Jury* (Cambridge, Mass.: Harvard University Press, 1983).

127. An extended discussion of these findings appears in Harry Kalven, "The Dignity of the Civil Jury," *Virginia Law Review,* 50 (1964), 1055–1075.

128. Kalven and Zeisel, *The American Jury,* p. 495.

129. *Ibid.,* pp. 63–64.

130. *Ibid.,* pp. 116, 469. Also see Dale W. Broeder, "Plaintiff's Family Status as Affecting Jury Behavior: Some Tentative Insights," *Journal of Public Law,* 14 (1965), 131–141.

Note the results of a Justice Department study that found the attitudes of jurors responsible for the Government's string of losses in its "political trials." See *New York Times,* April 19, 1975, p. 15.

131. Kalven and Zeisel, *The American Jury,* pp. 465, 466–468. Cf. Morton Hunt, "Putting Juries on the Couch," *New York Times Magazine,* November 28, 1982, pp. 70–72, 78, 82, 85–86, 88.

132. Dale W. Broeder, "University of Chicago Jury Project," *Nebraska Law Review,* 38 (1959), 748. Cf. Edmond Costantini and Joel King, "The Partial Juror: Correlates and Causes of Prejudgement," *Law and Society Review,* 15 (1980–81), 9–40; Edmond Costantini, Michael Mallery, and Diane Yapundich, "Gender and Juror Partiality: Are Women More Likely to Prejudge Guilt?" *Judicature,* 67 (1983), 120–133.

133. See Rita James Simon, "Jurors' Evaluation of Expert Psychiatric Testimony," *Ohio State Law Journal,* 21 (1960), 75–95; Stanley Sue and Ronald E. Smith, "How Not to Get a Fair Trial," *Psychology Today,* 7 (May 1974), 86–90; Saks, *Jury Verdicts;* Hastie et al., *Inside the Jury.*

134. Kalven and Zeisel, *The American Jury,* pp. 482–491.

135. *Ibid.,* p. 487.

136. *Ibid.,* p. 488.

137. *Ibid.,* p. 489. The more recent study by Hastie et al., *Inside the Jury,* suggests that this consensus-building process is significantly altered when nonunanimous juries are permitted. Also see this study, particularly chapter 7, for a wealth of findings concerning the effect of juror characteristics on their attitudes and decision making and on the jury deliberation process itself.

chapter 4

Input

Among the members of American society are constantly spawned needs, expectations, wants, desires, and disputes. These "disturbances"[1] are the raw material from which input is produced and injected into a political system. For example, such social systems as families, schools, street gangs, and voluntary associations indoctrinate or socialize maturing members into holding and acting out various beliefs, expectations, and codes of behavior. This produces members of society who are variously law-abiding and law-breaking, timid and aggressive, right-wing chauvinist and left-wing radical, productive and lazy, prudish and prurient, satisfied and dissatisfied, altruistic and selfish. The resulting "disturbances" often (but not always) become input to a political system.

In a similar way, through the workings of the economic system persons are employed as well as not employed, job conditions are found to be desirable as well as undesirable, people are encouraged by advertising to buy good as well as shoddy merchandise, wages and bills are paid as well as not paid, property is accumulated as well as lost, contracts are fulfilled as well as broken, customers are satisfied as well as swindled, and business firms compete fairly as well as unfairly. From this complex of activities, expectations and needs for reform, retribution, relief, and other types of action and inaction also arise. Many of the disturbances are resolved by third parties without any direct governmental interference at all. Employees change jobs. Complaining customers have their money returned or otherwise receive satisfaction. Defaulting employers and customers agree to pay what they owe. Thus, in one way or another, a vast number of mutually satisfying (or not so satisfying but still acceptable) accommodations are worked out. Still with the economic system, a vast number of calls for political action are generated by its activities.

One could look at other social processes and systems of behavior and note phenomena similar to those just mentioned. As students of politics, our interest, of course, is in those disturbances that eventually become input to a political system. Although our special concern is with the federal judicial system, that system is only one of many (both judicial and nonjudicial) within the larger American political system which receive political input.

Input may be characterized as being of two types: demands and support. *Demands,* in Eastonian analysis are "articulated statements, directed toward the authorities, proposing that some kind of authoritative allocation ought to be undertaken."[2] *Support* refers to the input of satisfaction or dissatisfaction on the part of the system's publics, both elite and mass, regarding the system's operations, structure, and output.

DEMANDS

Demands processed by the federal judicial system are those that satisfy the system's regime rules, which specify the form demands must take as well as certain substantive criteria. Although the federal courts are authorized to process a narrow range of administrative tasks (such as the approval of passport applications, naturalization of aliens, parole and probation of those convicted of federal crimes), the principal demands processed by the system are criminal and civil cases and controversies that meet the requirements of jurisdiction and justiciability. In processing both types of demands—administrative but most particularly litigative—there is also a set of formal regime rules relating to procedure that limits what information may be presented in the pressing of a demand.[3]

Administrative Demands

Administrative demands encompass certain direct and supervisory bureaucratic tasks as well as those relating to the system's internal administration.[4] The institutions or officials responsible for converting such demands into outputs as well as the number of such demands fed into the system in fiscal year 1982 (July 1, 1981 through June 30, 1982) are presented in Table 4.1.

These various demands are not "cases or controversies" as these terms are strictly used, and all have had the term "administrative" applied to them in one or another sense of that word. Demands concerning passport applications, alien naturalization, internal court administration, and even, to some extent, parole and probation do not typically present the conflict situation characteristic of litigation. Demands to institute bankruptcy proceedings, on the other hand, frequently do have such adversary characteristics. Yet traditionally these are also considered administrative matters.

Demands for the processing of passport applications and the naturalization of aliens are probably the least judicial of the administrative demands. Although large numbers are involved, they require little judicial time.[5] Bankruptcy as well as parole and probation supervision require somewhat more judicial time.[6] However, the main brunt of the work is carried on by others. In fiscal 1982, for

Table 4.1 ADMINISTRATIVE DEMANDS PROCESSED BY THE FEDERAL JUDICIAL SYSTEM DURING FISCAL 1982

Type of demand	Jurisdiction of[a]	Number[b]
Direct administrative functions:		
Passport applications	District courts (State Department)	15,018
Naturalization petitions	District courts	158,146
Supervisory administrative functions:		
Probation and parole	District courts (officers and staff of the Division of Probation)	58,373[c]
Bankruptcy		
Cases commenced	Bankruptcy courts (bankruptcy judges)	527,811
Cases appealed	Courts of appeals	509
Internal administration:		
Collection of statistics, payroll, budgeting, etc.	Administrative Office of the United States Courts	
Institutes for court personnel and research leading to recommendations for improvements of administrative practices	Federal Judicial Center	
Monitoring of caseloads and administrative supervision of lower courts	Judicial Council of each circuit	
Discussion of problems within each circuit and recommendations for improvements	Judicial Conference of each circuit	
Revision of rules of federal civil and criminal procedure	Supreme Court (Judicial Conference of the United States)	

Source: Administrative Office of the United States Courts, *Annual Report of the Director, 1982* (Washington, D.C.: Government Printing Office, 1982), *passim.*
[a]Institutions or officials in parentheses indicate those doing initial or main processing of demands if other than institution having ultimate authority.
[b]Number of applications, petitions, or cases *filed* in fiscal 1982.
[c]Number of those under supervision of federal probation officers on June 30, 1982.

example, 234 federal bankruptcy judges handled bankruptcy matters,[7] and 1637 probation officers of the Federal Probation Service prepared presentencing reports and supervised those on probation.[8]

Passport applications, naturalization petitions, bankruptcy petitions, and so forth, reflect political demands generated from the environment that one governmental agency or another must fulfill. On the other hand, demands concerned with the internal administration of the federal judicial system are generated from *within* the system and can only (and, indeed, must if the system is to operate) be processed *within* that system. These demands are considered in Eastonian analysis to be *withinputs.*[9] The most prosaic of these withinputs are concerned with the day-to-day tasks of the administration of minor court personnel, budgeting, disbursing, and the collection and reporting of court statistics. These demands are primarily handled by the Administrative Office of the U.S. Courts. Demands within the system for efficiency and consistency of behavior by court authorities are dealt with in part by the Federal Judicial Center through its various institutes (for example, sentencing institutes for judges, institutes for bankruptcy judges) and the research projects it sponsors and undertakes that may yield recommendations for improvements of administrative practices. The management of caseloads in terms of judicial personnel is in the hands of each circuit's judicial council. The councils monitor caseloads, call upon retired judges when the burdens become heavy, and request the temporary assignment of judges from other circuits. They have authority to discipline federal judges, short of removal from office. In one instance, a judicial council prevented a district judge, apparently for a variety of reasons including inefficiency, from handling any cases at all.[10] Problems within each of the circuits are discussed at the annual circuit judicial conferences. Perhaps the most important form of system withinput is handled by the Judicial Conference of the United States, which is officially described as "the governing body for the administration of the Federal judicial system as a whole."[11] By far its most important function is the promulgation and revision of the various rules of federal civil and criminal procedure (by which litigation is processed). The Judicial Conference solicits the views of a wide variety of judges and attorneys before making its recommendations. After usually receiving pro forma approval by the Supreme Court, the new rules are transmitted to Congress by the Chief Justice. If Congress does not issue a formal congressional resolution disapproving them within 90 days, the rules have the force of law.[12]

Litigative Demands: District Courts

The litigative input into the federal district courts is split into two formal categories, civil and criminal. As trial courts with original jurisdiction, the federal district courts process these demands for the first time.[13] In fiscal 1982, for example, civil cases accounted for 86 percent of the cases filed in the district courts,[14] and 68 percent of the trials. Table 4.2 gives an overview of the district courts' civil litigation in terms of cases filed in fiscal 1982. Noted in this table are both the jurisdiction heading under which the cases fall and the nature of the suits.

During the 1950s and most of the 1960s there was a slow but steady rise (about 2 to 3 percent) in the number of civil cases filed each year. A plateau of about 71,000 per year was reached in the fiscal 1966–1968 period. In fiscal 1969, however, there was an 8 percent increase in cases filed. Fiscal 1970 had a 13 percent rise, and in fiscal 1971 there was a 7 percent increase. In fiscal 1972 and 1973 the rate of increase was down to the pre-1966 level of between 2 and 3 percent, but fiscal 1974's 5 percent rate presaged a new round of litigation inflation. By fiscal 1974 there were over 100,000 civil cases filed in federal district courts and by fiscal 1982 the number of new civil cases exceeded 200,000. The sharp increases in filings can in part be attributed to the petitions filed by state and federal prisoners concerning demands for orders to vacate sentences, issue

Table 4.2 CIVIL CASES COMMENCED IN THE DISTRICT COURTS BY BASIS OF JURISDICTION AND NATURE OF SUIT, FISCAL YEAR 1982

Nature of suit	Total	Percent	United States cases			Private cases	
			Plaintiff	Defendant	Federal question	Diversity of citizenship	Local jurisdiction
Total cases	206,193	100.0	48,868	26,905	79,197	50,555	688
(Percent of total)			(23.7)	(13.1)	(38.4)	(24.5)	(0.3)
Contract actions	67,276	32.6	34,258	700	6,788	25,423	107
Real property	8,812	4.3	4,702	647	976	2,436	51
Tort actions	34,218	16.6	196	2,777	8,430	22,691	214
Actions under statutes	95,294	46.2	9,700	22,777	62,781	—	36
Antitrust	1,066		26	3	1,037	—	—
Bankruptcy	2,340		55	33	2,252	—	—
Civil rights: voting	170		4	11	155	—	—
Civil rights: employment	7,689		292	627	6,770	—	—
Civil rights: other	9,173		83	847	8,249	—	—
Commerce	1,057		77	10	970	—	—
Environmental matters	394		178	137	79	—	—
Deportation	134		5	129	—	—	—
Habeas corpus	9,986		—	1,927	8,036	—	23
Prisoner petitions: civil rights	17,575		—	834	16,739	—	2
Prisoner petitions: other	1,742		—	1,567	172	—	3
Forfeiture and penalty	3,340		3,340	—	—	—	—
Labor laws	10,227		1,525	161	8,541	—	—
Copyright, patent, trademark	4,592		4	3	4,585	—	—
Securities, commodities, exchanges	2,376		162	16	2,198	—	—
Social security	12,812		—	12,812	—	—	—
Reapportionment (state)	33		—		33	—	—
Tax suits	4,221		2,941	1,272	—	—	8
Freedom of Information	381		2	366	13	—	—
Other statutory actions	5,980		1,006	2,022	2,952	—	—
Other actions	593	0.3	12	4	312	5	260

Source: Administrative Office of the United States Courts, *Annual Report of the Director, 1982* (Washington, D.C.: Government Printing Office, 1982).

habeas corpus, grant parole, and modify living conditions in prisons and prison regulations.

Between 1966 and 1968, state prisoner petitions increased by one-third and federal prisoner petitions by almost one-fourth. (But, as there were decreases in other case categories, the overall case filings hardly increased.) Between 1969 and 1982, state prisoner petitions increased by 174 percent and federal prisoner petitions by 20 percent (though increases in most of the other case categories also affected the overall case filings). The large increase in prisoner petition input, particularly during the early 1970s, was doubtless a feedback effect from Supreme Court decisions dealing with criminal procedure and the utilization of federal *habeas corpus* by state prisoners. During the 1966–1968 period civil rights filings increased by one-fourth, between 1969 and 1974 the number of civil rights cases more than tripled,[15] and between 1974 and 1982 they more than doubled. During the 1973–1982 period, on the other hand, certain areas of civil litigation either remained stable or declined.[16] Thus, in recent years the civil suit input into the district courts has shifted somewhat away from the protection of property rights and toward the protection of civil rights and liberties, although as suggested by Table 4.2, property rights still dominate the civil case dockets.

A typology of the district courts' criminal case input (cases commenced) from fiscal years 1974–1982 is presented in Table 4.3. As suggested by the table, this demand input decreased through fiscal 1980 but then increased over 13 percent in fiscal 1982. As with civil cases, one can observe important fluctuations in the types of cases filed. Selective service cases increased as the Vietnam War progressed into the late 1960s and early 1970s, but by fiscal 1974, with the end of American participation in the war and the end of the draft, prosecutions for selective service violations dropped sharply and by fiscal 1978 had virtually disappeared. There were declines in forgery and counterfeiting, auto theft, sex offender, and illegal liquor manufacturing prosecutions. Narcotics prosecutions reached a high point in fiscal 1974, declined through fiscal 1980 (coinciding with the Carter Administration), then rose during fiscal 1982 (during the Reagan Administration) but not to the level of fiscal 1974. There were declines in some other areas as well, as is shown in Table 4.3.[17] In contrast, we can observe the increase through fiscal 1982 in prosecutions for embezzlement and fraud.[18]

One noteworthy characteristic of federal criminal cases is the relatively low proportion of cases dealing with violent crimes. This is largely due to the nature of federal offenses. The federal courts do not have jurisdiction over local crimes, which include most crimes of violence, except in federal territories outside the continental United States.

When we examine the district court processing of both civil and criminal litigation, we find that few cases are actually resolved by trial. Table 4.4 presents the data for fiscal 1982. Only about 8 percent of the civil cases and about 15 percent of the criminal cases were resolved by trial. In terms of completed trials in fiscal 1982 from which cases could be appealed, in the district court output pool there were 14,753 civil cases and 4860 losing criminal defendants. About four out of five civil cases and over nine out of ten criminal cases were appealed from the district courts to the appeals courts that same fiscal year.[19] In marked contrast,

Table 4.3 CRIMINAL CASES ORIGINATING IN THE DISTRICT COURTS, BY NATURE OF THE OFFENSE

Nature of offense	Fiscal 1974	Fiscal 1976	Fiscal 1978	Fiscal 1980	Fiscal 1982	Percent of 1982 total
Total	37,667	39,147	34,625	27,968	31,623	100.0%
General offenses:						
Homicide	160	158	144	141	151	0.5
Robbery	1,556	2,042	1,377	1,251	1,427	4.5
Assault	710	832	582	555	579	1.8
Burglary	271	354	207	151	143	0.4
Larceny and theft	3,565	4,006	3,995	3,033	2,887	9.1
Embezzlement	1,612	1,778	1,944	1,578	2,072	6.6
Fraud	3,073	3,930	4,637	4,632	4,709	14.9
Auto theft	1,790	1,430	810	381	369	1.2
Forgery and counterfeiting	4,360	3,972	3,818	2,124	2,128	6.7
Sex offenses	189	127	157	150	135	0.4
Narcotics	7,374	6,198	3,746	3,130	4,193	13.3
Miscellaneous	6,021	7,971	9,468	7,240	8,757	27.7
Special offenses:						
Immigration	1,921	2,070	1,734	1,821	1,803	5.7
Liquor, Internal Revenue	641	187	100	25	20	0.1
Antitrust	24	19	30	39	82	0.3
Civil rights	134	85	82	79	62	0.2
Food and Drug Act	116	61	101	104	77	0.2
Other federal statutes	4,150	3,927	1,693	1,534	2,029	6.4

Source: Administrative Office of the United States Courts, *Annual Report of the Director* (Washington, D.C.: Government Printing Office, 1974–1982).

of 412,852 bankruptcy cases terminated by the bankruptcy courts in fiscal 1982, 509 appeals were commenced.

Litigative Demands: Courts of Appeals

Demand input to the United States courts of appeals consists not only of civil and criminal appeals from the federal district courts, but also of petitions to review or enforce administrative agency orders and a small number of original proceedings. This demand input for fiscal 1982 is shown in Table 4.5. It should be noted that administrative agencies consider many tens of thousands of issues each year, most of which are resolved through informal proceedings. As one observer has noted, "Of the many thousands of formal administrative decisions reached each year, probably only one or two percent are appealed to the courts."[20] Another point worth noting is that the appeals courts have experienced major increases in their caseload. In the ten-year period from 1973 to 1983, the number of cases appealed from the district courts increased over 70 percent. And this was on top of close to a 90 percent increase from the previous five years (1968–1973). Criminal appeals had more than doubled between 1968 and 1973, but between 1973

Table 4.4 DISTRICT COURT CASE FLOW AND METHODS OF DISPOSITION, FISCAL 1982

	Cases pending June 30, 1981	Cases filed fiscal 1982	Terminated fiscal 1982	Cases pending June 30, 1982
Civil	188,714	206,193	189,473	205,434
Criminal	15,866	32,682 (31,301 original proceedings, 1,059 received by transfer, and 322 reopens)	31,889 (40,466 defendants)	16,659

Methods of termination		
	Number	*Percent of total*
Civil cases:		
Trial	*14,753*	*7.8*
Without trial	*174,720*	*92.2*
Criminal defendants:		
Not convicted	*8,214*	*20.3*
Dismissed	7,051	(17.4)
Acquitted after trial	1,163	(2.9)
Convicted	*32,252*	*79.7*
Plea of guilty or *nolo contendere*	27,392	(67.7)
Found guilty at trial	4,860	(12.0)

Source: Administrative Office of the United States Courts, *Annual Report of the Director, 1982* (Washington, D.C.: Government Printing Office, 1982).

and 1983 there was only a modest 7 percent increase. Criminal appeals accounted for about one out of six appeals. However, if the prisoner petition appeals (which also increased over 70 percent between 1973 and 1983) are added to the criminal cases, one finds that about two-fifths of the appeals from the district courts (and slightly over one-third of *all* appeals filed in the appeals courts) in fiscal 1982 were comprised of cases raising questions of personal rights and liberties in which the machinery of criminal justice was involved.[21] This is a profound change in demand input as compared to only two or three decades ago when the federal judicial system for the most part processed demands associated with property rights and other economic demands. One can plausibly infer a causal link between the massive social and cultural changes in the 1960s and the generation of new demands concerning personal rights and liberties, particularly when government has invoked the criminal process. It appears that the policy output of the Warren Court played no small part in fostering those changes and awakening people's sensitivities to their individual rights. But it should also be pointed out that the Burger Court has been far less receptive to claims of criminal defendants than was the Warren Court, and this swing back of the pendulum concerning the rights of criminal defendants may have discouraged some appeals. Thus we find that in fiscal 1973 close to half of all appeals filed in the appeals courts were criminal or prisoner petition cases, but by fiscal 1982 that proportion had decreased to about one-third.

**Table 4.5   COURTS OF APPEALS INPUT BY SOURCE AND NATURE OF CASE,
            FISCAL 1982**

Nature and source of case	Number	Percent of source input	Percent of total
District courts:	*23,551*	*100.0 %*	*84 %*
Civil	18,784	79.8	(67)
United States cases[a]	4,314	(18.3)	
Private cases[a]	9,636	(40.9)	
Prisoner petitions	4,834	(20.5)	[17]
U.S. cases	1,203	[5.1]	
Private cases (state prisoners)	3,631	[15.4]	
Criminal	4,767	20.2	(17)
Administrative agencies:	*3,118*	*100.0*	*11*
National Labor Relations Board	838	26.9	(3)
U.S. Tax Court	404	12.9	(1)
All other	1,876	60.2	(7)
Original proceedings	*768*	*100.0*	*3*
Bankruptcy courts	*509*	*100.0*	*2*
Total	*27,946*		*100*

Source: Administrative Office of the United States Courts, *Annual Report of the Director, 1982* (Washington, D.C.: Government Printing Office, 1982).
[a] Excludes prisoner petitions.

Table 4.6 shows how the courts of appeals disposed of their case input during fiscal 1982. About 34 percent of the cases filed during fiscal 1982 were disposed of by formal court decisions after a hearing or formal submission. Ten years earlier, the proportion had been 64 percent. The trend on the appeals courts

**Table 4.6   COURTS OF APPEALS CASE INPUT AND METHODS OF DISPOSITION,
            FISCAL 1982**

Cases pending July 1, 1981	Cases filed fiscal 1982	Cases terminated fiscal 1982	Cases pending July 1, 1982
21,548	27,946	27,984	21,510

Methods of disposition		
	Number	Percent
Cases disposed of after hearing or submission		
Affirmed or granted	9,560	75.2
Dismissed	657	5.2
Reversed	2,138	16.8
Other	365	2.9
Subtotal	12,720	100.1[a]
Without hearing or submission	11,060	
By consolidation	4,204	
Total	27,984	

[a] Total cases after hearing or submission.

has clearly been for more cases to be decided in a summary fashion.[22] Of the cases decided by formal decision, about one in six cases involved a reversal of the district court or administrative agency.

Litigative Demands: Supreme Court

The demand input into the Supreme Court in terms of cases filed has grown steadily in recent years. There were 1940 cases, for example, filed during the 1960 term. During the 1967 term the number had risen to 3106 cases. During the 1971 term, 3643 new cases were filed, and the 1973 term saw a startling 12 percent increase in filings, bringing the number of cases to the Supreme Court to 4187 new cases.[23] During the remainder of the 1970s to the present, there has generally been an increase in the number of cases coming to the Court. By 1981–1982, some 4422 cases were docketed, a new record high. Unlike the other courts in the federal judicial system, the Supreme Court's case input includes a large number of cases from state court systems. In recent years, the Court has been spending a large part (though not the major portion) of its time on state judicial activities.[24]

All cases filed by the Supreme Court are divided into three major categories and placed onto three different dockets. On the Original Docket go cases over which the Court has original jurisdiction. Typically the number of these cases filed is low. (The 1962–1967 term average was four cases per term; the 1978–1981 term average was 3.5.) On the Appellate Docket go (professionally drafted) appeals and petitions for writs of certiorari. Appellate Docket cases have risen over the last two decades. In 1962 there were 957 appeals and petitions for certiorari. By 1970 there were 1540 cases on the appellate docket, and by the end of 1981–1982 a record high of 2413 new cases on that docket was reached. On the Miscellaneous Docket are motions *in forma pauperis* (appeals and petitions for certiorari from impoverished state and federal prisoners). Prisoner petitions grew dramatically in the 1960s and early 1970s from a 1959–1962 mean of 1034, to a 1963–1967 mean of 1480, to a 1971–1973 mean of 2016. By the mid-1970s the number of prisoner petitions actually dropped, and the 1978–1981 mean was 1948.

The Supreme Court, unlike the other courts in the system, has been given under the system's regime rules considerable discretion as to how much of this demand input it need accept for formal processing and eventual output in opinions and court orders. Only with cases on the Original Docket is there any generally held expectation that a case filed will receive a formal court resolution. With petitions for certiorari and motions for leave to file writs on the Miscellaneous Docket, acceptance of these demands by the Court is completely discretionary. Such cases are accepted only if four or more judges so desire. Rejection of these case demands need not be, and almost always is not, accompanied by any comment. Even with appeals, a similar "rule of four" operates in making the decision of whether to note probable jurisdiction. Otherwise the case is dismissed with such pro forma and unilluminating notations as dismissed "for lack of jurisdiction" or "want of a substantial federal question." Even many appeals that are not dismissed never go to oral argument, and the decision of the lower court is merely "affirmed" or "reversed" in a summary order. The extent of the Court's discretion in these processes is illustrated in Table 4.7, which shows how the Court disposed of its Appellate and Miscellaneous Docket input from the 1978 through the 1982 terms.[25] Over the five terms from 1978 through the 1982 terms, the Court disposed of from about 3900 to over 4500 cases per term. Yet the number of cases decided on their merits averaged only about 298 cases per term, and the number of cases going to oral argument each term ranged from 154 in 1980 to 184 in the 1981 term. The number disposed of by full opinions, including long *per curiams,* never exceeded 216 in any one term. In these ways the Court handled its input so as to spend substantial judicial time only on those cases with which its members wished to deal.

PREVENTING DEMAND INPUT OVERLOAD

Demand input overload refers to two different empirical conditions: (1) an excessive number of demands each of which may take relatively little time to process, but whose great volume threatens the decision-making capacities of the system; and (2) demands, each of which takes an inordinate amount of time to process. If a political system is faced with processing demand input characterized by either one or both of these two conditions, its limited capacities for decision making are soon overwhelmed, and thus the system itself is in danger of collapse. Every system can therefore be expected to confront the problem of reducing demand input to that which can be adequately managed.

The federal judiciary, like the various state judiciaries, is subject to numerous demands. This in general seems to reflect the democratic ethic that everyone is entitled to one's day in court. But the federal judiciary has only so many courts and judges with which to process case input. It is appropriate, then, to examine some of the mechanisms by which input is regulated and overload prevented.

Table 4.7 SUPREME COURT DISPOSAL OF APPELLATE AND MISCELLANEOUS DOCKET CASES, 1978–1982 TERMS

	Term				
	1978	1979	1980	1981	1982
Appellate Docket total	2383	2509	2749	2935	2710
Appellate Docket cases disposed of	2021	2050	2324	2513	2297
By denial, dismissal, or withdrawn	1732 (85.7%)	1776 (86.6%)	1999 (86.0%)	2100 (83.6%)	1892 (82.4%)
Miscellaneous Docket total	2331	2249	2371	2354	2352
Miscellaneous Docket cases acted upon	1996	1838	2027	2039	2013
By denial, dismissal, or withdrawn	1938 (97.1%)	1757 (95.6%)	1968 (97.1%)	2014 (98.8%)	1995 (99.1%)

Source: *The United States Law Week,* 50 LW 3044 (1981) and 52 LW 3025 (1983).

Eastonian analysis suggests that two mechanisms—cultural and structural—discourage, limit, avoid, or otherwise inhibit demand input.[26]

Regime Rules as Cultural Inhibitors of Demand Input

The major cultural inhibitors of demand input (considered *cultural* inhibitors because they have grown out of our political and Anglo-American legal culture or traditions) are the formal and informal regime rules that serve to prevent, discourage, or modify the transformation of wants into formally articulated demands (i.e., litigation) calling for authoritative court judgments. They also serve to regulate the processing of litigation and operate at both the trial and appellate court levels. Such federal judicial rules include those concerning jurisdiction, standing to sue, justiciability, court costs, procedure, the role of the jury, and the availability of appellate review. Court costs, the uncertainties of jury behavior, and the complexity of the rules themselves (which makes it necessary to hire counsel or have one appointed by the court), suggest a long process until court judgment and do serve to discourage trials. At the appellate level, consideration of the cost in time and money imposed by the system's rules, special rules concerning the grounds and procedures of appeal, and (particularly as far as the Supreme Court is concerned) rules that give almost total discretion to the judges as to which demands to process further limit the system's demand input.

The system's rules of jurisdiction, standing, and justiciability allow the federal judiciary to avoid certain types of demands. *Jurisdiction*[27] refers to whether a particular court has the legal authority to process the demand. Does the subject matter of the demand raise a federal question? Does the demand involve states suing each other, or a suit concerning a foreign nation, or citizens of different states suing each other? If so, the federal courts have jurisdiction over the matter. If not, the courts will refuse to process the demand on the ground that it is outside their authority. The concept of *standing to sue* refers to those bringing demands to the courts and the criteria they must satisfy. For example, traditionally courts have only entertained demands presented within the framework of a case or controversy involving a legal right; that is, the litigation was expected to represent a genuine conflict over legal rights in which opposing parties personally involved contested their real interests. If administrative action were challenged, all available administrative channels for reversing that action must have been followed before going to court. Since the 1970s, the Burger Court has relaxed the rules of standing so that only injury, broadly defined, need be demonstrated[28] and organizations can bring suit on behalf of their injured members.[29] Furthermore, any conflict brought to the courts must be *justiciable,* that is, able to be resolved by the courts. Using such a notion of justiciability, the federal courts have, for example, refused to process (1) demands in which the controversial issue involved could not be conclusively determined by a court judgment because final authority was thought to rest or best lie with some other governmental body (the courts call these political question cases); (2) demands in which a court judgment would have no practical effect because of a change in the law, the status of the litigants, or some act of the parties involved that dissolves the controversy (moot cases);

and (3) demands in which there is no action that a court can prescribe to right the alleged wrong (lack-of-a-judicial-remedy cases).

Jurisdiction, standing, and justiciability determine whether a dispute will or will not be processed. However, a suit may contain not only the demand to resolve the dispute but the demand to resolve it in a particular manner, such as a special interpretation of the statute or Constitution. Here, too, there is wide latitude for the federal courts in processing demands. The courts can determine cases on broad or exceedingly narrow grounds, skirting controversy if they wish and certainly avoiding major constitutional issues.[30] Thus, even when the courts agree to process the case, there is no assurance that the case will be decided on the grounds argued by counsel. Of course, whether the system's regime rules will be used to avoid treating specific issues depends largely on the judicial philosophy and policy proclivities of the judges. The proponents of the judicial restraint philosophy urge that the courts avoid issues that can be better decided by the "political branches" of government. An underlying (but not the only) premise of this position is that to do otherwise would produce negative feedback, leading perhaps to a crisis in legitimacy concerning the Court's actions. Activist judges, presumably because they are more concerned with being "right" than popular, have often disregarded the rules and doctrines of restraint. Thus in *Pollock* v. *Farmers' Loan Association*[31] and *Carter* v. *Carter Coal Co.,*[32] "friendly" litigants were able to elicit wide-sweeping constitutional judgments from the Supreme Court that struck down an early version of the income tax and a major piece of New Deal legislation. In *Dred Scott* v. *Sandford,* the Court, in a burst of activism on the slavery issue, overturned the Missouri Compromise. In *Baker* v. *Carr* the Court reversed the precedent that had treated malapportionment of state legislatures as a nonjusticiable "political question."[33] The regime rules thus have some flexibility and can be used by judges to approach or avoid demands. Knowledge of previous judicial behavior of individual judges can aid in predicting how they will apply the regime rules in regulating demand input.

Kenneth Vines and Richard Richardson offered some insights into how the rules, the policy proclivities of the judges, and the desire of litigants to win interact in modifying demands at the different stages of trial and appellate review. They analyzed cases that raised civil liberties issues when appealed from the district courts to the Courts of Appeals for the Third, Fifth, and Eighth Circuits during the 1956–1961 period.[34] Of the cases studied, the authors found that only about one-third had a civil liberties content in the district courts, with the remainder not raising such issues. It was the latter cases that were specially examined, and it was found that at trial they were fairly routine cases having such low policy salience that they rarely resulted in a written opinion by the trial judge.

Vines and Richardson described two such cases. *Reyes* v. *United States*[35] was a narcotics case in which the judge realized after sentencing that the sentence he had given was below the statutory minimum. Thus, three days later he recalled the defendant and increased the sentence. The defendant appealed on grounds that his constitutional right to due process had been violated. *Proffer* v. *United States*[36] was a fraud case in which the defendant, a lawyer, waived his right to counsel and represented himself. After conviction the lawyer-defendant appealed on grounds that his constitutional right to counsel had been violated. In both cases the appeal was unsuccessful.

These two cases, and undoubtedly the others, suggest that the system's rules can generate an issue metamorphosis in litigation. Vines and Richardson suggested that appeal to the circuit courts is also encouraged by their collegial structure, their more deliberative atmosphere, and the more cosmopolitan backgrounds of their judges. This presumably makes them more receptive to civil liberties claims than the district courts, whose primary decision makers (judge and jury) are often rooted in local political cultures less sensitive to civil liberties claims. By their very complexity, the rules create opportunities for judicial "error" and as such serve to encourage appeals. When alleged errors occur, the almost absolute right to appeal given civil liberties claims and their high policy salience are seized upon as offering a second chance to trial court losers.

It might be further noted that the issue transformation observed here means that the courts of appeals in these cases can be conceived as forums of the first instance. Although the litigants remain the same as at trial, the legal issues and even the salient "facts" have changed. This conceptualization challenges conventional wisdom that conceives of these courts only as filters for demands initially raised and fully aired at trial as determining what are the issues of the case. In systems terms, this means that the courts of appeals often serve as forums in which new policy demands are put into the system. Thus, in this instance, the rules of the system, rather than inhibiting demand input, help generate it. One should also note that, since passage of the Criminal Justice Act of 1964, indigent criminal defendants are entitled to a cost-free appeal of their convictions. Without the financial burden, appeal may be an attractive option when it would postpone the imposition of imprisonment. Thus the act of 1964 represented a change in the rules that has resulted in the generation of demand input to the appeals courts. Interestingly, the Supreme Court, in the 1974 *Ross* v. *Moffitt* decision,[37] made it clear that indigents are entitled to free counsel only through the first appeal. The opinion of the Court seemed to be openly acknowledging the full implications that a change in the rules may have for demand input.

Gatekeeping

The major structural inhibitors of demand input are the *gatekeepers*.[38] These are systemic authorities who, by enforcing regime rules and through discretionary action, control demand input. The federal judicial system's gatekeepers include lawyers of potential litigants (including lawyers for interest groups that finance test cases), law enforcement officials, and, of course, the judges. Each has a part in controlling the system's demand input by such actions as advising clients, providing funds for litigation, making decisions as to what criminal cases to prosecute, and deciding which cases to accept on grounds of importance, jurisdiction, standing, and justiciability. Without stretching the truth too much it might be observed that lawyers, prosecutors, and judges typically act as if they were engaged in a vast conspiracy aimed at keeping litigants out of court. The effects of this "conspiracy" are most evident at the two levels of the court system (district court and Supreme Court) where authorities have perhaps the greatest discretion for playing their parts as systemic gatekeepers.[39]

In fiscal 1982, as we saw in Table 4.4, the district courts terminated 189,473 civil cases. Only 14,753 (about 8 percent) were terminated by trial. In fiscal 1982, 40,466 criminal defendants had their cases disposed of by the district courts. Only 6023 (about 15 percent) had trials. Thus, as far as the district courts are concerned, "justice without trial" is not only common, it is the norm.[40] How just this justice is and how and why litigants so overwhelmingly forfeit their right to trial are questions now to be considered.

Disposing of Civil Litigation Without Trial   Some typical statistics concerning the processing of tort cases (i.e., personal injury and personal property damage cases) illustrate how civil cases are settled without trial in the federal courts. Tort cases constituted about 17 percent of all civil cases filed in the district courts in fiscal 1982. Of these, only about 11 percent actually went to and completed trial, and of those that did about three out of five were appealed to an appeals court.[41] It is, therefore, apparent that tort claims are resolved with a large degree of finality at the district court level.

In analyzing the dynamics of tort claim processing it is useful to examine the studies of tort cases in the state courts because, in general, the law, fact situations, and even the participants (a victim/plaintiff and defendant's insurance company) are much the same in the federal and state courts. In fiscal 1982, for example, of the 34,218 tort cases filed in the district courts, 22,691 (about two-thirds) were diversity of citizenship cases. These differ from those tried in state courts only by the fact that federal procedure was used (although a number of states now use the same procedures) and that the amount of damages sought exceeded $10,000 (as required by federal law).[42]

In New York City during the late 1950s, there were approximately 193,000 accident victims each year who sought to recover damages on the grounds that their accidents were the fault of someone else. These were all potential litigants in personal injury actions, quantitatively the most important field of tort law. Only 40 percent of these potential litigants (about 77,000) even got as far as going to court and filing suits. Gatekeeping was thus under way in a substantial manner even before the courthouse doors were reached. Further gatekeeping is strongly evident at each subsequent step of the litigative process. In only about 48,000 cases were notes of issue filed, signifying that both plaintiff and defendant were ready for trial; in only about 7000 cases were trials actually commenced; and, finally, in only about 2500 cases was trial completed and a verdict given. To quote the authors of this study, "Less than 2 percent of the claims made each year in New York City are directly controlled by court adjudication. . . . [T]hese adjudications account for only 3 percent of the money that changes hands. The other 98 percent of the claims are disposed of, and the money moved, by a bargaining process in which victims, defendants, lawyers, and insurance companies' representatives are the chief participants."[43]

In considering why this radical attrition in claims occurred as a court verdict was approached, it is important to note that 84 percent of those making claims (about 162,000) did achieve some recovery. This high rate of recovery emphasizes the extent to which "out-of-court" case disposal is a negotiated process leading to results at least minimally satisfying to both parties. The crucial role played by lawyers must also be noted. Practically all defendants, being insured, are represented by their insurance company's counsel. This is not true for accident victims. With claims where the victim retained a lawyer, the recovery rate was 90 percent. With claims where the victim did not, the recovery rate was only 65 percent. In cases where the fact/law situations were similar, the size of recovery was about twice as high for victims with lawyers as for those without.[44] Since the authors could not find any other factor that might distinguish lawyer from nonlawyer cases, they concluded that the very presence of a plaintiff's lawyer is important for both the size and chances of recovery.

A lawyer undoubtedly can make a stronger legal claim than can the typical layperson. Furthermore, since the lawyer is paid only if recovery is made and the amount of payment varies directly with the size of recovery (contingent fee payment), the victim's lawyer has a direct interest in settling for as large an amount as possible. This makes it less likely that the victim can be bluffed into receiving no payment or an unfairly low one when there is a strong case. On the other hand, since lawyers are paid only if they win, some extremely weak claims are weeded out when victims go to a lawyer and are advised to drop the potential suit. The study's authors also suggested that a further reason why victims with lawyers do so much better than those without is that insurance companies sometimes will settle a relatively weak claim for a low amount when a lawyer is present to sustain "good will" for future cases. Whatever the reasons involved, lawyers emerge as significant participants in civil suit gatekeeping by the out-of-court settlement of claims.

Under federal rules of civil procedure, pretrial discovery procedures and the pretrial conference are vehicles for gatekeeping. Discovery procedures were instituted in 1938 to enable both sides to a civil suit to "discover" the facts and legal arguments the other side intends to use in the trial, thus eliminating surprises and cutting trial time. The implicit purpose of these rules is to encourage settlements before trial, thus saving all concerned much time and expense. In practice, there have been mixed results, and the rules have been used by some lawyers for dilatory purposes or for harassment or other strategic considerations.[45] Nevertheless, there is some evidence that for at least some parties to a civil dispute, discovery of the opponent's evidence and argument is followed by a settlement before the case comes to trial.[46]

Rule 16 of the Federal Rules of Civil Procedure for the U.S. District Courts authorizes the judge, at the judge's discretion, to "direct the attorneys for the parties to appear . . . for a conference to consider . . . matters as may aid in the disposition of the action." The judge thus has the opportunity to encourage a settlement and even to take an active part by, for example, stating what he or she thinks the case is worth (i.e., what would be a reasonable settlement). Although district judges vary in the manner and extent to which they utilize pretrial conferences, there is evidence that suggests that they are used widely. In fiscal 1960, for example, more than 15,000 such conferences were convened. About two out of five conferences produced a resolution of the cases.[47]

The fact that so few cases are resolved by a verdict after trial should not be taken to mean that trials are relatively unimportant for systemic operations. The "threat" of a trial verdict underlies out-of-court negotiations. The prediction by both plaintiff's and defendant's lawyers as to what a verdict might be is the benchmark toward which an out-of-court settlement is aimed. There are certain aspects of trial, however, that may make an out-of-court settlement a better resolution than a trial verdict. For the defendant, in particular, trials cost money. Even for a large insurance company with its own legal staff, going to trial consumes expensive legal time and energy. Even if an out-of-court settlement is slightly higher than a possible verdict, the costs saved may make it a bargain. Going to trial has its costs for the plaintiff also. Getting a trial judgment takes time. In the federal system as a whole, in recent years the median time from when a note of issue is filed (signifying that the parties are ready) until trial has been 14 months. It has been longer in some districts encompassing large metropolitan areas such as the District of Massachusetts (including the Boston metropolitan area), for which the median time in fiscal 1982 was 26 months.[48] Particularly with a not-too-wealthy accident victim, for whom a speedy financial recovery may be more important than a possible big one, "delay in court" can be a crucial factor in bringing about an out-of-court settlement.

Although judges and lawyers frequently state that certain cases are "worth" so much at trial, this does not mean that any particular jury will arrive at that amount. Rather, such statements are probabilistic in nature; that is, on the average such a case will yield such an award. The statistical nature of these predictions is well illustrated in an experiment by the Jury Project undertaken at the University of Chicago Law School.[49] An actual case was selected that was settled out of court for $42,000 just before verdict was to be rendered. The trial of this case was then reenacted before ten experimental "juries." The average verdict from the ten "juries" was, in fact, $41,000. This suggests that the lawyers in the real case were fairly accurate in assessing its worth in reaching settlement. The $41,000 average, however, was the result of verdicts that ranged all the way from $17,500 to $60,000. Only two verdicts were in accord with the average— one for $42,000 and one for $40,000.

In sum, the out-of-court resolution of a civil case may be less costly, is certainly more speedy, and perhaps (but not necessarily) is more "just" than its resolution by a verdict after trial. This has stimulated a relatively new movement among legal reformers for the development of alternative dispute-processing mechanisms such as neighborhood justice centers and mediation services.[50] However, the bulk of the work of these new modes of dispute processing, focusing on matters that ordinarily do not concern federal law, can be expected to have (and, it would appear, thus far has had) a minimal impact on the federal courts.[51]

Disposing of Criminal Cases Without Trial   Criminal case gatekeeping occurs at the trial court level of the federal judicial system both in the 91 district courts without local jurisdiction and the three (Guam, Northern Mariana Islands, Virgin Islands) *with* such jurisdiction. The criminal case demands processed by both types of courts, however, differ.

Districts with local jurisdiction typically process criminal cases that concern violations of the local criminal code (rather than a violation of a federal statute applicable nationwide) and include homicide, robbery, assault, and burglary. In fiscal 1982, over one-fourth of the criminal cases in the three districts with local jurisdiction concerned these crimes. In contrast, these offenses accounted for about 7 percent of the criminal cases commenced in the 91 district courts, which in turn have as their typical offenses fraud, forgery and counterfeiting, larceny, and violations of the narcotics and immigration laws. Criminal cases processed in the three district courts were more similar to those found in the state judicial systems than those found in the typical federal district court. However, both types of federal district courts process cases under the Federal Rules of Criminal Procedure, and there is reason to believe that their gatekeeping processes are similar.

The first step in the processing of a criminal case is typically arrest[52] (although some cases have as their first step—and are thus fed into the court system by—indictment as the result of a grand jury investigation). As soon after arrest as practicable, the accused must be presented before a judge or federal magistrate at which time he or she is formally advised of one's rights to remain silent and to have a lawyer[53] and is considered for release on bail or on his or her own recognizance. The accused is also informed of one's right to a preliminary examination by the court official. If from the evidence it appears to that official that there is probable cause to believe that an offense has been committed and that the defendant committed it, the case is then submitted by the U.S. attorney's office to the grand jury. If an indictment is obtained, the case is formally commenced. Misdemeanors and cases where the accused waives a grand jury may also be commenced by a U.S. attorney's filing of an Information. Whichever route is used, the accused is now a defendant and the case is commenced.

The next stage is arraignment. The defendant is taken before the trial judge where he or she is read the indictment or information, a lawyer is appointed if this has not already occurred, and the defendant enters a plea of guilty (including its substantial equivalent, *nolo contendere*) or not guilty.[54] If a guilty plea is entered, the next and final stage is sentencing by the judge. If the defendant pleads not guilty, preparation for trial begins. Any time before or during trial, the defendant's plea may be changed to guilty and the sentence imposed. If acquitted, the process ends with the defendant's release.

Throughout the process substantial gatekeeping aimed at the avoidance of trial occurs. It takes two forms: (1) a decision not to proceed with the case; and (2) plea bargaining. The decision not to proceed is made by any of three systemic authorities: the U.S. attorney's office (which is supervised by the Department of Justice), the initial committing judge or federal magistrate, or the grand jury. Of the three, most decisions not to proceed are made by the U.S. attorney's office. The decision may take the form of either the dismissal of all charges or, with cases in the District of Columbia District Court, which tries only felonies in which a federal crime is concerned (which also are violations of the District of Columbia Criminal Code), a reduction of charges to a misdemeanor or the dropping of federal charges and referral to the District of Columbia Court of General Sessions. Plea bargaining entails negotiations between defense attorney and prosecutor. The objective is to reach an agreement whereby the accused will enter a guilty plea in return for a reduced charge or a favorable sentence recommendation. Although there may be cases where the prosecutor feels that the seriousness or notoriety of the crime requires that "the book be thrown" at the defendant, there is evidence that suggests that plea bargaining occurs with some frequency in both the federal and state judicial systems.[55]

Figure 4.1 presents an analysis of felony case flow in the U.S. District Court for the District of Columbia for 1965.[56] Several characteristics of this case flow suggest criminal case gatekeeping. First, it should be noted that four out of five felony cases entering the system did not result in a felony conviction. Most of those cases that left the system did so because of decisions made by the prosecution, committing judge, or grand jury. Although most of these (over 60 percent) were referrals to the District of Columbia Court of General Sessions for processing as misdemeanors, the important point is that arrest for a felony is typically not the first step to a felony conviction. In this process the earlier the stage, the higher the exit rate. Sixty-six percent made their exit at the very start prior to or at the preliminary hearing. A further 9 percent left prior to or at the grand jury stage.

Commencement of the case by indictment or information marked a major watershed. Once that occurred, the chances for conviction were quite high. Of the approximately 1600 cases commenced, only 12 percent left by dismissal. Acquittal accounted for another 8 percent. The remaining 80 percent ended with convictions.[57]

In the District of Columbia there are formalized negotiations by way of hearings in the U.S. attorney's office prior to going to the grand jury.[58] In these hearings the assistant U.S. attorney in charge of the case, the arresting officer, defense counsel, and even the witnesses for both sides spend from 20 minutes to an hour discussing the case. In one study of such hearings, involving 64 felony complaints, the results were as follows: in 9 cases (14 percent) all charges were dropped; in 16 cases (25 percent) the original charge was maintained; in 39 cases (61 percent) the charge was reduced to a misdemeanor with the promise of a guilty plea.[59] Serious crimes were the most resistant to such bargaining. These, it might be noted, led to the highest number of sustained pleas of not guilty and thus the most trials.

Given the emphasis on plea bargaining before indictment, it is not surprising to find that the percentage of guilty pleas at arraignment, the next stage in the process, is low. Of the 1600 cases arraigned in 1965, over 90 percent of the defendants entered a plea of not guilty. Between arraignment and trial, however, pleading guilty was again common. Almost 58 percent of those originally pleading not guilty changed their pleas. Either the defendants decided to "throw themselves on the mercy of the court" or last-minute bargains were negotiated (e.g., some of the charges were dropped to assure a reduced sentence). When these guilty pleas were added to those made at arraignment, it was found that 75 percent of those convicted by the District of Columbia District Court never went to trial.

As in civil cases, we find doubtful (but not obviously weak) cases and cases

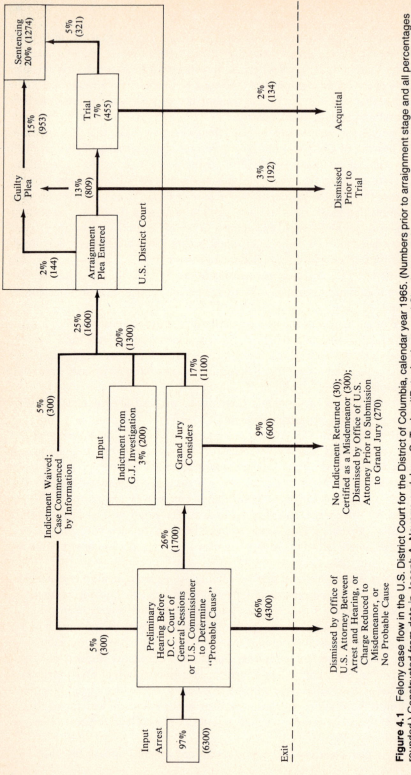

Figure 4.1 Felony case flow in the U.S. District Court for the District of Columbia, calendar year 1965. (Numbers prior to arraignment stage and all percentages rounded.) Constructed from data in Joseph A. Navarro and Jean G. Taylor, "Data Analyses and Simulation of Court System in the District of Columbia for the Processing of Felony Defendants," in *Task Force Report: Science and Technology* (The President's Commission on Law Enforcement and Administration of Justice) (Washington, D.C.: Government Printing Office, 1967), pp. 199–215.

involving the highest stakes most resistant (but certainly not immune) to gate-keeping. However, just as with most civil cases, the participants in most criminal cases want to avoid trial.[60] For the prosecution, trial is expensive in terms of organization time, energy, and money. Moreover, prosecutors do not like to stain their conviction records; therefore, except in the strongest cases, a negotiated guilty plea is preferable to the risk of an acquittal at trial. Defense counsel, too, is motivated to negotiate in order to get the client off as lightly as possible. As a Department of Justice study notes, "Many defense attorneys consider the plea bargain a vital part of their service to the defendant."[61] Defense counsel is encouraged to do this by the knowledge that trial may be long and fruitless. Moreover, since many such lawyers are court appointed and thus are not generously compensated by the court, or have private clients from whom chances of payment are questionable, it makes more financial sense to settle the case without going through a long and costly trial.

An obviously guilty defendant is discouraged from going to trial not only by the advice of counsel, but also by considerations of time and outcome. If bail cannot be provided, the time spent in jail prior to a trial judgment is normally not deducted from any subsequent prison term. In fiscal 1982, in the federal district courts, the median time from filing a case to sentencing after a guilty plea was four months while the median time where conviction was the result of a jury trial was six months.[62] Even more important in a defendant's calculation in deciding whether or not to plead guilty are the differences in sentences of those pleading guilty compared to those convicted by trial. An analysis of sentences received by defendants convicted in 89 district courts[63] in fiscal 1971 showed that those sentenced after trial received more severe treatment than those sentenced after pleading guilty. This was also true when prior criminal record was held constant.[64] Sentences after jury trial convictions were often two to three times more severe than sentences after guilty pleas for comparable crimes and defendants. There seems little doubt, therefore, that a trial—where the prosecution may "throw the book" at the defendant and the judge may discipline him or her with a harsh sentence for "wasting" the court's time—can be a risky business for the obviously guilty.

There is some evidence that suggests that the criminal case gatekeeping process was in a state of flux in the late 1960s and early 1970s. Generally, in the federal courts through fiscal 1973, the conviction rate declined as did the proportion of guilty pleas. The decline in the conviction rate, however, was not due to an increase in acquittals. In fact, conviction after trial increased. The decline in the conviction rate was almost solely due to an increase in dismissals between arraignment and trial. By the mid-1970s, the decline in the conviction rate stopped and stabilization of conviction rates, plea bargaining rates, and dismissal rates occurred. By 1982 there were even small increases over 1976 in the conviction and plea bargaining rates. This is shown in Table 4.8, which contains findings from the district courts. Separate findings for the District of Columbia District Court are also presented in Table 4.8. One should note two distinguishing characteristics of the District of Columbia District Court. First, until mid-1971 the court had local jurisdiction over felonies committed in violation of the District of

Table 4.8 TRENDS IN CRIMINAL CASE DISPOSAL IN U.S. DISTRICT COURTS AND THE U.S. DISTRICT COURT FOR THE DISTRICT OF COLUMBIA, BY FISCAL YEAR

	1964	1970	1976	1982
Types of disposition in districts:				
All defendants disposed of after arraignment	33,381	36,356	51,612	40,466
Total convicted	87.4 %	77.5 %	77.7 %	79.7 %
(By guilty plea)	(78.7)	(66.3)	(65.9)	(67.7)
(By trial)	(8.7)	(11.2)	(11.8)	(12.0)
Total not convicted	12.6 %	22.5 %	22.3 %	20.3 %
(Dismissed)	(8.8)	(18.2)	(18.9)	(17.4)
(Acquitted)	(3.8)	(4.3)	(3.4)	(2.9)
Types of disposition in D.C. District Court:				
All defendants disposed of after arraignment	1,442	2,311	1,004	632
Total convicted	77.3 %	72.7 %	84.9 %	80.1 %
(By guilty plea)	(56.5)	(54.6)	(71.1)	(68.5)
(By trial)	(20.8)	(18.1)	(13.8)	(11.6)
Total not convicted	22.7 %	27.3 %	15.1 %	19.9 %
(Dismissed)	(16.2)	(18.9)	(11.9)	(16.3)
(Acquitted)	(6.5)	(8.4)	(3.2)	(3.6)

Source: *Annual Report, Administrative Office,* 1964, 1970, 1976, 1982.

Columbia Criminal Code. Second, with no senators and party organizations involved in the judicial nomination process, the Nixon and Ford Administrations, as others before them, could select precisely the sorts of judges they would have liked to appoint throughout the country had they a free hand. This meant that by 1976 the Nixon appointees as well as the Nixon-appointed U.S. attorney's office could pursue a get-tough law-and-order policy. In any event, Table 4.8 suggests that for the District of Columbia District Court, in the 1970s there was a reversal of the trend of the 1960s, so that by 1976 criminal conviction and guilty plea rates were higher than the national norm. Where the acquittals of the District of Columbia District Court had been close to twice as high as those in the rest of the country, by 1976 they about matched the other districts. In 1970 the proportion of guilty pleas was markedly lower than in the other districts. By 1976 the proportion of guilty pleas had increased by about 30 percent and exceeded that for the other districts. In fiscal 1964 and 1970 the percentage of cases tried was over 26 percent, but by fiscal 1976 it had come down to about 17 percent (lower than the level of the other districts). By 1982, after both Carter and Reagan appointees had come to the court, the proportions on all these indicators were at about the same levels as for the rest of the country.

In contemplating these trends, it is difficult not to associate the fall in convictions in the districts to the Warren Court's policies concerning criminal procedure and the subsequent stabilization (if not modest rise) to the Burger

Court's more conservative approach. The intent of the Warren Court's policies was to discourage aggressive police questioning and thus confessions and guilty pleas. The Burger Court, however, has turned around the thrust of the Warren Court's policy-making in the criminal procedures area and has openly approved plea bargaining. In *North Carolina* v. *Alford*[65] the Court suggested that plea bargaining is constitutional as long as the guilty plea is voluntary and implied that the Court would broadly construe voluntariness. In *Santobello* v. *New York*[66] the Court appeared to recognize the necessity of plea bargaining to prevent demand overload, although the Court ruled that the prosecution must keep its end of the bargain.

Supreme Court Gatekeeping The Judiciary Act of 1925 included among its provisions one that authorized the Supreme Court to issue the writ of certiorari at its discretion in place of the writ of error that until then practically guaranteed Supreme Court review as a matter of right. This provision was instituted so that the Court could protect itself from being overwhelmed by a rising tide of litigation and instead focus its energies on those cases its members deemed of special importance.[67]

Petitions for certiorari come in two forms: petitions *in forma pauperis,* which since 1947 have been placed on the Court's Miscellaneous Docket; and other petitions, placed on the Appellate Docket. Usually a petition *in forma pauperis* consists of a single typewritten or handwritten document drafted without professional aid. It often contains much that is irrelevant and leaves out essential information. The single copies go to the office of the Chief Justice, whose clerks prepare memoranda analyzing the petitions; these go to the various justices. Only when a prisoner's life is at stake or the issue seems of distinct interest or importance is the petition itself circulated.

Petitions that go on the Appellate Docket are much more standardized. They are printed documents, from about 10 to 30 pages maximum (according to the Court's rules) in length, setting forth the basis for Supreme Court jurisdiction, the questions asked to be reviewed, the facts pertinent to them, and the reasons why the Supreme Court should review these questions. Also appended are the judgments and opinions of the lower courts and (if involved) administrative agencies as well as a copy of the record. Respondents may enter a brief as to why certiorari should be denied, and petitioners may file a supplementary brief in reply. Each justice receives a copy of these documents, and the law clerks prepare memoranda summarizing the issues raised in the petitions.

Each Miscellaneous and Appellate Docket petition is placed on the conference agenda[68] and discussed if at least one justice so desires.[69] If a minimum of four justices so vote, the petition is granted and the case is accepted for consideration on its merits. Otherwise it is rejected. However, any single justice can relist the petition on the agenda and have it reconsidered the following week.

Despite the low acceptance rate for petitions (in the 1982 term, less than one-half of one percent of Miscellaneous Docket petitions and about 8 percent of Appellate Docket petitions were accepted[70]), the large numbers involved have meant that in the past such petitions typically accounted for about 75 percent of all cases that went to oral argument (although starting in the early 1970s that proportion was reduced[71]). Thus a matter of keen interest to both practicing attorneys and to students of the Court has been determining what criteria the Court uses in accepting and rejecting cases.

Rule 17 of the Supreme Court's Rules ostensibly provides the gatekeeping criteria for the granting of the writ of certiorari. For example, Rule 17 specifies that certiorari will be granted if a lower court's ruling conflicts with a ruling of the Court, if a conflict in circuits exists, or if an "important" question is involved on which the Court has not ruled. Joseph Tanenhaus led a research team[72] that examined the opinions of cases for which certiorari had been granted and which were decided in the 1956–1958 terms and found that only about two out of three of them contained a reason for granting certiorari. In over half of these cases the reason given was the "importance of the issue," which of course is not a very illuminating reason. Tanenhaus concluded that Rule 17 reasons do not adequately explain the Court's certiorari gatekeeping. Rather, he hypothesized, the justices have had to develop some method for assessing the numerous petitions and for separating the frivolous ones from those that deserve careful study. This method, he suggested, is the search for readily identifiable *cues*. The presence of one or more of these cues would be a signal to the judge that the petition warrants careful study. The absence of cues would mean that the petition can be safely discarded without further expenditure of judicial time. Careful study of a petition with cues would then occur to determine if certiorari should nevertheless be denied because of defects concerning jurisdiction, inadequacies in the record, lack of ripeness, or tactical inadvisability. Only those not weeded out by this process would be granted certiorari and either summarily affirmed, reversed, or scheduled for oral argument with the preparation of full opinion anticipated. Tanenhaus's concept of cue, therefore, is obviously a gatekeeping concept.

Tanenhaus and associates conducted an empirical test of cue theory.[73] They tested for the presence of four cues and hypothesized that, if any one of the four cues was present alone, then the likelihood of certiorari being granted would be greater than when no cues were present. They found that three of the four hypothesized cues met this test. The most potent cue was whether the federal government was a party to the case and urged review. Next was whether the case contained a civil liberties issue. Finally, dissension (whether among the judges of the court immediately below or between two or more courts and agencies) was a cue. A case with all three cues would have a 4 out of 5 chance of having certiorari granted. A case with none of these three cues would only have a 7 out of 100 chance of having the certiorari petition granted.[74] Although other cues might be formulated and tested, the findings of the Tanenhaus study provide strong evidence that the Supreme Court's control of demand input by certiorari gatekeeping during the time period studied was far from policy neutral. The justices most assuredly were responding to policy-oriented cues.[75]

S. Sidney Ulmer and colleagues also tested cue theory,[76] but unlike Tanenhaus, who examined certiorari petitions that initially came to the Court, Ulmer studied those petitions that were not deadlisted and thus had been discussed at the weekly conferences. This information was obtained by study of Justice Harold

Burton's papers at the Library of Congress, which had not been available when Tanenhaus and his colleagues had conducted their study. The only cue that emerged from the statistical analysis of these conference-discussed cases was whether the federal government was a party to the case and wanted the Court to review it. This led Ulmer to suggest that a two-stage process may be at work. Initial screening may very well rely on a variety of cues such as those uncovered by Tanenhaus. But once these cases survive initial screening, and presumably many civil liberties cases were in this category, the most potent cue is the federal government's wishes concerning Supreme Court review.

Doris Marie Provine conducted an extensive analysis of case selection in which she, like Ulmer, placed great reliance on the data found in the Burton papers.[77] Provine's findings, however, cast some doubt on cue theory as suggested by Tanenhaus. She examined the cases that were special listed (for automatic denial of certiorari) during the period studied by Tanenhaus and that according to Tanenhaus' theory ought not to have contained cues. But this was not what she found. Sixteen percent of all civil liberties cases were deadlisted, as were 27 percent of the cases with dissension below. This compared to 45 percent of the cases with no cues being special listed.[78] This last figure was most important because it meant that over half the cases with no cues nevertheless survived the initial screening (that is, were not deadlisted) and were actually discussed in the conference. The presence of the cues hypothesized by Tanenhaus, particularly if the federal government wanted review, certainly were important for determining which cases would be selected for review. But so were a variety of other factors such as whether there were defects concerning jurisdiction, whether the record was muddled, whether the case was ripe for review, or indeed whether the justices believed it tactically advisable to confront the issues in the case.[79] Provine found that during the 1947–1957 terms of the Court, the period studied by Tanenhaus, not only was the federal government as petitioner enjoying a high success rate in the grant of review,[80] but so were organized labor when labor petitioned for review,[81] and civil rights–liberties petitioners.[82] Furthermore, when federalism issues were raised, that is, issues concerned with which level of government has authority over a particular dispute, the Court granted review in substantial numbers of cases.[83]

The cues identified by Tanenhaus were nevertheless found by Provine to have a statistical relationship to the granting of review. This has also been found by others.[84] One retest of cue theory by Virginia Armstrong and Charles Johnson examined two terms of the Warren Court and two terms of the Burger Court.[85] Armstrong and Johnson found that the three cues discovered by Tanenhaus also were related to the granting of review by both the Warren and Burger courts. There were no instances found of cases with all three cues present being denied review by either the Warren or Burger Court.[86] Armstrong and Johnson also found that for the Burger Court, when the lower court decision was a pro-civil liberties decision, the Court was more likely to grant review than when the lower court decision had been opposed to the civil liberties claim. With economic decisions, Armstrong and Johnson found that the Warren Court was more likely to accept for review conservative decisions of lower courts, particularly when the federal government sought review, while for the Burger Court precisely the opposite occurred—liberal lower court decisions received grants of review at a much higher rate than conservative lower court decisions.[87] This suggested to Armstrong and Johnson that the ideological direction of the lower court decision is a variable that, in conjunction with the presence or absence of one or more cues identified by Tanenhaus, will determine to a large extent whether review will be granted. As such, these findings are consistent with earlier findings of Donald Songer,[88] Provine,[89] and Ulmer.[90]

Over the years more and more cases have come to the Court, and this has been of special concern to Chief Justice Warren Burger, who has argued that demand input overload is overwhelming the Court. Unlike the lower federal courts whose demand overload, where it exists, is a result of the fact that these courts must decide the cases brought to them (assuming they have met such requirements as jurisdiction and standing), the Supreme Court's overload problem, such as it may be, lies in deciding what to decide. In 1972 Chief Justice Burger appointed a study group to examine this problem and to make recommendations.

Under the auspices of the Federal Judicial Center, the study group, under the chairmanship of Harvard Law Professor Paul Freund and composed of leading legal scholars, came up with a proposal for a new court that would make decisions as to what cases the Supreme Court should consider and what cases should be denied review.[91] If the Court could be relieved of the burden of having to select its cases for review, the justices presumably would be able to do a more thorough job on the cases they decide on the merits (the study commission was diplomatic in making this point). The new court would be *the national court of appeals* and would not only screen cases for the Court, but would also decide certain cases in which different circuit courts made conflicting rulings on points of law.[92]

Response from former and sitting members of the Supreme Court was negative. Former Justice Arthur Goldberg questioned the constitutionality of taking from the Court the responsibility for exercising its discretion in deciding which cases to hear.[93] Former Chief Justice Earl Warren opposed the proposed court as a political device that would hamper the Court from enforcing basic constitutional rights.[94] Justices Stewart,[95] Brennan,[96] and Douglas[97] came out in opposition to the new court recommendation, and Justice Douglas repeatedly made the point that the Court was not overworked and could handle the decisions to decide.[98]

In response to the study group's report, a federal commission was created by Congress to study the overload problem. In mid-1975, the federal Commission on Revision of the Federal Court Appellate System recommended its own version of a national court of appeals. Instead of deciding what cases the Supreme Court will decide, this court would decide cases referred to it by the Supreme Court.[99] There followed extensive congressional hearings but nothing came of the proposal. A study conducted by the Justice Department in 1976 recommended that the proposal be rejected as adding expense and delay to the process without appreciably relieving the caseload burden.[100] The issue appeared to fade from public view only to be revived in August, 1982, after the Supreme Court faced an unprecedented number of cases on its docket during 1981–1982. In an address before the American Judicature Society, Justice Stevens revealed that, because of the heavy burden of cases, he was forced to delegate to his law clerks the burden of reading certiorari petitions and that he himself examined less than 20 percent of the petitions. Stevens urged the creation of a national court of appeals along the lines originally suggested by the Freund study group.[101] Other justices soon spoke out. Justice Brennan, while rejecting Stevens's suggestion, nevertheless acknowledged for the first time that he recognized that there was a severe workload problem.[102] Justices Powell and White, speaking before the American Bar Association, urged fundamental changes to stem the flood of litigation.[103] Chief Justice Burger also spoke out about the caseload explosion at all court levels and warned that unless major changes were instituted the system "may literally break down before the end of this century."[104] In early 1983, Chief Justice Burger proposed the creation of a new court with the task of resolving conflicting decisions of two or more appeals courts. This, he argued, would relieve the Supreme Court of deciding as much as one-third of the cases it now hears. Burger also suggested that the new court be tried on an experimental basis and that Congress create a commission to look for long-term solutions to the overload problem.[105] Legislation was introduced to create an Intercircuit Tribunal of the United States Courts of Appeals along the lines suggested by the Chief Justice and hearings were held. However, opposition to the proposal emerged,[106] and it is likely that the Supreme Court will continue to retain its full gatekeeping and decisional powers. We can expect that other ways will be utilized to prevent the gatekeeping process itself from overwhelming the Court.[107]

SUPPORT

Systems analysis suggests that, in order to persist, a political system must maintain a minimum level of support among those who are politically relevant to it. This concept of support is distinct from the concept of feedback, although both are intimately related. (Each input to the system is instigated by systemic outputs; one way of inferring support attitudes is by looking at feedback activity.) Support, however, deals only with *attitudes* that may be related to systemic output, but may also be held as a result of early socialization or psychological predispositions toward governmental authority in general. Feedback, on the other hand, concerns only *behavioral* responses to output whose existence is transmitted back to the system. This includes *public expression* of support attitudes as well as a wide variety of actions (e.g., private and official noncompliance, court-curbing legislation, new litigation).

The concept of support, insofar as it attempts to aid in explaining judicial behavior, raises some problems. In American political and legal theory, federal judges are supposed to be insulated not only from the other branches of government and "politics" in general, but also from such considerations as whether their decisions are popular or not.[108] Judges who respond to the views of politicians, interest groups, or the public are considered by the organized bar to be acting "unprofessionally."[109] This makes it hard to know to what extent support is in fact an input variable processed by the judicial authorities.

Particularly unclear are both the effect and legitimacy of public opinion on judicial behavior. Some legal theorists have held that public opinion, insofar as it reflects contemporary community needs and values, should be considered in determining the general shape of judicial policy-making but not in specific cases concerning unpopular litigants. Similarly, advocates of judicial restraint have emphasized the need for some minimal attention to public opinion. Alexander Bickel, for example, who was one of the leading modern proponents of judicial restraint, argued that, although the courts should not enforce public opinion, the Supreme Court in particular should avoid cases and decisions that seriously violate community attitudes and values.[110] This, as Glendon Schubert noted, is a "strategy for survival."[111] It is, in other words, a working-out of a theory of support. Yet, many behavioralists have held that at the Supreme Court level, professions of judicial restraint are simply rhetoric. Harold Spaeth, for example, has presented evidence suggesting that judges who profess that certain decisions are based on considerations of judicial restraint are in fact using this as a rationale for arriving at decisions in accord with their more basic political attitudes and values.[112]

Nevertheless, the idea dies hard that, at least at some crucial turning points in judicial history, the Supreme Court, as Mr. Dooley commented long ago, "follows the election returns." To put it in the more scholarly language of David Easton, "Where . . . support threatens to fall below [some] minimal level, . . . the system must provide mechanisms to revive the lagging support or its days will be numbered."[113] One major way, notes Easton, by which such lagging support may be "revived," is through changing systemic policy output. Whether the public is a relevant source of support for the federal judicial system and, if so, whether it produces the type of response that both the fictional Mr. Dooley and the scholarly Mr. Easton suggest, are questions worth considering.[114]

The Analytical Dimensions of Support

Support may be highly different for different aspects or organizational units of the system.[115] Some aspects and units of the federal judicial system have appeared to have experienced substantial increases and decreases in support over time. With others, basic agreement as to their legitimacy appears so widespread that support has remained consistently high and unchanging. Since the Civil War, for example, there has been little disagreement as to the definition of the political community over which the authority of the federal judicial system extends. Similarly, such basic regime rules as the supremacy of federal law, judicial review, and the isolation of the courts from direct popular control have not been the subject of any serious support problems in recent times. On the other hand, particular judges, courts, and the judicial interpretation of some regime rules (e.g., various parts of the Federal Rules of Criminal Procedure, the extent of federal jurisdiction, and the scope of the judiciary's authority vis-à-vis Congress, the President, and the states) have from time to time been the objects of large negative inputs of support.

Another consideration to be taken into account is where support comes from: the legal profession or segments thereof; national, state, or local party leaders, elected politicians, and other public officials; or the general public. It would seem that different sources of support have different consequences for the system.

The kind of support involved is still another consideration. The distinction should be made between diffuse and specific support. *Diffuse support* concerns the general good will, loyalty, and sense of legitimacy directed toward a political system regardless of any specific rewards people may feel they have received. *Specific support* refers to the positive or negative feelings people have in direct response to their perceptions of specific policy outputs. These two kinds of support are both analytically and empirically separable. A person, for example, may express general approval of the Supreme Court as the legitimate forum for constitutional adjudication, while at the same time expressing strong disapproval of many of its constitutional decisions.

The focus here will be on the available evidence relating to both specific and diffuse support of the general public for the Supreme Court, particularly during the 1960s.

The Empirical Dimensions of the Supreme Court's Support Beginning in the 1940s and on through the 1960s, the Supreme Court was the object of increasing disenchantment by those members of the public who responded to the queries of the pollsters.[116] The trend was apparently not uniform, however. It least affected diffuse support among those members of the public least aware of Court activities (the Court's marginal public); it most affected specific support among persons most aware (the Court's attentive public). By 1966, net specific support was strongly negative and increasingly so in some major policy areas such as criminal procedures; net diffuse support was positive but decreasing.[117] Although the Court still had a substantial number of strong positive supporters within its attentive public, much of the reason for its comparatively high diffuse support was the large positive support from its marginal public. This is seen in Table 4.9, which is based on a study by Walter Murphy and Joseph Tanenhaus of support data collected nationally in 1966.[118]

The Court in some (but not all) surveys taken in 1966 can also be seen as doing relatively poorly in its input of support as compared to the other major national political institutions of Congress and the presidency. The results from three surveys are shown in Table 4.10. The Murphy-Tanenhaus survey asked respondents to compare the Court and Congress. The Dolbeare study was based on a survey taken only in Wisconsin. Both showed the Court doing comparatively badly in terms of support. However, the national Harris survey, also reported in Table 4.10, asked respondents about their level of confidence in American institutions, and the Supreme Court in 1966, unlike Congress or the presidency, was the recipient of a (bare) majority's positive diffuse support.[119] The reasons frequently mentioned by those who responded negatively in 1966 concerning the Court (and who had some knowledge of the Court's work) were its decisions concerning race, school prayers, and criminal procedures. (The reapportionment cases seemed to have elicited little awareness or negative support.)[120] In other words, the liberal-

Table 4.9 DISTRIBUTION OF SPECIFIC AND DIFFUSE SUPPORT AMONG SUPREME COURT'S ATTENTIVE AND MARGINAL PUBLICS, 1966

Type of support	Attentive public[a]		Marginal public[b]
	Specific support	Diffuse support	Diffuse support
Strong positive[c]	5.4%	26.8%	27.5%
Moderate positive	15.2	14.9	37.0
Pro/con[d]	10.8	16.7	14.8
Moderate negative	41.5	14.7	16.7
Strong negative[c]	27.0	19.9	4.0
Unclassified		7.4	
Total	99.9%	100.4%	100.0%
	N=596		N=357

Source: Percentages are derived from data presented in Walter F. Murphy and Joseph Tanenhaus, "Public Opinion and the United States Supreme Court: A Preliminary Mapping of Some Prerequisites for Court Legitimation of Regime Changes," *Law and Society Review,* 2 (1968), 370 (Table 5), 377 (Table 9).

[a]Attentive public defined as the 46.2 percent of all respondents in the Murphy-Tanenhaus survey who offered specific likes and dislikes about the Supreme Court.

[b]Marginal public defined as the 27.6 percent of all respondents in the Murphy-Tanenhaus survey who offered diffuse opinions about the Supreme Court, but could not articulate any specific likes or dislikes.

[c]Very strong and strong categories in the Murphy-Tanenhaus study combined for purposes of this table.

[d]Positive and negative comments were about evenly balanced.

Table 4.10 RELATIVE SUPPORT FOR THE SUPREME COURT AS COMPARED WITH OTHER BRANCHES OF GOVERNMENT (CONFIDENCE IN ACTIONS TAKEN BY INSTITUTIONS OF THE NATIONAL GOVERNMENT)

	Supreme Court	Congress	Presidency
Trust Congress/Trust Court? (1966)[a]	37%	51%	—
Confidence that right action taken by (1966)[b]	28	50	35%
Great deal of confidence[c]			
1966	51	42	41
1972	28	21	27
1973	33	30	19
1977	31	15	23
1980	27	18	17
1981	29	16	24
1983	14	6	—

[a]*Source:* Walter F. Murphy, Joseph Tanenhaus, and Daniel L. Kastner, *Public Evaluations of Constitutional Courts* (Beverly Hills, Calif.: Sage, 1973), p. 11, national sample survey. Proportions are of those answering the question of in which institution, Congress or the Court, did respondent place greater trust. Twelve percent gave on-the-fence responses.

[b]*Source:* Kenneth M. Dolbeare, "The Public Views the Supreme Court," in Herbert Jacob (ed.), *Law, Politics, and the Federal Courts* (Boston: Little, Brown, 1967), p. 197. 1966 Wisconsin Survey.

[c]*Source:* Louis Harris and Associates, Inc., national sample survey as reported in Subcommittee on Intergovernmental Relations of the Senate Committee on Government Operations, *Confidence and Concern: Citizens View American Government* (Washington, D.C.: Government Printing Office, 1973), p. 33; Louis Harris surveys as reported in Seymour Martin Lipset and William Schneider, *The Confidence Gap* (New York: Free Press, 1983), pp. 48–49. The 1983 survey was by Gallup, reported in *The Gallup Report,* Report No. 217, October, 1983.

activist Warren Court was viewed unfavorably by many of its critics in the public as too liberal and too activist. The criminal procedures area was particularly a source of increasing negative support of the Supreme Court and American court systems (federal and state) in general during the 1960s. This is suggested by Table 4.11, which was constructed from a series of Gallup poll responses to the question, "Do you think the courts in this area deal too harshly or not harshly enough with criminals?" Indeed, such negative attitudes extended through the 1970s into the 1980s.[121]

It is appropriate to examine more closely the "public" of the public-opinion polls. In the Murphy-Tanenhaus study mentioned earlier, the authors found that 53.8 percent of the entire survey could not state anything they liked or disliked about the Court, and 34.7 percent would not even venture a guess at "what the main job of the Court is."[122] Similarly, in a national poll made in 1945, 40 percent did not know how many justices were on the Court. In another poll taken in 1949, 14 percent were unable to even name the highest court in the land. In 1973, the Harris poll revealed that 20 percent of the national survey thought that the Supreme Court is a branch of Congress.[123] Analysis of these and other poll results indicates that the "public" of public-opinion polling can be stratified into a hierarchy of groups on the basis of awareness, concern, and information.

At the bottom level are those members of society who neither know nor care anything about Court behavior. Depending upon the survey question asked, this group's size varies between about 10 and 30 percent of the adult population as suggested by the various studies cited in Table 4.12. This segment of the public is generally unaware and apathetic about politics in general. They possess little or no general political knowledge. They tend not to vote.[124] Although the upper levels of this group sometimes respond to questions on "forced choice" public opinion polls, in general they are *politically irrelevant* as a source of either negative or positive support for the Court.

In setting the size of the Court's *politically relevant* public at from 70 to 90 percent of the adult population, there is serious danger of overstating the real percentage of those who hold meaningful opinions. Murphy and Tanenhaus noted, "Forced choice questions of the variety so typical in commercially conducted public opinion polls strenuously overestimate the Court's visibility be-

Table 4.11   PUBLIC ATTITUDES TOWARD TREATMENT OF CRIMINALS BY THE COURTS, 1965–1969

	Courts treat criminals:				
	Too harshly	Not harshly enough	About right	No opinion	Total
April 1965	2%	48%	34%	16%	100%
August 1965	2	60	26	12	100
February 1968	2	63	19	16	100
February 1969	2	75	13	10	100

Source: Gallup Opinion Reports, no. 4 (September 1965); no. 33 (March 1968); no. 45 (March 1969).

Table 4.12 DETERMINING THE SIZE OF THE SUPREME COURT'S POLITICALLY IRRELEVANT PUBLIC

	Percent
"No Opinion" about any Supreme Court decision or aspect of Supreme Court behavior (Seattle, 1965)[a]	21
"Don't Know" when asked to rate Supreme Court's performance (Wisconsin, 1966)[b]	19
"Unclassified"—i.e., "no response" or "no opinion" in testing for diffuse support (national poll, 1966)[c]	29
Cannot answer question about what Supreme Court is supposed to do (Missouri, 1968)[d]	26
"No opinion" when asked to rate Supreme Court's performance (AIPO national surveys)[e]	
1963	16
1967	9
1968	11
1969	13
1973	12

[a]*Source:* John H. Kessel, "Public Perceptions of the Supreme Court," *Midwest Journal of Political Science,* 10 (1966), 174.

[b]*Source:* Kenneth M. Dolbeare, "The Public Views the Supreme Court," in Herbert Jacob (ed.), *Law, Politics, and the Federal Courts* (Boston: Little, Brown, 1967), p. 203.

[c]*Source:* Walter F. Murphy and Joseph Tanenhaus, "Public Opinion and the United States Supreme Court: A Preliminary Mapping of Some Prerequisites for Court Legitimation of Regime Changes," *Law and Society Review,* 2 (1968), 374.

[d]*Source:* Gregory Casey, "The Supreme Court and Myth: An Empirical Investigation," *Law and Society Review,* 8 (1974), 397.

[e]*Source:* AIPO polls 1963, 1967, 1968, 1969, 1973.

cause they solicit responses from people who may possess no meaningful information."[125] Kenneth Dolbeare illustrated this point in his 1966 Wisconsin study by asking respondents to indicate whether the Court had recently made a decision in different policy areas including some in which the Court had not, for example, Medicare, urban renewal, and the John Birch Society. He found that 52 percent claimed that the Court had made a decision about Medicare, 26 percent about urban renewal, and 23 percent about the John Birch Society.[126] This suggests that many respondents to poll questions venture opinions that are based on no or false information. Perhaps even more revealing as to the extent of the Court's relevant public was a Survey Research Center poll conducted in 1964 that began with a question that asked whether the respondent had paid any attention to what the Supreme Court had done in recent years; 58.7 percent indicated they had not.[127] These and other data suggest that the Court's politically relevant public can be divided into two groups.

The attitudes of the members of the first group are meaningful inputs of support to the Court. Its members demonstrate knowledge about the Court, hold strong opinions either pro or con, are highly likely to have recently read or heard about the Court and its activities,[128] and are easily able to articulate specific likes and dislikes. This segment of the population is the Court's *attentive* public. It constitutes roughly about 40 percent of the adult population. Evidence for this estimate is presented in Table 4.13. Murphy, Tanenhaus, and Kastner have

**Table 4.13   DETERMINING THE SIZE OF THE SUPREME COURT'S ATTENTIVE
PUBLIC**

	Percent
Strong Court critic or supporter (Seattle, 1965)[a]	40.9
Intensity of attitude about the Supreme Court—"very strong" (Seattle, 1965)[b]	37.5
SRC polls—expression of specific likes and dislikes[c]	
1964	41.3
1966	46.2
"High knowledge" about the Supreme Court (Wisconsin, 1966)[d]	37.4
Awareness/Familiarity concerning Supreme Court decisions (Missouri, 1968)[e]	48.6

[a]*Source:* John H. Kessel, "Public Perceptions." "Strong critics" were those with scores of at least −2 and "strong supporters" with scores of at least +2 on the open-end questions scale presented in Kessel's Table 2.

[b]*Source:* Kessel, "Public Perceptions," derived from data presented in Table 12, p. 189.

[c]*Source:* Murphy and Tanenhaus, "Public Opinion," p. 360.

[d]*Source:* Dolbeare, "Public Views," p. 200. "High knowledge" defined as four or more correct identifications out of eight concerning policy areas in which the Court made a decision in recent years.

[e]*Source:* Gregory Casey, "The Supreme Court and Myth: An Empirical Investigation," *Law and Society Review,* 8 (1974), p. 415 n. 20. Those considered aware or familiar with Court decisions are those with scores of 2 and 3.

suggested that attitudes toward public policy best accounted for the variation in support levels of the knowledgeables in the 1966 survey, but they also acknowledged that party allegiance was related to support, with Democrats giving more positive diffuse support than Republicans.[129] In 1975, close to half the respondents surveyed in 1966 were reinterviewed and Murphy and Tanenhaus again found a strong relationship between public policy attitudes or ideology and support level. However, analysis of the 1975 interviews uncovered *no* relationship between party identification and diffuse support levels or any evidence backing the view that support levels are related to a partisan perspective according to which party controls the White House.[130]

Opinions of the remainder of the politically relevant public are much less meaningful. The persons holding them are characterized by a low knowledge of the Court and a propensity to express diffuse support attitudes or respond to forced-choice questions without having enough information to spontaneously be able to articulate specific support opinions. They are perhaps better characterized as on the threshold of political relevancy and can be considered the Court's *marginal* public.

Members of each public, whether friend or foe of the Court, tend to be more like one another than like their attitudinal partners in other publics. This is not only true in terms of knowledge, access to recent information, and propensity to hold strong opinions, but also in such demographic and political variables as education, income, partisanship, political involvement, and general political knowledge. Being in the Court's *attentive,* as compared to its *marginal,* public is positively correlated with greater formal education, income, and general political knowledge. Republicans tend to be better represented than Democrats, Democrats better represented than Independents.[131] Of even greater interest is that by the late 1960s being in the Court's attentive public was also positively associated with political involvement, alienation from government, and a high sense of political efficacy. It seems hard to overemphasize the importance of these latter tendencies. To quote Murphy and Tanenhaus, "Individuals who tend to be aware of the Court . . . [and] vote often, . . . are [also] apt to distrust government and feel that it is generally unresponsive to their desires."[132] Dolbeare states, "People [with high knowledge about the Court] are the [same] ones with a high sense of political efficacy, for they are also the ones who say that they would act in some way to change a Court decision of which they disapprove."[133] When one couples these latter tendencies with the relatively low positive specific and diffuse support levels within this same segment of the public, it is clear that the Court in the late 1960s was approaching a crisis in its input of support. Some of the evidence has already been presented in Table 4.9. Evidence from two other studies is provided in Table 4.14. It is rather ironic that much of the Court's net positive support was attributed to members of the public who were least aware of its activities. To know the Court was not necessarily to love it.[134]

The positive support from the Court's marginal public does not assure the viability of the system. The demographic and political involvement attributes of the Court's marginal public indicate relatively low social and political power. When compared to the attentive public, they tend generally to have less formal education, less income, less political knowledge, less sense of political efficacy, and less of a propensity to vote and be politically active. These attributes hardly indicate an inclination to fight in the political arena for the Court's integrity. Perhaps the most important contribution of positive support from the marginal public, however, is in how it affects the behavior of political leaders. In an age when elected politicians are reportedly sensitive to public opinion polls, this

Table 4.14   DIFFUSE SUPPORT FOR THE SUPREME COURT BY KNOWLEDGE OF THE COURT

Respondents' rating of the Court	Wisconsin Survey, 1966[a] Knowledge of the Court		
	High	Medium	Low
Very good/good	54%	65%	64%
Fair	28	29	33
Poor	18	7	4
Total	100%	101%	101%
N =	92	196	221

Type of support	Seattle Survey, 1965[b] Read or heard about the Court in last year?	
	Yes	No
Court supporter	51.7%	49.0%
Neutral	14.9	41.6
Critic	33.3	9.4
Total	99.9%	100.0%
N =	222	96

[a]*Source:* Dolbeare, "Public Views," p. 204.
[b]*Source:* Kessel, "Public Perceptions," p. 189, Table 12.

relatively large positive diffuse support may have discouraged most politicians from initiating a drastic frontal attack on the Court (e.g., an impeachment proceeding against the Chief Justice; fundamental contraction of the Court's jurisdiction).

It is of interest to speculate whether and how the attitudes of the marginal public would be affected by a concerted propaganda campaign by those unfriendly to the Court in the Congress, the White House, and the state capitals. On the one hand, because members of the marginal public are so resistant to receiving new information about the Court, one might speculate that such a campaign would only slightly affect the positive support level. On the other hand, if the message were able to penetrate the formidable perceptual barriers, it might well result—given the low intensity with which positive support attitudes are held and the paucity of information upon which they are based—in the formation of new negative attitudes. This may very well have occurred in 1981 and 1982 with the mobilization of anti-Court forces in Congress and the introduction of legislation (with the apparent approval of President Reagan) to contract the jurisdiction of the federal courts in the areas of school busing for the purpose of desegregation, the recitation of prayers in the public schools, and the ability of women to secure abortions. As it turned out, the legislation did not pass, but there appeared to be an absence of strong positive support among most Americans concerning the federal courts including the Supreme Court, as Table 4.10 suggests with the findings for 1983.

Perhaps a better indication of the relative weakness of support attitudes of the Court's marginal public is gained by a more detailed consideration of the drop in positive support for the judicial handling of criminal defendants. This is an area where public awareness has increased sharply since 1964. It is also an area where anti-Court propaganda has been intense. To indicate how this criticism has differently affected the members of the Court's attentive and marginal publics, the rate of decline in positive support for the courts among respondents with a grade-school education (who tend to be among the Court's marginal public) and among those with a college education (who tend to be among its attentive public) is considered.[135] To indicate what is presumed to be differences in how the policies affect members of the public, the attitudes of those living in cities of more than 500,000 are compared with those living in rural areas under 2500. (Inhabitants of major cities are most sensitized to crime as these cities have the highest crime rates.[136]) Since most studies seem to indicate that, at the most, local law enforcement officials have only been mildly hurt by Court decisions in their ability to make arrests and obtain convictions,[137] the statistics in Table 4.15 seem to indicate that anti-Court propaganda can significantly change support attitudes, particularly (but not exclusively) within the Court's marginal public. The effect is greatest in communities where respondents presumably feel most threatened by the decisions. By 1969, then, it appears that a majority of the marginal public had joined ranks with a majority of the attentive public to deny the Court positive support, particularly in the criminal procedures area. The July, 1969, Gallup survey found the smallest proportion (33 percent) of respondents giving the Court a favorable rating since such court-rating surveys were first conducted.[138]

The setting was ripe for a major assault on the Court, and in one sense the

Table 4.15 DECREASING SUPPORT FOR COURTS IN HANDLING OF CRIMINALS (BY RESPONDENT'S EDUCATION AND SIZE OF RESPONDENT'S COMMUNITY, 1965–1969)

Type of respondent/ response	Survey		
	August 1965	February 1968	February 1969
College education Courts treat criminals:			
Too harshly	1%	3%	3%
Not harshly enough	62	58	67
About right	28	20	18
No opinion	9	19	12
Total	100%	100%	100%
Grade school education Courts treat criminals:			
Too harshly	2%	3%	2%
Not harshly enough	56	63	78
About right	26	21	12
No opinion	16	13	8
Total	100%	100%	100%
Large urban community[a] Courts treat criminals:			
Too harshly	2%	2%	2%
Not harshly enough	63	68	78
About right	22	12	9
No opinion	13	18	11
Total	100%	100%	100%
Rural community[b] Courts treat criminals:			
Too harshly	1%	1%	2%
Not harshly enough	59	58	70
About right	30	24	19
No opinion	10	17	9
Total	100%	100%	100%

Source: AIPO Reports, no. 4 (September 1965); no. 3 (March 1968); and no. 45 (March 1969).
[a]"Large urban," defined in 1965 survey as cities with a population of 500,000 and over. In 1968 and 1969 surveys, "large urban" defined as cities with a population of one million and over.
[b]"Rural" defined as under 2500 population.

Nixon Administration actually mounted such an assault by successfully forcing Justice Fortas off the Court. Anti-Court sentiment was thereafter politically exploited through use of the law-and-order issue and the avowed nomination of conservatives to fill Court vacancies. When the dust finally settled, four appointments later, President Nixon had his Nixon Court. With the Court's major shift to the right of center, particularly in the criminal-procedures area, and the absence of the Court as a major partisan issue in the 1970s, it was reasonable to expect an increase in positive support.[139] The July, 1973, Gallup survey in fact showed an increase (4 percent) in favorable ratings of the Court from the previous 1969 survey and a decrease (8 percent) from the 1969 survey of the proportion giving the Court the poorest rating. A Survey Research Center study conducted during October and November, 1973, reported the results of a national sample survey in which people were asked how good a job each of 15 major institutions was doing for the country. The Supreme Court was found to be the governmental institution given the highest rating and was seen as having the highest integrity.[140] This trend continued and was demonstrated by the results of various Gallup polls taken in the 1970s and in 1981. In the 1981 survey, some 52 percent of the respondents said they had "a great deal" or "quite a lot" of confidence in the Supreme Court as an institution of government.[141] However, after the attacks on the federal courts in 1981 and 1982 in Congress and President Reagan's pronounced opposition to Court policies regarding busing, prayer in the public school, and abortion, the proportion of those surveyed with "a great deal" or "quite a lot" of confidence dropped to 42 percent.[142] Significantly, the Court in the 1983–1984 term moved sharply to the right and upheld the Reagan Administration's positions in several policy areas, most prominently on criminal procedures.[143]

The Court's longevity as a bastion of a particular political philosophy is not secure during periods of low specific support. However, attempts to change the Court through either blatantly or deviously untraditional means will probably not only fail, but may even be counterproductive for the attacker. A widespread lack of popular positive support for a particular set of justices should not be taken as indicative of a lack of positive support for the Court as an independent institution. It is just this error that President Franklin Roosevelt seems to have made in pushing his 1937 court-packing plan.

Roosevelt took the considerable evidence of widespread popular and congressional dissatisfaction with the "nine old men" of the Supreme Court as indicative of low support for the Court as an institution. His court-reform program was (and was almost immediately perceived as) not just an attack on the anti-New Deal justices, but also an attack on the Court's independence and decision-making procedures. The consequences for Roosevelt's own support were significant. Not only did he not get his plan passed, but, by pushing it, he provided a rallying point for his previously disorganized opposition.

President Roosevelt was not the only political authority to respond to the 1937 Court's low input of positive support. At least two crucial members of that Court, Hughes and Roberts, also seemed sensitive to its support problems. While FDR was attacking the Court as unresponsive to the nation's needs, they joined with the Court's liberal bloc of Stone, Brandeis, and Cardozo to renounce the Court's laissez-faire economic policies in favor of more progovernment policies.

The 1937 switch as an illustration of judicial responsiveness to a negative input of support raises a considerable number of questions as to the linkage between support input and judicial policy-making. To say the least, the degree of negative support the Court received during the early New Deal, especially in 1936, was dramatic. It was transmitted to the Court not only from Congress and the White House, but also through the mass media, law reviews, and the statements and writings of a number of scholars at universities and their law schools. This input of negative support was reinforced by a number of strongly negative feedback actions taken by the President, Congress, state legislatures, and the electorate. FDR's court-reform plan itself was such a feedback action. So also was the overwhelming reelection of FDR and his congressional colleagues in 1936 after a campaign in which the New Deal was the major issue. In the same vein were the actions of Congress and state legislatures, which passed new economic regulatory and social welfare legislation after their first attempts had been rejected as unconstitutional.

The 1937 episode represents what in systems terms one ought to expect to be the normal responsiveness of authorities to falling positive support. However, it appears that such responsiveness is at best episodic. Such falling support does not produce the automatic alterations in policy output in the federal judicial system to the extent that occurs with other social and political systems. This raises the fundamental question of what are the determinants of the judicial conversion process by which inputs are processed to produce policy outputs, which is the subject of the following chapter.

NOTES

1. David Easton, *A Framework for Political Analysis* (Englewood Cliffs, N.J.: Prentice-Hall, 1965), pp. 90–91.
2. *Ibid.,* p. 120.
3. For example, the data that establish the "facts" of a case at the trial level are presented through various physical and documentary evidence (contracts, signed statements, depositions) and through oral examination and cross-examination of witnesses and litigants.
4. Note that the review and enforcement of administrative agency orders are not considered an "administrative" function of the courts. Because of their form, content, and the courts' methods of processing them, such cases are considered litigative demands.
5. Since 1971, the United States Postal Service has assumed the bulk of the processing of passport applications. Passport applications, however, can be made to the clerks of the district courts. Applications are then processed by the State Department. Naturalization proceedings, however, are conducted exclusively in the federal district courts.
6. Note that employed within the federal district courts are federal magistrates who handle many of the preliminary steps prior to trial, thus freeing the judges for a variety of other administrative tasks. In 1979, Congress enacted legislation enlarging the authority of federal magistrates so that they are able to hold jury and nonjury trials in civil suits as well as criminal misdemeanor cases provided that both parties consent in writing. Furthermore, the legislation provided for direct appeal from magistrate proceedings to the appropriate U.S. Court of Appeals unless both parties agreed before trial to take any appeal to the U.S. District Court. See *Congressional Quarterly,* October 6, 1979, p. 2223.
7. They were assisted by 1985 clerks. See *Annual Report of the Director of the Administrative Office of the United States Courts, 1982* (Washington, D.C.: Government Printing Office, 1982) (hereafter cited as *Report, U.S. Courts, 1982*), Table 21. Note that under 1978 legislation, the referee in bankruptcy position was eliminated and replaced by the bankruptcy judge. Federal district judges appointed referees in

bankruptcy and would be allowed to appoint bankruptcy judges with the help of a screening panel until March 31, 1984, when the new system would go into operation. Under the terms of the 1978 act the President would then be authorized to appoint a new set of judges whose term of office would be increased from 6 to 14 years. Bankruptcy judges were authorized to hear *all* matters relating to bankruptcy whereas, before, ancillary proceedings were heard by the district judge. The Supreme Court in 1982, however, struck down part of the 1978 legislation that gave bankruptcy judges enhanced powers. The Court ruled that those powers can only be exercised by Article III judges appointed for life tenure and whose salary may not be reduced. The decision was Northern Pipeline v. Marathon Pipe Line, 458 U.S. 50. The Court gave Congress until October 4 and then to December 24, 1982, to establish a new bankruptcy program. The choices open to Congress were first to change the status of bankruptcy judges to Article III judges with the same status as federal district judges. If this were done, the new judges could be limited to bankruptcy matters or they could be able to be transferred to sit on the district courts and handle any business before the court. Alternatively, Congress could return to the pre-1978 process, or a variation thereof, but create additional district court positions to help handle the bankruptcy and presumably other litigative burdens on the courts. This last option was in fact what Congress chose when on June 29, 1984, it passed a bankruptcy act creating 61 new district court judgeships and 24 new appeals court judgeships. Under the new legislation, bankruptcy judges are considered adjuncts of the district court to whom clear-cut bankruptcy cases are assigned. The bankruptcy judges are, as before, Article I judges but now appointed by the appeals courts for 14-year terms. They consider generally uncontested, relatively uncomplicated bankruptcies.

8. They were assisted by 40 assistants, 68 pretrial services officers, and 1074 clerks. See *Report, U.S. Courts, 1982,* Table 21.

9. Easton, *A Framework for Political Analysis,* pp. 114–115.

10. That judge, Stephen S. Chandler, challenged the legality of the action, but the Supreme Court denied his motion for relief. See Chandler v. Judicial Council of the Tenth Circuit, 398 U.S. 74 (1970). See the discussion of the Chandler case and, in general, the findings of Beverly Blair Cook, "Perceptions of the Independent Trial Judge Role in the Seventh Circuit," *Law and Society Review,* 6 (1972), 615–629. Concerning Chandler, see Joseph C. Goulden, *The Benchwarmers* (New York: Weybright and Talley, 1974), pp. 206–249.

11. *The United States Government Manual, 1983–84* (Washington, D.C.: Government Printing Office, 1983), p. 65.

12. On April 28, 1983, Chief Justice Burger, on behalf of the Court, sent to Congress proposed certain changes in both the Federal Rules of Criminal Procedure and the Federal Rules of Civil Procedure. They became effective the following August 1. These changes, particularly concerning civil procedure, were of major significance and included limiting the use by lawyers of discovery as well as other legal devices to prevent harassment by one side of a suit of the other or unnecessary delay or needless costs. Judges were given new authority to enforce these new standards, including the authority to set time limits for the completion of pretrial proceedings.

13. But note that the district courts do review previous state and federal court proceedings when they consider petitions for *habeas corpus.*

14. Note that the number and proportion of civil cases has been increasing. Almost ten years earlier, in fiscal 1973, for example, civil cases accounted for "only" 70 percent of the cases filed in the district courts.

15. The overwhelming proportion of civil rights cases were initiated by private parties. Interestingly, the role of the federal government in civil rights litigation shifted from the Johnson Administration, where in fiscal 1967 the Administration was the plaintiff in 56 percent of the civil rights cases in which the federal government was involved, to the Nixon Administration in fiscal 1972 and the Reagan Administration in fiscal 1982, when the Administration was the *defendant* in 80 percent of the cases in which it was a principal party in the suit. The increase in civil rights litigation can most likely be attributed to the activity of legal services offices and the new public-interest lawyers and law firms that sprouted in the late 1960s and early 1970s as well as the expanded activities of the civil rights and civil liberties organizations.

16. For example, real property filings (most government mortgage foreclosures) were down 14 percent from 1966 to 1973. In fiscal 1966 they accounted for about 7 percent of civil cases commenced, and in both fiscal 1973 and 1982 they accounted for 4 percent. Antitrust suits dropped between 1973 and 1982.

17. The director of the Administrative Office of the U.S. Courts noted in the 1973 annual report: "The continued downturn of auto theft cases reflects Department of Justice policy to decline prosecution of joy riders and youthful auto thieves and center Federal efforts on prosecuting auto thefts connected with organized crime or multi-theft violations" (*Report, U.S. Courts, 1973,* p. II–57). The report also contained the observation that the decline in liquor law violations was due to these cases being handled by U.S. magistrates or being turned over to state authorities (p. II–58). It should also be mentioned that under the 1970 Court Reorganization Act for the District of Columbia there was a transfer beginning in part in fiscal 1972 from the federal district court to the "local" Superior Court of all offenses in violation of the District of Columbia Criminal Code except those that were also a violation of the United States Code (and also applicable nationwide). This brought about a dramatic drop in the criminal case input to the federal District Court of the District of Columbia from fiscal 1971 to fiscal 1974. In fiscal 1971, for example, 2306 criminal cases were begun, but in fiscal 1974 this was cut by almost two-thirds, to 835 cases. The biggest drop was in homicide, robbery, burglary, and sex offenses, precisely the areas in which the figures for all district courts nationwide in Table 4.3 indicated a drop for fiscal 1974. Thus in these areas, as in some others, cases were shifted out of the federal courts and were prosecuted elsewhere.

18. This trend continued in fiscal 1983. See *Report, U.S. Courts, 1983,* p. 164. The annual reports offer a detailed breakdown by circuit and district court.

19. The figures for civil cases may be misleading. Jerry Goldman has persuasively argued that one should consider all appealable decisions of district judges and not just completed trials. Goldman made use of unpublished data collected by the Administrative Office of the U.S. Courts categorized as "contested judgments" and considered *those* rather than completed trials as representing appealable decisions. On this basis his calculations for fiscal 1970 suggested approximately a one-in-four rate of appeals. See Jerry Goldman, "Federal District Courts and the Appellate Crisis," *Judicature,* 57 (1973), 211–213. If completed trials were used to determine the rate of appeal for fiscal 1970 the rate would be three out of four! Thus the four-out-of-five rate cited in the text should *not* be treated as the rate of all appealable civil decisions but only the rate in terms of completed trials. It should be recognized, as Goldman does in his article (p. 211), that the use of Administrative Office contested judgments has drawbacks in that the data are in aggregate form and individual cases are not traced through the system. Thus the figures for appeals for fiscal 1982 may contain cases begun in the district courts in fiscal 1981 or earlier as well as those begun in

fiscal 1982. One study that did keep track of cases from the appeals courts to the Supreme Court was conducted by J. Woodford Howard, Jr. See his "Litigation Flow in Three United States Courts of Appeals," *Law and Society Review,* 8 (1973), 33–53. The full report of this research is contained in his Report to the Federal Judicial Center, *The Flow of Litigation in the United States Courts of Appeals for the Second, Fifth, and District of Columbia Circuits,* Research Report No. 3 (Washington, D.C.: Federal Judicial Center, 1973). Also see his *Courts of Appeals in the Federal Judicial System: A Study of the Second, Fifth, and District of Columbia Circuits* (Princeton, N.J.: Princeton University Press, 1981), Chap. 2.

20. Martin Shapiro, *The Supreme Court and Administrative Agencies* (New York: Free Press, 1968), p. 262.

21. Goldman, in his study of the "Federal District Courts and the Appellate Crisis," documents what he appropriately calls the "startling" change in criminal appeals (in contrast to the rate of appeal in civil cases which fluctuated between 20 and 24 percent between 1951 and 1970): "In 1951, approximately 14 out of every 100 defendants found guilty after trial appealed their convictions. By 1970, more than half of all defendants found guilty after trial appealed their convictions" (p. 212). As noted earlier, this climbed to about two out of three by 1973. Goldman attributes the growth in appeals in part to the Criminal Justice Act of 1964 that began providing funds necessary to permit indigent defendants to enjoy free legal assistance.

22. There is also the trend of the appeals courts not publishing these decisions. In recent years, over half the criminal and civil appeals court decisions have not been published. Six appeals courts, including the Second Circuit, prohibit lawyers from citing unpublished appeals court decisions. See Marcia Chambers, "U.S. Appeals Court Restricts Use of Opinions by Lawyers," *New York Times,* February 21, 1983, pp. B1, B5. For a thoughtful essay on the implications of the burdensome caseload on appeals courts, see J. Woodford Howard, Jr., "Are Heavy Caseloads Changing the Nature of Appellate Justice?" *Judicature,* 66 (1982), 57–59, 102.

23. *U.S. Law Week,* 43 (1974), 3085.

24. This is particularly true for state criminal cases. For example, over five times as many state criminal cases were the subject of full written opinions during the 1966–1968 terms than during the 1948–1950 terms. In the 1972 and 1973 terms, about one out of four cases decided with full opinion by the Court either came from the state judicial systems or were *habeas corpus* cases concerning state prisoners. In the 1980 term the figure was also about one out of four cases, but by the 1982 term this fell to less than one in five. In the 1968 term, the last term of the Warren Court, over one-third of the cases decided with full opinion originated with the state judicial systems.

25. At the direction of Chief Justice Burger, the Clerk's office has not provided breakdowns of the docket in terms of appeal and certiorari cases since the 1970 term.

26. Easton, *A Framework for Political Analysis,* pp. 122–125.

27. A classic discussion of jurisdiction, standing, and justiciability can be found in Edward S. Corwin, *The Constitution of the United States of America: Analysis and Interpretation,* rev. ed. (Washington, D.C.: Government Printing Office, 1964), pp. 597–726. Also see Harold W. Chase and Craig R. Ducat, *Edward S. Corwin's The Constitution and What It Means Today* (Princeton, N.J.: Princeton University Press, 1973), pp. 167–195; Robert L. Stern and Eugene Gressman, *Supreme Court Practice,* 5th ed. (Washington, D.C.: Bureau of National Affairs, 1978), pp. 52–253.

28. See Karen Orren, "Standing to Sue: Interest Group Influence in the Federal Courts," *American Political Science Review,* 70 (1976), 723. Two of the landmark cases on

standing are Association of Data Processing Service Organizations, Inc. v. Camp, 397 U.S. 150 (1970) and Sierra Club v. Morton, 405 U.S. 727 (1972).

29. See, for example, Village of Schaumberg v. Citizens for a Better Environment, 444 U.S. 620 (1980).

30. Justice Brandeis discussed this point in his well-known opinion in Ashwander v. T.V.A., 297 U.S. 288 (1936), at 346–347. There he specified the circumstances under which the Court would or would not avoid deciding a case based on an interpretation of the Constitution.

31. 157 U.S. 429 (1895).

32. 298 U.S. 238 (1936).

33. Dred Scott v. Sandford, 19 How. 393 (1857). Baker v. Carr, 369 U.S. 186 (1962).

34. Richard Richardson and Kenneth N. Vines, "Review, Dissent and the Appellate Process: A Political Interpretation," *Journal of Politics,* 29 (1967), 597–616. A "civil liberties case" was defined as one in which a claim was made under the Bill of Rights, Thirteenth, Fourteenth, and Fifteenth Amendments, or Article I, Section 9 of the Constitution.

35. 262 F. 2d 801 (1959).

36. 288 F. 2d 182 (1961).

37. 417 U.S. 600.

38. They are considered "structural" because they occupy roles in the judicial structure; that is, they are "built into" the system. See Easton, *A Framework for Political Analysis,* p. 122.

39. Table 4.6 showed that a little more than half of courts of appeals cases in fiscal 1982 were disposed of by consolidation or without hearing or submission. Thus gatekeeping of course occurs at this level in the judicial system.

40. It should be noted that, with civil cases, judges adjudicate certain demands without a formal trial but rather by court hearings. The judge's rulings are appealable, for example, with prisoner petitions for the writ of *habeas corpus* or motions to reduce or vacate sentence. Thus while justice without trial may be common, justice without judicial adjudication is less frequent. Using unpublished data gathered by the Administrative Office of the U.S. Courts on contested judgments consisting of all actions by judges that are appealable, Jerry Goldman found that for fiscal 1970 some 23 percent (excluding prisoner petitions) resulted in contested judgments. When prisoner petitions were included the figure jumped to 37 percent. This still meant that justice without trial or adjudication was the norm, but it also meant that justice with adjudication was at least three and a half times greater than simply justice with trial. Jerry Goldman, unpublished Table One, "Ratio of Contested Judgements to Total Civil Terminations."

41. In comparison, it would appear that virtually all of the other types of civil cases completing trial in fiscal 1982 were appealed to an appeals court. However, this would be a misleading comparison since, as Jerry Goldman has pointed out in "Federal District Courts and the Appellate Crisis," there are many more appealable decisions than there are trials, and furthermore the figures do not represent the tracing of individual cases to determine if they were indeed appealed. What we can suggest, however, is that the maximum appeals rate for tort cases in fiscal 1982 was likely to have been considerably less than that for other types of civil cases.

42. Such procedural differences as exist are perhaps irrelevant. The difference in the size of the claims is not. Large claims are apparently more resistant to settlement than small claims. Thus, for the federal courts, about 10 percent of the cases filed are settled by a court judgment, while in the New York City courts in 1957 where the

median recovery was only $795 and the average $2058, only 3.2 percent required a court judgment (see the study cited in note 43). Nevertheless, if one keeps this difference in mind, an analysis of state tort claims settlement is illuminating for understanding the dynamics of civil suit gatekeeping within the federal courts.

43. Marc A. Franklin, Robert H. Chanin, and Irving Mark, "Accidents, Money and the Law: A Study of the Economics of Personal Injury Litigation," *Columbia Law Review,* 61 (1961), 1–39, reprinted in Rita James Simon (ed.), *The Sociology of Law: Interdisciplinary Readings* (San Francisco: Chandler, 1968), pp. 367–391. Quotation from pp. 373–374.

44. Insurance companies obviously prefer to deal directly with victims and avoid having to negotiate with lawyers. Insurance company adjustors as a consequence take the initiative in trying to settle before the claimant sees an attorney. See H. Laurence Ross, *Settled out of Court: The Social Process of Insurance Claims* (Chicago: Aldine, 1970). Ross also noted (pp. 193–198) that settlements were considerably larger when an attorney represented the victim. Even for victims with lawyers, one study found that those who took an active interest in their case and shared decision making concerning the litigation with their lawyer wound up much better than those who were passive and had little participation in their own case. See Douglas E. Rosenthal, *Lawyer and Client: Who's in Charge?* (New York: Russell Sage Foundation, 1974).

45. See William A. Glaser, *Pretrial Discovery and the Adversary System* (New York: Russell Sage Foundation, 1968), pp. 3–37, 91 (especially note 4), 117–161.

46. *Ibid.,* pp. 91–101. However, in the Glaser study, pretrial settlement was even more likely when neither party utilized the discovery procedures! Furthermore, Glaser also found (pp. 102–103) that use of discovery procedures was associated with increased trial time. His data (p. 106) further suggested that discovery "might be associated with *more* surprise." Clearly, pretrial discovery is not the gatekeeping mechanism its proponents once suggested, and this has led to a movement to curb the abuses associated with discovery. The Judicial Conference of the United States and the Supreme Court proposed new rules that became effective in 1983 that require lawyers who use discovery to certify that their requests were made in "good faith" and were not being made "to harass or to cause unnecessary delay or needless increase in the cost of litigation." Judges now have the authority to impose sanctions on lawyers who violate these standards. Also, judges are empowered to set time limits on the discovery process. See *Supreme Court Reporter,* 103 (June 15, 1983), yellow pages 52. For a review of studies on discovery see Daniel Segal, *Survey of the Literature on Discovery from 1970 to the Present: Expressed Dissatisfactions and Proposed Reforms* (Washington, D.C.: Federal Judicial Center, 1978).

47. Richard J. Richardson and Kenneth N. Vines, *The Politics of Federal Courts* (Boston: Little, Brown, 1970), p. 86. Also see their discussion on pp. 85–88. In general, see Maurice Rosenberg, *The Pretrial Conference and Effective Justice* (New York: Columbia University Press, 1964) and John Paul Ryan, Allan Ashman, Bruce D. Sales, and Sandra Shane-DuBow, *American Trial Judges: Their Work Styles and Performance* (New York: Free Press, 1980), chap. 8.

48. In the eastern federal district of both Tennessee and Virginia, the median was only five months. *Report, U.S. Courts, 1982,* Table C-10.

49. Harry Kalven, Jr., "The Jury, the Law and the Personal Injury Damage Award," *Ohio State Law Journal,* 19 (1958), 158–178.

50. See, for example, Jerold S. Auerbach, *Justice Without Law?* (New York: Oxford University Press, 1983); Roman Tomasic and Malcolm M. Feeley, eds., *Neighborhood Justice: Assessment of an Emerging Idea* (New York: Longman, 1982); and

Christine B. Harrington, "Delegalization Reform Movements: A Historical Analysis," in Richard L. Abel, ed., *The Politics of Informal Justice,* volume 1 (New York: Academic Press, 1982), pp. 35–71, and other studies in the Abel edited volume. Also see the major study by Christine B. Harrington, *Shadow Justice* (Westport, Conn.: Greenwood Press, in press).

51. This is not to suggest that alternative dispute processing is limited to the modes mentioned. There are a wide variety of institutions and mechanisms for dispute resolution outside of court processes, but their effectiveness has been seriously questioned. See Laura Nader, ed., *No Access to Law: Alternatives to the American Judicial System* (New York: Academic Press, 1980). But see Tamar Lewin, "New Alternatives to Litigation: Companies Bypass Courts," *New York Times,* November 1, 1982, p. D1. Also note that in 1980 Congress enacted the Dispute Resolution Act, which established within the Justice Department a dispute resolution resource center to serve as a clearinghouse for state and local governments concerning the establishment of alternative dispute resolution programs. A federal grant program was also established to help existing programs and to develop new ones. See *Congressional Quarterly,* February 2, 1980, p. 274.

52. Prior to arrest, substantial gatekeeping may also occur by the police or other public and private law enforcement officials. See James Q. Wilson, *The Varieties of Police Behavior* (Cambridge, Mass.: Harvard University Press, 1968), for a systematic study of different patterns of gatekeeping behavior by local police. Also see John A. Gardiner, *Traffic and the Police: Variations in Law-Enforcement Policy* (Cambridge, Mass.: Harvard University Press, 1969), especially pp. 150–165. In general, see the discussion and the citations within James Eisenstein, *Politics and the Legal Process* (New York: Harper & Row, 1973), pp. 84–97, 216–233; Michael K. Brown, *Working the Street: Police Discretion and the Dilemmas of Reform* (New York: Basic Books, 1981); and George F. Cole, *The American System of Criminal Justice,* 3rd ed. (Monterey, Calif.: Brooks/Cole, 1983), pp. 125–219. Federal prosecutors have discretion whether or not to proceed with criminal referrals from federal government agencies, for example, referrals from the Internal Revenue Service for income tax fraud or from the Department of Agriculture of those suspected of violating provisions of the food stamp program. Referrals that go unprosecuted can range from 10 percent to over 90 per cent, depending on the agency. See Robert L. Rabin, "Agency Criminal Referrals in the Federal System: An Empirical Study of Prosecutorial Discretion," *Stanford Law Review,* 24 (1972), 1036–1091.

53. Since Miranda v. Arizona, 384 U.S. 436 (1966), state law enforcement officials also have been required to inform the accused of these rights upon the commencement of questioning. In 1984, the Court permitted what it called a "public safety" exception to this rule. Police need not give the warning when extreme circumstances that immediately endanger the public (such as a loaded revolver hidden in a supermarket) require that a suspect be questioned. See New York v. Quarles, 104 S. Ct. 2626 (1984).

54. Under the provisions of the Speedy Trial Act (1974), and amending legislation enacted in 1979, the period from indictment to the start of trial may not exceed 70 days. See *Congressional Quarterly,* August 4, 1979, pp. 1606, 1608. For a discussion of the legislation and its implementation, see Malcolm M. Feeley, *Court Reform on Trial: Why Simple Solutions Fail* (New York: Basic Books, 1983), pp. 156–188.

55. A landmark study of plea bargaining is by Abraham S. Blumberg, "The Practice of Law as a Confidence Game: Organizational Cooptation of a Profession," *Law and Society Review,* 1 (1967), 15–39. Also see Linda Ann Carstarphen, "Sentence Bargaining at the Local Level: Perceptions and Attitudes of Judges, Prosecutors, and

Defense Attorneys," Ph.D. dissertation, University of Georgia, 1970; Jonathan D. Casper, *American Criminal Justice: The Defendant's Perspective* (Englewood Cliffs, N.J.: Prentice-Hall, 1972), pp. 77–99; George F. Cole, *Politics and the Administration of Justice* (Beverly Hills, Calif.: Sage, 1973), pp. 195–208; Lynn M. Mather, *Plea Bargaining or Trial?* (Lexington, Mass.: Heath, 1979); Herbert Jacob, *Urban Justice: Law and Order in American Cities* (Englewood Cliffs, N.J.: Prentice-Hall, 1973), pp. 96–118; David W. Neubauer, *Criminal Justice in Middle America* (Morristown, N.J.: General Learning Press, 1974), especially pp. 194–223; James Eisenstein and Herbert Jacob, *Felony Justice: An Organizational Analysis of Criminal Courts* (Boston: Little, Brown, 1977); Milton Heumann, *Plea Bargaining* (Chicago: University of Chicago Press, 1978). The *Law and Society Review* devoted an entire issue to plea bargaining. See Volume 13, Number 2 (1979), 189–687. This issue contains numerous articles, book reviews, and an extensive bibliography on the subject of plea bargaining. Also see Peter F. Nardulli, James Eisenstein, and Roy B. Flemming, "Unraveling the Complexities of Decision Making in Face-to-Face Groups: A Contextual Analysis of Plea Bargained Sentences," *American Political Science Review,* 78 (1984), in press.

56. Figure 4.1 has been constructed from data contained in Joseph A. Navarro and Jean G. Taylor, "Data Analyses and Simulation of Court System in the District of Columbia for the Processing of Felony Defendants," in *Task Force Report: Science and Technology* (The President's Commission on Law Enforcement and Administration of Justice) (Washington, D.C.: Government Printing Office, 1967), pp. 199–215. This was a study of felony cases in the U.S. District Court for the District of Columbia for calendar year 1965. Unfortunately only two figures are presented with any high degree of certainty: 6300 arrests and 1600 cases commenced. All other figures are computed from percentages contained in the study. Moreover, in comparing the data found in this study with data, admittedly less precise, from Harry I. Subin, *Criminal Justice in a Metropolitan Court: The Processing of Serious Criminal Cases in the District of Columbia Court of General Sessions* (Washington, D.C.: Department of Justice, 1966), serious discrepancies are found. In that study, the number of felony cases begun in the U.S. District Court in 1965 is put at 1200. Furthermore, in checking the number of cases commenced in the U.S. Courts, *Federal Offenders, 1967* (a publication that gives data by the fiscal rather than the calendar year), it appears that no more than about 1100 cases were commenced. In sum, the figures presented in this analysis are somewhat in controversy. Therefore, they should be treated only as approximations. However, the Navarro and Taylor data are likely to be dependable since their study was based on the actual inspection of documents relating to each case. A more recent case flow analysis (prepared by a Washington, D.C., criminal justice research firm) of a typical trial court estimated that 32 percent of those arrested on a felony charge are sentenced. See *U.S. News and World Report,* November 1, 1982, p. 41. The *Bureau of Justice Statistics Bulletin* reported the results of a four-state survey which showed a 31 percent conviction rate for those arrested on felony charges. For the District of Columbia, the figures were 7 percent of felony cases presented to the prosecutor went to trial (2 percent resulted in acquittals; 5 percent in guilty verdicts—the same proportions that are reported in Figure 4.1) and 42 percent were guilty pleas. See *Bureau of Justice Statistics Bulletin,* November 1983, pp. 1–3.

57. Note that the conviction rate in the District declined by 1970, but then turned around so that by 1976 it exceeded the 1965 level and by 1982 was still high (although under the 1976 but at the 1965 level). See Table 4-8 and the discussion in the text.

58. Subin, *Criminal Justice,* pp. 42–48.

59. *Ibid.*, p. 44.
60. Note that the highest New York state court, the New York Court of Appeals, endorsed and even encouraged plea bargaining in a series of three cases decided in October, 1974. Chief Judge Charles D. Breitel, writing for a unanimous court, observed: "In budget-starved urban criminal courts, the negotiated plea literally staves off collapse of the law enforcement system, not just as to the courts but also as to local detention facilities." As quoted in the *New York Times,* October 13, 1974, p. 70.
61. Subin, *Criminal Justice,* p. 43.
62. *Report, U.S. Courts, 1982,* Table D-6.
63. The District of Columbia, Guam, the Canal Zone, and the Virgin Islands were excluded from analysis. The middle district of Louisiana and the Northern Mariana Islands district had not yet been created.
64. *Federal Offenders, 1971* (Washington, D.C.: Administrative Office of the U.S. Courts, 1973), pp. 14–17. This was found to be true at the state level as well. See "Wide Disparities Mark Sentences Here," *New York Times,* September 27, 1972, pp. 1, 57.
65. 400 U.S. 25 (1970).
66. 404 U.S. 257 (1971). Chief Justice Burger speaking for the Court observed: "The disposition of criminal charges by agreement between the prosecutor and the accused, sometimes loosely called 'plea bargaining,' is an essential component of the administration of justice. Properly administered, it is to be encouraged. If every criminal charge were subjected to a full-scale trial, the States and the Federal Government would need to multiply by many times the number of judges and court facilities. Disposition of charges after plea discussions is not only an essential part of the process but a highly desirable part for many reasons. It leads to prompt and largely final disposition of most criminal cases; it avoids much of the corrosive impact of enforced idleness during pre-trial confinement for those who are denied release pending trial; it protects the public from those accused persons who are prone to continue criminal conduct even while on pre-trial release; and by shortening the time between charge and disposition, it enhances whatever may be the rehabilitative prospects of the guilty when they are ultimately imprisoned," 404 U.S. 257 (1971) at 260–261. The Supreme Court, in its Amendments to the Federal Rules of Criminal Procedure sent to Congress in 1974, included Rule 11(e), which specifies the plea bargaining procedure to be used in federal courts. Within Rule 11(e)(1) there is the stipulation that the judge is not to participate in any such plea bargaining discussions.
67. While accomplishing this purpose, the rationale for the Judiciary Act also, in the words of one study, "made dissenting more acceptable and expected" since the major controversial cases on which the Court would be likely to focus its attention "are not necessarily and ineluctably subject to one 'correct' solution." The authors of the study, Stephen C. Halpern and Kenneth N. Vines, documented the sharp rise in dissent rates and behavior after the 1925 act and concluded that the act may have been a necessary condition to maintain, promote, and legitimate that development. See their "Institutional Disunity, the Judges' Bill and the Role of the U.S. Supreme Court," *Western Political Quarterly,* 30 (1977), 471–483, especially p. 481.
68. See the discussion of the "special list" procedure by David J. Danelski, "The Influence of the Chief Justice in the Decisional Process of the Supreme Court," in Sheldon Goldman and Austin Sarat (eds.), *American Court Systems: Readings in Judicial Process and Behavior* (San Francisco: Freeman, 1978), p. 508. Also see S. Sidney Ulmer, William Hintze, and Louise Kirklosky, "The Decision to Grant or Deny

Certiorari: Further Consideration of Cue Theory," *Law and Society Review,* 6 (1972), 643, n. 6.

69. Starting in 1950, Miscellaneous Docket petitions were treated differently. Those petitions the Chief Justice wanted discussed at the conference were placed on a special discussion list. Any justice could add to the list. Miscellaneous Docket cases not placed on the discuss list were automatically denied review. Chief Justice Burger in the early 1970s extended this procedure to all cases. See William J. Brennan, Jr., "The National Court of Appeals: Another Dissent," *University of Chicago Law Review,* 40 (1973), 478–479.

70. *The United States Law Week,* 52 LW 3025 (1983).

71. See *Harvard Law Review,* 88 (1974), 277; and Mark W. Cannon, "Administrative Change and the Supreme Court," *Judicature,* 57 (1974), 338, n. 29.

72. Joseph Tanenhaus, Marvin Schick, Matthew Muraskin, and Daniel Rosen, "The Supreme Court's Certiorari Jurisdiction: Cue Theory," in Glendon Schubert (ed.), *Judicial Decision-Making* (New York: Free Press, 1963), pp. 111–132. Note that before June 30, 1980, when new rules went into effect, the rule governing certiorari was Rule 19. To avoid confusion, references in the text are to the renumbered Rule 17.

73. *Ibid.*

74. *Ibid.,* p. 129.

75. Ulmer found a relationship between voting to grant certiorari and voting on the merits of the cases. See S. Sidney Ulmer, "The Decision to Grant Certiorari as an Indicator to Decision 'On the Merits,' " *Polity,* 4 (1972), 429–447; and his "Supreme Court Justices as Strict and Not-So-Strict Constructionists: Some Implications," *Law and Society Review,* 8 (1973), 13–32.

76. Ulmer, Hintze, and Kirklosky, "The Decision to Grant or Deny Certiorari."

77. Doris Marie Provine, *Case Selection in the United States Supreme Court* (Chicago: University of Chicago Press, 1980).

78. *Ibid.,* p. 81.

79. *Ibid.,* p. 61.

80. When the federal government was the petitioner, in 66 percent of the cases review was granted, but when the government was respondent, only 15 percent were granted review. Provine, p. 87. Provine also found that the government's success rate depended on the subject matter of the case, with 86 percent of the antitrust cases being granted review, 82 percent of other federal regulatory decisions, 73 percent of criminal prosecutions, down to 49 percent of contracts and condemnation disputes. Provine, p. 90.

81. Twenty-six percent of the cases in which labor petitioned for review were granted. Provine, p. 85. When civil liberties claims were involved in these cases, the proportion rose to 38 percent. When corporations were the petitioners in labor disputes, only 9 percent were granted review. Provine, p. 93.

82. Provine found that 37 percent of the cases were granted review, but when states or private individuals petitioned arguing against civil liberties claimants, only 7 percent were successful in terms of review. Provine, p. 95.

83. Overall the rate was 39 percent of the cases granted review. But this also varied by petitioner, with labor having 58 percent of its cases heard when federalism was an issue to Indians having only 9 percent of their cases heard. Provine, p. 100.

84. Another test of cue theory was conducted by Niel Thomas Zimmerman, who examined the actual documents filed with the Court by the litigants in a random sample of all cases (not just certiorari petitions) brought over a ten-year period (1957

through 1966). Zimmerman found that the most important cue was the position of the government. See his "The Decision to Decide: A Statistical Analysis of the Preliminary Decision-Making Process of the United States Supreme Court," Ph.D. dissertation, University of California (Riverside), 1970. Also see Stuart H. Teger and Douglas Kosinski, "The Cue Theory of Supreme Court Certiorari Jurisdiction: A Reconsideration," *Journal of Politics,* 42 (1980), 834–846.

85. Virginia C. Armstrong and Charles A. Johnson, "Certiorari Decisions by the Warren & Burger Courts: Is Cue Theory Time Bound?" *Polity,* 15 (1982), 141–150.
86. *Ibid.,* p. 146.
87. *Ibid.,* pp. 148–149.
88. Donald R. Songer, "Concern for Policy Outputs as a Cue for Supreme Court Decisions on Certiorari," *Journal of Politics,* 41 (1979), 1185–1194. Similar findings for the California Supreme Court were first reported by Lawrence Baum in his two articles "Policy Goals in Judicial Gatekeeping: A Proximity Model of Discretionary Jurisdiction," *American Journal of Political Science,* 21 (1977), 13–35, and "Judicial Demand-Screening and Decisions on the Merits," *American Politics Quarterly,* 7 (1979), 106–119.
89. Provine, pp. 94–96, 104–130.
90. Ulmer's research is of particular importance because he demonstrated a policy-oriented linkage between the vote to grant review and the vote on the merits. See his "Selecting Cases for Supreme Court Review: An Underdog Model," *American Political Science Review,* 72 (1978), 902–910. Also see Saul Brenner, "The New Certiorari Game," *Journal of Politics,* 41 (1979), 649–655. Research by Gregory A. Caldeira has shown a linkage between ideological divisions on the Court and the proportion of all full opinions term by term that concern criminal matters. Caldeira found that when the Court was dominated by liberals, the Court was more likely than when conservatives were dominant to write full opinions on criminal justice. See his "The United States Supreme Court and Criminal Cases, 1935–1976: Alternative Models of Agenda Building," *British Journal of Political Science,* 11 (1981), 449–470.
91. *Report of the Study Group on the Case Load of the Supreme Court.* Excerpts from the report are reprinted in Walter F. Murphy and C. Herman Pritchett (eds.), *Courts, Judges and Politics,* 2nd ed. (New York: Random House, 1974), pp. 83–87. The entire report can be found in 57 Federal Rules Decisions 573–628 (1972).
92. Under the proposal, membership on the court would be limited to regularly serving appeals courts judges who have had a minimum of five years of appellate bench service. Appointments would be automatic from lists of judges by seniority and would alternate between the most senior and the most junior judges with the minimum of five years' experience and would rotate by circuit. Seven judges would serve at any one time and appointments would be for three-year terms, with the terms staggered to give continuity on the bench. A case denied review would be at the end of the legal line, although under the proposal the Supreme Court could, if it wished, take the initiative and call up the case on its own (how the justices would know very much about the case was not clear from the study group report).
93. *New York Times,* January 1, 1973, sec. 4, p. 6.
94. *New York Times,* May 2, 1973, p. 50.
95. *New York Times,* January 9, 1973, sec. 4, p. 6.
96. William J. Brennan, Jr., "National Court of Appeals: Another Dissent," *University of Chicago Law Review,* 40 (1973), 473–485.
97. *New York Times,* January 9, 1973, sec. 4, p. 6.
98. See, for example, *New York Times,* October 25, 1974, p. 14. For a systematic

empirical analysis of the problem and a critique of the proposal, see Gerhard Casper and Richard A. Posner, "A Study of the Supreme Court's Caseload," *Journal of Legal Studies,* 3 (1974), 339–375.

99. See Commission on Revision of the Federal Court Appellate System, *Structure and Internal Procedures: Recommendations for Change,* Preliminary Report, (Washington, D.C.: 1975), pp. 8–53. Chief Justice Burger and Justices White, Blackmun, Powell, and Rehnquist were reported as being favorably disposed toward the commission's proposal, while Justices Stewart, Marshall, Brennan, and Douglas were reported as being opposed to it. *New York Times,* June 21, 1975, p. 20.

100. See *New York Times,* August 15, 1982, p. E9.

101. John Paul Stevens, "Some Thoughts on Judicial Restraint," *Judicature,* 66 (1982), 177–183.

102. William J. Brennan, Jr., "Some Thoughts on the Supreme Court's Workload," *Judicature,* 66 (1983), 230–235.

103. *New York Times,* August 15, 1982, p. E9.

104. *New York Times,* November 19, 1982, p. B1.

105. *New York Times,* February 7, 1983, p. 1. The proposed new court would have a membership composed of judges drawn from all the federal circuits. The court's decisions could be appealed to the Supreme Court, but the working assumption is that the Supreme Court would not ordinarily hear such appeals.

106. For example, see Donald P. Lay, "Will the Proposed National Court of Appeals Create More Problems than It Solves?" *Judicature,* 66 (1983), pp. 437, 476; Arthur D. Hellman, "Caseload, Conflicts, and Decisional Capacity: Does the Supreme Court Need Help?" *Judicature,* 67 (1983), 28–48.

107. There is the proposal before Congress to virtually end the Court's obligatory jurisdiction so that cases coming to the Court on appeal would be treated the same way that petitions for certiorari are treated. Another proposal, to end the federal court's diversity jurisdiction, has aroused the opposition of some lawyers who fear that state courts are more biased than federal courts in dealing with out-of-state litigants (see, for example, Jerry Goldman and Kenneth S. Marks, "Diversity Jurisdiction and Local Bias: A Preliminary Empirical Inquiry," *Journal of Legal Studies,* 9 [1980], 93–104), but if enacted would also relieve the Supreme Court and lower federal courts. To discourage frivolous appeals, the Supreme Court, on June 13, 1983, ordered the petitioner of an appeal deemed frivolous to pay $500 damages to the respondent. See Tatum v. Regents of University of Nebraska—Lincoln, 103 S. Ct. 3084 (1983). Although authorized by the Court's rules, this was the first time that this was done, and Justices Brennan, Marshall, and Stevens dissented.

108. The classic statement concerning the insulation of the judicial branch is contained in *The Federalist,* No. 78. See Jacob E. Cooke (ed.), *The Federalist* (New York: World, 1961), pp. 521–530.

109. On the other hand, the organized bar and members of the legal profession frequently express *their* views. This is seen by at least one legal commentator as an important check on judicial decision making. For example, the late Dean of Harvard Law School, Roscoe Pound, once observed that "Every [judicial] decision is subject to criticism by a learned profession, to whose opinion the judge, as a member of the profession, is keenly sensitive." See Pound's "Justice According to Law, III," *Columbia Law Review,* 14 (1914), 108.

110. Alexander Bickel, *The Least Dangerous Branch* (Indianapolis: Bobbs-Merrill, 1962).

111. Glendon Schubert, *Constitutional Politics* (New York: Holt, Rinehart and Winston, 1960), p. 213.

112. Harold J. Spaeth, "Judicial Power as a Variable Motivating Supreme Court Behavior," *Midwest Journal of Political Science,* 6 (1962), 54–82. But compare Joel B. Grossman, "Role-Playing and the Analysis of Judicial Behavior: The Case of Mr. Justice Frankfurter," *Journal of Public Law,* 11 (1962), 285–309.

113. Easton, *A Framework for Political Analysis,* p. 124. Also see David Easton, "Theoretical Approaches to Political Support," *Canadian Journal of Political Science,* 9 (1976), 431–448.

114. For a general survey and assessment of the literature on public opinion and law, see Austin Sarat, "Studying American Legal Culture: An Assessment of Survey Evidence," *Law and Society Review,* 11 (1977), 427–488. Also see William J. Daniels, "The Supreme Court and Its Publics," *Albany Law Review,* 37 (1973), 632–661. A major analysis of survey data relating to support for the principal institutions of American society including the Supreme Court can be found in Seymour Martin Lipset and William Schneider, *The Confidence Gap: Business, Labor and Government in the Public Mind* (New York: Free Press, 1983).

115. Note that in this discussion of support, there is no consideration of intrasystemic support. This form of withinput is of interest as it is manifested by affirmance and reversal rates of judges and courts by the next court level as well as additional actions and remarks of judges and other authorities in the system. The empirical dimensions of such withinput have not been subjected to much scholarly scrutiny. An important exception is Richardson and Vines, *Politics of Federal Courts,* Chaps. 6 and 7. Also see Robert A. Carp, "The Scope and Function of Intra-Circuit Judicial Communication: A Case Study of the Eighth Circuit," *Law and Society Review,* 6 (1972), 405–426; Greg A. Caldeira, "Judges Judge the Supreme Court," *Judicature,* 61 (1977), 208–219; Stephen L. Wasby, "Internal Communication in the Eighth Circuit Court of Appeals," *Washington University Law Quarterly,* 58 (1980), 583–605; and Donald R. Songer, "Consensual and Nonconsensual Decisions in Unanimous Opinions of the United States Courts of Appeals," *American Journal of Political Science,* 26 (1982), 225–239.

116. See the 1949 and 1956 Gallup polls, the 1964 Michigan Survey Research Center, and 1964 Berkeley Survey Research Center surveys cited in Kenneth M. Dolbeare and Phillip E. Hammond, "The Political Party Basis of Attitudes toward the Supreme Court," *Public Opinion Quarterly,* 32 (1968), 23–24.

117. According to the Gallup polls, positive diffuse support continued its downward plunge, reaching a low point in July, 1969. The Gallup surveys asked respondents to rate the Court as either "Excellent," "Good," "Fair," or "Poor." The proportion of "Excellent" and "Good" ratings dropped from 60 percent in the 1949 poll to 45 percent in 1967, 36 percent in 1968, and finally 33 percent in the 1969 poll. Conversely, the relatively unfavorable ratings of "Fair" and "Poor" rose from 14 percent in 1949 to 46 percent in 1967, 53 percent in 1968 to 54 percent in the 1969 survey. (The balance consisted of those unable or unwilling to rate the Court.)

118. Walter F. Murphy and Joseph Tanenhaus, "Public Opinion and the United States Supreme Court: A Preliminary Mapping of Some Prerequisites for Court Legitimation of Regime Changes," *Law and Society Review,* 2 (1968), 357–384. Murphy and Tanenhaus, along with Daniel L. Kastner, reanalyzed the 1966 survey and tested a number of alternative hypotheses to explain differences in diffuse support. See Walter F. Murphy, Joseph Tanenhaus, and Daniel L. Kastner, *Public Evaluations of Constitutional Courts: Alternative Explanations,* Sage Professional Papers in Comparative Politics, Vol. 4, series no. 01-045 (Beverly Hills, Calif.: Sage, 1973). Although the reanalysis used a smaller number of respondents than utilized in the earlier Murphy

and Tanenhaus articles based on the same 1966 survey, and the methodology employed in the reanalysis was more rigorous, the general findings of the earlier studies that are used in the discussion here remain unrefuted. The reanalysis by Murphy-Tanenhaus-Kastner supports the basic proposition illustrated by Table 4.9. See Murphy, Tanenhaus, and Kastner, *Public Evaluations,* pp. 41, 51–52. Respondents from the 1966 survey were reinterviewed in 1975, and diffuse support level shown in 1966 was positively correlated (.53) with diffuse support level in 1975. Joseph Tanenhaus and Walter F. Murphy, "Patterns of Public Support for the Supreme Court: A Panel Study," *Journal of Politics,* 43 (1981), 30.

119. By 1972, as suggested by Table 4.10, positive diffuse support had plummeted across the three institutions. By 1973, however, Congress and the Court had made some very modest gains in regaining public confidence while the Watergate-mired Nixon presidency plunged still lower in the public's esteem. But in 1977 confidence in Congress took a plunge, while in 1980 both the Court and the presidency lost ground; however, both made rebounds in the 1981 survey. In general, see Lipset and Schneider, *The Confidence Gap,* Chaps. 1–5.

120. Murphy, Tanenhaus, and Kastner, *Public Evaluations of Constitutional Courts,* p. 46. This was also true in 1975. Tanenhaus and Murphy, "Patterns of Public Support," p. 33.

121. Follow-up surveys in February, 1971, and December, 1972, revealed that three out of four respondents continued to feel that the courts did not treat criminals harshly enough. The 1971 survey was conducted by the Gallup organization for and reported in *Newsweek,* March 8, 1971, p. 39. The 1972 Gallup survey was reported in the *New York Times,* January 16, 1973, p. 15. In 1981, a Gallup poll conducted for *Newsweek* and reported in the March 23, 1981, issue, p. 49, noted that 71 percent of the respondents had little or no confidence in the courts to sentence and convict criminals.

122. Murphy and Tanenhaus, "Public Opinion and the United States Supreme Court," pp. 360, 365.

123. Both the 1945 and 1949 polls are cited in Kenneth M. Dolbeare, "The Public Views the Supreme Court," in Herbert Jacob (ed.), *Law, Politics, and the Federal Courts* (Boston: Little, Brown, 1967), pp. 194–212. The Harris poll is cited in *Confidence and Concern: Citizens View American Government* (Washington, D.C.: Government Printing Office, 1973), p. 250. Note that even 12 percent of the college-educated thought that the Court was a branch of Congress.

124. Murphy and Tanenhaus, "Public Opinion," p. 368; note that 42 percent of these "unknowledgeables" did not vote in the 1964 Presidential election.

125. *Ibid.,* p. 360.

126. Dolbeare, "Public Views," pp. 199–201.

127. Murphy and Tanenhaus, "Public Opinion," pp. 360–361.

128. John H. Kessel, "Public Perceptions of the Supreme Court," *Midwest Journal of Political Science,* 10 (1966), 189, Table 12.

129. Murphy, Tanenhaus, and Kastner, *Public Evaluations of Constitutional Courts,* pp. 32–33. See Dolbeare and Hammond, "The Political Party Basis of Attitudes toward the Supreme Court," pp. 23–24. The argument, however, can be made that the partisans of the party in control of the White House will observe their President making appointments to the Court and will consider the Court part of their "government." Thus, when Republicans control the White House, Republicans should give more positive diffuse support than Democrats. The opposite should be true when Democrats control the White House. During the Republican Eisenhower Adminis-

tration, a 1956 Gallup survey asking people to rate the Court found that, nationally, Republicans gave greater positive diffuse support than did Democrats (although when the South was excluded there was little difference in support levels). In the 1973 Gallup court-rating poll, with another Republican administration in power, Republicans gave greater positive diffuse support than did Democrats. The greatest gains in positive support from the previous survey, taken at the end of the last term of the Warren Court, were in the South. See *Current Opinion,* 1 (1973), 91. More specialized segments of the attentive public, however, may base support levels not on the basis of attitudes toward the party in power generalized to the Court but rather more on the basis of policy positions. For example, a survey in 1970 of congressional candidates revealed marked differences between Democrats and Republicans in terms of their positive support for the Court in the criminal procedures areas. Democrats gave considerably more positive support than did Republicans. *Congressional Quarterly,* October 16, 1970, pp. 2564–2565.

130. Tanenhaus and Murphy, "Patterns of Public Support," pp. 24–39, especially pp. 30, 36.

131. Note that party identification was found to be unrelated to knowledge of Court decisions in the 1968 sample survey of Missouri reported in Gregory Casey, "The Supreme Court and Myth: An Empirical Investigation," *Law and Society Review,* 8 (1974), 385–419 at 405–406.

132. Murphy and Tanenhaus, "Public Opinion," p. 366. Also see Lipset and Schneider, *The Confidence Gap.*

133. Dolbeare, "Public Views," p. 201.

134. Cf. Murphy, Tanenhaus, and Kastner, *Public Evaluations of Constitutional Courts,* pp. 41–43. The public opinion findings raise serious questions about traditional assumptions concerning the "role" of the Court as a legitimizer of the actions of government. See the extensive discussion on this matter by David Adamany, "Legitimacy, Realigning Elections, and the Supreme Court," *Wisconsin Law Review* (1973), 790–846. There is evidence from a case study involving a federal district court that suggests that agreement with a court decision leads to an increase in specific support and disagreement with a court's decision leads to a substantial decrease of specific support. However, diffuse support did not change significantly for either those agreeing or those disagreeing with the particular decision. See Thomas R. Hensley, *The Kent State Incident: Impact of Judicial Process on Public Attitudes* (Westport, Conn.: Greenwood, 1981), pp. 179–184. The results from another study suggested that there is no evidence of the Supreme Court having the power to legitimate specific controversial policies. See Larry R. Baas and Dan Thomas, "The Supreme Court and Policy Legitimation," *American Politics Quarterly,* 12 (1984), 335–360. In general, see David Adamany and Joel Grossman, "Support for the Supreme Court as a National Policymaker," *Law and Politics Quarterly,* 5 (1983), 405–437.

135. Murphy and Tanenhaus, "Public Opinion," pp. 367–368, note "the strength of the association between education and awareness [is strong] ($r = .44$). . . . Thirty-nine point six percent of the totally unaware group completed less than nine years of schooling and only 6.7 percent had any college work at all. For those aware of both the Court's activity and responsibilities, the comparable figures are almost reversed, 12.4 percent and 40.4 percent."

136. *Uniform Crime Report for the United States* (Washington, D.C.: Federal Bureau of Investigation, 1968), pp. 96–97, Table 6. Victimization surveys conducted by the Census Bureau for the Law Enforcement Assistance Administration in 13 cities

found that residents experienced at least two or three times more crime than was reported by the police. The results of the study were reported in some detail in the *New York Times,* April 15, 1974, pp. 1, 51. A Gallup survey reported in 1973 that 60 percent of the residents of the center cities said there was *more* crime in their areas than in the previous year. Half of the residents of the suburbs and 45 percent of the residents in the rural areas thought that crime had increased over the year (*New York Times,* January 16, 1973, p. 15). Perhaps most to the point, a national Gallup crime victimization survey taken in December, 1972, revealed that one out of three residents of central cities had been the victim of a major crime (robbed, mugged, suffered property damage) during the previous 12 months. The figure was about one out of five for residents of suburbs and about one out of eight for residents of rural communities. See *Current Opinion,* 1 (1973), 24.

137. An early study that established this point was "Interrogations in New Haven: The Impact of *Miranda," Yale Law Journal,* 76 (1967), 1521–1648.
138. *Current Opinion,* 1 (1973), 91.
139. Note there is the suggestion in data presented by Dolbeare, "Public Views," p. 209, that believers in the judicial myth (i.e., that judging is a mechanical business and that Supreme Court judges "decide cases strictly on the basis of what the Constitution says") have a greater tendency than nonbelievers to give the Court positive diffuse support. Presumably as long as there are believers in the myth, the Court is assured of some positive diffuse support. The Casey study, "The Supreme Court and Myth," suggests that members of the attentive public are the ones likely to be the myth-holders; thus the Court has perhaps more leeway in terms of diffuse support than its friendly critics have feared.
140. *Institute for Social Research Newsletter,* 1 (1974), 8.
141. Lipset and Schneider, *The Confidence Gap,* p. 57.
142. *The Gallup Report,* Report No. 217, October, 1983.
143. See, for example, the review of the Court's 1983 term in the *New York Times,* July 8, 1984, p. 1, and the more caustic personal assessment by Anthony Lewis in the *New York Times,* July 9, 1984, p. A-19.

chapter 5

Conversion

The study of judicial conversion is the study of decision making whereby input is processed by judges into output. How and why judges decide the way they do has for many decades held a certain fascination for lawyers, political scientists, and even judges themselves. We first examine the more traditional concepts and briefly describe the development of the field of judicial behavior which has used more advanced tools for the systematic study of conversion. The subsequent sections discuss various behavioral approaches and the facets of the conversion process that are explored by utilizing them.

FROM TRADITIONALISM TO BEHAVIORALISM

The oldest and most discredited explanation of conversion has been derisively called "mechanical jurisprudence." This was, for over a century, the official and widely accepted explanation of judicial and, notably, Supreme Court behavior. In the words of President Calvin Coolidge, "Men do not make laws. They do but discover them."[1] Judges, in an exact, logical, and absolutely detached manner, merely "find" the law that already exists and apply it mechanically to the case in hand. Or to use another metaphor, the judge is a legal slot machine. You put in the case and out comes *the law,* law that is only discovered and known by the oracle–slot-machine judge. Justice Owen Roberts restated this view of judicial conversion in an often-quoted passage in the important case of *United States* v. *Butler,*[2] which declared the Agricultural Adjustment Act of 1933 unconstitutional. Roberts observed that "This Court neither approves nor condemns any legislative policy. Its delicate and difficult office is to ascertain and declare whether the legislation is in accordance with, or in contravention of, the provisions of the Constitution." How does the Court make this determination? Roberts suggested that what the Court does is "to lay the article of the Constitution which is invoked beside the statute which is challenged and to decide whether the latter squares with the former."

At odds with the notions of mechanical jurisprudence were the outspoken lawyers and judges associated with what became known as the legal realism movement. Paternity is often attributed to Oliver Wendell Holmes, who for a time before the turn of the century stood in the forefront of the assault on mechanical jurisprudence. Soon he was joined by others who developed the thesis that judging is a human process and judges have their own notions of public policy that are often absorbed into their decisions. These scholars stressed the wide range of discretion at the disposal of judges. They emphasized the opportunities for exercising choice in the interpretation or application of facts, statutes, the Constitution, rules of procedure and precedent. The high point of legal realism occurred in the 1930s. The major legal realists undertook to study judges, courts, and justice to "see it as it works."[3]

The legal realists of the 1930s, for the most part law professors, constituted a small minority of the legal profession. Their common bond was a rejection of traditional jurisprudence and an ardent desire to grasp the reality of the judicial process. Most were what have been called "rule skeptics."[4] They were skeptical of the legal rules and legal norms ostensibly used by judges. Instead they were concerned with what was actually being decided, what values were being promoted. Another type of legal realist was the "fact skeptic," a position developed by Jerome Frank.[5] At the heart of this approach was a skepticism about the ability of trial courts to discover "facts." According to Frank, each judge has idiosyncrasies that cannot help but affect performance as a judge. The process of conducting a trial and the facts that emerge are in large part attributable to the judge: likes and dislikes; what was had for breakfast; relations with spouse and family; anxieties, hopes, and aspirations; religious, social, economic, and political beliefs. For Frank each judge was unique, and the variables associated with each judge's decision making were viewed as so complex that without knowledge gained from a psychoanalysis of the judge it would be impossible to predict judicial behavior.[6]

Frank implicitly rejected empirical research on decision making. Some rule skeptics did attempt such research, but with few exceptions their work remained crude, as the realists were not concerned with developing rigorous methodology and theory to guide their research. Legal realism made little impact on the law school curriculum, and legal education has continued more or less as usual.[7] Today the stock in trade at most law schools is the case analysis approach, which assumes that case law develops rationally so that one may trace the logical connection between one case and the next. The focus is on legal logic and not the judges themselves. The basic implication is that *stare decisis* is the rule, not the exception, and as such guides judicial conversion. Much legal scholarship is thus in the more traditional vein: that is, a concern with case law in specific areas of the law, in particular, how the law developed or should develop; professional criticism of court policies concerning the standards, precedents, or reasoning of courts; or criticism of the unarticulated changes in policy. This scholarship, of course, is a source of feedback and is undoubtedly valuable in pointing the way to policy change or even change of the regime rules.

About the same time that legal realism was in its heyday, the political science profession was undergoing an analogous upheaval that was destined to change the discipline radically.[8] Political science traditionalism, with its heavy emphasis on formal rules and institutions, was challenged by political science "realists" who insisted that the first order of the discipline is to focus on how politics and our political institutions really work. How are decisions in fact really made? Who gets what, when, and how? This quest for realism among political scientists was accompanied by the development and increasing use of quantitative and statistical techniques as well as a commitment to the scientific method.[9]

Political scientists who specialized in the field of constitutional or public law had largely followed the lead of the legal academics, and the thrust of their work was on legalistic analyses of cases. An increasing number of scholars, however, no doubt influenced by the trends in the other areas of the discipline, began to produce judicial biographies, political histories of the Supreme Court, case studies of particular decisions, descriptive studies of the social characteristics and selection processes of judges and other participants in the judicial process, and descriptive analyses of the activities of interest groups in their attempts to influence decision making.[10]

The breakthrough that began the development of the behavioral approach to judicial conversion was achieved by Professor C. Herman Pritchett, who began where the legal realists left off.[11] His attention was on the Supreme Court, and his concern was with the voting alignments and policy preferences of the justices. His theory of conversion was that all courts, but especially the Supreme Court, are political agencies and that judges are political actors whose attitudes toward the substantive issues are often decisive in shaping their votes and opinions. Pritchett focused on nonunanimously decided Supreme Court cases because they offered the most compelling evidence that the judges "are operating on different assumptions, that their inarticulate major premises are dissimilar, that their value systems are differently constructed and weighted, that their political, economic, and social views contrast in important respects."[12]

In the late 1950s, Glendon Schubert, Joseph Tanenhaus, Sidney Ulmer, and others began to build on Pritchett's work and also to develop new methodologies for the study of judicial behavior. They were innovators in their use of cumulative scaling of judicial decisions and the use of the phi coefficient, factor analysis, and other statistical techniques to analyze judicial behavior. By the late 1960s, attention had turned to other American courts aside from the Supreme Court, further development of theories of judicial behavior (some by way of causal models), and the use of techniques developed to study the Supreme Court to study the courts of other countries.[13] These trends have continued well into the 1980s.

ATTITUDES AND DECISION MAKING

The attitudinal approach to conversion is the approach perhaps most identified with the field of judicial behavior. From the pioneering work of Pritchett to the work of the current generation of behavioral scholars, discovery and analysis of patterns of behavior that could be shown to represent judicial attitudes has been of primary research interest.[14] Voting behavior of individual judges is studied in order to discern regularities of behavior that might exist. The central hunch is that attitudes and values guide voting behavior and that the votes in specific cases—*what the authorities actually do*—are more important in revealing their attitudes and values than are the rationalizations they provide in their written opinions telling us why they voted as they did.

This focus on *voting* behavior as providing the clue to judges' attitudes and values does not necessarily mean that written opinions are considered irrelevant for these concerns. They can and have been used as data for behavioral analysis, and the computerized content analysis method in particular has been used to discover underlying attitudinal dimensions.[15]

Among the principal methodologies used individually or in concert in judicial attitudinal research are bloc analysis and Guttman scaling. Many studies have used other statistical tools as well.[16] Some of the major studies using these various methods will be briefly discussed, particularly in terms of research concerning federal judges. It should be acknowledged, however, that blocs, scale patterns, or issue voting support scores cannot be used to conclusively *prove* (in the scientific sense of the term) the attitudinal hypothesis as there is no measure of judges' attitudes and values independent of their votes. Thus we cannot say that attitudes *cause* votes when we have defined those attitudes in terms of the same votes. Nevertheless, it is clear that if the attitudinal hypothesis were invalid, neither repeated findings of bloc voting, scale patterns, nor consistent issue-oriented voting would be found. It is therefore reasonable to suggest that judges tend to behave *as if* their attitudes and values governed their voting choices. One can, therefore, have a firm basis for evaluating the attitudinal hypothesis taking into account the close to three decades of research results from numerous studies.

Bloc Analysis

C. Herman Pritchett was the first to study systematically judicial bloc voting. In his analyses of the Supreme Court, he theorized that attitudes are the key to judicial conversion, that nonunanimously decided cases can best reveal attitudinal differences, and that judges with similar attitudes and values will tend to agree with each other in these cases and thus vote together forming "blocs." Pritchett analyzed the voting data in various ways, including the construction of matrices[17] of agreement scores (i.e., the percentage of nonunanimous cases in which every two-judge combination voted alike). He found two principal voting blocs, one consisting of judges who usually voted for "liberal" decisional results, and the other consisting of judges who typically opted for the more "conservative" solutions.[18]

Table 5.1 SUBGROUPS IN THE U.S. SUPREME COURT, 1946–1983 TERMS

	1946 (3)	
BL, MU, DO, RU	RE, BU	FR, JA, VI
	1947 (3)	
BL, MU, DO, RU	RE, BU, VI	FR, JA
	1948 (4)	
BL, DO MU, RU	RE, BU, VI	FR, JA
	1949 (3)	
BL, DO	RE, BU, VI, CL, MI	FR, JA
	1950 (4)	
BL, DO	RE, VI, CL BU, MI	FR, JA
	1951 (2)	
BL, DO, FR, JA	RE, BU, VI, CL, MI	
	1952 (4)	
BL, DO	RE, BU, MI VI, CL	FR, JA
	1953 (4)	
BL, DO	RE, BU WA, CL	FR, JA, MI
	1954–1955 (3)	
BL, DO, WA, CL	RE, BU, MI	FR, HA
	1956 (3)	
BL, DO, WA, BR	RE, CL	FR, HA, BU
	1957 (3)	
BL, DO, WA, BR	WH, BU, CL	FR, HA
	1958–1961 (2)	
BL, DO, WA, BR	WH, CL, ST, FR, HA	
	1962 (3)	
BL, DO, WA, BR, GO	WI, ST	CL, HA
	1968 (2)	
BL[a], DO, WA, BR, MA, FO	WI, ST, HA	
	1969 (3)	
DO, BR, MA	WI, HA	ST, BG, BL[a]
	1970 (2)	
DO, BR, MA		ST, BG, BL[a], HA, WI, BM
	1971 (2)	
DO, BR, MA, ST		BG, WI, BM, PO, RN
	1972 (2)	
DO, BR, MA		BG, WI, BM, PO, RN, ST
	1973 (3)	
DO, BR, MA	ST, PO, WI	BM, BG, RN
	1974 (2)	
DO, BR, MA		BM, BG, RN, ST, PO, WI
	1975 (2)	
BR, MA		BG, BM, RN, PO, WI, ST, SV
	1976 (2)	
BR, MA, SV		BG, BM, RN, PO, WI, ST
	1977 (3)	
BR, MA	PO, BM	BG, RN, WI, ST, SV[b]
	1978 (3)	
BR, MA, SV	WI, BM	BG, RN, PO, ST
	1979 (3)	
BR, MA, SV	PO, ST	BG, RN, WI, BM
	1980 (2)	
BR, MA		BG, BM, RN, PO, WI, ST, SV[b]
	1981 (3)	

Table 5.1 *(Continued)*

BR, MA	SV, BM	BG, RN, PO, WI, OC
	1982 (3)	
BR, MA, SV, BM	BG, PO, WI	RN, OC
	1983 (2)	
BR, MA, SV		BG, PO, WI, RN, OC, BM

Legend:

BG	Burger	GO	Goldberg			RN	Rehnquist
BL	Black	HA	Harlan			RU	Rutledge
BM	Blackmun	JA	Jackson			ST	Stewart
BR	Brennan	MA	Marshall			SV	Stevens
BU	Burton	MI	Minton			WA	Warren
CL	Clark	MU	Murphy			WH	Whittaker
DO	Douglas	OC	O'Connor			WI	White
FO	Fortas	PO	Powell			VI	Vinson
FR	Frankfurter	RE	Reed				

Source: The 1946–1961 subgroups from S. Sidney Ulmer, "Toward a Theory of Sub-Group Formation in the United States Supreme Court," *Journal of Politics,* 27 (1965), p. 146, Table 1. Note that the positions of subgroups in the table should *not* be taken to mean that they were either "left," "right," or "center," in terms of their attitudes and values. The 1962 and 1968–1983 subgroups were derived from voting behavior on civil liberties cases only.

[a]Black's placement in this subgroup is an artifact of the method (the McQuitty technique) that requires that each justice be placed with the justice with whom he or she has the greatest correlation. Justice Black, however, exhibited such idiosyncratic behavior that in no meaningful sense can he be said to have "belonged" with a subgroup. For more on Justice Black, see note 22.

[b]Stevens's placement is an artifact of the method. Link with subgroup tenuous at best.

Glendon Schubert, in the late 1950s, suggested refinements to Pritchett's method and introduced several indices including the index of interagreement (i.e., the average agreement score of the justices in the hypothesized bloc).[19] In later years other methods of undertaking bloc analysis were devised and utilized.[20]

One scholar, S. Sidney Ulmer, undertook an extensive bloc analysis of the Supreme Court.[21] He began by assuming that the existence of a voting bloc at one point in time does not necessarily demonstrate that common attitudes and values account for the bloc-voting phenomenon. It is possible, Ulmer suggested, for a voting bloc to represent a coalition of judges with a diversity of views who find it mutually advantageous to vote together in the short run because, for example, they wish to dominate the Court by being on the winning side. A subgroup or bloc can be interpreted as representing common attitudes and values only if the voting bloc persists and thus has stability over time. The results of Ulmer's study of voting in nonunanimous cases decided by the Supreme Court from the 1946 term through the 1961 term are presented in Table 5.1 (along with similar analyses for more recent terms). Ulmer found not only that voting blocs occurred during each term of the Court, but that there was a large extent of stability in the alignments over time. Although the nonunanimous cases studied covered a wide variety of issues, Ulmer found that the voting blocs actually voted together for the most part in a large proportion of nonunanimous decisions. Ulmer concluded that common attitudes and values underlie the formation of voting blocs. As Table 5.1 suggests, the blocs of more recent years continue to demonstrate enduring stability of membership, although there has been some fluctuation when new members have joined the Court. There have been three justices, however—Black, Blackmun, and Stevens—who have behaved atypically.[22]

It is beyond serious question today that the judges of the Supreme Court have their own conceptions of public policy and that their attitudes and values affect the thrust of their decision making. Bloc analysis of the Supreme Court has been instrumental not only in specifically demonstrating differences of views on the Court but in suggesting their magnitude.

Bloc analysis of the courts of appeals has also repeatedly uncovered evidence of voting blocs on these courts,[23] lending further credence to the attitudinal approach to *judicial* and not just Supreme Court conversion.

One further word about bloc analysis is in order. The existence of voting blocs *suggests* that judicial attitudes are instrumental for judicial conversion. The existence of voting blocs, however, does *not* imply that judges consider themselves members of a bloc, or that they caucus to discuss strategy, or that the bloc assumes a life of its own, with bloc loyalties independent of attitudes affecting voting behavior. The assumption is simply that judges who have similar attitudes and values independently examine the issues before them and then vote alike. As one critic of bloc analysis concedes, bloc analysis "may still be a useful tool in describing the commonality of views shared by Justices."[24] However, the technique has a major drawback in that it can only provide a crude measure of attitudes and values. No account is taken of the variation in the case stimuli and thus the variations of the voting responses. The methodology of Guttman scaling, on the other hand, is attuned to this problem and has been used by students of judicial behavior for precisely this purpose.

Guttman Scaling

Guttman scaling, sometimes referred to as cumulative scaling or scalogram analysis, was first developed by Louis Guttman in the early 1940s to determine whether a series of attitude questions on interview schedules measured the same underlying attitude.[25] Guttman suggested that if the questions in fact tap the same underlying attitudinal dimension, then the questions and responses can be arranged so that there is an attitudinal continuum indicating varying degrees of intensity of the underlying dimension. This pattern of responses is a *scale* and as such contains certain properties. We are able to determine where each question (i.e., stimulus) falls on the attitudinal continuum. We can also determine the break-off point of each respondent, that is, the point at which the stimulus will produce a negative response in terms of the underlying attitudinal dimension. The scale is cumulative in that it represents a continuum and each item is ordinally related (i.e., contains more, less, or the same) to the items above and below it on the scale. Perhaps the most interesting property of a scale is that once you know a respondent's scale score, you can exactly predict the response to the items in the scale or, if the respondent did not respond to certain items, what the responses ought to have been were the respondent attitudinally consistent.

The conventional example of a scale is one in which the questions relate to the respondent's height, and the underlying dimension is thus height. For example, the following questions will normally produce a perfect scale:

1. Are you five feet tall or more?
2. Are you five feet, eight inches, tall or more?
3. Are you six feet tall or more?

These responses fall on a continuum. If we know the respondent's scale score (derived from the scale position which is fixed by the last consistent positive response) we can accurately predict the responses to the questions as well as fill in nonresponses.

Typically with attitude measurement the empirically obtained pattern of response differs from the perfect scale pattern because of a variety of reasons. For example, the respondent misunderstood or misinterpreted the question or had great difficulty deciding how to respond. It is useful then to be able to measure the extent to which the empirically obtained scale corresponds to the perfect scale and indeed to formulate a criterion to determine when a pattern of responses can be said to represent a scale. Guttman proposed the coefficient of reproducibility (CR) for these tasks.[26] A CR of 0.90 (90 percent reproducibility) or more was suggested as indicating that the response pattern was a scale characterized by "unidimensionality," that is, a common attitudinal dimension.

Glendon Schubert took the lead in developing Guttman scaling for the analysis of Supreme Court voting behavior.[27] What Schubert did was to consider the cases as representing questions and the votes (*not* the opinions) of the justices to be the responses. Unanimously decided cases are eliminated from the scales, and in practice decisions with only one dissenting vote are eliminated from the computations of CR to decrease the likelihood that CR will be spuriously high. In addition to CR, other measures of scalability have been devised such as the coefficient of scalability (S), which takes into account all inconsistent responses and the maximum number of opportunities for inconsistent votes.[28]

Before a scalogram is constructed, it is necessary to hypothesize the existence of an attitude underlying the cases. The hypothesized attitude should be plausible; that is, it should make some sense to begin with and should not be trivial (in order to reduce the possibility of constructing a spurious scale).

Through the use of cumulative scaling of voting responses, Schubert, Ulmer, Danelski, Spaeth, and other students of judicial behavior have presented ample evidence *suggesting* that the justices have varying attitudes toward the substantive issues before them.[29] It has been fairly well established that, at least since 1946, two major underlying attitudinal dimensions have characterized most Supreme Court voting behavior in nonunanimously decided cases. They have been represented by two scales; the C (for civil liberties) and the E (for economic liberalism). The C scale, according to Schubert, contains all cases in which the primary issues involved a conflict between individual rights and liberties and the exercise of governmental authority.[30] The E scale, Schubert has suggested, contains cases whose underlying characteristic is that they involve "an underdog economic relationship . . . conflicts of interest between the economically affluent and the economically underprivileged."[31]

Harold Spaeth and associates also undertook extensive scaling of Supreme Court decisions. Particularly noteworthy about this work was the detailed development of attitude and value theory[32] and Spaeth's newspaper and radio predictions of pending Court decisions and votes (his high rate of correct predictions itself won media attention[33]). Spaeth's method involves the use of refined category scales that differentiate between and among subject matter (attitude toward the situation) and the litigants or interests involved (attitude to-

Table 5.2 1982 TERM C SCALE

Cases	M	Br	Sv	Bl	W	P	Bu	O'	R	Totals
103/2398			$\underline{x}$							1–8
103/2532			$\underline{x}$							1–8
103/321	x									1–8
103/394	x									1–8
103/1548	x									1–8
103/673	x		$\underline{x}$							2–7
103/916	x		$\underline{x}$							2–7
103/1736	x	x								2–7
103/2733	x	x								2–7
103/3308	x	x								2–7
103/1108	x	x		$\underline{x}$						3–6
103/1974	x	x		$\underline{x}$						3–6
103/3383	x	x		$\underline{x}$						3–6
103/3418	x	x		$\underline{x}$						3–6
103/1741	x	x	x							3–6
103/2261	x	x	x							3–6
103/2317	x	x	x							3–6
103/2573	x	x	x							3–6
103/3319	x	x	x							3–6
103/3330	x	x	x							3–6
103/3469	x	x	x							3–6
103/3513	x	x	x							3–6
103/3517	x	x	x							3–6
103/948	x	x	x			$\underline{x}$				4–5
103/843	x	x	x	x						4–5
103/864	x	x	x	x						4–5
103/1660	x	x	x	x						4–5
103/1684	x	x	x	x						4–5
103/1933	x	x	x	x						4–5
103/2517	x	x	x	x						4–5
103/2830	x	x	x	x						4–5
103/3043	x	x	x	x						4–5
103/3062	x	x	x	x						4–5
103/3446	x	x	x	x						4–5
103/1564	x	x	x	x			$\underline{x}$			5–4
103/3001	x	x	x	x		$\underline{x}$				5–4
103/969	x	x	x	x	x					5–4
103/1625	x	x	x	x	x					5–4
103/3133	x	x	x	x	x					5–4
103/1319	x	x	x	—	x	x				5–4
103/2517	x	x	x	x	—	x	x			6–3
103/416	x	x	—	x	x	x	x			6–3
103/2481	x	x	x	x	—	x	x			6–3
103/2764	x	x	x	x	—	x	x	x		7–2
103/1855	x	x	x	x	—	x	x	x		7–2
103/505	x	x	x	x	x	x	x	x		8–1
103/1365	x	x	x	x	x	x	x	x		8–1
103/608	x	x	—	x	x	x	x	—	x	7–2
103/3164	x	x	x	x	x	x	—	x	x	8–1
										191–250
										441

Table 5.2 (Continued)

Cases	M	Br	Sv	Bl	W	P	Bu	O'	R	Totals
Totals	47–2	42–7	37–12	28–21	9–40	12–37	9–40	5–44	2–47	191–250
Scale positions	47	42	35	25	13	10	9	6	2	
Scale scores	+0.918	0.714	0.429	0.020	−0.469	−0.592	−0.633	−0.755	−0.918	

$$CR = 1 - \frac{17}{369} = .954 \qquad\qquad S = 1 - \frac{20}{79} = .747$$

Legend:
Bl	Blackmun	M	Marshall	R	Rehnquist
Br	Brennan	O'	O'Connor	Sv	Stevens
Bu	Burger	P	Powell	W	White

* nonparticipation
x consistent vote in support of civil liberties claim
<u>x</u> inconsistent vote in favor of civil liberties claim
(blank) represents consistent negative vote
−inconsistent negative vote
Case citations from *Supreme Court Reporter* advance sheets. The numbers preceding the slash bar refer to the volume number; the numbers following the slash bar refer to the page citations.

ward the object). The refined category scales provide the basis for determining attitudes, while values are defined as sets of interrelated attitudes. Spaeth and associates identified three major values for the Warren and Burger Courts: Freedom (including rights of criminal defendants and First Amendment freedoms scales), Equality (encompassing political, economic, and racial discrimination scales), and New Dealism (covering economic activity and government regulation scales). Spaeth made his predictions after subjectively determining what attitudes were involved in pending cases and the strength of the claims being made. Spaeth then compared the past behavior of the judges on the particular refined category scale and made his predictions accordingly.[34] Spaeth was able to correctly predict over nine out of ten decisions. Over a decade earlier Schubert, who originated a similar method, correctly predicted reapportionment cases that were then coming to the Court.[35] By successfully predicting Supreme Court voting behavior using past behavior as measured through the use of cumulative scaling, we have still more evidence of the plausibility of the attitudinal hypothesis (although such prediction techniques make some observers uncomfortable because of the subjective aspects of identifying the strength of the case stimuli).

Three scales from the 1982–1983 term are presented in Tables 5.2, 5.3, and 5.4. Table 5.2 is the C scale without the equality cases. Table 5.3 is the EQ or

Table 5.3 1982 TERM EQ SCALE

Cases	M	Bl	W	Br	Sv	O'	Bu	P	R	Totals
103/1838	x									1–8
103/998	x	x	x							3–6
103/2985	x	x	x							3–6
103/2690	x	x	x	x						4–5
103/3221	x	x	—	x	x					4–5
103/3493[a]	x	—	x	x	x					4–5
103/3352	x	x	—	x	—	x				4–5
103/3493[a]	x	—	x	x	x	x				5–4
103/2653	x	x	—	x	x	x				5–4
103/530	x	x	x	x	x	—	x			6–3
103/2622	x	x	x	x	x	x	x			7–2
103/2017	x	x	x	x	x	x	x	x		8–1
										54–54
Totals	12–0	9–3	8–4	9–3	7–5	5–7	3–9	1–11	0–12 / 54–54	108
Scale positions	12	11	11	9	8	6	3	1	0	
Scale scores	+1.000	0.833	0.833	0.500	0.333	0.000	−0.500	−0.833	−1.000	

$$CR = 1 - \frac{7}{90} = .922 \qquad\qquad S = 1 - \frac{7}{24} = .708$$

Legend: Same as that for C scale with exception that votes are in support or opposition to the equality claim.
[a]Two separate votes in this case.

equality scale that includes cases raising issues of racial, sexual, political, or economic discrimination. Table 5.4 is the E scale. It is of interest to note the different positions of the justices on the three scales. For example, Justice O'Connor's scale scores on the C and E scales place her with Justice Rehnquist as the two most conservative justices on these dimensions, while on the EQ dimension she is seen as considerably more liberal than Rehnquist and, relative to her colleagues, in a middle-of-the-road position. It is not unreasonable to infer that her experience as a woman in a male-dominated society sufficiently sensitized her to equality issues so as to counter in part her more conservative tendencies. These scales also suggest the continuing polarization on the Burger Court.

It should be clear, however, that only collegial courts with a constant membership are best suited for scalogram analysis. The three-judge appeals court panel with shifting membership, the specially constituted ad hoc three-judge district court panel, and the single-judge district court are generally not appropriate subjects for this method. Although most appeals courts occasionally decide

Table 5.4 1982 TERM E SCALE

Cases	M	Br	W	Bl	Bu	Sv	P	R	O'	Totals
103/897	x									1–8
103/2045	x									1–8
103/3172	x	x					x			3–6
103/2266	x	x	x				*			3–5
103/1587	x	—	x							2–7
103/3255	x	x	—	x						3–6
103/3024	x	x	x	x						4–5
103/2218	x	x	x	x	x					5–4
103/2856	x	x	x	x	—	x				5–4
103/2706	x	x	x	x	x	x				6–3
103/1453	x	x	x	x	x	x				6–3
103/1011	x	—	x	x	x	—	x			5–4
103/2281	x	x	x	x	x	—	x	x		7–2
103/665	x	x	x	x	x	x	x	x		8–1
103/634	x	x	x	x	x	—	x	x	x	8–1
										67–67
										134
Totals	15–0	11–4	11–4	10–5	7–8	4–11	5–9	3–12	1–14 / 67–67	
Scale positions	15	13	12	10	8	7	4	3	1	
Scale scores	+1.000	0.733	0.600	0.333	0.067	−0.067	−0.047	−0.600	−0.867	

$$CR = 1 - \frac{7}{98} = .929 \qquad\qquad S = 1 - \frac{8}{33} = .758$$

Legend: Same as that for C scale with exception that votes are in support of or opposition to the economic liberalism claim.

cases *en banc* (i.e., the entire membership of the particular appeals court decides the case), such cases for most circuits tend to be too infrequent to allow for meaningful cumulative scaling, although by combining several years' worth of *en banc* cases it has been possible to construct some scales for some circuits.[36]

Guttman scaling has been the subject of some criticism,[37] in part over the criteria used to establish a valid scale and the manipulations used to achieve the least number of inconsistencies. There has also been serious question of the assumption of unidimensionality, the argument being that cases often concern many issues and that to focus on one dimension distorts the complexity and neglects the richness of "law." These charges have been answered by Glendon Schubert and Sidney Ulmer[38] (the precise rebuttal need not concern us here). What is of great importance is that all but the most adamant antibehavioralists concede that cumulative scaling is useful *at least* as the beginning of analysis. It is also apparent that the continued successful cumulative scaling of Supreme Court decisions underscores the plausibility of the attitudinal interpretation of judicial conversion.

Other Methods

The attitudinal assumption has also been tested by other methods such as simple correlational analysis of support or opposition scores (e.g., concerning civil liberties or subcategories thereof) based on the votes of judges. This method has been used particularly for the analysis of voting behavior of lower federal court judges; for example, one study examined the voting behavior of appeals court judges and found that there were significant positive correlations in the voting behavior of judges on various issues.[39] There was a marked tendency for a judge who tended to support the claims of the criminally prosecuted to support the individual presenting a civil liberties claim against the actions of government, the labor union or employee in controversies with management, the underdog claim in private economic cases, and claims by the physically injured. The interpretation of these results was that a liberalism-conservatism voting syndrome exists on the appeals courts just as it does on the Supreme Court.[40] A study by Burton Atkins of voting behavior on the District of Columbia circuit involved the scaling of *en banc* criminal procedures decisions and the determination of pro-defendant (liberal) and anti-defendant (conservative) judges on that broadly defined set of issues.[41] Atkins found that panels dominated by judges identified by the scale as liberal produced a considerably larger proportion of liberal decisions than those panels dominated by previously identified conservatives. For the deep South (the pre-1981) Fifth Circuit on the racial segregation issue, Atkins and Zavoina found convincing statistical evidence suggesting that the attitudes of the judges during the tense period of the early 1960s were likely to have been taken into account by the chief judge of the circuit in making panel assignments in race cases.[42] Other work as well concerning the appeals courts has lent support for the attitudinal explanation of judicial voting behavior.[43]

BACKGROUNDS AND DECISION MAKING

Closely associated with the attitudinal approach to judicial conversion is the backgrounds approach. The focus of this approach is on the various socioeconomic, political, and professional backgrounds (or attributes) of judges and whether they may be linked with judicial behavior. The types of questions asked in background/behavior analysis are: Does it make a difference in terms of how a judge will decide cases if he or she is, for example, Catholic rather than Protestant? older rather than younger? a Democrat rather than a Republican? from a lower social class rather than a higher social class? has an Ivy League law school education rather than a public law school education? from a small law firm rather than a large Wall Street–type firm? white rather than black? male and not female? The assumption has been that, just like all people, a judge is a product of his or her attributes and experiences, and that a knowledge of certain backgrounds may be the key to understanding that judge's decisional behavior. The problem, of course, is to differentiate between those backgrounds that may be directly relevant for judicial behavior and those that are not. Earlier, in Chapter 3, some backgrounds of federal judges were discussed. The implication was that these were likely to be related to their decision making. This implication deserves closer scrutiny.

Essentially, background studies suggest that certain backgrounds are conducive to the formation of certain attitudes that in turn may affect the decisional behavior of the judge; that is, these backgrounds provide the foundation or the setting for the development of attitudes and values. However, each judge's attitudes and values have been tempered by a host of experiential, institutional, and interpersonal variables once on the bench. Political party affiliation is one background variable that has been thought to be a summary variable of relevant backgrounds and attitudes. But party affiliation, as well as other attributes, has not been considered identical to attitudes or values. Nevertheless, those undertaking background/behavior analysis hypothesize that some relationships between discrete backgrounds and judicial behavior can be found, and the testing of these hypotheses has been at both the group and individual levels.

Aggregate background/behavior analysis of the Supreme Court has posed some problems because only a small number of justices sit at any one time and generalizations from such a small group may not be too reliable. Similarly, consideration of the entire past and present membership of the Supreme Court for purposes of analysis raise methodological problems, such as the comparability of attributes from different social and economic periods. However, S. Sidney Ulmer, in an exploratory study of 14 justices who served during the 1947–1956 time period, found that three background variables were strongly related in a statistical sense to the voting of the justices on criminal justice issues.[44] A more elaborate test with Supreme Court justices was conducted by C. Neal Tate.[45] Tate examined the relationship of some 20 attributes to the civil liberties and economic liberalism voting behavior of 25 justices who had served on the Court between 1946 and 1978. He found that the political party affiliation of the justices, the appointing President, the type of prosecutorial experience, and the extent of judicial experience were strongly associated with both civil liberties and economic liberalism voting. Tate's attribute models explained from 72 to 87 percent of the variance.

Lower federal courts with larger numbers of judges with which to conduct analyses have been examined in terms of the relationship of attributes to behavior. One extensive study of appeals court judges and the cases they decided during fiscal 1965 through fiscal 1971 included tests of the relationships of certain background variables to decision making.[46] The findings were that, *in the aggregate,* most of the demographic variables for the most part could not be directly related to voting behavior. Party affiliation, however, proved to have a moderately strong association with voting behavior on issues involving economic liberalism and, to a lesser extent, political liberalism. The age variable seemed to be associated to some extent with political liberalism issues and to a lesser extent with economic issues. Religion had a relatively minor association with primarily economic issues. Thus, judges who were Democrats, younger judges, and Catholics *tended* to be more "liberal" than those who were Republicans, older judges, and Protestants. However, background variables were much weaker than attitudinal variables in their association with judicial behavior. The study did not downplay background variables, but rather concluded that their primary importance lies in the part they play in shaping the hierarchy of values, the philosophy, outlook, and attitudes of *individual* judges. Further work with appeals judges revealed that past judicial voting behavior was primarily associated with subsequent voting behavior, with certain background variables adding only somewhat to the explanation of variation in voting behavior among the judges.[47] Still other recent work suggests that gender and race may be linked to judicial voting behavior tendencies in certain areas of civil liberties.[48]

Several studies of federal district court judges also tested the nexus of backgrounds to behavior. Kenneth Vines conducted a study concerned with southern district court judges and their decisional behavior in cases involving civil rights of blacks. He found somewhat of a tendency for southern judges with cosmopolitan backgrounds (e.g., they were born outside the state in which they served as district judges, they went to a law school in a state other than the one in which they sat as judges, they had ties and contacts outside the district) to render more pro–civil rights decisions than those without such backgrounds.[49] Micheal Giles and Thomas Walker also conducted an analysis of southern district judge behavior, but only in the school desegregation realm.[50] Their study covered a later time period than that studied by Vines. Giles and Walker found that the background variables discovered by Vines to be significantly associated with district judge behavior in race relation cases were (with the exception of the judge's educational background) minimally related to the level of school desegregation ordered by the judge. They found that the percentage of black students enrolled, the size of the school district, and, most interestingly, whether the school district was located geographically in the heart of the area in which the district court was physically located were most important for determining the level of segregation allowed by the district judge.[51]

Kenneth Dolbeare studied the voting behavior of a sample of federal district judges situated in urban areas, but did not discover any relationship between backgrounds (including party affiliation) and decisional behavior.[52] Thomas Walker's study of federal district judges found little association between party and civil liberties voting behavior.[53] However, the most extensive study of federal district judge behavior, conducted by Robert Carp and C. K. Rowland, came up with sharply different findings.[54] The Carp and Rowland study contained sufficient numbers of cases (i.e., a large enough data base) so that they could more rigorously test background/behavior hypotheses than could Dolbeare and Walker.[55] The most significant finding of Carp and Rowland is that the appointing President and, to a somewhat lesser extent, the party affiliation of the judges were closely associated with district judge voting behavior.

When the unit of analysis is the individual and not the group, the relationship of backgrounds to behavior becomes more apparent. The mainstay of such analysis is judicial biography. One assessment of 15 major judicial biographies (all but two of them concerned Supreme Court justices) found that, with only one exception, every biographer sought to demonstrate the relationship of the particular judge's backgrounds to subsequent judicial behavior.[56] In a study of the appointment of Pierce Butler to the Supreme Court, David Danelski utilized cumulative scaling to demonstrate the relationship of Butler's experience as a railroad lawyer (in the context of his previous experiences) to his subsequent voting behavior in support of railroads and utilities in rate and valuation cases.[57] Danelski also suggested that Butler's Roman Catholicism accounted for his dissenting behavior in at least two cases (one in which the Court upheld the constitutionality of Virginia's law authorizing compulsory sterilization of the feeble-minded and the other in which the Court ruled that a former resident alien, an unmarried woman who was living with a married man, was entitled to readmission to the United States).[58] In a study of Justice Harold Burton, Danelski convincingly linked Burton's American Legion background to his policy orientation as a justice.[59]

It would appear, then, that the investigation of the relevance of backgrounds to behavior is essentially an examination of those life experiences (and attributes that presumably characterize those experiences) that mold certain attitudes, shape the value hierarchies, and affect the way the individual perceives and interprets reality. Life experiences and attributes are numerous, and the combinations of different backgrounds are obviously countless. Even the same discrete attribute—such as religion, race, sex, type of law school attended, or type of law practice engaged in—may mask a multitude of varying individual experiences. It should therefore be no surprise that, although several aggregate analyses have shown some statistical relationships, analysis of individual judges strongly suggests a relationship of an individual's backgrounds to subsequent decision making. The point, of course, is not that judges are necessarily prisoners of their past, but that at least part of their judicial behavior is probably accounted for by their attitudes and philosophical outlook as it has been shaped by their life experiences.

SMALL GROUP ANALYSIS

A judge comes to the bench with numerous attitudes and a hierarchy of values formed during a lifetime of experiences and, perhaps, even an inchoate judicial philosophy. If appointed to a collegial court, he or she discovers that decision making is a group endeavor and not simply an individual act made in isolation. It is this small group nature of collegial court decision making that provides another perspective on judicial conversion. This perspective, sometimes with explicit reference to social psychological concepts, suggests a focus on various types of group interaction in the process of rendering decisions and suggests that the group condition itself affects the kinds of decisions made.[60] The principal data are mined from the private papers of deceased judges.[61]

Walter Murphy suggested that much of the interaction among the justices (and presumably judges on other collegial courts) may be governed by strategic considerations of individual justices. In his classic study, *Elements of Judicial*

Strategy, Murphy considered various interpersonal activities in which policy-oriented justices could engage and which would directly or indirectly enhance their influence with their colleagues and thus promote acceptance of their strongly held policy views.[62] Such activities include persuasion, bargaining, friendship, and social amenities. A brief discussion of each follows. Small group leadership analysis that explicitly utilizes social psychological concepts will also be examined, along with some additional considerations of the small group approach.

Persuasion

One course of action open to a judge on a collegial court is to attempt to persuade the other judges through logical argument of the correctness of his or her view of the particular case before them. With the Supreme Court, the weekly judicial conferences offer the primary forum for such activity. Subsequent face-to-face meetings and the circulation of memoranda and drafts of majority, concurring, and dissenting opinions are other vehicles for maintaining a dialogue among justices as well as permitting policy-oriented justices to press their views.

Were all the justices to hold their policy views on the same matter before them with equal intensity of commitment, negotiation rather than persuasion would characterize all interpersonal relationships. But the available evidence suggests[63] that (1) the attitudes of all justices on all matters are not held with the same intensity; (2) some issues before the Court are sufficiently novel or present a multiplicity of conflicting values so that at least some justices are open to persuasion; and (3) in complex cases some justices may have initial difficulty in identifying issues, and they may be swayed by a policy-oriented justice's arguments concerning the depiction of the problem.

Several examples of the use of persuasion by a justice with strongly held policy views under these varying circumstances can be found in the papers of Supreme Court justices. For example, in 1947 the Vinson Court considered the issue of indirect state aid to parochial schools by way of subsidizing the transportation costs of parochial school students (the case *Everson* v. *Board of Education*[64] concerned a New Jersey statute permitting such subsidies).[65] This forced the Court to consider the prohibition against the establishment of religion found in the First Amendment and its application to the states through the Fourteenth Amendment. When the transportation subsidy was first discussed in conference, Justice Rutledge vigorously articulated his policy view that there must be an absolute separation between church and state and that the line must be drawn with the subsidy in question. Rutledge argued, "First it has been books, now buses, next churches and teachers. Every religious institution in the country will be reaching into the hopper for help if you sustain this. We ought to stop this thing at the threshold of the public school."[66] Justice Frankfurter was the only other justice who voted in the preliminary voting against the subsidy, and his policy views, too, were strongly held and expressed. Rutledge's and Frankfurter's use of logical argument won over only Justices Jackson and Burton, one vote short of a majority. Frankfurter made an unsuccessful effort to gain the support of Justice Murphy. In one note to Murphy, Frankfurter spiced his intellectual arguments with an emotional appeal by writing "You have a chance to do for your country and your Church such as never come to you before—and may never again."[67] Justice Black, writing for the majority, agreed with the minority's insistence on absolute separation of church and state, but held that the subsidy to the parents of parochial school students did not violate that standard. For Justice Black, the New Jersey statute was essentially a secular public welfare measure that the Court had no business invalidating. Justice Black's persuasive powers kept the votes of Chief Justice Vinson and Justices Douglas, Reed, and Murphy. Justice Murphy, a devout Catholic[68] and undoubtedly the most cross-pressured of all the justices in this case, told confidants that he had *prayed* over the church-state issue[69] before allowing himself to be persuaded by Black's opinion.

Another example of persuasion at work in the small group milieu of the Supreme Court can be seen with the case of *Martin* v. *Struthers,*[70] decided in 1943.[71] The case concerned the constitutionality of an anti-doorbell-ringing ordinance of the city of Struthers, Ohio, that sought to protect the daytime repose of night-shift industrial workers. Proselytizing Jehovah's Witnesses had violated the ordinance, setting in motion the litigation that came before the Court. Chief Justice Stone argued in conference that the ordinance violated the "preferred freedoms" of the First Amendment, and Justices Murphy, Douglas, and Rutledge agreed. A majority including Justice Black disagreed, and Justice Roberts, being the senior justice with the majority, exercised his opinion-assignment prerogative and assigned the task to Black. Black saw the Struthers ordinance as protecting the privacy of the home and believed that the right to privacy in the home was a legitimate subject of concern for a municipality. After Justice Black circulated a second revision of his majority opinion, and after he read the sharply worded dissent by Justice Murphy in which Murphy was joined by Douglas and Rutledge, Black changed his mind. The Chief Justice generously permitted Black to write the opinion for the new majority, and in it Black made clear that First Amendment considerations had priority over privacy in this case, but that both values are not necessarily mutually exclusive. Struthers was invited to write a more carefully drafted ordinance protecting both rights.

Still another example of persuasion is suggested by the decision making in the case of *Terminiello* v. *Chicago.*[72] Terminiello was convicted of inciting a breach of the peace by delivering a virulently racist speech at an indoor rally while an angry crowd protested outside the hall. Justice Douglas first perceived that speech as the functional equivalent of throwing a burning stick into a warehouse of dynamite. He initially voted with Vinson, Frankfurter, Jackson, and Burton to sustain the conviction. However, after considering the views of Murphy, Rutledge, and Black, Douglas reevaluated the case and perceived it as clearly a case in which freedom of speech was abridged. Joined by Justice Reed, a new majority was formed, and Justice Black assigned Douglas to write for the majority. Douglas's opinion contained a stirring defense of free speech and did not betray his initial "misperception" of the matter.[73]

Bargaining

Another principal form of intracourt activity is bargaining and negotiating over votes and opinions. A judge with strongly held views can be expected to do this, and the small group literature contains many examples attesting to this phenomenon. It is now believed that Justice Brandeis engaged in either tacit or explicit bargaining during the Taft Court (the 1920s), often circulating a dissenting opinion and then withdrawing it once he was able to make changes in the majority opinion.[74] Brandeis himself admitted that the "great difficulty of all group action, of course, is when and what concession to make."[75] When there is a close division on a case, any one justice's bargaining power may be enhanced. For example, in an 1889 case, Justice Gray put the squeeze on Justice Miller, who had written the majority opinion in a case where the vote was 5–3. Gray, in a note sent to Justice Miller, said:

> After a careful reading of your opinion in *Shotwell* v. *Moore,* I am very sorry to be compelled to say that the first part of it (especially in the passage which I have marked in the margin) is so contrary to my convictions, that I fear, unless it can be a good deal tempered, I shall have to deliver a separate opinion on the lines of the enclosed memorandum.
>
> I am particularly troubled about this, because, if my scruples are not removed, and Justices Field, Bradley and Lamar adhere to their dissent, your opinion will represent only four judges, half of those who took part in the case.[76]

Justice Miller made the necessary revision.

Justice Stone frequently negotiated with his colleagues both as an associate justice and as Chief Justice. For example, one note to Justice Frankfurter contained the following: "If you wish to write, placing the case on the ground which I think tenable and desirable, I shall cheerfully join you. If not, I will add a few observations for myself."[77]

Another documented example of intracourt bargaining occurred during the deliberations over the 1941 *Meadowmoor Dairies* case.[78] Only the year before, Justice Murphy, speaking for the Court in the *Thornhill*[79] and *Carlson*[80] cases, had stated that picketing was a constitutionally protected exercise of freedom of speech. The *Meadowmoor* case involved a state court injunction prohibiting picketing in a labor dispute that had a context of bloodshed and violence. The Court was split on this issue. Justice Frankfurter circulated a draft of the majority opinion and Justices Black and Reed prepared separate dissents. Justice Murphy first considered writing an opinion expressing his own views, but then took the advice of his law clerk, who in a memo urged Murphy:

> [T]ake advantage of your eminently strategic position. All three will try to woo you. Wouldn't it be better to work out your own views? Then pick the opinion that comes the closest. Then start work (à la Stone) on that. The name of Murphy in this case means much. It adds great weight to the opinion bearing it since you wrote Thornhill. I'd act accordingly.[81]

Murphy found that Frankfurter's opinion came closest to his views, and he transmitted them to him. Frankfurter revised his opinion accordingly and sent the revision to Murphy along with a memorandum stating in part: "You know how eager I have been—and am—to have *our* Milk opinion reflect your specially qualified expert views. . . . So here is my effort to translate the various suggestions into terms that would fit into, and truly strengthen, *our* opinion. *Of course* I am open for any further suggestion."[82] In the published decision, Frankfurter emphasized the extreme violence that underlay the labor dispute and justified the injunction. Frankfurter specifically noted, "We do not qualify the Thornhill and Carlson decisions. We reaffirm them." Murphy's *Thornhill* opinion was quoted to demonstrate that it was not inconsistent with the *Meadowmoor* decision.

There is a suggestion in the literature that the nature of the negotiations may vary from Court to Court. It appears that the justices of the Taft Court were more likely to bargain over votes than opinions than were the justices of the Stone or Vinson Courts.[83] One reason was that, unlike the later Courts, the custom on the Taft Court was not to dissent unless absolutely necessary.[84] The type of leadership provided by the Chief Justice, the various personalities and role and value orientations of the justices, the type of issues coming to the Court, and the level and nature of specific and diffuse support for the Court may also be relevant for the kind and extent of negotiations that take place.

There is some evidence that a negotiations process similar to that on the Supreme Court occurs on the various courts of appeals.[85] One appeals judge, the late Simon Sobeloff of the Fourth Circuit, observed in an interview:

> It is very difficult to get unanimity on the court but the judges on the circuit try to reach consensus. It is a bargaining, give-and-take process as each judge is a different being with different views. Often a judge would rather bargain with his peers and achieve a decision, although not as broad-sweeping as he would want but nevertheless in the right direction, than write a ringing dissent while having no influence on the outcome of the case.[86]

Judge Oliver Koelsch from the Ninth Circuit remarked, "We don't like to dissent. It's a last resort. To avoid it, the judges engage in further conferences, additional research, and exchange of memos."[87] The nature and kind of bargaining, however, may vary with the circuit, the issues, and the personalities and value orientations of the judges (just as, of course, with the Supreme Court).

Friendship and Social Amenities

Those using the small group approach are also interested in the friendship and social amenity patterns among the judges insofar as they may be related to the exercise of influence. For example, it appears that Justice Stone's transformation from a conservative to what Chief Justice Taft considered a "radical" was in part due to his close friendship with Holmes and Brandeis. As an intimate friend of Stone suggested, it was "respect and liking for Holmes and Brandeis that turned him from his earlier attitudes."[88] A close friendship can reinforce attitudes as well, as is suggested, for example, by Justice Murphy's close friendship with Justice Rutledge.[89] Justice Arthur Goldberg's revelation that he and Chief Justice Warren had daily conferences with each other raises an interesting question about the friendship patterns on the Warren Court.[90] Justice Brennan was also apparently close to Chief Justice Warren.[91] On the Burger Court, Justice Harry Blackmun made a transition from conservative to moderate and this might in part be attributed to his developing relationship with Justice Brennan.[92]

When a newly appointed justice first takes a seat on the Court, he or she may be the subject of wooing from several judicial colleagues.[93] Once on the bench, a new justice in particular, but undoubtedly others as well, will appreciate praise for his or her written opinions. Examples of praise adorn the papers of most justices. For example: "I congratulate you most sincerely and heartily on having written an opinion which . . . will be a landmark in the history of the Court,"[94] or "If Justice Brandeis could read it [the opinion] he would be proud of his successor."[95] However, unlike persuasion and bargaining, the relationship of friendship and social amenity patterns to decision making is uncertain.[96]

Leadership

Social psychologists have conducted numerous investigations of the nature of small group decision making.[97] From this research two types of leadership have been defined: task leadership and social leadership.[98] David Danelski utilized these concepts in his study of the influence of the Chief Justice in the small group situation of the Supreme Court, in particular at the weekly Court conferences.[99] Danelski suggested that the task leader of the conference is that member who is concerned with getting the job done and who consequently "makes more suggestions, gives more opinions, orients the discussion more frequently, and successfully defends his ideas more often than the others."[100] The task leader is held in high esteem by colleagues. The social leader of the conference is concerned with maintaining friendly relations within the group. Acting as a diplomat who strives to lessen tension and to promote consensus, the social leader "attends to the emotional needs of his associates by affirming their value as individuals and Court members"[101] and consequently is well liked.

Danelski suggested that Chief Justices, by virtue of the fact that they preside over the conferences, have the best opportunity to be either or both task and social leaders. Relying on the private papers of several justices, Danelski studied leadership patterns on the Taft, Hughes, and Stone Courts. He found that during the Taft Court, Taft was the social leader of the conference in coalition with Van Devanter, who was task leader. This positive sharing of leadership led to a productive and congenial Court despite ideological differences on the bench. Justice Brandeis attested to this with his observation, "Things go happily in the conference room. The judges go home less tired emotionally and less weary physically than in [former Chief Justice] White's day."[102]

Chief Justice Hughes was apparently both task and social leader, and conference productivity reached a new high.[103] However, the situation under Chief Justice Stone was substantially different. Stone was a poor task leader and

was challenged by Justice Black. Stone was unprepared to assume social leadership, and cleavages on the Court became more pronounced and more personal.
Conferences were long, frequently continuing into the evening and requiring
additional days. It took the Court twice the amount of conference time to decide
the same number of cases decided by the Hughes Court.[104] Chief Justice Vinson
had difficulty exercising task leadership because of his own intellectual limitations
and social leadership because of the sharp personality clashes on the Court.[105] Earl
Warren, on the other hand, demonstrated strength in both the task and social
leadership arenas.[106] Although it may be premature to assess the leadership of
Warren Burger as Chief Justice, there is some evidence that, at least in the task
leadership realm, he has not been as effective as Earl Warren.[107]

All Chief Justices have the opportunity to exercise some influence during
the course of the decisional process. At the first stage of the process, that of
deciding which cases will be heard by the Court, Chief Justices have an advantage
by virtue of the special list procedure. During the conference discussions of
certiorari petitions as well as cases to be decided, the Chief Justices present their
views first, and their ability to structure discussion can be a source of influence.
When voting with the majority, the Chief Justice self assigns the writing of the
Opinion of the Court or assigns it to another with the majority. This assignment
power of the Chief Justice is one of great importance because the particular justice
chosen to speak for the Court[108] (1) may approach the case differently than would
another majority justice in terms of the grounds on which the opinion is based
or its narrowness or breadth (thus possibly furthering the Chief Justice's own
policy preferences), (2) may make the decision more or less acceptable to the
public, (3) may enable the Chief Justice to retain the narrow majority, and (4)
may win over dissenters to the majority.[109] There are other considerations in the
use of the assignment power. A Chief Justice may wish to distribute the work load
equally, or may wish to take advantage of the expertise of a particular justice,[110]
or may have a special regard for the ability of an associate. However, as Danelski
points up, "every assignment presents the Chief Justice with an opportunity for
influence."[111] The final stage is when the opinions have been circulated and are
being debated, modified, or rewritten. The Chief Justice, as the administrative
head of the Court, is at the nucleus of activity. Ordinarily the Chief Justice will
know the status of each case and the position of each justice, and can potentially
use this knowledge for policy goals by, for example, delaying the announcement
of a case in order to work for unanimity, trying to persuade a wavering justice,
or taking the lead in accommodating differences. In sum, the office of Chief
Justice provides "an opportunity for influence, but it does not guarantee it."[112]

One of the outstanding examples of leadership on the Supreme Court was
Chief Justice Earl Warren's skillful, patient, persuasive, and diplomatic marshall-
ing of the Court to a unanimous vote and opinion in *Brown* v. *Board of Education.* [113] Today one might think that the justices ought to have had no hesitation
in striking down racial apartheid as violating the Constitution, but there is
evidence that reveals otherwise. Three of the justices were southerners and one
of the nonsoutherners had given some indications that he might harbor some
racial prejudice.[114] The legislative history of the Fourteenth Amendment was

ambiguous as to the intent of the framers concerning racially segregated public schools. As soon as he came to the Court in October, 1953, Chief Justice Warren was faced with the school segregation cases, and he realized that there was division on the Court on the issue.[115] At an early conference on the school cases, Warren gave his view that racial segregation was based on a premise of Negro inferiority and that such a premise was inconsistent with the Thirteenth, Fourteenth, and Fifteenth Amendments to the Constitution. Warren also persuaded his colleagues not to take a formal vote, but instead to discuss the issues during subsequent conferences. As Warren himself later observed: "We did not polarize ourselves at the beginning."[116] Usually at the end of other business at the weekly conferences, Warren would turn the group's attention to the *Brown* and companion cases. Warren was also active outside the conference room, and there is evidence that suggests he personally sought to persuade doubting justices.[117] The justices finally voted, and Warren assigned himself the job of writing the Opinion of the Court. In the spring of 1954, Warren personally circulated drafts of the opinion and sought to accommodate various suggestions of his colleagues as well as to work on those whose support was shaky.[118] On May 17, 1954, the Supreme Court announced its historic *unanimous* decision, and it is clear that unanimity was the result of the task and social leadership exercised by the Chief Justice.

Other Aspects of Small Group Analysis

Experimental research by social scientists with small groups in a laboratory setting has resulted in studies that suggest that group decision making is a markedly different enterprise than individual decision making and that groups make different kinds of decisions than individuals do acting alone. We have already seen how this appears to be true in terms of the federal judicial system when we previously considered interaction patterns, particularly on the Supreme Court, and when we discussed leadership. There are other small group concepts, most of which have not been put to use by students of courts primarily because of the difficulties involved in so doing. Nevertheless such small group concepts as group accuracy (groups have been found to make fewer errors than individuals), reference group (a group with which an individual identifies), communication net (who communicates with whom in the small group), conformity and deviance (to group norms and decisions) and the "risky shift" (the greater willingness to take risks as one shifts from the individual to the group) may have potential for aiding our understanding of collegial court processes.[119] One student of courts, Thomas Walker, tested the risky-shift concept by comparing the behavior of federal district judges in civil liberties cases when they sat alone to when they served as members of three-judge district courts.[120] He found that the same judges tended to give greater support to the civil liberties claim when they served on three-judge courts than when sitting alone (i.e., they behaved differently in a group context, thus leaving open the possibility that they took greater risks). In a survey of the judges, Walker found that about four out of five respondents claimed they had no preference in terms of a single judge or collegial court when it came time to make an unpopular decision. But of those with a preference, over three out of four claimed they preferred the three-judge court as opposed to the one-judge court as the vehicle for making controversial decisions.[121]

Evaluation of the Approach

Ideally, the investigation of collegial courts utilizing the tools and approach of small group analysis should be conducted by firsthand observation of the judicial conference at work. Of course, this is impossible. Thus, the major reliance must be on the reports of justices or persons who were the recipients of revelations by the justices as to the interpersonal relationships and conference proceedings on the Court. Such reports and revelations are available from several sources: the private papers of deceased judges; private interviews with judges; and the public writings, speeches, or interviews of judges and their close associates or relatives.

Several Supreme Court justices and Chief Justices have kept voluminous files of their correspondence, exchange of memoranda with their colleagues, drafts of opinions with the comments of colleagues, diaries or notes taken of the conference proceedings, and other pertinent papers related to their work. Such collections of private papers of justices have been indispensable to the judicial biographer. They are of equal value to the small group analyst. Small group analysts following the lead of David Danelski and Walter Murphy have mined the unusually extensive private papers of Chief Justices Taft and Stone as well as of other justices. Students of the appeals courts are beginning to investigate the wealth of private papers of appeals court judges that can shed light on the small group behavior on those courts.[122] Perhaps the most valuable papers are those of justices who have died before having had the opportunity to edit their papers.

However, the use of private papers has several distinct drawbacks. First, not all judges keep extensive accounts of court deliberations. Second, most justices stipulate that their papers are not to become available for public inspection until their colleagues who served with them are no longer on the bench. This, of course, means that there is a considerable lag between the time the justice sat and the time that the papers become available for examination by scholars. Third, the conference notes taken by one justice may not necessarily be complete and objective reportage. The justice's strongly held policy views and the nature of interpersonal relationships with colleagues may affect a justice's papers so as to distort events and mislead the scholar. Similarly, after a justice has the opportunity to edit the papers in order to dispose of confidential or potentially embarrassing materials, the papers may be of little value to the small group analyst.

Personal interviews with Supreme Court justices are extremely difficult, if not impossible, for most scholars to arrange. Access has been somewhat easier to lower federal court judges, but judges tend to be cautious about revealing specifics about the intracourt relationships and maneuverings—precisely the sort of information so vital for small group analysis. Memoirs, public interviews, the writings and speeches of justices and their close associates and relatives may occasionally contain pertinent data suitable for analysis.

One of the difficulties with most data sources for small group analysis is that the analyst has little control over the extensiveness of the data to be collected.

Small group processes, however, have been inferred from quantitative analysis of voting behavior of the sources and nature of conflict and consensus and the extent to which the Chief Justice has exercised leadership to further policy goals by use of the opinion-assigning powers.[123] Reliance on justices' papers has with few exceptions resulted in less precise analyses than studies dependent upon other behavioral approaches to conversion. Yet the value of the small group studies and of the approach itself is considerable. The small group studies, for example, have fleshed out the workings of the Supreme Court, suggesting a more sophisticated and complex decision-making context than might be surmised from the more quantitative attitudinal analyses. What is more, these studies are compatible with the attitudinal approach and in a general sense provide additional evidence supporting the attitudinal thesis. If the justices display some fluidity and not rigidity in their responses to the cases before them, if they have some difficulty perceiving or digesting the facts of a case within their attitudinal frame of reference, if their votes can be swayed by persuasion, negotiation, interpersonal relationships, the leadership of the Chief Justice, or appeals to their sense of institutional loyalty, it is because the justices are human beings and not judicial slot machines. The small group studies have sensitized students of courts to these considerations.

One further observation is in order. While our attention in this section was focused exclusively on collegial court decision making, evidence has begun to accumulate that suggests that trial judges also are part of a small group negotiations process when plea-bargained sentences are determined. Trial judges, prosecutors, and defense attorneys constitute these small informal work groups that jointly arrive at sentencing decisions.[124] Research thus far has concerned state courts, and it is unknown to what extent such small work group activity occurs at the federal district court level.

FACT PATTERN ANALYSIS

The fact pattern approach to judicial conversion seems to bear somewhat of a resemblance to the more traditional approach still used by most of the legal profession. Both suggest that judicial decisions turn on the facts presented in the case, and both seemingly underplay individual attitudes in favor of a focus on institutional decision making. However, unlike traditional legal analysis, fact pattern analysis does not contain the assumption that courts examine the law and apply it to the legally relevant facts of the case. Fact pattern analysis is not only concerned with legally relevant facts (i.e., those facts that clearly fall within the purview of the statute invoked in the case), but also with legally irrelevant facts (such as the race of the defendant in criminal cases). Furthermore, fact pattern analysis, unlike traditional analysis, hypothesizes but does not assume that courts are consistent in the type of facts used as a basis of decision. Finally, unlike traditional analysis, fact pattern analysis enables the researcher to determine what combinations of facts are more important than others for reaching a result for one or the other party involved in the litigation. Fact pattern methods (provided the court has been found to be consistent) can potentially yield precise weightings or combinations of facts that permit the researcher to predict the decisional results of future cases.

Essentially, then, fact pattern analysis is concerned with uncovering, by systematic examination of a set of decisions, the patterns of facts that are related to decisional results. In the words of Fred Kort, who did path-breaking work in this realm, the objective is "to obtain a precise and exhaustive distinction between combinations of facts that lead to decisions in favor of one party and combinations of facts that lead to decisions in favor of the opposing party."[125] The approach originated in the 1930s with legal realist Herman Oliphant[126] and was developed by Kort, Reed Lawlor, Stuart Nagel,[127] and S. Sidney Ulmer.[128]

The study of fact patterns requires content analysis to ascertain the facts in a predetermined set of decisions. Fred Kort has demonstrated two different methods for studying fact patterns.[129] One method, utilizing algebraic solutions to simultaneous equations, allows one to calculate the weight of each fact. Equations are written expressing the facts present in the cases and the number of judges voting for or against the plaintiff or defendant. Because there may be many facts whose weights are unknown and relatively few cases, factor analysis is used to reduce the number of facts to factors. Once the weights of different facts or factors are determined, it is possible to predict the decision of future cases given their facts. Both the factor analysis and the solving of simultaneous equations are done by computer.

The second method Kort has demonstrated utilizes Boolean algebra. Unlike the method of simultaneous equations, the objective is not to calculate weights for each fact or factor, but rather to derive a compound statement that will precisely indicate what combination of facts is necessary in order for the court to render a pro or con decision. Because there may be thousands of combinations of facts (if not more), it is necessary to rely on computers to derive the compound statement. Other fact pattern analysts, although using different statistical techniques, either have essentially been concerned with deriving the weights of facts in order to ascertain their relative importance or have been concerned with the combinations of facts that produce pro or con decisions.

Theoretical Basis for Fact Pattern Analysis

Reed Lawlor and S. Sidney Ulmer in particular have used fact pattern analysis to study individual judicial behavior, and both developed theories of conversion. Lawlor theorized that each judge follows personal stare decisis; that is, the judge is logically consistent in behavior from case to case as to the weights assigned to different facts.[130]

Ulmer's theory of conversion is more elaborate. Ulmer has argued that although human behavior is a function of the interdependence and interaction of three basic dimensions—the psychological, the organic, and the environmental—it is useful to abstract the last dimension for purposes of empirical analysis.[131] Ulmer assumed that a judge's decision is "a behavioral response to some perceived aspect of environment."[132] More specifically, Ulmer contended that judges

respond to signs or signals contained within or associated with the cases before
them. These signs designate or represent something (e.g., an occurrence or state
of affairs), and they are interpreted by the judge in accordance with the judge's
values and the calculus of the costs involved in choosing decisional alternatives.
Ulmer's focus was on the individual judge, and he used the statistical technique
of discriminant analysis to establish the weights and direction (either pro or con)
of the signs.

Although Ulmer's fact pattern approach, and to some extent Lawlor's, is
consistent with the attitudinal approach, the principal empirical research concerns an analysis of the statistical relationship between facts or signs and the
decisions of judges. This raises the question of whether the facts cited by judges
and their perceptions of what these facts represent are substantially subjective or
whether they accord with objective reality. Ulmer considered this and argued that
"the judge is not free to dream signs or to ignore those that all others see. Thus
the fact that the judge identifies a particular sign does not mean that the signs
exist only in his subjective."[133] Where many identify signs and agree as to what
they represent (such as a beating with a rubber hose signifying coercion), their
beliefs may be considered to represent objective reality.[134]

In his study of Justice Frankfurter, Ulmer relied on lower court records to
identify the presence or absence of the hypothesized relevant signs. Lawlor, too,
concerned himself with the question of subjectivity and objectivity and furthermore conducted an empirical analysis in which he compared the fact content of
briefs with the fact content of judicial opinions.[135] He found that the court asserted
that certain facts were present or absent in contradiction to the assertions in the
briefs in only a minute portion of the cases.[136]

Race as a Fact

One fact that has been considered by fact pattern analysis is the race of the litigants,
in particular whether black Americans are involved. This fact is ordinarily not
legally relevant in criminal cases. Yet fact pattern studies of the Supreme Court by
Kort, Nagel, and Ulmer have found that the fact that a criminal defendant was
black was related to a decision *favorable* to the defendant. This is not to suggest
that all black defendants received favorable judgments, but rather that race was
one of many facts that led toward favorable decisions. Kort, in his study of
involuntary confession cases, found that the fact that the defendant was black was
associated along with 21 other variables with a prodefendant decision.[137] Nagel also
examined involuntary confession cases and found that the fact that the defendant
was a black American in a southern jurisdiction was relevant to a decision in favor
of the defense.[138] Ulmer, in his study of Justice Frankfurter, found that the fact (or
sign) that the complaining party was black (or a lower court judge or attorney
defined the case as one of Negro rights) was related to Frankfurter's decisions. In
the 1959–1960 terms, Frankfurter responded favorably (13 of 15 cases) with the
appearance of the "Negro sign."[139] On the other hand, there is evidence that
suggests that in the past many southern and more recently some lower court judges
throughout the country have responded negatively to black litigants because of
their race,[140] particularly in criminal sentencing.

Sex as a Fact

Only recently has the question been raised whether the sex of the litigant as plaintiff or defendant in civil cases or defendant in criminal cases is associated with decisional outcomes. There has been no systematic study of sex or gender as a fact in Supreme Court or lower federal court decision making. Nevertheless, there is some fragmentary evidence that suggests that in criminal cases women criminal defendants may be treated more leniently by male judges than by female judges.[141] Of course this also suggests that gender may not only be a relevant variable in terms of the facts of a case but that gender is also relevant in terms of attributes of judges.

Sentencing Behavior and Fact Patterns

Sentencing behavior of trial court judges has come under increasing scrutiny in recent years. There is evidence that suggests that trial judges are often arbitrary and inconsistent from the standpoint of legal criteria in their sentencing patterns and that there are wide disparities among judges in their sentencing of similar defendants convicted under the same statutes. Legally irrelevant considerations seem to frequently influence sentencing. Blacks have been found to be sentenced to longer prison terms than whites convicted of the same offense. For example, the Federal Bureau of Prisons records reveal that in fiscal 1970 the average sentence for whites convicted of income tax evasion was 12.8 months, but was 28.6 months for nonwhites. For drug offenses the average sentence for whites was 61.1 months, but for nonwhites it was 81.1 months.[142] In 1983 an extensive Rand Corporation-sponsored study of minority convicts in California, Michigan, and Texas was published. The study, conducted by criminologist Joan Petersilia, revealed that black and Hispanic felons tended to draw lengthier prison sentences than whites for the same crimes, taking into account their criminal records.[143]

Socioeconomic considerations—that is, whether the crime and criminal were white collar or blue collar—have also been related to sentencing patterns. In fiscal 1980, for example, 33 percent of those convicted of the white-collar crime of bank embezzlement were sentenced to prison for an average sentence of 2 years and 7 months, while 93 percent of those convicted of the blue-collar crime of bank robbery were sentenced to prison for an average sentence of 12 years and 2 months.[144]

There appears to be a relationship between still other legally irrelevant facts and criminal sentencing. Whether the defendant entered a plea of guilty (and plea bargained) or was convicted after a jury trial is apparently an important consideration, as shown by the much more severe sentences for those who go to trial and are convicted. With some offense categories such as marijuana and other narcotics laws violations, sentences in fiscal 1971 were from two to three times longer than for defendants who entered a plea of guilty and presumably had plea bargained.[145] Defendants with no lawyer (or their own privately retained counsel) come off better at sentencing time than those with assigned counsel.[146] Other legally irrelevant facts that seem to be related to some judges' sentencing patterns have been discussed by former Federal District Judge Marvin Frankel in his study of criminal sentences appropriately subtitled "Law Without Order."[147] Another study, by a psychoanalyst who is also a law school professor, was based on interviews with judges and demonstrated that even the "best" judges continually use legally irrelevant criteria in their sentencing, often without realizing it.[148]

One of the most rigorous studies of sentencing disparity in the federal courts was conducted by a subcommittee of the Second Circuit Committee on Sentencing Practices in conjunction with the Federal Judicial Center.[149] The 1974 study involved all 43 active district court judges and 7 senior judges who participated in a sentencing simulation experiment. The judges were given the same set of presentence reports and asked to render sentences. For the first time in sentencing studies it was possible to control the case stimuli by having different trial judges respond to the same "cases." Furthermore, most of the "cases" were based on real cases previously decided in the circuit.

The results were startling. Second Circuit district judges responding to the same presentence reports varied widely in their sentences. For example, in one case half the judges gave a sentence from one to three years of *probation,* while one-fourth of the judges gave prison sentences from 6 months to 3 years. In another case, the sentences varied from 5 years to 18 years and a fine, with the median sentence being 10 years.[150] The study also found that it made no difference in terms of disparity whether judges had a number of years of trial court experience or whether they were relative newcomers to the bench.[151]

In some respects the search for fact patterns that are associated with individual judges' sentencing behavior is similar to the study of attitudes. One can consider the response of a judge to a particular combination of facts as representing the judge's attitudes toward the litigant and situational characteristics of the cases. The fact pattern approach as applied to collegial courts, in the hands of some practitioners, has provided more of a focus on institutional responses. The approach, whether in the context of individual or institutional decision making, by examining all the legally relevant *and* legally irrelevant facts alerts us to the wide range of discretion available and used by judges. Perhaps, most importantly, it also aids us in documenting the use of that discretion by courts and individual judges.

JUDICIAL ROLE ANALYSIS

Of all the approaches discussed, judicial role analysis offers perhaps the most ambiguous and yet potentially the most comprehensive explanation of judicial conversion. It is ambiguous in that the concept of judicial role can and has been defined differently, and only recently has systematic attention been devoted to formulating and testing judicial role hypotheses. It is comprehensive in that, in its broadest form, the judicial role concept can be used to order the just discussed conversion variables to provide a general model of conversion.

The concept of role as used by social scientists is tied to the concept of position; that is, the researcher examines the role of those who occupy particular positions such as federal district court judge, federal appeals judge, or associate justice of the Supreme Court. The judicial role may be defined as the "set of normative expectations concerning the official behavior of an incumbent of a . . . [judicial] position."[152] Judicial role behavior may be defined as those activities of a judge that manifest his or her perceptions of what he or she ought to and can do (as well as the converse) as a judge.[153] Thus, the judge's attitudes and values are filtered through a role screen and are manifested by role behavior. From the more traditional legal literature as well as from some behavioral analyses, there appear to be some elements of role for which there is wide consensus among judges, that is, common role behavior. These may be considered the *institutional role elements.* There also appear to be some elements of role that, on the basis of divergent patterns of judicial behavior, suggest the absence of common interpretations and perceptions. These may be considered *variable role elements.* Both will be discussed and followed by a consideration of the potential of role analysis to provide the basis for a comprehensive causal model of conversion.

Institutional Role Elements

Institutional role elements, as just defined, are those about which a wide consensus apparently exists in terms of normative expectations and about which a uniformity exists for the most part in actual behavior. They are likely to have been initially fostered during the ongoing legal socialization process that law students undergo and to which practicing lawyers are constantly exposed. New judges, too, are socialized in terms of the judicial role.[154] Institutional role elements may be considered insofar as they concern or relate to public behavior of judges, procedural aspects of decision making, and substantive aspects of decision making.

Public Behavior   There is an image of a federal judge that is probably widely perceived by most Americans, that of a late middle-aged or elderly black-robed, dignified, and learned individual. This institutional image is in part fortified by an accepted judicial etiquette whereby judges are treated with deference by other authorities (particularly other court personnel). Judges also address each other on the bench and in their opinions with at least surface respect and courtesy.

It is also expected that judges will appear to be and will be in fact impartial when processing litigation. A judge who has or had any involvement with one or more of the litigants or any substantial stake in the resolution of the controversy is expected not to participate in the case. Judges on appellate courts are also expected to maintain secrecy about conference deliberations. Prior to judgment day, judges do not reveal their views of the case nor do they predict how the case will be decided. Even then, it is traditional for judges not to reveal the course of deliberations and not to elaborate upon the decision itself.[155] These institutional elements of the judicial role as well as others (some of which are specified in the American Bar Association's Canons of Judicial Ethics) are associated with the distinctive public image of the judiciary.

Procedural Aspects of Decision Making   There are various institutional role elements related to procedural aspects of decision making. The special judicial position of federal district judge, the trial judge of the federal system, connotes particular activities in the conduct of trials, for example, the maintenance of decorum in the courtroom and scrupulous attention to correct trial procedures. The positions of appeals court judge and associate justice of the Supreme Court also suggest institutional role elements concerned with procedure. One study of appeals judges suggested that panel conferences on most circuits are conducted in a spirit of give-and-take or accommodation in an effort to reach decisional consensus and thus avoid public dissension. The extent of accommodation in practice, however, apparently depends upon the circuit, issue, ideological or attitudinal gaps that must be spanned, and personal relationships of the judges with one another.[156] Nevertheless, the role of appellate judge or associate justice contains the element of negotiation institutionalized through the conference and the practice of circulating drafts of opinions for comments and suggestions.[157]

The position of Chief Justice of the Supreme Court is also a specialized role, as will be recalled from previous discussion of leadership and the small group approach. The Chief Justice chairs the conference, makes opinion assignments when voting with the majority, first presents a view of the issues and indicates a voting inclination[158] (followed by the colleagues in order of seniority), and has special gatekeeping responsibilities (preparation of the conference agenda). The Chief Justice also has the opportunity to exercise task and social leadership in order to promote an efficient and harmonious Court.

Other institutional role elements include the norm that judges on a collegial bench will not change their votes just before the decisions are to be announced. A court would be in a constant turmoil if this were not common practice.

Substantive Aspects of Decision Making   Institutional role elements that concern or affect the substance of decisions include the norms of *stare decisis* and adherence to the obvious requirements and intent of the law. The uses of dissent, at least on the Supreme Court, also appear to fit the pattern of institutional role elements.

Although the legal realists argued forcefully that *stare decisis* is a meaningless norm because precedents are plentiful and can always be found to support one's view, the rule of precedent is still maintained by the bar and bench as a decision-making norm. The crucial question, however, is whether *stare decisis* is merely pro forma or whether it does in fact shape the substance of decisions. The answer is that there is some evidence suggesting that to a limited extent *stare decisis* is related to substantive decision making. The majority of all decisions (with *per curiams* included) decided by the Supreme Court are decided unanimously, and many (particularly the *per curiam* decisions) are specifically decided on the authority of precedent. One scholar, Werner Grunbaum, who conducted a computer simulation of the 1962 and 1963 terms, concluded that "judicial attitudes alone are insufficient to explain judicial behavior" and that in unanimously decided cases "justices are influenced by the lawyers' model governing traditional *stare decisis.*"[159] There is other evidence that concerns the appeals courts.

Typically, at least four out of five cases are unanimously decided by the various appeals courts. One study involving interviews with a large sample of appeals judges found that most judges not only recognized the expectation that they follow Supreme Court precedent, but suggested that when the precedent involves policy set by the Supreme Court, *stare decisis is* largely responsible for encouraging decisional consensus on the appellate courts. This should not be taken to mean that all or even most unanimous appellate panels achieve unanimity *because* of precedent alone, but the limited evidence suggests that *stare decisis* is probably responsible for at least a part of those decisions.[160]

Of course, *stare decisis* as an institutional role element raises some problems. It is difficult to conclusively prove that *stare decisis* operates for all judges on some minimal basis to influence the substance of policy-making. A judge may claim to be following precedent, but it may also be that the precedent coincides with the judge's attitudes and values. The empirical analyses of *stare decisis,* such as Glendon Schubert's analysis of Justice Clark[161] and his later work in *The Judicial Mind,* suggested that *stare decisis* is really a role variable, that justices differ in their perceptions and evaluations of *stare decisis* as a norm. Sophisticated qualitative analysts such as Martin Shapiro have argued that *stare decisis* is typically a facade for what really amounts to incremental changes in policy.[162] Further role behavior research may be able to establish the extent to which *stare decisis* can be considered an institutional role element with import for substantive decision making.

When one examines the norm that judges should follow the obvious requirements and intent of the law, one turns to what has always been considered a given of the judicial function. To some scholars the mention of this as an institutional role element may seem superfluous, indeed, belaboring the obvious. Yet the emphasis of political analyses of judges' behavior is on their use of discretion, and one may lose sight of the fact that not every case offers judges a wide range, or perhaps even any range, of legitimate decisional alternatives.

One classic example of this is the famous 1833 Court opinion in the case of *Barron* v. *Baltimore,*[163] in which Chief Justice John Marshall was compelled to rule that the Bill of Rights provided limitations on Congress but not the individual states. One obscure example concerns another activist justice, some 110 years later, who wrote to a colleague explaining his vote in a case, "I am constrained to concur, though I wish, as I know you do, that there was some tenable way to reach the opposite result."[164] There are undoubtedly other examples that could be mentioned. However, it should be noted that there have been no studies demonstrating more precisely the extent to which there are cases with no meaningful decisional alternatives because of the requirements of law. Presumably the Supreme Court, which determines for the most part which cases it hears, is *least* concerned with such cases. The district courts and the appeals courts, which do not have a similar discretionary power over their dockets, would be expected to be *most* concerned with such cases.

There is some evidence that suggests that before 1940 the accepted norm of the Supreme Court was not to dissent unless absolutely necessary, that is, unless a great principle and/or major constitutional issue was at stake.[165] This, of course, affected the strategy and tactics of negotiation related to the substance of the Court's opinion (as will be recalled from the discussion of small group behavior). Since 1940 this expectation appears to have been changed. Certainly the much greater frequency of dissents and concurrences suggest as much. As for the operating norms on the appeals courts, not much is known except that the rate of dissent is markedly less than that of the Supreme Court and also that dissent rates vary by circuit.[166]

Role Variables

A norm more difficult to define than those just discussed is that judges are expected to dispense "justice." Although "rendering justice" is a norm widely recognized by judges, their role behavior suggests vastly different perceptions and interpretations of justice. This indeed goes to the essentials of conversion—the backgrounds and conditioning experiences of the judges and the emergent attitudes and values that may culminate in a judicial philosophy that may lead one judge to view the equities of a case in an entirely different manner from another judge. For example, one study reported the contrasting views of criminal justice of two judges on the United States circuit court for the District of Columbia. One judge, Judge John Danaher, remarked in an interview, "Our main goal is to see that no man loses his life, liberty, or indeed, his property unless he is clearly guilty. . . . [However] if a man is guilty I will not look for procedural niceties. [What is important is that] justice should be done."[167] His colleague, Judge J. Skelly Wright, on the other hand, stated:

> The primary goal of the judge is to do justice. . . . Settled principles of law are used to guide a court to a just result. When it is clear that these principles or precedents will produce an injustice, then you must strain the principles to get a just result. . . . I feel our society is responsible for Negro crime and my position is that society must dot the i's and cross the t's when it brings a criminal case [with a black defendant] before me.[168]

Another role variable, one that has especially occupied the attention of students of the Supreme Court, concerns each justice's perception of what the higher courts ought to do and can do in determining public policy for the nation. The popular discussion usually centers around the catch-all terms of "activism" (i.e., the position that courts should not hesitate to foster policies beneficial to society) and "restraint" (i.e., the courts should defer to the popularly elected branches of government in *their* determination of suitable public policy).[169] Obviously one can be activist on one issue and restrained on another. Justice Frankfurter was closely identified with the restraint philosophy, particularly when the issue involved state criminal procedures. He observed, for example, in a 5–4 decision in which his vote was the deciding vote in allowing Louisiana authorities to attempt a second time to execute a young black teenager after the first attempt was unsuccessful due to a malfunctioning electric chair:

> I cannot rid myself of the conviction that were I to hold that Louisiana would transgress the Due Process Clause if the State were allowed, in the precise

circumstances before us, to carry out the death sentence, I would be enforcing my private view rather than that consensus of society's opinion, which for purposes of due process, is the standard enjoined by the Constitution.[170]

Justice Frankfurter, however, was apparently less restrained in his embrace of more conservative economic positions in his later years on the bench.[171] In sum, it is apparent both from the more traditional analyses of decisional output and philosophical statements by judges as well as from empirical analyses[172] that judges differ as to the proper function of higher courts in a democracy. Although the terms "activism" and "restraint" may be an oversimplification of a complex reality, they do suggest the variable nature of this role element.

The varying personality characteristics of judges also can be thought of as affecting their role behavior. Jerome Frank[173] and Harold Lasswell,[174] among others, suggested in their studies that the personality variable may lurk beneath the ostensible philosophical and attitudinal differences of judges.[175]

Role and a Dynamic Causal Model of Conversion

The role concept may be utilized in the construction of a causal model of judicial conversion. Such an endeavor represents a level of analysis different from that presented thus far in that a causal model seeks to account for all the relevant variables and to specify precisely how they are interrelated.[176] Building a causal model in the mathematical sense involves developing a system of equations the solution of which determines which variables are causes and which are effects (as well as specifying which variables serve as linking mechanisms).[177] Implicit in such analysis is the assumption that there are regularities of behavior and that the discovered uniformities suggest a dependence of effect on cause under specified conditions, all other things being equal. There are various alternative methods of causal model building, the details of which are more appropriately discussed in more advanced technical writings.[178] Neither is it necessary to be concerned here with their mathematics, for what is described here is a theoretical model that might be able to be tested but as of now essentially consists of hypotheses that are grounded in the research results discussed earlier in this chapter.[179]

Figure 5.1 presents an arrow diagram of a dynamic causal model of judi-

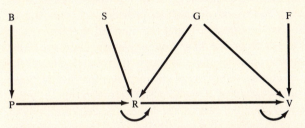

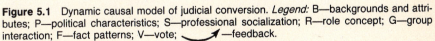

Figure 5.1 Dynamic causal model of judicial conversion. *Legend:* B—backgrounds and attributes; P—political characteristics; S—professional socialization; R—role concept; G—group interaction; F—fact patterns; V—vote; ⌣⟋—feedback.

cial conversion in which the role concept is central. As can be observed, the model suggests that backgrounds are causally related to certain political characteristics (such as party affiliation, partisan activism, and political attitudes and values). These political characteristics, in turn, are causally related to the role concept espoused by the judge. Attitudes and values are at the heart of a judge's role concept, but they are assumed to be not as baldly political as they were before ascending the bench. Rather, attitudes and values are manifested in terms of what the judge believes he or she can and ought to do and how the judge in fact acts as a judge. Or, as concisely put by James Gibson, "Judges' decisions are a function of what they prefer to do, tempered by what they think they ought to do, but constrained by what they perceive is feasible to do."[180] The kind and extent of professional socialization is also causally related to the judge's role concept, as are various on-the-bench collegial experiences. The model, however, takes into consideration that the judge's role concept (i.e., the judge's attitudes and values in the context of how he or she believes judges should decide cases) is subject to change over time due to feedback from previous decisional output. Increased age and experience can also be taken into account by this dynamic aspect of the model. The judge's role concept as well as the facts of the case and the group experience related to discussing the case (conferences, circulation of drafts of opinions and memoranda, etc.) cause the collegial court judge to vote as he or she does.

The challenge of such a model is to devise operational procedures by which to quantify and then measure the variables. It would be necessary to specify the types of cases and voting responses to be studied. It would also be necessary to devise indices by which to measure the variables. For example, B (backgrounds) might be a composite of weighted attributes;[181] P (political characteristics) could consist of a composite index of party affiliation and activism as well as political attitudes and values held before ascending the bench (perhaps determined through a content analysis of pre-judicial speeches or writings[182] or perhaps as ascertained through extensive interviewing of the judge and those who knew the judge in the pre-court days); S (professional socialization) could weight bar association activism, legal honors and writings, and types of legal experience; R (role concept) could perhaps be operationally determined through extensive use of scaling of previous voting behavior[183] and/or determined by content analysis of previous opinions; G (group interaction) might possibly be discerned through a combined index measuring the amount of conference time spent on a case, the number of drafts circulated, the extent and nature of behind-the-scenes negotiations (presumably conference notes and diaries can provide such data but of course only years after the case was decided), and the number of concurrences and dissents and how they are in accord or differ from previously discovered bloc patterns; and F (fact patterns) can be found through the use of any of the established techniques. V, of course, refers to the vote or votes that we hypothesize are caused by the preceding variables. It should also be stressed that the votes to be explained (the dependent variable) cannot also be used to determine any of the variables (the independent variables) that presumably cause those votes. Only past behavior would be used for those measures.

These, then, are the rudiments of what a causal model of judicial conversion looks like. It should be apparent, however, that serious difficulties are involved in such an enterprise. Not only are there problems of operationalizing the variables and measuring them, there are also formidable technical problems as well.[184] Perhaps the greatest utility of such a model as presented in Figure 5.1 (which was suggested in part by the studies reported earlier in this chapter) is that it is a working model of behavior that suggests a more complex empirical theory of judicial conversion than those presented earlier.[185]

NOTES

1. As quoted by Jerome Frank in *Law and the Modern Mind* (Garden City, N.Y.: Anchor, 1963), p. 35, n. 1.
2. 297 U.S. 1 (1936) at 62–63.
3. The phrase was coined by Karl Llewellyn. See his *The Common Law Tradition: Deciding Appeals* (Boston: Little, Brown, 1960), pp. 508–510.
4. See the discussion in Wilfred E. Rumble, *American Legal Realism* (Ithaca, N.Y.: Cornell University Press, 1968), Chap. 2.
5. See the discussion in Rumble, *American Legal Realism,* Chap. 3.
6. Frank, *Law and the Modern Mind,* pp. 398–399.
7. Cf. Rumble, *American Legal Realism,* pp. 238–239.
8. See Albert Somit and Joseph Tanenhaus, *The Development of American Political Science* (Boston: Allyn & Bacon, 1967), Chaps. 9–14.
9. At the heart of the scientific method is a concern with assertions that can be proven true or false by empirically verifiable procedures. In order for an assertion or hypothesis to be testable, it is necessary to establish operational definitions of the phenomenon about which a hypothesis or hypotheses have been formulated. Typically, five steps or procedures are involved in the scientific method: (1) identifying a particular research question; (2) specifying one or more hypotheses; (3) gathering data that test the hypothesis; (4) analyzing the findings in terms of the hypothesis; and (5) assessing the findings in the context of other knowledge. See the discussion of these five steps by S. Sidney Ulmer in "Scientific Method and the Judicial Process," *American Behavioral Scientist,* 7 (December 1963), 21–22, 35–38.
10. These areas of concern, along with an interest in the processing of cases at all court levels and the impact of court decisions, represent much of the research in the judicial area undertaken by political scientists in recent decades. See David J. Danelski, "Public Law: The Field," *International Encyclopedia of the Social Sciences,* 13 (1968), 175–183; Glendon Schubert, "Judicial Process and Behavior, 1963–1971," in James A. Robinson (ed.), *Political Science Annual,* Vol. III (Indianapolis: Bobbs-Merrill, 1972), pp. 73–280; Lawrence Baum, "Judicial Politics: Still a Distinctive Field," in Ada Finifter (ed.), *Political Science: The State of the Discipline* (Washington, D.C.: The American Political Science Association, 1983), pp. 189–215.
11. C. Herman Pritchett, "Divisions of Opinion among Justices of the U.S. Supreme Court, 1939–1941," *American Political Science Review,* 35 (1941), 890–898; and his two books, *The Roosevelt Court: A Study in Judicial Politics and Values 1937–1947* (New York: Macmillan, 1948), and *Civil Liberties and the Vinson Court* (Chicago: University of Chicago Press, 1954).
12. Pritchett, *Roosevelt Court,* p. xii.
13. See, for example, Glendon Schubert, "Behavioral Jurisprudence," *Law and Society*

Review, 2 (1968), 407–428; and C. Herman Pritchett, "Public Law and Judicial Behavior," *Journal of Politics,* 30 (1968), 480–509. Also see Glendon Schubert and David J. Danelski (eds.), *Comparative Judicial Behavior* (New York: Oxford University Press, 1969); Schubert, "Judicial Process and Behavior, 1963–1971"; and Baum, "Judicial Politics: Still a Distinctive Field."

14. See James L. Gibson, "From Simplicity to Complexity: The Development of Theory in the Study of Judicial Behavior," *Political Behavior,* 5 (1983), 7–50.

15. See Glendon Schubert, "Jackson's Judicial Philosophy: An Exploration in Value Analysis," *American Political Science Review,* 59 (1965), 940–963, and his "The Dimensions of Decisional Response: Opinion and Voting Behavior of the Australian High Court," in Joel B. Grossman and Joseph Tanenhaus (eds.), *Frontiers of Judicial Research* (New York: Wiley, 1969), pp. 163–195 for examples of the use of opinion data. See Werner F. Grunbaum, "Analytical and Simulation Models for Explaining Judicial Decision-Making," in Grossman and Tanenhaus (eds.), *Frontiers of Judicial Research,* pp. 307–334, and his "A Quantitative Analysis of the 'Presidential Ballot' Case," *Journal of Politics,* 34 (1972), 223–243, for examples of the use of computerized content analysis.

16. For an examination of judicial behavior methods, see C. Neal Tate, "The Methodology of Judicial Behavior Research: A Review and Critique," *Political Behavior,* 5 (1983), 51–82.

17. A matrix is a rectangular array of entries by row and columns.

18. See the Pritchett works cited in note 11.

19. Glendon Schubert, *Quantitative Analysis of Judicial Behavior* (New York: Free Press, 1959), Chap. 3.

20. See S. Sidney Ulmer, "The Analysis of Behavior Patterns in the United States Supreme Court," *Journal of Politics,* 22 (1960), 629–653; Glendon Schubert, *The Judicial Mind* (Evanston, Ill.: Northwestern University Press, 1965); David J. Danelski, "Values as Variables in Judicial Decision-Making: Notes toward a Theory," *Vanderbilt Law Review,* 19 (1966), 721–740; John D. Sprague, *Voting Patterns of the United States Supreme Court* (Indianapolis: Bobbs-Merrill, 1968); Glendon Schubert, "Dimensions of Decisional Response." See the discussion by Walter Murphy and Joseph Tanenhaus, *The Study of Public Law* (New York: Random House, 1972), pp. 159–176, 190–194.

21. S. Sidney Ulmer, "Toward a Theory of Sub-Group Formation in the United States Supreme Court," *Journal of Politics,* 27 (1965), 133–152. But cf. S. Sidney Ulmer, "Subset Behavior in the Supreme Court," in Sven Groennings, E. W. Kelley, and Michael Leiserson (eds.), *The Study of Coalitional Behavior* (New York: Holt, Rinehart and Winston, 1970), pp. 396–409; and David N. Atkinson and Dale A. Neuman, "Toward a Cost Theory of Judicial Alignments: The Case of the Truman Bloc," *Midwest Journal of Political Science,* 13 (1969), 271–283.

22. Justice Black's voting behavior during the last half-dozen terms in which he sat was markedly different from his previous civil libertarian voting record. The annual surveys published by the American Jewish Congress demonstrated this. Prior to the 1963 term, Black was second only to Justice Douglas in his support of civil liberties as measured by the simple percentage of votes each term favoring civil liberties. In the 1963 and 1964 terms, Black moved to third place. In the 1965 and 1966 terms, he occupied fifth place. By the end of the 1967 term, Black was recorded in seventh place, and after the 1968 term, he earned placement in ninth place (i.e., the Justice *least* sympathetic to claims of civil liberties during the 1968 term). (As cited by Wallace Mendelson, "Hugo Black and Judicial Discretion," *Political Science*

Quarterly, 85 [1970], 38–39.) Interestingly, in his last two terms (which coincided with the first two terms of the Nixon Court), Black was the most liberal of the *non*liberal wing of the Court.

Black's shift from liberal to idiosyncratic conservative and his shift in bloc alignment as noted in Table 5.1 has met with conflicting explanations. Black's defenders found consistency in his behavior. See, for example, Mendelson, "Hugo Black"; A. E. D. Howard, "Mr. Justice Black: The Negro Protest Movement and the Rule of Law," *Virginia Law Review,* 53 (1967), 1030–1090; John M. Harlan, "Mr. Justice Black—Remarks of a Colleague," *Harvard Law Review,* 81 (1967), 1–3; Howard Ball, *The Vision and the Dream of Justice Hugo L. Black* (University: University of Alabama Press, 1974). Black defended himself in *A Constitutional Faith* (New York: Knopf, 1968). Also see S. Sidney Ulmer, "The Longitudinal Behavior of Hugo Lafayette Black: Parabolic Support for Civil Liberties, 1937–1971," *Florida State Law Review,* 1 (1973), 131–158. But cf. Glendon Schubert, *The Constitutional Polity* (Boston: Boston University Press, 1970), pp. 118–129; Glendon Schubert, "Hugo Black: Conservatism as an Exponential Function," *Micropolitics* (in press); James J. Magee, *Mr. Justice Black: Absolutist on the Court* (Charlottesville, Va.: University Press of Virginia, 1980); and Mark Silverstein, *Constitutional Faiths: Felix Frankfurter, Hugo Black, and the Process of Judicial Decision Making* (Ithaca, N.Y.: Cornell University Press, 1984).

Note that Ulmer has argued in general that "no judge exhibits absolutely constant behavior patterns from one year to the next . . . [and] that over a long-enough period, marginal changes can lead cumulatively to major change in judge or behavior." See S. Sidney Ulmer, "Dimensionality and Change in Judicial Behavior," in James F. Herndon and Joseph L. Bernd (eds.), *Mathematical Applications in Political Science, VII* (Charlottesville: University Press of Virginia, 1974), p. 66. Justice Harry Blackmun perhaps is a good example of marginal changes leading to major change. In his first term on the Court, the 1970 term, Blackmun was tied with Chief Justice Burger as the most conservative justice on the Court in matters of civil liberties. By the end of the 1982 term, Blackmun had become the fourth most liberal justice. Blackmun himself has publicly acknowledged his shift from a conservative to a more liberal position. See the interview with Blackmun in John A. Jenkins, "A Candid Talk with Justice Blackmun," *New York Times Magazine,* February 20, 1983, pp. 20–29, 57, 61, 66.

Justice Stevens is atypical in that he has not been firmly allied with a bloc on the Court although he generally appears closest to the liberals. In general, see Edward V. Heck, "Consensus and Conflict in the Supreme Court: Changing Voting Patterns in the Warren and Burger Courts," in Sheldon Goldman and Charles Lamb (eds.), *Judicial Conflict and Consensus: Behavioral Studies of American Appellate Courts* (Lexington: University Press of Kentucky, in press). The above notwithstanding, the evidence also suggests that some justices display broad attitudinal consistency over long periods of time. See, for example, Saul Brenner and Theodore Arrington, "William O. Douglas: Consistent Civil Libertarian or Parabolic Supporter?" *Journal of Politics,* 45 (1983), 490–496.

23. See the two studies by Sheldon Goldman, "Conflict and Consensus in the United States Courts of Appeals," *Wisconsin Law Review* (1968), 461–482, and "Conflict on the U.S. Courts of Appeals 1965–1971: A Quantitative Analysis," *University of Cincinnati Law Review,* 42 (1973), 635–658. Also see Burton M. Atkins, "Decision-Making Rules and Judicial Strategy on the United States Courts of Appeals," *Western Political Quarterly,* 25 (1972), 626–642, and Charles M. Lamb, "Warren Burger

and the Insanity Defense: Judicial Philosophy and Voting Behavior on a U.S. Court of Appeals," *American University Law Review,* 24 (1974), 91–128.

24. Joel B. Grossman, "Dissenting Blocs on the Warren Court: A Study in Judicial Role Behavior," *Journal of Politics,* 30 (1968), 1089.

25. See the discussion and materials cited in Schubert, *Quantitative Analysis,* Chap. 5. In general, see Gary M. Maranell (ed.), *Scaling: A Sourcebook for Behavioral Scientists* (Chicago: Aldine, 1974).

26. The coefficient of reproducibility is 1 minus the number of inconsistent responses (in terms of a perfect scale) divided by the number of items scored. CR measures the extent to which one is able to correctly reproduce the responses from the respondents' scale positions or scale scores. See the discussion in Schubert, *Quantitative Analysis,* pp. 271–272.

27. See Schubert, *Quantitative Analysis,* pp. 269–270, for references to other early work in adapting Guttman scaling for judicial research.

28. See the discussion in Schubert, *Judicial Mind,* pp. 79–81.

29. Glendon Schubert, in particular, developed an attitudinal or (as he named it) a *psychometric model* of judicial conversion and constructed an elaborate and sophisticated methodology with which to test it. See *Judicial Mind* and also his *The Judicial Mind Revisited: Psychometric Analysis of Supreme Court Ideology* (New York: Oxford University Press, 1974). Simply stated, the psychometric model considers cases to be stimuli and judicial votes to be responses that represent attitudes toward the substantive issues. What is important is the nature of the stimulus and the point where it falls along the value continuum as well as the individual judge's attitude and its point on the value continuum. For a thorough consideration of Schubert's extensive contributions see Fred Kort, "The Works of Glendon Schubert: The History of a Subdiscipline," *The Political Science Reviewer,* 4 (1974), 193–227.

30. See the discussion in Schubert, *Judicial Mind,* pp. 99–127. The different types of civil liberties cases are discussed in *ibid.,* Chap. 6.

31. *Ibid.,* pp. 127–128; also see pp. 127–146. Types of economic liberalism cases are discussed in *ibid.,* Chap. 6. Note that cases involving government economic regulation of business are included. A vote favoring government regulation in the public interest (the public being the "underdog") is considered to be the economically liberal position.

32. See Harold J. Spaeth and Douglas R. Parker, "Effects of Attitude toward Situation upon Attitude toward Object," *Journal of Psychology,* 73 (1969), 173–182; Harold J. Spaeth and David J. Peterson, "The Analysis and Interpretation of Dimensionality: The Case of Civil Liberties Decision-Making," *Midwest Journal of Political Science,* 15 (1971), 415–441; Harold J. Spaeth, David B. Meltz, Gregory J. Rathjen, and Michael V. Haselswerdt, "Is Justice Blind: An Empirical Investigation of a Normative Ideal," *Law and Society Review,* 7 (1972), 119–137; and Harold J. Spaeth and David W. Rohde, *Supreme Court Decision Making* (San Francisco: Freeman, 1976). Spaeth and colleagues draw heavily on the attitude and value theory developed by Milton Rokeach. See Rokeach's *Beliefs, Attitudes and Values* (San Francisco: Jossey-Bass, 1968) and his "The Nature of Attitudes," *International Encyclopedia of the Social Sciences,* 1 (1968), 449–457. In general, see Jarol B. Manheim, *The Politics within: A Primer in Political Attitudes and Behavior* (Englewood Cliffs, N.J.: Prentice-Hall, 1975). For an application of scaling and attitude and value theory to the pre-1945 Supreme Court, see Donald Leavitt, "Changing Issues, Ideological and Political Influences on the U.S. Supreme Court, 1893–1945," paper presented at the 1974 Annual Meeting of the American Political Science Association. Also see Roger

Handberg, Jr., "Decision-Making in a Natural Court, 1916–1921," *American Politics Quarterly,* 4 (1976), 357–378, and David J. Danelski, "Values as Variables in the Judicial Process," *Vanderbilt Law Review,* 19 (1966), 721–740.

33. See, for example, "Computer Helps Predict Court Rulings," *New York Times,* August 15, 1971, sec. 1. p. 75; "Court Handicappers: Computer Predictions of Supreme Court Decisions," *Newsweek,* 84 (August 12, 1974), 53.

34. Spaeth and Rohde, *Supreme Court Decision Making,* Chap. 7.

35. Glendon Schubert, "Prediction from a Psychometric Model," in Glendon Schubert (ed.), *Judicial Behavior: A Reader in Theory and Research* (Skokie, Ill.: Rand McNally, 1964), pp. 548–587.

36. See Goldman, "Conflict on the U.S. Courts of Appeals, 1965–1971," pp. 652–656. Also see Charles M. Lamb, "Warren Burger and the Insanity Defense: Judicial Philosophy and Voting Behavior on a U.S. Court of Appeals," *American University Law Review,* 24 (1974), 118. But cf. John P. McIver, "Scaling Judicial Decisions: The Panel Decisionmaking Process of the U.S. Courts of Appeals," *American Journal of Political Science,* 20 (1976), 749–761.

37. See, for example, Joseph Tanenhaus, "The Cumulative Scaling of Judicial Decisions," *Harvard Law Review,* 79 (1966), 1583–1594; Sprague, *Voting Patterns,* pp. 9–11, 73–77, 157–160. In general, see C. Neal Tate, "The Methodology of Judicial Behavior Research: A Review and Critique," *Political Behavior,* 5 (1983), 65–70.

38. Glendon Schubert, "Ideologies and Attitudes, Academic and Judicial," *Journal of Politics,* 29 (1967), 3–41; S. Sidney Ulmer, "The Dimensionality of Judicial Voting Behavior," *Midwest Journal of Political Science,* 13 (1969), 471–483.

39. Sheldon Goldman, "Voting Behavior on the United States Courts of Appeals, 1961–1964," *American Political Science Review,* 60 (1966), pp. 378–379, and Sheldon Goldman, "Voting Behavior on the United States Courts of Appeals Revisited," *American Political Science Review,* 69 (1975), pp. 491–506.

40. Note that the study of ideological voting patterns has also made use of factor analysis, a mathematical technique, enabling one to extract the underlying dimensions in a correlation matrix. The method is a data-reduction method in that it cuts through the multitude of surface relationships to uncover the essential commonalities. Factor analysis of a matrix of phi coefficients is an integral part of the methodology used by Schubert (see *Judicial Mind* and *Judicial Mind Revisited*). Schubert discusses another data-reduction technique, smallest space analysis, in his "Dimensions of Decisional Response," pp. 181–185. See the discussion of factor analysis in Murphy and Tanenhaus, *Study of Public Law,* pp. 208–212.

41. Burton M. Atkins, "Decision-Making Rules and Judicial Strategy on the United States Courts of Appeals," *Western Political Quarterly,* 25 (1972), 626–642. Also see Burton M. Atkins, "Judicial Behavior and Tendencies toward Conformity in a Three Member Small Group: A Case Study of Dissent Behavior on the United States Court of Appeals," *Social Science Quarterly,* 54 (1973), 41–53.

42. Burton M. Atkins and William Zavoina, "Judicial Leadership on the Court of Appeals: A Probability Analysis of Panel Assignments in Race Relations Cases on the Fifth Circuit," *American Journal of Political Science,* 18 (1974), 701–711.

43. See the citations contained in Goldman, "Voting Behavior, 1961–1964," p. 375, n. 6; Goldman, "Conflict on the U.S. Courts of Appeals 1965–1971," p. 636, n. 3; and Goldman, "Voting Behavior Revisited," p. 491, n. 2. Also see Burton M. Atkins and Justin Green, "Consensus on the United States Courts of Appeals: Illusion or Reality?" *American Journal of Political Science,* 20 (1976), 735–748; Charles M. Lamb, "Exploring the Conservatism of Federal Appeals Court Judges," *Indiana Law*

Journal, 51 (1976), 257–279; Sheldon Goldman, "The Effect of Past Judicial Behavior on Subsequent Decision-Making," *Jurimetrics Journal,* 19 (1979), 208–217; J. Woodford Howard, Jr., *Courts of Appeals in the Federal Judicial System: A Study of the Second, Fifth, and District of Columbia Circuits* (Princeton, N.J.: Princeton University Press, 1981); Donald R. Songer, "Consensual and Nonconsensual Decisions in Unanimous Opinions of the United States Courts of Appeals," *American Journal of Political Science,* 26 (1982), 225–239; Justin J. Green, "Parameters of Dissensus on Shifting Small Groups," in Goldman and Lamb (eds.), *Judicial Conflict and Consensus;* Stephen L. Wasby, "Of Judges, Hobgoblins, and Small Minds: Dimensions of Disagreement in the Ninth Circuit," in *Judicial Conflict and Consensus;* Donald R. Songer, "Factors Affecting Variation in Rates of Dissent in the U.S. Courts of Appeals," in *Judicial Conflict and Consensus;* and Charles M. Lamb, "A Micro-Analysis of Appeals Court Conflict: Warren Burger and His Colleagues on the D.C. Circuit," in *Judicial Conflict and Consensus.*

44. S. Sidney Ulmer, "Social Background as an Indicator to the Votes of Supreme Court Justices in Criminal Cases: 1947–1956 Terms," *American Journal of Political Science,* 17 (1973), 622–630. Also see his earlier study, "Dissent Behavior and the Social Background of Supreme Court Justices," *Journal of Politics,* 32 (1970), 580–598.

45. C. Neal Tate, "Personal Attribute Models of the Voting Behavior of U.S. Supreme Court Justices: Liberalism in Civil Liberties and Economic Decisions, 1946–1978," *American Political Science Review,* 75 (1981), 355–367.

46. Goldman, "Voting Behavior Revisited."

47. Sheldon Goldman, "The Effect of Past Judicial Behavior on Subsequent Decision-Making," *Jurimetrics Journal,* 19 (1979), 208–217.

48. Jon Gottschall, "Carter's Judicial Appointments: The Influence of Affirmative Action and Merit Selection on Voting on the U.S. Courts of Appeals," *Judicature,* 67 (1983), 164–173; Thomas R. Hensley and Joyce Baugh, "The 1978 Omnibus Judgeships Act: Impact on the Federal Judiciary," paper delivered at the 1983 annual meeting of the American Political Science Association. But cf. Thomas G. Walker and Deborah J. Barrow, "The Diversification of the Federal Bench: Policy and Process Ramifications," paper delivered at the 1982 annual meeting of the Southern Political Science Association.

49. Kenneth N. Vines, "Federal District Judges and Race Relations Cases in the South," *Journal of Politics,* 26 (1964), 338–357.

50. Micheal W. Giles and Thomas G. Walker, "Judicial Policy-Making and Southern School Segregation," *Journal of Politics,* 37 (1975), 917–936.

51. Larger school districts, those with a higher concentration of black students, school districts in which the federal courthouse was geographically situated, and districts in which the presiding federal judge's undergraduate and law school education was entirely within the South had higher levels of court-approved school *segregation* than smaller districts with lower black enrollments situated away from the federal courthouse and presided over by judges whose higher education was outside the South.

52. Kenneth M. Dolbeare, "The Federal District Courts and Urban Public Policy: An Exploratory Study (1960–1967)," in Grossman and Tanenhaus (eds.), *Frontiers of Judicial Research,* pp. 373–405.

53. Thomas G. Walker, "A Note Concerning Partisan Influences on Trial-Judge Decision Making," *Law and Society Review,* 6 (1972), 645–649.

54. C. K. Rowland and Robert A. Carp, "The Relative Effects of Maturation, Time Period, and Appointing President on District Judges' Policy Choices: A Cohort Analysis," *Political Behavior,* 5 (1983), 109–133, and Robert A. Carp and C. K.

Rowland, *Policy Making and Politics on the Federal District Courts* (Knoxville: University of Tennessee Press, 1983).

55. It is possible that the methods used by Dolbeare and Walker were responsible for their finding no relationship between backgrounds and decisional results. Because there were insufficient numbers of cases for each judge to enable the researchers to quantify individually the behavioral tendencies of each judge, it was necessary to treat the judges and cases as fungible. Studies that *have* found some relationship between backgrounds (such as party) and voting behavior have generally been based on aggregating the decision scores of individual judges (i.e., judges were not considered to be fungible). However, Carp and Rowland's method was similar to that used by Dolbeare and Walker, but the large numbers of cases Carp and Rowland worked with enabled them to use controls that Dolbeare and Walker were unable to use.

56. J. Woodford Howard, Jr., "Judicial Biography and the Behavioral Persuasion," *American Political Science Review,* 65 (1971), 712.

57. David J. Danelski, *A Supreme Court Justice Is Appointed* (New York: Random House, 1964), pp. 186–189.

58. *Ibid.,* pp. 189–190.

59. David J. Danelski, "Legislative and Judicial Decision-Making: The Case of Harold H. Burton," in S. Sidney Ulmer (ed.), *Political Decision-Making* (New York: Van Nostrand Reinhold, 1970), pp. 121–146. In general, see Mary Frances Berry, *Stability, Security and Continuity: Mr. Justice Burton and Decision-Making in the Supreme Court, 1945–1958* (Westport, Conn.: Greenwood Press, 1978).

60. See in general S. Sidney Ulmer, *Courts as Small and Not So Small Groups* (Morristown, N.J.: General Learning Press, 1971).

61. Cf. Eloise Snyder, "The Supreme Court as a Small Group," *Social Forces,* 36 (1958), 232–238. Snyder's study relied on voting data; her work, however, is perhaps closest in approach to the attitudinal studies. Thomas Walker's work also relied in large part on voting data. See the reference in note 120. Note that the popular journalistic account by Bob Woodward and Scott Armstrong, *The Brethren* (New York: Simon & Schuster, 1979), was a study of the Supreme Court as, in effect, a small group. The principal data sources consisted of interviews with then current and former law clerks to the justices.

62. See Walter F. Murphy, *Elements of Judicial Strategy* (Chicago: University of Chicago Press, 1964), especially Chaps. 3, 7, and 8.

63. See, for example, the biographies cited in Howard, "Judicial Biography," and the various empirical analyses cited in this chapter.

64. 330 U.S. 1 (1947).

65. The discussion in the text is drawn from J. Woodford Howard, Jr., "On the Fluidity of Judicial Choice," *American Political Science Review,* 62 (1968), 54.

66. *Ibid.* Note that the source for Rutledge's remarks was the conference notes of Justice Murphy.

67. J. Woodford Howard, Jr., *Mr. Justice Murphy* (Princeton, N.J.: Princeton University Press, 1968), p. 450.

68. *Ibid.,* p. 444.

69. *Ibid.,* p. 450.

70. 319 U.S. 141 (1943).

71. The discussion is drawn from Howard, *Mr. Justice Murphy,* pp. 291–294.

72. 337 U.S. 1 (1949).

73. Howard, *Mr. Justice Murphy,* p. 484. But note that in the aggregate, for the overwhelming majority of cases, the evidence suggests virtually no vote changes from the

votes in judicial conference to the public announcement of the decision. Saul Brenner, "Fluidity on the Supreme Court: 1956–1967," *American Journal of Political Science,* 26 (1982), 388–390, found that in 87 percent of the votes the justices' final votes were the same as the original votes in conference. Also see Brenner's earlier article, "Fluidity on the United States Supreme Court: A Reexamination," *American Journal of Political Science,* 24 (1980), 526–535.

74. Alexander Bickel (ed.), *The Unpublished Opinions of Mr. Justice Brandeis* (Cambridge, Mass.: Harvard University Press, 1957); and Murphy, *Judicial Strategy,* p. 201.

75. Quoted in Bickel, *Unpublished Opinions,* p. 18, as cited by Murphy, *Judicial Strategy,* p. 57.

76. As quoted by Murphy, *Judicial Strategy,* pp. 57–58.

77. *Ibid.,* p. 59.

78. Milkwagon Drivers Union v. Meadowmoor Dairies, 312 U.S. 287 (1941).

79. Thornhill v. Alabama, 310 U.S. 88 (1940).

80. Carlson v. California, 310 U.S. 106 (1940).

81. As quoted in Murphy, *Judicial Strategy,* p. 58.

82. *Ibid.,* p. 59. Italics added.

83. *Ibid.,* p. 198.

84. David J. Danelski, "The Influence of the Chief Justice in the Decisional Process of the Supreme Court," in Thomas P. Jahnige and Sheldon Goldman (eds.), *The Federal Judicial System* (New York: Holt, Rinehart and Winston, 1968), pp. 158–160.

85. See Goldman, "Conflict and Consensus," pp. 479–480; Marvin Schick, *Learned Hand's Court* (Baltimore: Johns Hopkins Press, 1970); Howard, *Courts of Appeals,* pp. 207–221.

86. Goldman, "Conflict and Consensus," p. 479.

87. *Ibid.*

88. Alpheus T. Mason, *Harlan Fiske Stone: Pillar of the Law* (New York: Viking, 1956), p. 254, as cited in Murphy, *Judicial Strategy,* p. 53.

89. Howard, *Mr. Justice Murphy,* pp. 425–426.

90. Television interview with former Justice Arthur Goldberg on NET Journal: Documentary on Earl Warren, July 7, 1969.

91. See Edward V. Heck, "Justice Brennan and the Heyday of Warren Court Liberalism," *Santa Clara Law Review,* 20 (1980), 841–887. Also see Woodward and Armstrong, *The Brethren,* p. 47.

92. See Woodward and Armstrong, *The Brethren,* p. 362. Cf. John A. Jenkins, "A Candid Talk with Justice Blackmun," *New York Times Magazine,* February 20, 1983, pp. 20–29, 57, 61, 66.

93. See, for example, Murphy, *Judicial Strategy,* pp. 49–50.

94. *Ibid.,* p. 51.

95. *Ibid.,* p. 52.

96. James Sterling Young, *The Washington Community 1800–1828* (New York: Harcourt Brace Jovanovich, 1969), pp. 76–77, notes that until 1845 the justices of the Supreme Court roomed and took meals at a common table in the same lodging house on Capitol Hill. Quoting Justice Story, "'The Judges here live with perfect harmony . . . in the most frank and unaffected intimacy. We are all united as one.'" Young himself observed that "The unanimity of their [the Supreme Court's] case decisions provides little food for political analysis beyond the observation that their single-mindedness on policy questions conformed to the fraternal character of their life

style." John R. Schmidhauser has argued that this constant social interaction helped Chief Justice John Marshall to dominate the Court. See Schmidhauser's *The Supreme Court: Its Politics, Personalities, and Procedures* (New York: Holt, Rinehart and Winston, 1960), pp. 111–114.

97. See, for example, the studies cited in Thomas W. Madron, *Small Group Methods* (Evanston, Ill.: Northwestern University Press, 1969). Also see Graham S. Gibbard, John J. Hartman, and Richard D. Mann (eds.), *Analysis of Groups: Contributions to Theory, Research and Practice* (San Francisco: Jossey-Bass, 1974).

98. See the citations in Danelski, "Influence of the Chief Justice," pp. 151–152, nn. 22–25.

99. *Ibid.*

100. *Ibid.,* p. 151.

101. *Ibid.,* p. 152.

102. As quoted in *ibid.,* p. 153.

103. *Ibid.,* p. 154.

104. *Ibid.,* p. 156.

105. See the discussion and references in Sheldon Goldman, *Constitutional Law and Supreme Court Decision-Making* (New York: Harper & Row, 1982), pp. 423–427.

106. *Ibid.,* pp. 427–430.

107. *Ibid.,* pp. 543–546. Also see Woodward and Armstrong, *The Brethren, passim,* but note that no documentation is provided and that the authors accept at face value the comments and perspective of the young law clerks, whose objectivity is questionable.

108. Discussion of the assignment power is drawn from Danelski, "Influence of the Chief Justice," pp. 156–158.

109. Examples can be found in David J. Danelski, "The Assignment of the Court's Opinion by the Chief Justice," paper presented at the Annual Meeting of the Midwest Conference of Political Scientists, 1960; also see Danelski, "Legislative and Judicial Decision-Making," p. 139.

110. Justice Brennan observed of Chief Justice Warren: "He bent over backwards in assigning opinions to assure that each Justice, including himself, wrote approximately the same number of Court opinions and received a fair share of the more desirable ones." William J. Brennan, Jr., "Chief Justice Warren," *Harvard Law Review,* 88 (1974), 2. But see the contrary empirical evidence in S. Sidney Ulmer, "The Use of Power in the Supreme Court: The Opinion Assignments of Earl Warren, 1953–1960," *Journal of Public Law,* 19 (1970), 49–67; William P. McLauchlan, "Research Note: Ideology and Conflict in Supreme Court Opinion Assignment, 1946–1962," *Western Political Quarterly,* 25 (1972), 16–27; and David W. Rohde, "Policy Goals, Strategic Choice, and Majority Opinion Assignments in the U.S. Supreme Court," *Midwest Journal of Political Science,* 16 (1972), 652–682. On the other hand, some empirical support for Brennan's assertion can be inferred from the findings of Gregory James Rathjen, "Policy Goals, Strategic Choice, and Majority Opinion Assignments in the U.S. Supreme Court: A Replication," *American Journal of Political Science,* 18 (1974), 713–724. These studies are not contradictory but rather suggest that Warren in civil liberties but *not* in economic cases (according to the Rathjen study) assigned majority opinions to himself or to the justice closest to his views on the particular civil liberties issue raised in order to have the Court make policy closest to his own policy preferences. Opinion assignment in the economic cases may have been used in part to equalize the work load. In general, see the following three articles by Elliot E. Slotnick: "The Chief Justices and Self Assignment of Majority Opinions: A Research Note," *Western Political Quarterly,* 31

(1978), 219–225; "Judicial Career Patterns and Majority Opinion Assignment on the Supreme Court," *Journal of Politics,* 41 (1979), 640–648; and "Who Speaks for the Court? Majority Opinion Assignment from Taft to Burger," *American Journal of Political Science,* 23 (1979), 60–77. See Saul Brenner, "Strategic Choice and Opinion Assignment on the U.S. Supreme Court: A Reexamination," *Western Political Quarterly,* 35 (1982), 204–211. Also note the analysis of opinion assignment on the Burger Court which demonstrates that Chief Justice Burger in the 12 terms from 1969 through 1980 tended to assign each justice a roughly equal number of opinions. See Harold J. Spaeth, "Distributive Justice: Majority Opinion Assignments in the Burger Court," *Judicature,* 67 (1984), 299–304. Note also that there is some evidence of expertise being a consideration in opinion assignments on the courts of appeals. See Burton M. Atkins, "Opinion Assignments on the United States Courts of Appeals: The Question of Issue Specialization," *Western Political Quarterly,* 27 (1974), 409–428; and Howard, *Courts of Appeals,* pp. 232–258.

111. Danelski, "Influence of the Chief Justice," p. 158.

112. *Ibid.,* p. 160.

113. The definitive account of the decisional process involved in the *Brown* cases and preceding events is provided by Richard Kluger, *Simple Justice* (New York: Knopf, 1975). Also see S. Sidney Ulmer, "Earl Warren and the *Brown* Decision," *Journal of Politics,* 33 (1971), 689–702. For a brief general overview see Goldman, *Constitutional Law,* pp. 427–429. Also see Irving F. Lefberg, "Chief Justice Vinson and the Politics of Desegregation," *Emory Law Journal,* 24 (1975), 243–312.

114. See S. Sidney Ulmer, "Bricolage and Assorted Thoughts on Working in the Papers of Supreme Court Justices," *Journal of Politics,* 35 (1973), 306–308; Jack Anderson and Carl Kalvelage, *American Government . . . Like It Is* (Morristown, N.J.: General Learning Press, 1972), p. 69.

115. Ulmer, "Earl Warren and the *Brown* Decision," pp. 690–692. Chief Justice Warren also indicated this in an interview on public television, broadcast and produced by WGBH (Boston), on December 11, 1972, and reprinted in part in Sheldon Goldman and Austin Sarat (eds.), *American Court Systems: Readings in Judicial Process and Behavior* (San Francisco: Freeman, 1978), pp. 520–522. In general, see Kluger, *Simple Justice,* vol. 2, pp. 830–883.

116. Warren television interview reprinted in Goldman and Sarat (eds.), *American Court Systems,* p. 522.

117. Ulmer, "Earl Warren and the *Brown* Decision," p. 699. Anderson and Kalvelage report that Warren took the draft of his *Brown* opinion to Justice Robert Jackson, who was in a hospital, and by Jackson's bedside Warren explained it to him *(American Government,* p. 69). See Kluger, *Simple Justice,* vol. 2, pp. 857–883.

118. Ulmer, "Earl Warren and the *Brown* Decision," pp. 698–699; Kluger, *Simple Justice,* vol. 2, pp. 879–882.

119. See the discussion in Ulmer, *Courts as Small and Not So Small Groups.*

120. Thomas G. Walker, "Judges in Concert: The Influence of the Group on Judicial Decision-Making," Ph.D. dissertation, University of Kentucky, 1970.

121. *Ibid.,* pp. 99–104. Walker found that southern judges preferred the collegial court more than judges from the other regions (pp. 103–104).

122. See, for example, Schick, *Learned Hand's Court.*

123. See, for example, the studies cited in footnote 110. Also see the numerous studies by S. Sidney Ulmer that have utilized the diary and papers of Justice Harold Burton, such as "The Decision to Grant Certiorari as an Indicator to Decision 'On the Merits,'" *Polity,* 4 (1972), 429–447. Also see Glendon Schubert, "Policy without

Law: An Extension of the Certiorari Game," *Stanford Law Review,* 14 (1962), 284–327; Saul Brenner, "The New Certiorari Game," *Journal of Politics,* 41 (1979), 649–655.

124. Peter F. Nardulli, James Eisenstein, and Roy B. Flemming, "Unraveling the Complexities of Decision Making in Face-to-Face Groups: A Contextual Analysis of Plea Bargained Sentences," *American Political Science Review,* 78 (1984), in press.

125. Fred Kort, "Simultaneous Equations and Boolean Algebra in the Analysis of Judicial Decisions," in Jahnige and Goldman (eds.), *Federal Judicial System,* p. 167.

126. Herman Oliphant, "Facts, Opinions, and Value Judgments," *Texas Law Review,* 10 (1932), 127–139. See the discussion of Oliphant's work in Rumble, *Legal Realism,* pp. 159–161.

127. See Reed C. Lawlor, "Personal Stare Decisis," *Southern California Law Review,* 41 (1967), 73–118, and his other works cited therein. Also see Stuart S. Nagel, *The Legal Process from a Behavioral Perspective* (Homewood, Ill.: Dorsey, 1969), Chaps. 10–13.

128. See the following articles by S. Sidney Ulmer: "Supreme Court Behavior in Racial Exclusion Cases: 1935–1960," *American Political Science Review,* 56 (1962), 325–330; "Mathematical Models for Predicting Judicial Behavior," in Joseph Bernd (ed.), *Mathematical Applications in Political Science—III* (Charlottesville: University of Virginia Press, 1967), pp. 67–95; "The Discriminant Function and a Theoretical Context for Its Use in Estimating the Votes of Judges," in Joel Grossman and Joseph Tanenhaus (eds.), *Frontiers of Judicial Research* (New York: Wiley, 1969), pp. 335–369.

129. Kort, "Simultaneous Equations and Boolean Algebra."

130. Lawlor, "Personal Stare Decisis."

131. Ulmer, "Discriminant Function," p. 339.

132. *Ibid.,* p. 342.

133. *Ibid.,* p. 358, n. 45.

134. *Ibid.*

135. Reed C. Lawlor and H. T. Fehn, "A Study of Appellate Briefs," Report no. 4, in Reed C. Lawlor, *Judicial Opinions: Analysis and Prediction* (Reports to the National Science Foundation, 1968), mimeographed.

136. *Ibid.,* p. 22. For an analysis of search and seizure cases see Jeffrey A. Segal, "Predicting Supreme Court Cases," *American Political Science Review,* 78 (1984), in press.

137. Fred Kort, "Content Analysis of Judicial Opinions and Rules of Law," in Glendon Schubert (ed.), *Judicial Decision-Making* (New York: Free Press, 1963), p. 137.

138. Stuart S. Nagel, "Using Simple Calculations to Predict Judicial Decisions," *American Behavioral Scientist,* 4 (1960), 24.

139. Ulmer, "Discriminant Function," p. 365. Also see Ulmer's study of Earl Warren, "Support for Negro Claimants in the Warren Court: The Case of the Chief Justice," *Jurimetrics Journal,* 11 (1971), 179–188.

140. See, for example, Kenneth N. Vines, "The Role of Circuit Courts of Appeal in the Federal Judicial Process: A Case Study," *Midwest Journal of Political Science,* 7 (1963), 305–319; Jack W. Peltason, *Fifty-Eight Lonely Men: Southern Federal Judges and School Desegregation* (New York: Harcourt Brace Jovanovich, 1961); Comment, "Judicial Performance in the Fifth Circuit," *Yale Law Journal,* 73 (1963), 90–133; Charles V. Hamilton, *The Bench and the Ballot: Southern Federal Judges and Black Voters* (New York: Oxford University Press, 1973). Also see Marvin E. Wolfgang and Marc Riedel, "Race, Judicial Discretion, and the Death Penalty," *The Annals of the American Academy of Political and Social Science,* 407 (1973), 119–133; Isaac D. Balbus, *The Dialectics of Legal Repression: Black Rebels*

Before the American Criminal Courts (New York: Basic Books , 1973); Walter G. Markham, "Chromatic Justice: Color as an Element of the Offense," paper presented at the Annual Meeting of the A.P.S.A., 1974. But note that a reanalysis of the major empirical studies of sentencing behavior and the race of the defendant found the statistical evidence for racial discrimination in sentencing by judges to be weak. See John Hagan, "Extra-Legal Attributes and Criminal Sentencing: An Assessment of a Sociological Viewpoint," *Law and Society Review,* 8 (1974), 357–383. But cf. James L. Gibson, "Race as a Determinant of Criminal Sentences: A Methodological Critique and a Case Study," *Law and Society Review,* 12 (1978), 455–478; Cassia Spohn, John Gruhl, and Susan Welch, "The Effect of Race on Sentencing—A Re-Examination of an Unsettled Question," *Law and Society Review,* 16 (1981), 71–88. Also see the findings of Charles R. Pruitt and James Q. Wilson, "A Longitudinal Study of the Effect of Race on Sentencing," *Law and Society Review,* 17 (1983), 613–635. A persuasive statistical critique of the studies that *fail* to find racial discrimination in sentencing is offered by Samuel L. Myers, Jr., "Statistical Tests of Discrimination in Punishment," paper presented at the 1984 annual meeting of the Law and Society Association. Also see his "Race and Punishment: Directions for Economic Research," *The American Economic Review,* 74 (1984), 288–292.

141. John Gruhl, Cassia Spohn, and Susan Welch, "Women as Policymakers: The Case of Trial Judges," *American Journal of Political Science,* 25 (1981), 308–322. Also see Herbert M. Kritzer and Thomas M. Uhlman, "Sisterhood in the Courtroom: Sex of Judge and Defendant as Factors in Criminal Case Dispositions," *Social Science Quarterly,* 14 (1977), 77–88, and Candace Krutschnitt, "Social Status and Sentences of Female Offenders," *Law and Society Review,* 15 (1980), 247–265. But cf. Freda F. Solomon, "Factors Affecting Disposition of Urban Felony Cases: Sex as a Critical Variable," Ph.D. dissertation, Northwestern University, 1983.

142. This was reported in the *New York Times,* September 27, 1972, pp. 1ff. But note that these analyses did not take into consideration prior convictions; thus, John Hagan's reservations concerning other studies as reported in "Extra-Legal Attributes" may be applicable here. Note that James Eisenstein and Herbert Jacob also found that race did not emerge as statistically important in sentencing. See their *Felony Justice.* But cf. Gibson, "Race as a Determinant of Criminal Sentences."

143. *Racial Disparities in the Criminal Justice System* (Santa Monica, Calif.: Rand Corp., 1983). Petersilia noted that minorities were treated differently at the sentencing stage and that in part one main reason for this was that minority criminal defendants tended to do relatively less plea bargaining and to have relatively more jury trials than white defendants. See pp. vii, ix.

144. Annual Report, Administrative Office of the U.S. Courts, Fiscal 1980, Table D-5. Also see Marvin E. Frankel, *Criminal Sentences: Law Without Order* (New York: Hill & Wang, 1973), pp. 23–24. Also see John Hagan and Ilene Nagel Bernstein, "The Sentence Bargaining of Upperworld and Underworld Crime in Ten Federal District Courts," *Law and Society Review,* 13 (1979), 467–478.

145. *Federal Offenders, 1971,* pp. 14–15. Also see David Brereton and Jonathan D. Casper, "Does It Pay to Plead Guilty? Differential Sentencing and the Functioning of Criminal Courts," *Law and Society Review,* 16 (1981), 45–70. The attributes and attitudes of prosecutors and defense attorneys appear to be important for plea-bargained sentencing. See Nardulli, Eisenstein, and Flemming, "Unraveling the Complexities of Decision Making."

146. *Federal Offenders, 1971,* pp. 8–9. Also see Stuart S. Nagel, "Effects of Alternative Types of Counsel on Criminal Procedure Treatment," *Indiana Law Journal,* 48

(1973), 404–426. The reasons for this are not entirely clear. Perhaps privately retained lawyers tend to be more experienced and more skillful at persuading judges to be lenient than are assigned counsel. Perhaps judges are more lenient when no lawyer is present in order to "bend over backwards" to be fair to the defendant. Also, it is possible that the finding is a spurious relationship and a result of coincidence. See David Willison, "The Effects of Counsel on the Severity of Criminal Sentences: A Statistical Assessment," *Justice Systems Journal,* 9 (1984), 87–101.

147. Frankel, *Criminal Sentences.* Also see Stuart Nagel and Lenore J. Weitzman, "Double Standard of American Justice," *Society,* 9 (1972), 18–25, 62–63, and their study "Women as Litigants," *Hastings Law Journal,* 23 (1971), 171–198, for evidence of sexual discrimination in the judicial process. Cf. Hagen, "Extra-Legal."

148. Willard Gaylin, *Partial Justice: A Study of Bias in Sentencing* (New York: Knopf, 1974). Also see Keith D. Harries and Russell P. Lura, "The Geography of Justice: Sentence Variations in U.S. Judicial Districts," *Judicature,* 57 (1974), 392–401.

149. Anthony Partridge and William B. Eldridge, *The Second Circuit Sentencing Study: A Report to the Judges of the Second Circuit* (Washington, D.C.: Federal Judicial Center, 1974).

150. *The Second Circuit Sentencing Study,* pp. 6–7.

151. *Ibid.,* pp. 34–35.

152. David J. Danelski, "Conflict and Its Resolution in the Supreme Court," *Journal of Conflict Resolution,* 11 (1967), 76.

153. Joel B. Grossman, "Dissenting Blocs on the Warren Court: A Study in Judicial Role Behavior," *Journal of Politics,* 30 (1968), 1071. Also see Russell Wheeler, *Extrajudicial Behavior and the Role of the Supreme Court Justice* (Morristown, N.J.: General Learning Press, 1975); and Bruce Allen Murphy, *The Brandeis-Frankfurter Connection: The Secret Political Activities of Two Supreme Court Justices* (New York: Oxford University Press, 1982).

154. See Robert Carp and Russell Wheeler, "Sink or Swim: The Socialization of a Federal District Judge," *Journal of Public Law,* 21 (1972), 359; Beverly Blair Cook, "The Socialization of New Federal Judges: Impact on District Court Business," *Washington University Law Quarterly* (1971), 253–279. In general, see Charles H. Sheldon, *The American Judicial Process: Models and Approaches* (New York: Dodd, Mead, 1974), Chap. 3.

155. But see the revelations in Nina Totenberg, "Behind the Marble, Beneath the Robes," *New York Times Magazine,* March 16, 1975, 15, 58–67. Totenberg claims to have obtained interviews with justices, law clerks, and friends of the justices, among others. The article contains juicy accounts of conference deliberations over cases involving school busing, abortion, and the Nixon tapes. That such information could be obtained brings into doubt notions of widespread consensus concerning conference secrecy. On the other hand, given the unflattering portrait of Chief Justice Burger unveiled in the article, one could speculate that perhaps only one disgruntled justice and his entourage might have spilled the beans to Ms. Totenberg. Four years later, Bob Woodward and Scott Armstrong's book *The Brethren* appeared, and that, too, raised questions about the confidentiality of conference deliberations in light of the book's many "revelations." Woodward and Armstrong relied heavily on personal interviews, primarily with law clerks; however, they claim to have personally interviewed several of the justices.

156. Goldman, "Conflict and Consensus," p. 479. In general, see J. Woodford Howard, Jr., *Courts of Appeals in the Federal Judicial System: A Study of the Second, Fifth, and District of Columbia Circuits* (Princeton, N.J.: Princeton University Press, 1981).

157. See the comments of Howard, "Fluidity of Judicial Choice," p. 55.

158. Chief Justice Earl Warren explained in a television interview what happens next: "[We] go on until everybody has spoken . . . [and] generally stated his views. . . . [If] everyone is agreed that the outcome should be one way there's no need of taking a [formal] vote. But if there is a division [of opinion] . . . we start with the junior member of the Court and vote upwards instead of going from the Chief Justice down to the junior member of the Court." Warren television interview (WGBH), Boston, December 11, 1972, transcript pp. 7–8, as reprinted in Sheldon Goldman and Austin Sarat (eds.), *American Court Systems: Readings in Judicial Process and Behavior* (San Francisco: Freeman, 1978), p. 521.

159. Werner F. Grunbaum, "Analytical and Simulation Models for Explaining Judicial Decision-Making," in Grossman and Tanenhaus (eds.), *Frontiers of Judicial Research,* p. 329.

160. Note that cases which are unanimous affirmances at the appeals court level or at the Supreme Court level, with no lower court judge disagreement, are likely to be those decisions in which *stare decisis* plays the greatest part. See the discussion in Sheldon Goldman, "Backgrounds, Attitudes and the Voting Behavior of Judges," *Journal of Politics,* 31 (1969), 214–222. Also see Donald R. Songer, "Consensual and Nonconsensual Decisions in Unanimous Opinions of the United States Courts of Appeals," *American Journal of Political Science,* 26 (1982), 225–239; Francis M. Rich, Jr., "Role Perception and Precedent Orientation as Variables Influencing Appellate Judicial Decision-Making: An Analysis of the Fifth Circuit Court of Appeals," Ph.D. dissertation, University of Georgia, 1967. Also of interest in terms of the general research problem is the article by Bradley Canon and Dean Jaros: "External Variables, Institutional Structure and Dissent on State Supreme Courts," *Polity,* 3 (1970), 175–200. For some suggestive evidence concerning state trial and appellate court judges, see Thomas D. Ungs and Larry R. Baas, "Judicial Role Perception: A Q-Technique Study of Ohio Judges," *Law and Society Review,* 6 (1972), 343–366. Also see John T. Wold, "Political Orientation, Social Backgrounds, and Role Perceptions of State Supreme Court Judges," *Western Political Quarterly,* 27 (1974), 239–248. For an analysis based on mail questionnaire responses by middle-level appellate court judges in Austria and Switzerland, see Victor E. Flango, Lettie M. Wenner, and Manfred W. Wenner, "The Concept of Judicial Role: A Methodological Note," *American Journal of Political Science,* 19 (1975), 277–289. In general, see James L. Gibson, "The Role Concept in Judicial Research," *Law and Policy Quarterly,* 3 (1981), 291–311.

161. Glendon Schubert, "Civilian Control and Stare Decisis in the Warren Court," in Schubert (ed.), *Judicial Decision-Making,* pp. 55–77.

162. Martin Shapiro, "Stability and Change in Judicial Decision-Making: Incrementalism or Stare Decisis?" *Law in Transition Quarterly,* 2 (1965), 134–157; and see, in general, Martin Shapiro, "Toward a Theory of *Stare Decisis,*" *Journal of Legal Studies,* 1 (1972), 125–134.

163. Barron v. Baltimore, 7 Peters 243 (1833).

164. As quoted in Howard, "Fluidity of Judicial Choice," p. 49.

165. Danelski, "Conflict and Its Resolution," pp. 78–79.

166. Goldman, "Conflict and Consensus," pp. 463–464; and Goldman, "Conflict on the U.S. Courts of Appeals 1965–1971," pp. 638–639. Also see, in general, Howard, *Courts of Appeals in the Federal Judicial System.*

167. Goldman, "Conflict and Consensus," p. 478.

168. *Ibid.* There is some evidence that different urban political systems recruit judges with

markedly different role concepts in terms of rendering justice. See Martin A. Levin, "Urban Politics and Judicial Behavior," *Journal of Legal Studies,* 1 (1972), 193.

169. In general, see Stephen C. Halpern and Charles M. Lamb (eds.), *Supreme Court Activism and Restraint* (Lexington, Mass.: Lexington Books, Heath, 1982).

170. Louisiana ex rel Francis v. Resweber, 329 U.S. 459 (1947) at 471. As quoted in Danelski, "Conflict and Its Resolution," p. 76. On the Francis case, see Arthur S. Miller and Jeffrey H. Bowman, " 'Slow Dance on the Killing Ground': The *Willie Francis* Case Revisited," *DePaul Law Review,* 32 (1982), 1–75.

171. Harold J. Spaeth, "Warren Court Attitudes toward Business: The 'B' Scale," in Schubert (ed.), *Judicial Decision-Making,* pp. 79–108. Also see Anthony Champagne and Stuart S. Nagel, "The Advocates of Restraint: Holmes, Brandeis, Stone, and Frankfurter," in Halpern and Lamb (eds.), *Supreme Court Activism and Restraint,* pp. 303–318. In general, see Harry N. Hirsch, *The Enigma of Felix Frankfurter* (New York: Basic Books, 1981).

172. See in particular, Harold J. Spaeth, "Judicial Power as a Variable Motivating Supreme Court Behavior," *Midwest Journal of Political Science,* 6 (1962), 54–82. J. Woodford Howard, Jr., interviewed appeals court judges on the Second, Fifth, and District of Columbia Circuits and found some differences in the judges' role concept. Five judges saw their judicial work as innovating (akin to the activist position). Nine took the opposite position and asserted that their job was not to judicially legislate, but to confine themselves to the case at hand and avoid innovation whenever possible (similar to the restraint stand). Most (20) had what Howard considered the "realist" role concept; that is, they acknowledged more restraints than did the "innovators," but also more need and room for innovation than did the "interpreters" (or restraint-oriented judges). "Role Perceptions and Behavior in Three U.S. Courts of Appeals," *Journal of Politics,* 39 (1977), 916–938. See Howard, *Courts of Appeals in the Federal Judicial System.* In general, see the studies in Halpern and Lamb (eds.), *Supreme Court Activism and Restraint.*

173. *Law and the Modern Mind.*

174. Harold Lasswell, *Power and Personality* (New York: Norton, 1948), pp. 61–88.

175. In general, see Fred I. Greenstein, *Personality and Politics: Problems of Evidence, Inference, and Conceptualization* (Chicago: Markham, 1969).

176. See Abraham Kaplan, *The Conduct of Inquiry* (San Francisco: Chandler, 1964), pp. 327–369, for a discussion of what distinguishes causal explanations from predictive and functional ones.

177. See Hayward R. Alker, Jr., "Causal Inference and Political Analysis," in Joseph L. Bernd (ed.), *Mathematical Applications in Political Science, II* (Dallas: Southern Methodist University Press, 1966), pp. 7–43. In general, see Fred Kort, *A Special and a General Multivariate Theory of Judicial Decisions,* Sage Professional Papers in American Politics (Beverly Hills, Calif.: Sage, 1977).

178. See the discussion and citations in *ibid.*

179. Also see Edward J. Weissman, "Mathematical Theory and Dynamic Models," pp. 367–395; Glendon Schubert, "Two Causal Models of Decision-Making by the High Court of Australia," pp. 335–366, in Schubert and Danelski (eds.), *Comparative Judicial Behavior;* and David J. Danelski, "Causes and Consequences of Conflict and Its Resolution in the Supreme Court," in Goldman and Lamb (eds.), *Judicial Conflict and Consensus.*

180. James L. Gibson, "From Simplicity to Complexity: The Development of Theory in the Study of Judicial Behavior," *Political Behavior,* 5 (1983), 32.

181. Possibilities are suggested in the classic work of Rodney L. Mott, Spencer D. Alb-

right, and Helen R. Semmerling, "Judicial Personnel," *Annals of the American Academy of Political and Social Science,* 67 (1933), 143–155.

182. See Danelski's use of content analysis in his "Values as Variables" and "Legislative and Judicial Decision-Making: The Case of Harold H. Burton." Also see Carp and Rowland, *Policy Making and Politics on the Federal District Courts.*

183. The Schubert method as presented in the original and revisited *Judicial Mind,* and that used by Harold Spaeth and David Rohde, *Supreme Court Decision Making,* seem to be suggestive for classifying judges as to role concept. Also see Howard, *Courts of Appeals in the Federal Judicial System.*

184. See Weissman, "Mathematical Theory and Dynamic Models," pp. 389, 394, n. 18; Schubert, "Two Causal Models"; Alker, "Causal Inference," p. 13. Also see Dennis J. Palumbo, "Causal Inference and Indeterminancy in Political Behavior: Some Theoretical and Statistical Problems," paper presented at the Annual Meeting of the American Political Science Association, 1969. But see Kort, "A Special and a General Multivariate Theory."

185. Also see Gibson, "From Simplicity to Complexity: The Development of Theory in the Study of Judicial Behavior," *Political Behavior,* 5 (1983), 7–49.

chapter *6*

Output

In studying judicial output, we are primarily concerned with the formal decisions by which demands fed into the federal judicial system are finally and authoritatively disposed. This concern also includes a focus on the rules and norms that underlie the disposition of particular demands. In discussing output within the framework of political systems analysis, Easton distinguishes three different subconcepts as relevant to the main concept of output. These are *authoritative* output (the binding decisions of the authorities), *associated* output (which includes the statements that interpret, clarify, or build on authoritative output, but also encompasses other activities related to the judge's official position), and *outcomes* (the immediate effects or consequences of authoritative and associated outputs). In this chapter these concepts are considered (but with special attention to authoritative output and to the U.S. Supreme Court).

Traditionally, in their analyses of federal judicial output, historians, political scientists, and legal scholars have tended to focus almost exclusively on the decisions (authoritative outputs) and opinions (associated outputs) of the Supreme Court, especially in the "important" cases. The most highly regarded scholars have supplemented their keen analyses of Court decisions and opinions with extensive historical and judicial biographical research. They have used the Court's output as the springboard for understanding the place of the federal courts in American democracy. The literature produced by the major traditionalist (in method) legal scholars is rich and, indeed, indispensable for serious students of the federal judicial system.

Despite the fact that Supreme Court decisions and opinions constitute the most analyzed and perhaps the most interesting single species of output of the federal judicial system, their study must be approached with some care and sophistication. Although Supreme Court decisions and opinions (and the policies they represent) often have broad effect on the behavior of persons and institutions both in and out of government, the Court is, after all, only one of over 100 courts in the federal system. The combined output of the lower federal courts greatly exceeds that of the Supreme Court. Furthermore, Supreme Court (as well as lower court) decisions and opinions are but one species of output among a whole set of political outputs that determine the shape of public policy and the nature of social behavior in America. Consistent judicial gatekeeping—that is, the application of such systemic rules as those dealing with jurisdiction and justiciability —has meant that over broad periods of time some areas of public policy and social life, potentially within the Supreme Court's jurisdiction, have been left almost exclusively under the control of the state courts or other political institutions such as Congress, the state legislatures, or local governments.

When the Supreme Court decides an issue "on the merits," its decision does not unambiguously determine the decisions of subsequent cases raising similar questions, particularly in the lower courts. Even when the Court has made specific authoritative rulings, compliance problems can occur under the rules of the system. When the Supreme Court acts as an appellate court, its decisions and opinions are technically intrasystemic in nature. The Supreme Court (after it rules on the merits) may affirm the lower court's ruling or send the case back to the lower court for final disposition "not inconsistent" with the decision and opinion of the Court. Some lower courts have thus been able to turn a Supreme Court "winner" into a "loser" after all.[1] Therefore, to understand the outcome and impact of Supreme Court output, we must consider not only that output itself, but also the systemic rules and processes that influence or bear upon it.

THE RELATIONSHIP OF INPUT RULES TO OUTPUT

The federal judicial system's rules of jurisdiction and justiciability mean that certain areas of public policy never or almost never become the object of authoritative judicial output. Excluded are most questions of foreign policy, including decisions about diplomatic recognition, foreign aid, treaty making, whether to go to war, and military operations. Rather, judicial policy-making has been almost solely concerned with domestic affairs. Even in this area, broad questions involving governmental spending for public works, natural resource and technological development, and the raising of revenue have typically not been subjected to judicial control. Only in those areas where constitutionally protected individual rights are threatened—for example, in cases concerning equal treatment, just compensation for expropriated property, and political freedom—have the courts played an autonomous policy-making role. Judicial interference is also rare in the internal organization, procedures, and activities of the legislative and executive branches of government. Although cases are litigated concerning the hiring and firing of certain specific classes of employees, the validity of election procedures and districting, and the treatment of private citizens by legislative committees and executive officials, the questions involved rarely change the essential structure, procedures, or policy-making proclivities of the legislative and executive branches of government. The important exceptions to this generalization (and these *are* extremely important exceptions) are judicial policies concerning racial and sexual discrimination by or within governmental agencies, legislative malapportionment, and, of course, the behavior of law enforcement officials, an area of executive action closely related to the judiciary's control over criminal law.

In assessing the extent to which systemic rules limit judicial output, one should recognize the fact that these rules are to a broad degree self-defined and self-enforced. They are, therefore, subject to change. On rare occasions they have been changed by Congress either by legislation (e.g., the removal of the federal judiciary's jurisdiction over certain classes of *habeas corpus* cases following the Civil War)[2] or in conjunction with the states through constitutional amendment (e.g., the Eleventh and Sixteenth Amendments). Historically, however, most changes in the rules determining systemic input have been engineered by the federal judicial system itself through Supreme Court decisions.

Sometimes the change in jurisdictional rules is explicit, as in *Fay* v. *Noia*[3] (expanding the availability of federal *habeas corpus* for state prisoners) and *Baker* v. *Carr*[4] (announcing that state legislative malapportionment was a justiciable federal question). Other times the triggering judicial decision is more substantive in nature, but because the social or governmental behavior involved is widespread, a specific decision or set of decisions has the effect of promoting or stifling large amounts of litigation. *Brown* v. *Board of Education,*[5] for example, was a substantive decision that, by overruling the "separate but equal" doctrine of *Plessy* v. *Ferguson,*[6] generated vast amounts of litigation attacking segregationist laws and official activities which had developed under the protective mantle of the *Plessy* decision. Conversely, the many post-1937 economic decisions in which the Supreme Court left standing most state and almost all federal laws concerning the power to regulate economic life, as well as the frequent denial of certiorari in cases challenging the constitutionality of such legislation, have served to stifle litigation raising similar questions in more recent years.

GATEKEEPING AND THE NATURE OF SUPREME COURT OUTPUT

Many cases and controversies that are disposed of by gatekeeping contain issues that might well be fit subjects for Supreme Court review and decision making. In Chapter 4 the mechanisms of gatekeeping and some of its empirical dimensions were discussed in the analysis of how the judicial system protects itself from demand input overload. If gatekeeping were carried on in a completely random manner, then these processes would be of no greater interest than as an economical way by which a vast number of cases are disposed of with minimal expenditure of judicial time, energy, or resources.

But this is not so. Gatekeeping processes, at least at the Supreme Court level, have important implications by determining at any particular time which issues will be the subject of Court output and which will not. This is clearly understood by the justices and was and is the basis for the opposition on the part of so many justices and former justices to proposals that would diminish or eliminate the Court's gatekeeping authority. It is of interest to examine, by way of a formal model, litigant and judicial gatekeeping to see how these processes affect the Court's policy output.

At the outset it is apparent that, despite the policy dimension to gatekeeping, individual gatekeeping decisions in themselves generally stimulate little public controversy or interest.[7] This is not hard to understand, for when the members of the Court gatekeep by dismissing an appeal or denying a petition for certiorari, only rarely is the decision accompanied by a display of sharp intracourt dissension. Such decisions ordinarily do not make good copy for the communications media. Perhaps more important is the fact that there is generally no one point upon which criticism of gatekeeping decisions can focus, since only the result is announced and not the reasons behind the decisions. With denials of certiorari, the decisions even formally lack any assessment of the merits of the claims pressed. At the most, a denial of certiorari may represent an approval of lower court decision making; at the least, it is a nondecision, that is, a decision not to do anything. Because they involve the Court neither in new policy departures nor in the overt responsibility for existing policy, such nondecisions are generally perceived as not being politically salient. Nondecisions, however, when consistently made, are a form of policy-making. Until the 1920s, for example, the consistently made nondecision that First Amendment liberties would not be enforced by the federal courts on the states was a policy with profound political implications. Not until the 1925 case of *Gitlow* v. *New York*[8] did the Court finally reverse its position.

Most gatekeeping is a product of decision making by litigants and their lawyers. These include decisions to settle civil cases out of court, to plead guilty (with and without promises of a prosecutorial *quid pro quo*), plaintiff and prosecution decisions not to proceed to trial, and the decision of the losing party not to appeal the trial or intermediate appellate court decision. We therefore start our model of gatekeeping by a consideration of the factors involved in making such decisions.[9]

Litigant-lawyer gatekeeping doubtless involves some rough-and-ready form of cost-benefit analysis. Initially involved are calculations by the litigant of (1) the utility of a favorable judgment in terms of psychic satisfaction, prestige, money, freedom, and so forth; (2) the cost of going on with litigation in terms of time, money, psychic frustration, and so forth; and (3) the perceived probability of a favorable decision from a trial or appellate court. Representing the utility by U, the cost of litigation by C, and the perceived probability of a favorable judgment by p, we note that for any litigant, a, if[10]

$$U_a p_a \gg C_a$$

then the litigant will be inclined to press for a formal court judgment. If, on the other hand,[11]

$$U_a p_a \ll C_a$$

the litigant will be inclined to avoid further litigation by a gatekeeping solution. These solutions are of two types: (1) complete renunciation of all reward *(non-*

negotiated gatekeeping)—for example, no recovery in a civil suit or full payment of requested damages, a nonbargained guilty plea or the decision not to prosecute, complete acceptance of a trial or circuit court's (unfavorable) judgment—and (2) a negotiated settlement or bargained guilty plea *(negotiated gatekeeping)*. If the first option is exercised, then a gatekeeping solution is resorted to regardless of litigant *b*'s calculations.[12] If the second option is sought, then *b*'s calculations become important. If *b*'s calculations indicate that

$$U_b p_b \ll C_b$$

then negotiated gatekeeping is sought. What then must be determined is the worth, *W*, of the case for both *a* and *b*: for example, the size of the damages, the acceptable criminal charge with its projected penalties, and so on. If[13]

$$W_a = W_b$$

then a negotiated settlement or plea bargain occurs. If, however,[14]

$$W_a \neq W_b \quad \text{or} \quad U_b p_b \gg C_b$$

then a formal systemic resolution in terms of an authoritative court judgment will still be sought.

Litigant-lawyer gatekeeping is encouraged by a number of aspects of the judicial process. The costs of litigation, *C*, for both *a* and *b* are often high as compared to their utilities, *U*. This is particularly true for civil litigation and appellate review. The legal skill and familiarity with judicial and jury behavior of both litigants' lawyers mean that the perceived probabilities of a favorable court judgment for one side or the other tend to be the same; that is, there is a tendency for

$$p_a = 1 - p_b$$

Usually these probabilities approach zero for one side and unity for the other; that is, there is often little doubt by both lawyers as to what the *general* court judgment will be. At the same time, the *specific* decision is typically less pre-dictable. There is always the chance that an "unexpected" assessment of dam-ages or sentence will occur in terms of leniency or severity for the "losing" party. The specific result of a negotiated settlement, on the other hand, is much more predictable.

Stated conversely, this means that cases that go to trial and are pressed for appellate review for an authoritative output are those where either U_a or U_b or both are high (e.g., cases involving high stakes in monetary value, criminal penalties, prestige, or issues of public policy) and cases where p_a and p_b approach 0.5 (cases whose decisional results are ambiguous). Most favored, of course, are cases that combine both features.

Whether a case leads to the highest authoritative output of a Supreme Court ruling accompanied by a written opinion is dependent upon how the Court's members respond to the demand for such treatment by a petitioner for certiorari or appellant. Here we are interested in the exercise of judicial rather than litigant-lawyer gatekeeping. At this stage, questions of utility and decisional predictability once again play an important role. Utility considerations are suggested by the Court's giving special scrutiny and a higher acceptance rate to petitions where a prisoner's life is at stake as well as cases where the federal government favors review. But of greatest import are the justices' calculations of their own utilities in having the Court render an authoritative judgment on the specific questions of public policy presented. The process of filtering out cases where judicial utilities are low, either because the case is considered frivolous or its treatment would involve the Court in unwanted political controversy, is highly formalized in the exercise of granting certiorari petitions through the mechanisms of the Chief Justice's special discussion list and the "rule of four."

It should not be thought that Supreme Court gatekeeping only allows acceptance of cases involving important social interests or policy questions, while rejecting cases lacking these characteristics. Cases that are avoided because of the tactical consideration that a judicial decision would place the Court in the center of a storm of controversy are rejected not because the issues or interests are unimportant, but rather because they are considered too important. Even many frivolous cases that are rejected may contain important issues affecting widespread and powerful interests. It is not their lack of important issues that make these cases frivolous; rather it is because the points of law challenged are considered so well settled as to be beyond question, at least for the time being. This is the current status of cases questioning the constitutionality of state and federal authority to regulate the economy or the lack of governmental authority to regulate political speech. Importance or utility, therefore, as a criterion for judicial selection of cases for Supreme Court review, refers to the subjective evaluation by each member of the Court. In other words, to pass Supreme Court gatekeeping, a case must present issues upon which at least four members of the Court feel it is time for the Court to act. As already suggested, the cue of the federal government's favoring review and the question of a litigant's life or death are two objective criteria creating this subjective importance. A further, and perhaps as important, variable giving a case subjective importance is whether the issue raised falls into an area of stable judicial policy or not; that is, *is* the decisional result of the case in doubt?

Decisional ambiguity as an important criterion is indicated by the findings of Tanenhaus and his colleagues that both lower court dissension and conflict in circuits are relevant for the granting of certiorari.[15] Its importance is further suggested by the fact that the reversal rate for cases accepted on certiorari, at least in the past, has run about 50 percent.[16]

When it affects a whole area of the law, decisional ambiguity doubtless springs from deeply felt societal tensions. It may be created by changing patterns in social life (e.g., economic and technological development) that render old rules and norms inapplicable to the newly created modern conditions. For example, American industrialization generated severe economic and social dislocations that gave rise to numerous demands on the larger political system as well as the federal and state judicial systems. As a result, during most of the latter nineteenth and early twentieth centuries, there was widespread instability in the law governing economic life, especially involving employer-employee and manufacturer-consumer relationships. The Supreme Court as well as Congress and the state legislatures spent considerable time and energy on redefining the law of business regulation. This example suggests a simple causal model for explaining the surge and decline in cases that are considered important and thus deserving of Supreme Court time and policy-making creativity.

Old patterns of stable social life are broken by (economic and technological) developments leading to new patterns of social interaction. Such increasing social conflict generates increasing demands on legislative and judicial systems for new rules and norms. Legislative and/or lower level judicial authorities may respond by creating such new rules and norms, and the Supreme Court may then legitimize them by reinterpreting or changing the previously established legal norms. This cycle continues until a new pattern of stable social relationships is established.

A similar process occurs when previously thwarted demands are made amenable to authoritative treatment by decisions made solely by the judicial authorities. Such a situation has characterized the Court's confrontation with the issues of racial segregation, sexual equality, and legislative malapportionment. In fact, it has often been stated by admirers of the judiciary that one contribution that the courts, and especially the Supreme Court, uniquely make for conflict resolution in American society is to offer oppressed groups a forum for treating demands that otherwise are untreatable because of the control exercised by entrenched majorities, whether they be in a national or local electorate, a legislative body, or a local governmental area such as a school district. Here a favorable judicial decision encourages litigation calling for new judicial decisions and often legislation creating new rules and norms. In the broader sense, conflict is thereby enhanced rather than resolved as new issues demand the attention of political authorities. Thus legal instability continues to make such issues subjectively important for members of the Court.

This demand-flow/gatekeeping model of what cases and issues ultimately become formal output following Supreme Court review illuminates some empirical characteristics of Court policy-making. First, it has often been noted that the Court concentrates its energies on certain questions of public policies during certain specific historical periods, for example, economic issues from after the Civil War until the mid-1930s, civil rights and civil liberties since then. These policy proclivities of the Court are often explained in terms of judicial attitudes, backgrounds, or political sensitivities. However, as just suggested, an understanding of Court output also requires consideration of the nature of the demands made on the system as well as the nature of gatekeeping at any one point or period in time.

It has also been suggested by some observers of the American judiciary that trial courts typically enforce norms, while the Supreme Court makes policy.[17] The norm-enforcement role of trial courts is suggested by such facts as: Only rarely do specific cases at trial generate much public or professional attention or controversy; few trial judgments, particularly at the state judicial level, are accompanied by a written opinion which then stands as a precedent for lawyers and other courts; and, last, only somewhat less rarely is the basic decision of who will win

win (but not the size of the damages or the severity of the sentence) a matter of considerable doubt. In other words, individual cases within the trial courts are typically fairly routinized affairs affecting and of interest to only the specific parties involved. Cases that the Supreme Court reviews, especially those involving oral argument and a written opinion, tend to have just the opposite characteristics.

The norm-enforcement policy-making dichotomy is at heart a qualitative distinction. An analysis of gatekeeping, however, suggests that the real distinction is more properly a quantitative one. Because the district courts, especially at the pretrial stage but also at trial, handle predominantly routine cases that are important only to the specific litigants involved, this dichotomy is doubtlessly reinforced. Although some trial judges do show a propensity for creative policy-making when called upon to do so, both the hierarchical nature of the system and the general atmosphere created by handling mostly routine cases discourages this even when a novel situation begs such a response. Moreover, the pressing of questions calling for judicial creativity may not even occur until after the trial record has been searched, and thus such questions are not raised as the central issue of the case until the first appeal.[18]

As cases move up the court system hierarchy, litigant-lawyer and judicial gatekeeping filter out the routine cases and promote for extensive Supreme Court consideration cases that on the whole call for judicial creativity. The very expectation that the Court will concentrate on such cases—as well as the knowledge that the Supreme Court is the court of last resort with constitutional equality, if not superiority, to the states, Congress, and the executive—encourages its members to be creative policymakers. As Wells and Grossman have pointed out,[19] the case or controversy context of adjudication has meant that *both* the Supreme Court and the lower courts are involved in the problem-solving exercise of authoritatively resolving unique conflicts between specific individuals and institutions through the application of certain standards (provided by such legal sources as the Constitution, statutes, and the body of precedent that makes up the evolving legal tradition) to specific sets of facts.

ADJUDICATION AS POLICY-MAKING

The concrete specific context of adjudication has important implications for the manner in which judicial policy-making proceeds, the types of questions that can be handled successfully, and the ability of the federal judiciary and especially the Supreme Court to change social behavior through its power to define legal rules and norms. Like the authorities of bureaucratic systems in general, the authorities of a judicial system strive to bring decisional ambiguity under control in the areas over which it has competence. This makes adjudication more than just a process by which concrete conflicts are resolved in the here and now. It is also an enterprise by which judges try to eradicate decisional ambiguity through the authoritative announcement of what norms are currently being applied to cases. Each decision, therefore, may be seen as a declaration of current policy. Appellate court decisions in particular and the opinions associated with them stand as a communications output telling other judges, public officials, members of the bar, and private citizens what to expect from litigation. In effect, when any court authoritatively decides a case it says, "This is what this court will do when presented with this situation again." When that court is the highest court in the system, its decision in a case in effect states, "This is what all courts [in the system] will [should] do when presented with this situation again."

Without this future orientation to judicial outputs, court judgments would be like the arbitrary granting of favors by a capricious sovereign. Such a situation would have serious implications for the legitimacy of the judiciary. Moreover, it would probably result in an intolerably high level of demands for trial and appellate review as litigants pressed their cases until all remedies were exhausted in the search for a favorable decision. When one combines this antigatekeeping effect of unpredictability with the cultural concepts that posit that judicial decision making is only legitimate when it represents the consistent application of known law, then it should be obvious that the pressures toward predictability in judicial decision making are great. This drive toward consistency is, of course, at the heart of the legal concept of *stare decisis*.

Before the days when legal philosophers recognized that courts ought to be responsive to changing social needs and conditions as well as to be consistent, *stare decisis* was emphasized as *the legal norm*. The law that courts enforced was seen as stable and knowable through the analysis of constitutional provisions, statutes, and past precedents. Each judicial output was seen as an application of that knowable law. Since, however, trial judges could err in making decisions, appellate courts, particularly the one court of last resort (the Supreme Court), were a structural necessity to see that lower court consistency and correctness were maintained. Supreme Court decisions and opinions, therefore, were conceptualized as the vehicles by which the lower court judges—and all other interested persons, for that matter—were informed as to what *the law* was.

As our demand-flow/gatekeeping discussion of appellate review suggests, the situation is not as simple. Stability in the law is constantly broken by new legislation and judicial interpretations aimed at making legal norms more responsive to contemporary social needs, demands, and ideas. Thus, as the courts, especially the Supreme Court, focus on legal areas at which such demands for change are aimed, that law enters into a state of becoming rather than being.

Judicial gatekeeping and the case-by-case aspect of adjudication allow the Court to engineer legal change incrementally. For example, in attacking racial segregation in the public schools, the landmark case that announced the major policy that such practices are forbidden by the "equal protection clause" of the Fourteenth Amendment *(Brown v. Board of Education)* was preceded by a series of less dramatic and less far-reaching cases that had slowly chipped away at the separate-but-equal doctrine in law and graduate schools.[20] Even the Brown case itself was announced in a way that allowed for further incremental change. The separate-but-equal doctrine upon which segregation laws had rested was not declared unconstitutional per se. Such a ruling would have meant that all legally required segregation in every aspect of social life from residential housing to miscegenation laws would immediately have been struck down. Rather, the doctrine was declared unconstitutional in *public education* because social science research indicated that such segregation had a deleterious effect on black children. This attempt at social theorizing made the decision less comprehensive in scope than would have the ruling of per se unconstitutionality. The incremental effect of the Court's reasoning should be plain. It meant that for other segregation laws to be struck down, the Supreme Court had to take up these laws one at a time (e.g., public parks, public transportation, public libraries) and consider whether they, too, would be declared unconstitutional.

The Court's method of disposing of the *Brown* case, the "all deliberate speed" formula, also contained an obvious incremental aspect. Here, however, the incrementalism was concerned more with the pace of implementation at the district court level than with the shape or scope of the basic policy. Yet even this created a certain step-by-step growth in judicial policy-making. First, state laws that met the letter of the *Brown* ruling but evaded its spirit (e.g., closing of all public schools and state financing of private "whites only" schools) were struck down. Then the more substantive plans (e.g., freedom of choice) that allowed marginal but did not provide for total desegregation were attacked. Eventually even delaying tactics based on the "all deliberate speed" formula itself were declared invalid. Finally, the lower courts began to move on various forms of *de facto* (i.e., what occurs in practice although not legally required, as opposed to legally imposed or *de jure*) segregation. Ultimately, the Supreme Court made it clear in *Keyes* v. *School District Number 1, Denver, Colorado,*[21] that *de facto* school segregation as a result of actions deliberately taken by the local school authorities, which had the effect of maintaining the separation of the races, was indistinguishable from *de jure* segregation and was thus in violation of the equal protection clause of the Fourteenth Amendment. The Denver case was to northern school segregation what *Brown* v. *Board of Education* was to southern school segregation.[22]

The incremental approach in the articulation of legal norms dealing with civil rights meant that it took the Court almost two decades to erect the necessary legal structure for the elimination of *de jure* segregation, and almost another two decades to strike down *de facto* segregation. Even now, many of the behavioral remains of the old patterns of segregation still exist in both North and South. Their final eradication depends in part on continued litigation in the lower courts and determined administrative action such as the withholding of tax-exempt status from colleges that have racially discriminatory policies.[23] This has led some to charge that the "all deliberate speed" formula was itself responsible for the long delay. However, it should be kept in mind that the pressures for incrementalism in striking down *de jure* (and even *de facto*) segregation were strong. Broad areas of social life and deeply held cultural mores have had to be changed. To prevent the Brown decision from becoming a gigantic "self-inflicted wound" that would have severely undermined the Court's support and been unenforceable as well, time had to be given to allow for Congress, the executive branch, and the nation at large to adjust. Indeed, it should be noted that incrementalism can be found in practically all subject areas where the Court has fashioned new policies, be they the civil rights of black Americans or the civil rights of women.

In pointing to Supreme Court incrementalism, a word of caution is in order. Although from time to time members of the Court as well as various legal scholars have called attention to the merits of such an approach, it should not be implied that a step-by-step growth in judicial policy is necessarily due to the fact that certain policy goals are set and then a crablike movement toward those goals is undertaken in order to "break the news gently." Although there is statistical evidence that suggests that such a tactic may be consciously carried out by certain members of the Court,[24] when one looks at the Court as a whole, much less conscious psychological mechanisms seem to be involved.

The Supreme Court's dual appellate jurisdiction over federal and state courts also leads to a certain type of incrementalism, that is, initially fashioning policies that only apply to its federal jurisdiction and then extending them through constitutional interpretation to the states. This process is quite obvious in the Court's policy-making in the area of criminal procedure. The reasons the Supreme Court initially had been more creative in handling cases dealing with federal rather than state criminal procedure included the lack of any inhibitions arising from considerations of federalism, the direct supervisory role formally given the Supreme Court over the lower federal courts, its participation in rule making for the federal system as a whole, and the fact that in federal cases the Court is typically involved in statutory interpretation rather than constitutional adjudication. Members of the Court have had fewer qualms about the legitimacy, informational base, or ability to do irreparable harm in modifying federal rules than they have had with state rules. Not only are the Court's statutory interpretations amenable to remedial congressional action through legislation, but also the number of persons affected is much smaller, given the difference between federal and state criminal jurisdiction. Thus we see, particularly in the areas of search and seizure, and post-arrest and appellate procedures, that policy thrusts through federal rule making and case decisions preceded similar thrusts into state criminal procedures.

Policy-making by adjudication implies a number of limits on the scope and impact of judicial policies. Some of these have already been suggested in the discussion of the system's regime rules concerning jurisdiction and justiciability, gatekeeping, and incremental decision making. Other limitations are inherent in the adversary method of processing cases, the nature of legal remedies, and the format (i.e., court rulings and opinions) by which policies are announced. It is to these latter limitations that we now turn.

The adversary method means that for a case to arise there must exist social conflicts between identifiable persons and/or institutions.[25] The impact of judicial policy thrusts is furthered when the injured parties readily attack evasion of those policies either because they are well organized (e.g., the NAACP and civil rights) or because of the strong personal interests involved (e.g., when the rights of criminal defendants are involved). The adversary method also limits judicial output in that it limits information input. American trial judges are not expected to independently gather evidence and search for the truth. Federal District Judge John J. Sirica's handling of the Watergate-related trials raised some eyebrows because of his insistence at getting at the truth as much as at the sensational aspects of the revelations.[26] Trial courts ordinarily process only information provided them by opposing counsel as that information survives cross-examination and standards of evidence. Although appellate courts may receive, in addition to the trial record and standard appellate briefs, additional informational input from factual Brandeis-type and *amicus curiae* briefs (and from each new crop of law clerks as well), even these courts are limited to an extent by the adversary method.

Judicial policy-making (and constitutional policy-making, in particular) is also limited by the nature of legal remedies.[27] The Court essentially says either yes or no to governmental activity. Because where the line falls between the permissible and the forbidden is difficult to pinpoint and the affected instances of behavior are numerous, the promotion of a judicial policy may take numerous cases extending over many years. The Court normally does not articulate its policies in the form of codes of what is permissible and what is forbidden;[28] thus, even after years of adjudication, there still may be substantial confusion as to just what is judicial policy. For example, this confusion was long apparent in the law dealing with obscenity.[29] In short, judicial remedies are relatively unsuccessful for controlling policy in an area that requires a comprehensive plan of positive action. In such areas often the most appropriate judicial response is to return these problem areas to Congress or the executive, whose regime rules do allow for comprehensive plans of positive action.[30] This is in effect what the Court did after 1936 with regard to the regulation of economic life.

The impact of judicial policy-making where it implies new patterns of social behavior is strongly limited by the format in which policies are announced. The bare outlines of each case disposed of by the Supreme Court—that is, the facts, the legal questions considered, and who won—provide important cues as to contemporary judicial policy for the area of the law under consideration. Yet because each case is always to some extent unique and the factual and legal questions may be many and complex, a case decision (absent an opinion) may leave many questions in doubt. In "important" cases, therefore, associated output by way of the Court's opinion can be seen as a device to clarify and interpret the underlying considerations behind the case's disposal.

But there are opinions and opinions. Some serve to clarify, others confuse. In *Brown* v. *Board of Education,* for example, the fact that the Court was able to produce a unanimous opinion helped to establish Court policy in what was bound to be a controversial and complex subject. In *Reynolds* v. *Sims,* [31] the "one person–one vote" policy announced in the Court's opinion served as a fairly definitive guide for subsequent district court action. However, the Court is often unwilling or unable to agree on only one policy option. Sometimes this occurs because members of the Court in fact *want* to leave open more than one option. Other times a consensus is lacking among the members of the Court majority as to what policy considerations lie behind a specific decision; that is, a Court majority may agree on authoritative but not associated output.

Youngstown Sheet and Tube v. *Sawyer* [32] is a good example of such a case. Although the Court ruled that the federal government's seizure of the nation's steel mills was forbidden when based on presidential authority alone, the opinions that represented the views of the justices in the majority had little to offer as policy guides for future presidents and courts. The case was decided 6–3 against the government. Justice Black wrote the opinion for the Court. Each of his colleagues on the winning side also wrote a concurring opinion, and each disagreed to some extent with the Black opinion as well as with each other's concurrences. The same phenomenon was demonstrated, to give other examples, with the Pentagon Papers case in 1971[33] and with the famous *Bakke* decision concerning affirmative action in higher education.[34]

Although these cases are perhaps extreme examples, most opinions representing the majority's view suffer from their ambiguities. This is perhaps unavoidable, as the Court's opinion reflects the negotiations and bargaining that were necessary to attract a majority. Such compromises mean that areas of intramajority contention and conflict will be papered over by ambiguous phrases. Moreover, often the thrust of this opinion is made less understandable by concurrences and dissents that misstate or exaggerate the majority's intent.

Needless to say, opinion ambiguity and intra-Court dissension can seriously affect the impact of the case on social behavior. They can be seized upon by the Court's critics for challenging the rationality and legitimacy of the Court's ruling.[35] They can provide the opportunities for subsequent private, official, and judicial evasion and noncompliance.

In summary, as our analysis of judicial output indicates, the nation is not ruled by the Supreme Court. This is true even for those areas of the law in which there are frequent judicial policy pronouncements. Instead, we have a much more complex situation. There are important and broad areas of national policy where there is no judicial policy. In those areas where federal judicial policy does exist, although the Supreme Court often plays a primary role in setting this policy, it does so in conjunction with the lower federal and state judiciaries. Often intervention by the Court is sporadic and aimed more at legitimizing governmental policy or preserving the status quo rather than creating new legal norms. However, when judicial policy-making is aimed at the definition of new norms of behavior, the results of the new policy may be in doubt. There are numerous instances where Court policies have been totally or partially nullified. This has occurred quite legitimately, for example, when Congress has passed new legislation overturning a Court ruling on statutory interpretation or in the few instances when a constitutional ruling of the Court has been repudiated by a constitutional amendment. Of course, there are less legitimate ways of avoiding compliance that run the gamut from benign neglect to outright defiance. There are other occasions when Court policy defining new legal norms may be followed by official action and social behavior that complies with both the letter and spirit of that policy. In such instances it may truly be said that the Court exercises a "final say" in national policy-making.

OUTPUT TRENDS: SOME GENERAL CONSIDERATIONS

Although detailed discussion of the substantive policies promoted by the Supreme Court and the lower federal courts is beyond the scope of this book, a few very general comments in addition to the preceding references to substantive output are in order.

In terms of constitutional policy-making, the basic trend since 1937 has been apparent.[36] The Court in 1937 and beyond rejected the legal doctrines so carefully built in the preceding half-century that stated that economic regulatory legislation could be constitutionally challenged because the judges thought that the law was inherently a deprivation of liberty or property without due process of law. Rejected, too, were allied doctrines in the commerce and taxation areas, all of which allowed the Court to preempt economic policy-making for the nation. The Court, of course, had used its laissez-faire economic policies in favor of powerful corporate and financial interests, and in turn the Court had received potent political support. After the so-called Constitutional Revolution of 1937, the Court has almost always conceded to government the right to control economic policy. However, the Court has not removed itself from economic policy-making. Rather, the Court has been very heavily involved in statutory interpretation of the glut of economic regulatory legislation that thickens the statute books. Thus, less dramatically than through constitutional adjudication, the Court has nevertheless influenced economic policy.[37] However, the most prominent thrust of Court policy-making since 1937 has been in the realm of civil liberties, and it is here that Court output has had a profound effect on American life.

Why civil liberties came to dominate the constitutional output of the Court in the last several decades can perhaps be answered. First, it must be recognized that the Roosevelt pro–New Deal appointees to the Court were sympathetic to these issues. Second, the members of the Court, as most perceptive Americans, undoubtedly became more self-conscious of basic freedoms in an age that saw the rise of brutal fascist and communist totalitarianisms. Third, it should be kept in mind that the Court as an institution has historically been activist on behalf of one or another set of values. Historically, the Court has played an active role in American life. Had it not embraced and promoted some constitutional values, the Court would have been surrendering a vital portion of its institutional power. Finally, individuals and groups emerged willing to press civil liberties claims. Three broad areas of civil liberties in which the civil libertarian activism of the post-1937 Court (especially during the last half of Chief Justice Warren's tenure) was pronounced concerned First Amendment freedoms, constitutional rights of criminal defendants, and the equal protection of the law (i.e., racial and electoral discrimination, and starting in the 1970s, sexual discrimination).[38]

As suggested earlier (and as considered in the following chapter), the federal judicial system entered a new constitutional era fashioned by the Burger Court. Unlike the 1937 constitutional revolution, the Court has not made, at least through the 1983 term, wholesale reversals of liberal Warren Court doctrines, nor has it repudiated constitutional doctrines that permit the exercise of power in any subject matter area. Rather the Burger Court has sought to limit and reinterpret those policies particularly in (but not confined to) the realm of criminal procedures.[39] The strategy seems to be that of incrementalism, so that policies disliked by the Burger Court majority—for example, the exclusionary rule and also the Miranda policy—will eventually be so eroded that by the time the Court comes around to formally announcing their demise, for all intents and purposes those policies will long have been reversed.

Yet it should be emphasized that not only has the Court *not* given up the broad constitutional doctrines that permit substantive policy-making, but the Burger Court has revived the substantive due process doctrine and has used it as the constitutional basis in certain areas of civil liberties, for example, the abortion decision of *Roe* v. *Wade.* This decision, a decidedly "liberal" one, also suggests that new areas of civil liberties, such as the rights of women, have been developed by the Burger Court. Thus, while many important Warren Court policies have in effect been turned around, there are other and even new areas in which the Court has demonstrated a creative will of its own (thereby being true to the institutional traditions of the Court). Thus the Nixon, Ford, and Reagan appointments to the Supreme Court and the staffing of the lower judiciary with Nixon, Ford, Carter, and Reagan appointees have had an effect on substantive output.[40]

ASSOCIATED OUTPUT

In some respects, the distinction between authoritative and associated judicial output is difficult to discern. After all, in accord with the definitions proposed at the beginning of this chapter, a judicial policy can consist of both a binding decision by the authorities (authoritative output) and the opinion elaborating upon the principle used to decide the case (associated output). The previous considerations in fact did blur any distinction between the two forms of output, and it is plausible to argue that, for purposes of analysis of judicial policies as they are articulated in decisions and opinions, such a distinction is unnecessary.[41] However, there are other forms of judicial output that intuitively are not of the same character as binding judicial decisions and policies. In judicial opinions, for example, *obiter dicta* (judicial asides) may anticipate new policy directions or may imply certain consequences of the policy that were not actually decided upon by the Court. Incrementalism in policy-making, as suggested earlier, is largely fostered by such dicta.

Furthermore, there are other on-the-bench aspects of judicial behavior that can be considered a form of output, for example, the attitudes and demeanor of trial judges toward the attorneys and litigants appearing before them. One of the serious charges brought against G. Harrold Carswell during the Senate controversy over his Supreme Court nomination in 1970 was that, as a federal trial judge, he was openly hostile to civil rights lawyers appearing before him.[42] His behavior can be considered to have represented a policy output for which he ultimately was held accountable. Participating in a case in which one has some (however minor) tangible interest can also be thought of as a form of output. Judge Clement Haynsworth's nomination to the Supreme Court in 1969 suffered badly because of such charges brought against him.[43]

Off-the-bench activities of judges can also be conceptualized as forms of output when they concern the judge by virtue of his or her official capacity. The financial dealings of Justice Fortas and what they purportedly represented made him a vulnerable member of the Court and ostensibly began the chain of events that led to his resignation.[44] A book written by political scientist Bruce Murphy revealed that Justice Brandeis had quietly made financial gifts to then–Harvard Law School Professor Felix Frankfurter to enable Frankfurter to promote worthy social and public policy causes important to Brandeis. When it was published in 1982, the book was page-one news in the *New York Times* and raised questions about the propriety of justices engaging in such activity.[45] As a justice, Frankfurter himself, as documented by Murphy, engaged in behind-the-scenes activities in order to influence the course of governmental policy.[46] When such behavior comes to public attention, it is treated as if it were output in that it is evaluated in light of the individual's position as a justice of the Supreme Court.

The speeches and writings of judges are also output-type activities, particularly when they concern matters of controversy. When he was on the Court of Appeals for the District of Columbia, Judge Warren Burger delivered several speeches setting out his views on criminal procedures.[47] One of these caught the attention of Richard Nixon and eventually led to Burger's elevation to the chief justiceship of the Supreme Court.[48] As Chief Justice, Burger has spoken often on questions of the administration of justice, such as legislation affecting the work load of judges, the training and ethics of lawyers, and the problem area of bail. The writings of Justice Douglas, particularly his book *Points of Rebellion,*[49] led to a serious congressional campaign for his impeachment. In announcing his intent to press for Douglas's impeachment, then–Republican House Minority Leader Gerald Ford stated that Judges Carswell and Haynsworth "have been denied seats on the bench for statements that are much less reprehensible than those made, in my opinion, by Justice Douglas."[50]

Associated output, then, encompasses those actions of the judicial authorities that are not direct orders and rulings in specific cases. As such, associated output covers a wide variety of on- and off-the-bench behavior that has the imprimatur of the judge in his or her official position. That output, too, can be thought of as resulting from processing input and feedback. Just as with authoritative output, it can be expected to change under certain circumstances. No doubt the Fortas-Haynsworth-Douglas controversies and the revelations about Brandeis and Frankfurter have affected many forms of associated output.[51]

Until the last decade or two, analysis of judicial decision making normally ceased after a consideration of the results of particular rulings in terms of the behavior and fortunes of those directly affected. Such results or *outcomes* of judicial output include, for example, the exchange of money in the payment of damages, the imprisonment of those convicted of crimes, the release of those not convicted, and the dropping of legal actions against those accused of violating statutes declared invalid.

The reason that analysis of output ended with a consideration of outcomes was because it was generally assumed that specific decisions, particularly by the Supreme Court, had the effect of settling the issues raised, at least for the time being. As the recent history of civil rights and school prayer decisions has shown, however, what is legally a settled question may, in terms of behavioral compliance, not be a settled question at all. Sometimes, but certainly not always, private citizens and public officials evade, resist, and even openly defy the Court's policy.

Thus it is necessary to study not only what the courts decide, but also the rate of compliance or *impact* to gain a full understanding of the judicial system's contribution to the governing of society.

Sometimes, too, but not always, once a case is decided its outcome gives rise to forces in society that have the effect of creating new systemic inputs or *feedback*. Included are new litigation, new information about how current Court policy channels social behavior, and even the institution of new regime rules concerning substantive and/or procedural law. Attention is given to these processes in the following chapter.

NOTES

1. For example, in a study of all cases remanded by the Court to state courts between 1941 and 1951, it was found that of the 175 cases involved there was further litigation in 46, and in just under half of these the party successful in the Supreme Court was unsuccessful in the state court following remand. See "Evasion of Supreme Court Mandates in Cases Remanded to State Courts since 1941," *Harvard Law Review,* 67 (1954), 1251–1259. Jerry K. Beatty's study of the last ten years of the Warren Court revealed that in about 27 percent of the cases remanded to the state courts, the winners at the Supreme Court level ultimately became losers. See his study, "State Court Evasion of United States Supreme Court Mandates during the Last Decade of the Warren Court," *Valparaiso University Law Review,* 6 (1972), 260–285.
2. See Ex Parte McCardle, 6 Wall. 506 (1869).
3. 372 U.S. 391 (1963). Note that the Burger Court 14 years later for most intents and purposes shut the jurisdictional door opened by the *Fay* decision. See Wainwright v. Sykes, 433 U.S. 72 (1977). In general, see Neil D. McFeeley, "A Change of Direction: Habeas Corpus from Warren to Burger," *Western Political Quarterly,* 32 (1979), 174–188.
4. 369 U.S. 186 (1962).
5. 347 U.S. 483 (1954).
6. 186 U.S. 537 (1896).
7. In recent decades, plea bargaining has become more controversial and newspaper stories have focused on it in the coverage of certain "newsworthy" cases. The case of James Earl Ray, the man convicted of murdering Nobel Peace Prize winner the Reverend Martin Luther King, Jr., stimulated much public debate and criticism. By confessing to the crime, Ray avoided a trial and also the death penalty. This example of plea bargaining aroused widespread criticism. See *New York Times,* March 11, 1969, p. 16. Ray later maintained that he was pressured into the plea bargain by his lawyer and claimed he did not commit the murder. See *New York Times,* October 22, 1974, p. 25.
8. 268 U.S. 652 (1925).
9. It should be emphasized at this point that the model presented is a formal model. As such it is based on considerations of how the various actors involved in litigation should behave if they wish to maximize their interests with a minimal risk of extreme loss. As a formal description of how rational participants in litigation should act, it is valid even if no real-life persons act in the way described (though if this were the case, we would want to know why). However, there is suggestive evidence, some of it previously discussed in Chapter 4, that leads us to believe that many litigants behave in accordance with the formal model.

10. This inequality may be read: "For litigant a the utility of a favorable judgment multiplied by its probability is *much greater* than the cost of litigation."

11. This inequality may be read: "For litigant a the utility of a favorable judgment multiplied by its probability is *much less* than the cost of litigation."

12. This is not quite true since if it is *known* that b is willing to negotiate, negotiated gatekeeping may still occur. However, if it is known that b will not negotiate or b's calculations are unknown or disguised (b is bluffing), nonnegotiated gatekeeping will occur by a.

13. $W_a = W_b$ is not meant to represent an exact equality. This is because the W's do not represent exact figures but rather zones of acceptability. If we represent the situation by two overlapping circles, $W_a = W_b$ is the intersection between the two circles. The case is negotiated in the area of intersection, with the exact settlement or bargain being determined by the negotiating skill of the respective parties and their lawyers. $W_a \neq W_b$ represents the condition when W_a and W_b do not intersect. Thus there is no possible negotiated result.

14. Both the utility of winning the case, $U,$ and its worth, $W,$ must be separately considered because these are not the same things. The latter includes only such settlement-related factors as the amount of damages or length and nature of a criminal sentence. The former also includes such other factors as psychic satisfaction of winning, prestige, and the desire to establish a formal policy ruling. For example, in a tax case a business firm may not be very much concerned with the amount of money it would have to pay as a settlement. It may, however, be very much concerned with obtaining a formal ruling on a point of tax law, particularly if there is a good probability that the ruling will be in the firm's favor.

15. Joseph Tanenhaus, Marvin Schick, Matthew Muraskin, and Daniel Rosen, "The Supreme Court's Certiorari Jurisdiction: Cue Theory," in Glendon Schubert (ed.), *Judicial Decision-Making* (New York: Free Press, 1963), pp. 111–132.

16. Glendon Schubert, *Quantitative Analysis of Judicial Behavior* (New York: Free Press, 1959), pp. 43, 62.

17. See Herbert Jacob, *Justice in America,* 4th ed. (Boston: Little, Brown, 1984), pp. 25–46. But also note that trial courts sometimes break new policy ground and the Supreme Court sometimes enforces previously determined norms, so the distinction is in reality at times blurred.

18. Richard J. Richardson and Kenneth N. Vines, "Review, Dissent, and the Appellate Process: A Political Interpretation," *Journal of Politics,* 29 (1967), 597–616.

19. Richard S. Wells and Joel B. Grossman, "The Concept of Judicial Policy-Making," *Journal of Public Law,* 15 (1966), 286–307.

20. Missouri ex. rel. Gaines v. Canada, 305 U.S. 337 (1938); Sweatt v. Painter, 339 U.S. 629 (1950); McLaurin v. Oklahoma State Regents, 339 U.S. 637 (1950), among others. Also see Albert P. Blaustein and Clarence C. Ferguson, Jr., *Desegregation and the Law,* 2nd ed. (New York: Random House [Vintage Books], 1962), pp. 95–113; Richard Kluger, *Simple Justice* (New York: Knopf, 1975). In general, see Stephen L. Wasby, Anthony A. D'Amato, and Rosemary Metrailer, *Desegregation from Brown to Alexander* (Carbondale, Ill.: Southern Illinois University Press, 1977).

21. 413 U.S. 921 (1973).

22. The Burger Court, however, in a subsequent sharply divided decision concerning the Detroit metropolitan area, ruled that desegregation plans can only be imposed on the local governmental unit in which it has been proven that official actions by the school authorities promoted racial segregation. Thus, even when the problem is shown to be an areawide one fostered by state action or inaction in terms of discriminatory real-estate practices or nonenforcement of antidiscrimination statutes, school desegrega-

tion remedies are limited strictly to the geographical locality in which it is proved that the actions of *school authorities* have maintained segregation of the races. Milliken v. Bradley, 418 U.S. 717 (1974).

23. The action of the Internal Revenue Service in denying such tax-exempt status was upheld by the Supreme Court in Bob Jones University v. United States, 103 S. Ct. 2017 (1983).

24. See Schubert, *Quantitative Analysis,* pp. 214–254. Cf. Saul Brenner, "The New Certiorari Game," *Journal of Politics,* 41 (1979), 649–655.

25. When social consensus exists, judicial control is very difficult to establish and maintain. This seems evident, for example, in the fate of the school prayer decisions, where noncompliance has been substantial. Cf. Richard M. Johnson, *The Dynamics of Compliance* (Evanston, Ill.: Northwestern University Press, 1967); William K. Muir, *Prayer in the Public Schools* (Chicago: University of Chicago Press, 1967); and Kenneth M. Dolbeare and Phillip E. Hammond, *The School Prayer Decisions: From Court Policy to Local Practice* (Chicago: University of Chicago Press, 1971).

26. See, for example, Robert M. Smith, "T-r-u-t-h or T-r-i-a-l?," *New York Times,* November 4, 1974, p. 37. Note that the Court of Appeals praised Sirica when it upheld the conviction of Watergate conspirator G. Gordon Liddy. The appeals court wrote: "Judge Sirica's palpable search for truth in such a trial [involving the integrity of the nation's political system] was not only permissible, it was in the highest tradition of his office as a federal judge. And although his execution of this objective presented problems, as must be acknowledged, they were not of a kind that deprived defendants of a fair trial." United States v. Liddy, 509 F. 2d 428 at 442 (1974). For Judge John J. Sirica's perspective, see his *To Set the Record Straight: The Break-in, the Tapes, the Conspirators, the Pardon* (New York: Norton, 1979).

27. It has been argued by John Brigham that the special language of constitutional law itself limits the range of judicial policy-making and legal remedies. See his *Constitutional Language: An Interpretation of Judicial Decision* (Westport, Conn.: Greenwood, 1978). Also see Timothy J. O'Neill," The Language of Equality in a Constitutional Order," *American Political Science Review,* 75 (1981), 626–635.

28. One famous decision that seems to be an exception to this general statement was Miranda v. Arizona, 384 U.S. 436 (1966), the opinion of which includes detailed instructions to police as to how they should behave when they wish to question a criminal suspect. Another is Roe v. Wade, 410 U.S. 113 (1973), in which the Court sought to specify what sort of legislation regulating abortion would pass constitutional muster and what would not.

29. When the Burger Court sought to change but also clarify matters in the key 1973 obscenity decisions, the Court's efforts only resulted in continued confusion. See Miller v. California, 413 U.S. 15 (1973); Paris Adult Theatre v. Slaton, 413 U.S. 49 (1973); United States v. 12 200-Ft. Reels of Super 8mm Film, 413 U.S. 123 (1973); and United States v. Orito, 413 U.S. 139 (1973).

30. The Burger Court would have liked to have been able to turn obscenity back to the state legislatures and Congress, but obscenity may be such a unique policy area that it is impossible for the courts to remove themselves from deciding the constitutional questions that invariably arise without an absolutist policy of total permissibility. Thus, in 1974, the Court had to clarify its 1973 position in the case over the alleged obscenity of the film *Carnal Knowledge.* See Jenkins v. Georgia, 418 U.S. 153 (1974). In 1982, the Supreme Court ruled on so-called kiddie porn, upholding a strict New York state law forbidding the distribution or promotion of sexual materials showing a sexual performance of children. See New York v. Ferber, 458 U.S. 747.

31. 377 U.S. 533 (1964).

32. 343 U.S. 579 (1952).

33. New York Times Company v. United States, 403 U.S. 713 (1971).

34. Regents of the University of California v. Bakke, 438 U.S. 265 (1978).

35. Some justices appear to be alerting the opposition with their dissents. For example, Justice Black in one dissent noted, "I regret very much that this Court by its hasty, summary reversal, is providing its critics with such choice ammunition for their attacks." Recznik v. City of Lorain, 393 U.S. 171 at 174 (1968). Another apparent example of this is a dissent by Justice Stewart in which he observed, "It seems to me that those of us who dissented in Miranda v. Arizona . . . remain free not only to express our continuing disagreement with that decision, but also to oppose any broadening of its impact." Orozco v. Texas, 394 U.S. 324 at 331 (1969). Justice Marshall in Milliken v. Bradley declared: "The Court today takes a giant step backwards. . . . I cannot subscribe to this emasculation of our constitutional guarantee of equal protection of the laws and must respectfully dissent. . . . Today's holding, I fear, is more a reflection of a perceived public mood that we have gone far enough in enforcing the Constitution's guarantee of equal justice than it is the product of neutral principles of law." 418 U.S. 717 at 782, 814 (1974). Justice Blackmun, to give another example, charged in one dissent that the Opinion of the Court "perpetuates confusion in an area where clarification and uniformity are urgently needed." Michigan v. Doran, 439 U.S. 282 (1978) at 292.

36. See Glendon Schubert, *The Constitutional Polity* (Boston: Boston University Press, 1970), Chap. 1; Alpheus T. Mason, *The Supreme Court from Taft to Warren* (New York: Norton, 1964), Chaps. 3–6; Robert G. McCloskey, *The American Supreme Court* (Chicago: University of Chicago Press, 1960), pp. 136–231; Sheldon Goldman, *Constitutional Law and Supreme Court Decision-Making* (New York: Harper & Row, 1982), pp. 321–787.

37. See Martin Shapiro, *Law and Politics in the Supreme Court* (New York: Free Press, 1964); and also his book, *The Supreme Court and Administrative Agencies* (New York: Free Press, 1968).

38. In general, see, for example, Andrea L. Bonnicksen, *Civil Rights & Liberties* (Palo Alto, Calif.: Mayfield, 1982); Lucius J. Barker and Twiley W. Barker, Jr., *Civil Liberties and the Constitution: Cases and Commentaries,* 4th ed. (Englewood Cliffs, N.J.: Prentice-Hall, 1982); C. Herman Pritchett, *Constitutional Civil Liberties* (Englewood Cliffs, N.J.: Prentice-Hall, 1984); John Brigham, *Civil Liberties and American Democracy* (Washington, D.C.: C.Q. Press, 1984). For a Marxist interpretation of the Warren Court's civil liberties decisions, see Joan Roelofs, "Judicial Activism as Social Engineering: A Marxist Interpretation of the Warren Court," in Stephen C. Halpern and Charles M. Lamb (eds.), *Supreme Court Activism and Restraint* (Lexington, Mass.: Lexington Books, Heath, 1982), pp. 249–270.

39. See, in general, James F. Simon, *In His Own Image: The Supreme Court in Richard Nixon's America* (New York: McKay, 1973); and Leonard W. Levy, *Against the Law: The Nixon Court and Criminal Justice* (New York: Harper & Row, 1974). Cf. Vincent Blasi (ed.), *The Burger Court: The Counter-Revolution That Wasn't* (New Haven, Conn.: Yale University Press, 1983).

40. See Sheldon Goldman, "Voting Behavior on the U.S. Courts of Appeals Revisited," *American Political Science Review,* 69 (1975), p. 497, n. 24; Jon Gottschall, "The Nixon Appointments to the United States Courts of Appeals: The Impact of the Law and Order Issue on the Rights of the Accused," Ph.D. dissertation, University of Massachusetts, 1975; Donald R. Songer, "The Policy Consequences of Senate Involvement in the Selection of Judges in the United States Courts of Appeals," *Western*

Political Quarterly, 35 (1982), 107–119. Also see Jon Gottschall, "Carter's Judicial Appointments: The Influence of Affirmative Action and Merit Selection on Voting on the U.S. Courts of Appeals," *Judicature,* 67 (1983), 164–173; Thomas R. Hensley and Joyce Baugh, "The 1978 Omnibus Judgeships Act: Impact on the Federal Judiciary," paper delivered at the 1983 Annual Meeting of the American Political Science Association; Robert A. Carp and C. K. Rowland, *Policy Making and Politics on the Federal District Courts* (Knoxville: University of Tennessee Press, 1983).

41. This is the position taken by Joel B. Grossman in his "A Model for Judicial Policy Analysis: The Supreme Court and the Sit-In Cases," in Joel B. Grossman and Joseph Tanenhaus (eds.), *Frontiers of Judicial Research* (New York: Wiley, 1969), p. 420.

42. *New York Times,* February 3, 1970, p. 15.

43. See *Congressional Quarterly,* September 26, 1969, pp. 1766–1767; November 14, 1969, pp. 2244–2245; November 21, 1969, pp. 2310–2311.

44. See the discussion in Chapter 1.

45. Bruce Allen Murphy, *The Brandeis-Frankfurter Connection: The Secret Political Activities of Two Supreme Court Justices* (New York: Oxford University Press, 1982). The *New York Times* story appeared on February 14, 1982.

46. Murphy, *ibid.*

47. Julius Duscha, "Chief Justice Burger Asks: 'If It Doesn't Make Good Sense, How Can It Make Good Law?' " *New York Times Magazine,* October 5, 1969, p. 30.

48. *Ibid.*

49. William O. Douglas, *Points of Rebellion* (New York: Random House, 1970).

50. *New York Times,* April 14, 1970, p. 27.

51. Note that in August, 1972, the American Bar Association approved a revised and stricter set of Canons of Judicial Ethics. The Judicial Conference of the United States, in April, 1973, went even further in the first code of ethics for federal judges that body had ever adopted. Among the provisions of the new code were requirements of periodic disclosure of compensation, gifts, and other outside income, and that judges should refrain from business dealings or from participating in any case in which they have a financial interest in the matter that might raise questions of their impartiality. See *Congressional Quarterly,* April 14, 1973, p. 820. Congress later in 1974 passed the Judicial Disqualification Act that incorporated the ABA and Judicial Conference codes. Under the legislation that affects Supreme Court justices, lower federal court judges, magistrates, and bankruptcy judges, these officials are *required by law* to disqualify themselves in any proceeding in which their impartiality is plausibly open to question, including cases in which the official has even a small financial stake that could be affected by the court's decision. For other circumstances requiring disqualification, see *Congressional Quarterly,* November 30, 1974, p. 3226. In general, see the discussion of off-the-bench behavior of justices in Russell R. Wheeler, *Extrajudicial Behavior and the Role of the Supreme Court Justice* (Morristown, N.J.: General Learning Press, 1975).

Impact and Feedback

The concepts of impact and feedback, although analytically distinguishable, are empirically closely related to each other. Information on the rate of compliance, the mechanisms used to affect that rate, and the broad social, economic, and political consequences of the implementation and attempts to implement policy output are important feedback data and activities. Various feedback responses in turn may vitally affect impact. Thus these analytically separate concepts are treated here as an empirical whole. Impact and feedback phenomena take a variety of forms, such as oral or written comment by the communications media, politicians, and interest group leaders; various actions of evasion, noncompliance, and protest by lower court judges, public officials, and the public-at-large; new litigation aimed at narrowing or broadening court policy; and various responses by the major national political institutions of Congress and the presidency in enforcement, legislation, and judicial selection. It will be recalled that impact and feedback phenomena were earlier considered in our analyses of judicial selection and the input of support. Here some other aspects of these two highly interrelated phenomena will be considered.[1]

Compliance to court decisions is an important aspect of the study of impact and feedback. Compliance is not at issue when a court says "yes" and legitimates ongoing practices without requiring a change in behavior. It is only when a court, in effect, says "no, what you are doing violates *the law*" that our interest in compliance is sparked. Of course, decisions of the federal district courts can be appealed to the courts of appeals and ultimately can be taken to the Supreme Court. The rulings of a trial court that can be appealed to a higher court are not considered final while an appeal is in progress. Those who are potentially within a court's jurisdiction and may be affected by but are not a party to the suit need not comply with the court's ruling as long as the possibility remains that a higher court may reverse the lower court. Thus when compliance is studied, it is compliance to the authoritative rulings in cases that have run the course of appeal. This means that the United States Supreme Court, as the ultimate expounder of constitutionality in the federal judicial system, is the focus of attention in the compliance-to-court-decisions literature. The Supreme Court will also be our focus here in terms of compliance and other impact/feedback phenomena.

There are, of course, several dramatic episodes in American history when politically unpopular Supreme Court decisions triggered anti-Court responses. These include, for example, the attempt by a Jeffersonian- dominated Congress to use impeachment as a weapon for removing offensive Federalist judges from the federal courts; the overturning of *Chisholm* v. *Georgia*[2] and *Pollock* v. *Farmers' Loan*[3] by the Eleventh and Sixteenth Amendments; and President Franklin Roosevelt's attempt to change Supreme Court policy by potentially manipulating its size (a tactic used by Republicans of the 1860s and by others earlier). Obviously such court-curbing activities were immensely important negative feedback to the Court. However, not all feedback is either as dramatic or as tinged with partisan and ideological controversy. Neither is all feedback as episodic as the preceding examples imply, nor is it always so bound up with basic questions of constitutional law, judicial powers, and constitutional legitimacy. There are such clearly standard forms of congressional and presidential feedback as the passage of remedial legislation and the use of the appointment process to staff the courts with those in ideological agreement with the appointing authorities. Furthermore, the common law tradition allows extensive room for certain other kinds of feedback, including the use of litigation as a feedback device and the recognition by judges of professional comment and criticism in court opinions.

LITIGATION AS A VEHICLE FOR FEEDBACK

Litigation is one of the most important ways by which the Supreme Court receives feedback. In fact, the incremental nature of judicial policy-making suggests that such feedback is not only expected, but it is even invited. When it ventures to change long-standing legal norms or practices, the Supreme Court's initial decision rarely so settles the law as to make subsequent appeals appear frivolous and only appropriate for routine lower court enforcement. Rather, the initial decisions may be so ambiguous as to invite further appeals, thus allowing for additional policy consideration, definition, and clarification.

Baker v. *Carr* illustrates this phenomenon well. That decision was a landmark in that it broke with precedent and made legislative apportionment a justiciable question, but it provided very little guidance as to what standard should be applied not only by the District Court for the Middle District of Tennessee to which the case was remanded, but also to other district courts which would obviously receive similar litigation. The Court's opinion stated, "The right asserted is within the reach of judicial protection under the [Equal Protection Clause of the] Fourteenth Amendment." It was also asserted that "Judicial standards under the Equal Protection Clause are well developed and familiar.''[4] But, of course, at that time the judicial standards provided by the Equal Protection Clause concerning legislative apportionment were anything but well developed and familiar. Thus this case, rather than stifling further appeals by "settling" the law, invited them by "unsettling" it. Such cases of course came, and two years later in *Reynolds* v. *Sims*[5] the Court again took up the issue and provided the one person–one vote standard. After that, other cases made their way to the Court asking for greater clarification of the new standard, such as whether it applied to local governing boards and special purpose districts, as well as the extent of permissible deviation from perfect mathematical equality. As late as 1983, the Court was dealing with reapportionment. It ruled in *Karcher* v. *Daggett*[6] that congressional districts must adhere as closely as possible to the one person–one vote standard and that any deviation from precise population equality (even under 1 percent, as was the case here with New Jersey districts) violated the Constitution unless it was proven that such deviation was made for legitimate public policy reasons. This decision means that further litigation will be coming to the Court in order to precisely define what legitimate public policy reasons are acceptable in justifying population variation in congressional districting. To complicate matters further, at the same time the *Karcher* decision was handed down by a 5–4 majority, the Court, with a different 5–4 majority (Justice Sandra O'Connor switched sides), *upheld* a population variation as large as 89 percent for *state* legislative districts in Wyoming because the new majority approved as a legitimate public policy reason the state's desire to have each county with at least one representative of its own (the case was *Brown* v. *Thompson*[7]). This means that in future reapportionment cases coming to the Court, the Court will also be receiving feedback from its two contradictory decisions, *Karcher* and *Brown.*

Other policy areas in which the Supreme Court has been involved can also illuminate the use of litigation as a vehicle for feedback. In the obscenity area, the Burger Court sought to change the more liberal Warren Court standards in order to permit state and local authorities to crack down on "hard core" pornography. The 1973 cases, which announced the new more restrictive standards,[8] far from resolving the issues, exposed the Court to much new litigation as the problems of differentiating obscenity from constitutionally protected free speech remained as difficult as before. Indeed, in 1974 the Supreme Court decided a case in which the Georgia Supreme Court had ruled that the widely acclaimed motion picture *Carnal Knowledge* was obscene.[9] Another facet of the obscenity issue came before the Court in 1982 in *New York* v. *Ferber,*[10] and the Court received feedback concerning its obscenity policy. In this decision, the Court upheld a New York law that made it a felony to distribute sexually explicit material in which children 16 years of age or younger were portrayed, even though the material itself did not meet the legal definition of obscenity. The vote was unanimous and the Court was clearly sensitive to both feedback and the impact of its decision. In this policy area, new litigation then continues to keep the Court apprised of the impact of its obscenity policy and the difficulties of implementation.

The same is true, to take another example, with the Court's policy concerning the admissibility of confessions. *Miranda* v. *Arizona*[11] was the culmination of a series of cases that brought feedback information to the Court as to the implementation of its previous "due process" policy concerning the questioning of suspects and the use of statements and confessions against the defendant in court. Finally, in *Miranda* the Court spelled out the procedures that must be followed before statements and confessions extracted from the suspect can be used to prosecute (the constitutional basis was the Fifth Amendment right against self-incrimination and the Sixth Amendment right to counsel as these rights have become part of the Fourteenth Amendment due process guarantees that the states must respect). But here, too, litigation continued transmitting (negative) feedback responses to the Court. Then in *Harris* v. *New York,* after several years of intense negative feedback and with the emergence of the Burger Court, a new majority shifted gears and modified *Miranda.* Under *Harris,* statements and confessions obtained in violation of the *Miranda* standards can be introduced at the trial to impeach the credibility of the defendant's on-the-stand-testimony (when it contradicts what was said during interrogation).[12] Confession cases continued to come to the Court into the 1980s, and the *Miranda* policy, close to two decades after its launching, seemed not to have accomplished the broad purposes for which it was designed (i.e., the elimination of *any* form of coercion to produce statements or confessions from those arrested). Finally, in 1984 the Court ruled that *Miranda* need not be followed when public safety is immediately threatened, thereby sealing the eventual doom of *Miranda* but also inviting feedback by way of continued litigation.[13]

Feedback via litigation occurs to some extent in every case that is appealed and even with many that never proceed beyond the trial stage. Interest groups use test cases quite deliberately to channel feedback to the courts. At times legislative and executive officials also use their powers in lawmaking and law enforcement to generate feedback. One of the more dramatic (and controversial) examples of such feedback occurred after the National Industrial Recovery Act (NIRA) was declared unconstitutional in the *Schechter* case.[14] President Roosevelt then urged Congress to pass a new NIRA-like statute for regulating the bituminous coal industry. In the face of charges that the proposed law was unconstitutional, Roosevelt wrote a letter to the chairman of the House subcommittee in which the bill was pending. This letter said in part,

> Manifestly, no one is in a position to give assurance that the proposed act will withstand constitutional tests. . . . But the situation is so urgent and the benefits of the legislation so evident that all doubts should be resolved in favor of the bill, leaving to the courts, in an orderly fashion, the ultimate question of constitutionality. A decision by the Supreme Court relative to this measure would be helpful as indicating, with increasing clarity, the constitutional limits within which this Government must operate.[15]

The bill became law. It was soon struck down as unconstitutional in *Carter* v. *Carter Coal Co.*[16] But within a year, quite similar legislation did withstand the test of constitutionality in *National Labor Relations Board* v. *Jones and Laughlin*

Steel Corporation, [17] and within five years after *Carter* was announced it was explicitly overturned in *United States* v. *Darby.* [18] This switch in judicial policy, of course, followed sustained and forceful negative feedback concerning the Court's conservative activism.

PROFESSIONAL COMMENT AND CRITICISM AS FEEDBACK

Students of the law have long recognized the legitimacy and potential ability of professional comment and criticism in influencing judicial outputs. The dual notion of the courtroom lawyer as advocate and officer of the court, the casebook approach in law schools where opinions and decisions are analyzed and criticized, the role given the organized bar in suggesting changes in legal procedure, and the existence and the prominence of law reviews and professional journals all suggest that feedback from the legal profession is widely accepted and expected. Much of this feedback occurs within the context of litigation itself, for example, through briefs and oral argument. It also occurs within the context of opinion writing and in off-the-bench activities of fellow judges. In this section two aspects of professional feedback to the Supreme Court are considered: feedback from members of the lower courts and feedback from the law reviews.

Lower Court Feedback to the Supreme Court

Decisions of the Supreme Court articulate norms that lower courts are supposed to follow in deciding cases. With the lower federal courts, the supremacy of the Supreme Court theoretically extends to all matters within their jurisdiction, while with the state courts, it extends to all questions touching matters of federal law and ultimately even the determination of whether federal law is applicable. Although the complexities and courtesies created by the doctrine of federalism generally mean that the Supreme Court supervises the federal courts more closely than it does the state courts, state judges have long acknowledged that Supreme Court rulings indeed represent the highest judicial voice in the land. As Walter Murphy noted in his analysis of southern state judicial attitudes toward the Supreme Court's school desegregation rulings, "When pressed, no state supreme court has yet failed to concede that the School Segregation cases are the law of the land and binding on the lower [state] courts."[19]

The Court's supremacy, however, has not made lower court judges merely its silent servants. The most common form of feedback from lower court judges has been both on- and off-the-bench praise and condemnation of the Court's decisions. A dramatic instance of off-the-bench criticism was the 1958 report by the Conference of State Chief Justices on federal-state relationships. In this report, adopted by a vote of 36–8, the Court was strongly chastised for "press[ing] the extension of federal power [over the states] and press[ing] it rapidly."[20] Significantly, however, the chief justices prefaced their report by noting that they have an "obligation . . . to uphold respect for the law" and that this obligation includes being bound even by those Supreme Court policy pronouncements that they believe to be wrong. Interestingly, about a quarter of a century later, when the federal courts were under attack in Congress and legislation was being considered to strip the federal courts of jurisdiction in such areas as busing and abortion, the Conference of State Chief Justices came out opposed to such legislation and expressed support for the Supreme Court and the federal courts.[21]

Closely related to off-the-bench verbal feedback is that rendered by lower court judges from the bench. For example, in 1969 the Court of Appeals for the Second Circuit sitting *en banc* reversed the dismissal by two district judges of state prisoners' applications for writs of *habeas corpus.*[22] The prisoners had asserted that their guilty pleas were not voluntary, but had been induced by illegally obtained confessions that their lawyers allegedly refused to attempt to challenge. The dissent suggested the dissenters' disagreement with the Warren Court's liberal policies in the confessions area. This prompted a concurring (with the majority) opinion by Judge Irving Kaufman that chided the dissenters with the observation that "Judges must be careful lest their personal predilections lead them to ignore the constitutional requirements set forth by the Supreme Court, by indulging in sophistic games of distinction-making because they do not approve of the Court's constitutional determinations."[23]

Mere verbal feedback may have little direct effect on case outcomes and the rate of compliance, but lower court judges do not always limit themselves to unhappy compliance when they disagree with Supreme Court policy. Such judges have at times provided encouragement for legislative attempts to circumvent a Court decision. For example, following the Court's ruling in *Mallory* v. *United States*[24] that a ten-hour delay between Mallory's arrest and arraignment represented an "unnecessary delay" under Rule 5(a) of the Federal Rules of Criminal Procedure, Federal District Judge Alexander Holtzoff [the trial judge on the *Mallory* case and a member of the advisory committee that had drafted Rule 5(a)] testified before a Senate subcommittee concerning the *Mallory* case. He told the senators that when the rule had been drafted, a proviso that confessions obtained during a period of "unnecessary delay" be forbidden had been considered and rejected because it was felt that this would punish the public more than delinquent police officials. He furthermore reminded the subcommittee that the *Mallory* case was an instance of statutory interpretation and therefore could be overturned by a simple act of Congress. Congress did in fact follow Holtzoff's suggestion some years later in the Omnibus Crime Act of 1968. To cite another example, U.S. Court of Appeals Judge Henry Friendly demonstrated his dismay with the *Miranda* policy when he publicly advocated severe restrictions by way of constitutional amendment on the use of the self-incrimination guarantee of the Fifth Amendment.[25] Lower court judges have also on occasion used less legitimate means to blunt a Supreme Court decision. The most illegitimate means is, of course, outright defiance of a Supreme Court ruling. However, open and publicized defiance is usually corrected by the processes of appellate review.

Outright refusal to comply is not the only on-the-bench option left to lower court judges who disagree with Court policies. Working in the interstices of the law and making use of the ambiguities inherent in Supreme Court opinion writing, lower court judges are often able to evade the spirit of current Court policies while observing the letter of its decisions. For example, of the approximately 20 cases decided between 1941 and 1951 where Supreme Court "winners" became state court losers on remand, in only one case was there outright defiance.[26] In all the others, the case outcome was changed by a lower court's interpretation of the Supreme Court's ruling. A similar finding of state court evasion was revealed in a study of the last decade of the Warren Court that determined that over one out of four winners at the Supreme Court level eventually became state court losers.[27]

Evasion, of course, does not only concern cases on remand. It is a phenomenon that affects much trial and intermediate appellate court decision making. The pervasiveness of evasion is difficult to ascertain and is, of course, more characteristic of some fields of law, levels of the judiciary, and areas of the nation than others. In recent history perhaps the most systematic evasion occurred during the 1950s, and 1960s when southern state courts had responsibility for implementation of the Supreme Court's decisions dealing with the civil rights of black Americans. Some evasion by some state courts of the Supreme Court's criminal procedures decisions has also been documented.[28]

The most obvious effect of evasion is to retard the impact of Supreme Court decisions and to stifle broad extension of rulings into areas of social behavior related to those the Court has dealt with explicitly. This dual effect was quite obvious in southern court response to *Brown* v. *Board of Education*. Evasion itself may lead to direct litigative feedback to the Court as cases marked by lower court resistance are appealed. This gives the Court an opportunity to reiterate more clearly its initial policy. It also provides the chance for a second judicial look at the policy in light of its impact. With the school segregation cases, the result of reexamination was for the Court to call for even more forceful and far-reaching implementation as well as an extension of the decision to other areas of social life and governmental action. In some other areas of the law, the second look offered by a lower court's narrow interpretation of a Supreme Court ruling has led, at least temporarily, to the Court's accepting that interpretation and thus indicating the limits of its initial decision.[29]

Not all judicial feedback is aimed at retarding the thrust and impact of Supreme Court policy-making. Lower court judges off the bench often publicly express support for newly articulated Court rulings and even urge their expansion. Positive feedback to evolving judicial policy also occurs within the context of lower court decision making. Some lower court judges on occasion have even decided cases in anticipation of how the Supreme Court was likely to rule. An example of such action can be found in a decision by Fourth Circuit Court of Appeals Judge John J. Parker concerning a West Virginia law compelling all children attending public school to salute the flag. This included children of the Jehovah's Witnesses sect, for whom the flag salute represents a violation of their religious beliefs. Parker held the law unconstitutional despite the fact that just two years earlier a similar Pennsylvania law had been upheld by the Court in the *Gobitis* case.[30] In rendering his decision, Parker noted that three of the *Gobitis* majority had subsequently publicly changed their minds and that two others had retired. Upon appeal to the Court, Parker's prediction held true, and *Gobitis* was formally overruled.[31]

However, second-guessing the Court is far from being an accepted tactic. A number of jurists have, in fact, disavowed it, and in the words of one, "We should leave it to the Supreme Court to overrule its own cases."[32] Furthermore, second-guessing is not necessarily a successful tactic. Some 30 years after Judge Parker's decision, another Fourth Circuit Judge (and another senatorial reject on ideological grounds for a Supreme Court seat), Clement Haynsworth, who was no doubt aware of the Court's consistent extension of the right to counsel during the previous decade, ruled that the right of indigents to free counsel applied to their taking their appeals beyond the first appeal to the highest state court and the U.S. Supreme Court. Judge Haynsworth, as it turned out, incorrectly anticipated the Burger Court, which by a divided vote in *Ross* v. *Moffitt,* [33] overruled him.

The Court and the Law Reviews

Prior to the 1930s, there were very few citations of law reviews in Supreme Court opinions.[34] By the early 1930s citations became more numerous. Those who cited reviews during this period and those who did not fell into two groups, corresponding to the Court's liberal and conservative wings. Those who most cited review articles were Brandeis, Stone, and Cardozo—all members of the Court's liberal, pro–New Deal bloc. McReynolds, Van Devanter, Butler, Sutherland, and Roberts—the five justices who were most anti–New Deal—practically never cited reviews. Since the early 1940s, however, when the number of opinions with citations to reviews reached about 20 per term, there have been no obvious ideological or background differences between those who cite law review articles and those who do not. In the 1982 term, for example, there were law review citations in one or more opinions in about 47 percent of the decisions decided with opinion and every justice could be found citing law reviews on at least several occasions. In 28 percent of the majority opinions, there were citations to law reviews.

The citation of review articles is an important modern manifestation of how professional comment and research is fed into judicial policy-making. To a surprisingly large degree (over 80 percent of the time in one study[35]), review citations in Supreme Court opinions are not taken from references within briefs, but rather reflect the justices' and their clerks' own research efforts.

Reviews are edited by the best students at each law school. Issues contain unsigned articles called "Notes" written by individual editors as well as signed articles by legal scholars, judges, and legal administrators. In the last two decades an increasing number of the signed articles have also been contributed by political scientists. Obviously not all reviews are of equal quality nor, of course, are members of the Court equally responsive to all reviews or all commentators. As a result, a few reviews and authors have been found to have been cited quite frequently, while most others are cited only rarely or never. In an analysis of citations to law reviews in Supreme Court opinions between 1924 and 1956, Chester A. Newland found that the *Harvard Law Review* was cited most frequently (399 times), followed by the *Yale Law Journal* (194), and the *Columbia*

Law Review (176). Thereafter the number of citations to particular reviews fell off rapidly. As for the authors most frequently cited, Newland found that Felix Frankfurter (28) and Charles Warren (27) led the list.

One must be careful in assessing such quantitative data. Most citations stand only as minor references in an opinion. A citation may be used to support a position reached independently by the justice and in no way can be considered to have influenced the opinion. Citations may also reflect the interests and research of the law clerk rather than the justice. Articles from such often-cited sources as the *Harvard Law Review* may be inconsequential, while a single reference to a rarely cited journal may be important. Only a few times has an article apparently had a major influence on an opinion.

A classic instance of such an influential article concerned one by Charles Warren, which appeared in 1923 in the *Harvard Law Review*.[36] It was a critique of Justice Story's opinion in *Swift* v. *Tyson*[37] interpreting the Federal Judiciary Act of 1789. The Court's ruling in that case resulted in the establishment of a federal "common law" for diversity cases in the federal courts, while equivalent cases tried in state courts were subject to the "common law" of the respective states. Since the federal courts' diversity jurisdiction is nonexclusive (i.e., either a state or federal court can try the case), litigants were encouraged to shop around for the court system with the most favorable common law.

In analyzing the historical background to *Swift*, Warren wrote,

> It now appears from an examination of the Senate Files . . . that if Judge Story and the Court had had recourse to those Files in preparing the decision . . . it is highly probable that the decision would have been different, and that the word "laws" in Section 34 would have been construed to include the common law of a State as well as the statute law. This conclusion will probably be reached by anyone who examines the original slip of paper on which the amendment containing Section 34 was written, and which is, with little doubt, in Ellsworth's handwriting.[38]

In a 1928 case, Holmes used the Warren article as a basis for his dissent, writing, "An examination of the original document by a most competent hand has shown that Mr. Justice Story probably was wrong if anyone is interested to inquire what the framers of the instrument meant."[39] Thereafter criticism of *Swift* proliferated in the reviews. Finally, in *Erie R.R.* v. *Tompkins*,[40] *Swift* was overruled. In writing the opinion, Brandeis cited 22 different articles. In commenting on the Warren article, Brandeis wrote, "[I]t was the more recent research of a competent scholar, who examined the original document, which established that the construction given to it by the Court was erroneous." As Newland noted, "The decisive influence of Warren's article in Brandeis' interpretation of the Judiciary Act of 1789 could hardly be made more plain."[41]

Thus far only activities within the legal community have been surveyed.[42] Now we turn to a consideration of phenomena occurring outside the courts and the legal profession. The activities of the communications media, local officials, interest group spokesmen, private citizens, Congress, and the President will be discussed in terms of how they affect impact and contribute to feedback. Attention is first focused on the media because they link judicial output to citizen and even official response. Typically, the only information that most Americans have about court decisions—and this includes many public officials as well as private citizens —is through the media. How the media report and cover court activities, in particular those of the Supreme Court, goes a long way in illuminating how and why private citizens and public officials respond to judicial output the way they do.

THE COURTS AND THE COMMUNICATIONS MEDIA

To understand the relationship of the communications media to the courts, it is necessary to understand how the media in general influence governmental policy and affect its implementation. Through newspapers, news magazines, radio, and television, the "newsworthy" events of the daily lives of the political authorities and the decisions they make or are in the process of making are reported and interpreted. Information about policy decisions is transmitted outward to those who are the objects of that policy, and information about the reception and impact of decisions is fed back to the policymakers. Through their operations, the communications media serve not only to transmit information about the activities of others but also as a source of feedback itself, in that the media highlight and bring to consciousness various problem areas of social life and governmental activity, interpret them for both the public at large and governmental policymakers, and render value judgments. Obviously, the media are neither so monolithic nor so universally believed that they can make and break policy and policymakers at will. However, the media are widely acknowledged to have a major influence on the public. Thus, the way news is handled, interpreted, and evaluated in editorials can help to stimulate positive or negative attitudes about governmental institutions and policies. This, in turn, may be an important variable in what policies are made and how they are received.

The influence of the media is generally well understood by those who aspire to and hold positions of political power. It is also generally recognized that those who collect, report, and interpret the news are not totally unbiased as to either persons or policies.[43] In practice, most of those with some policy to promote make use of these biases (along with the media's need for news) to generate approval for some policies and to destroy it for others. News releases, press conferences, speeches, and even demonstrations and acts of civil disobedience are used for getting one's name and face (and, of course, views) onto the printed page and on the television screen. Through these devices even those with few friends in the press can get into the headlines, but those with even just a few friends can do much more. Favored reporters and columnists are fed "leaks" and given access to otherwise inaccessible materials. Through background sessions, off-the-record briefings, and other similar devices, high-ranking government officials are able to get potential policies aired to test public reactions without having to have their names associated with the proposed policy. In sum, through these and other ways, political authorities use an often-willing press to create public opinion supporting the making and implementation of governmental policies.

In this scramble for media attention and favor, the courts are at a distinct disadvantage. The judiciary's critics in Congress, in the executive branch, in local officialdom, and at the head of pressure groups can all use the devices just outlined in attacking the courts. At the same time, long-standing traditions and expectations related to the judicial role discourage judges from responding in like manner. Although some individual judges have made their views known through public speeches, interviews, and writings, it is largely the official and formal aspects of courtroom activity and its end products of case disposition and published opinions that constitute the sources for reporters covering the courts. Some crucial aspects of case processing and policy-making, such as what occurs in Supreme Court conferences and what policies are considered only to be subsequently rejected, are never disclosed at the time. "Trial balloons" and news "leaks" are forbidden. Many judges refuse to be interviewed privately by reporters. Thus, to a large degree, judicial authorities must rely upon the perceptions of reporters and commentators in the transmission of judicial policy to the American people.

A number of aspects of judicial decision making and of media reporting, however, serve to blur and distort the policy messages that judicial opinions and decisions are meant to convey. This is especially true of Supreme Court decision making, where the decisions are often the subject of sharp professional disagreement and where the interests rallying behind the opposing sides are highly organized and vocal.

Many judicial policy pronouncements and decisions enunciate or are based on threshold criteria. For example, in the *Mallory* case, the Court ruled that the ten-hour delay between arrest and arraignment exceeded the threshold implied by the term "unnecessary delay" in Section 5(a) of the Federal Rules of Criminal Procedure. Thus Mallory's conviction, resulting from a trial in which a confession made during this ten-hour period was admitted, was declared invalid and he was set free. It was irrelevant to the Court's ruling that Mallory was a chronic criminal and that a brutal rape was the crime to which he had confessed. Similar irrelevancies also marked the *Escobedo* and *Miranda*[44] cases, yet it was just these irrelevancies that made the cases newsworthy for the media. By emphasizing their outcomes rather than the rules of law being articulated, the media stressed the fact that the Court through its actions had freed chronic and violent criminals. "Good" civil libertarian decisions, in other words, often result in a bad press. On the other hand, when the Burger Court handed down its numerous pro-police decisions during the 1983–1984 term that, among other things, greatly undermined the exclusionary rule and the *Miranda* policy, press coverage—with the exception of civil liberties oriented editorial writers—was favorable. The Court was seen as protecting society from convicted rapists and murderers who no longer would be set free on legal technicalities that bore no relationship to innocence or guilt.

A second source of news distortion has been the lack of professional training by most of those who write about the Court. Only a handful of reporters who cover the Court have had some legal training, and even fewer (three were mentioned in a study published in 1968) have law degrees.[45] Although there is a high level of reporting found in the major newspapers serving the Washington community (such as the *New York Times, Washington Post, Wall Street Journal,* and *Christian Science Monitor*), news distortion grows rapidly as one retreats to the hinterland. Most non-Washington-oriented papers get their first and often only news on Court decisions from the wire services (AP and UPI), although many papers also subscribe to either the *New York Times* or *Los Angeles Times* press services, which also have regular Court reporters. Rarely in covering the Court is the text of an opinion itself sent out. With the wire services the pressure for speed, brevity, and dramatic news content results in the initial stories written by Court "regulars" being constantly cut and revised both by wire service rewrite persons and local reporters and editors. Much accuracy is lost in this process as inexact journalistic language replaces the exact language of the Court, and background information and speculation of the initial reporter is taken as the content of the Court's opinion. "Denial of certiorari" becomes "dismissal of an appeal." A reporter's background inclusion of the language of the lower court's opinion may result in that language being attributed to the Supreme Court, when in fact the lower court's decision was merely summarily affirmed in a memorandum order. The far-ranging language of a concurrence or even a dissent may form the basis of a story purporting to portray what actually was decided.

Adding to distortion in press coverage of what the Court did is that by the second day after the decision is rendered, stories focus on reaction to the Court's decision rather than the decision itself. This often means that reporters without legal training who have not read the full text of the opinion ask similarly untrained and uninformed people, whose interests may be strongly affected by the decision, for their views of the Court's action. In the stories thus generated, extreme and highly contentious statements are generally played up to the detriment of those more restrained and ambiguous, since the former are more "newsworthy."

Often, in fairness to the media, many of the extreme views found in such stories are indeed worth reporting, since they may coincide with the opinions of highly placed members of the legal community, including even members of the Court itself. This is well illustrated in the media's coverage of reaction to the Court's ruling in *Engel* v. *Vitale,*[46] the New York School Prayer case.

In his majority opinion, Justice Black reasoned that since the prayer in question was drafted and recommended by the New York State Board of Regents (a governmental agency) for reading in the state's public schools, this represented a violation of the Establishment Clause of the First Amendment (as applied to the states through the Fourteenth Amendment) and was thus unconstitutional. Even before it was announced, the opinion was already marked by extreme controversy and misstatement. Justice Douglas, in a concurring opinion, suggested that the Court's interpretation of the Establishment Clause raised serious questions about the validity of numerous governmental activities in the religious realm. In a footnote he included such practices as the hiring of chaplains for Congress, the armed forces, and the service academies; the use of the Bible for administering oaths; governmental aid for busing of parochial school students; tax deductions for contributions to religious institutions; and even the Treasury's use of the motto "In God We Trust." Justice Stewart, in dissent, suggested that the decision also extended to the Court's practice of having its marshal declare "God save the United States and this Honorable Court," as well as the prayers said at the beginning of each daily session of the House and Senate, and the presidential practice of calling on God's aid at inaugurations.

Douglas's concurrence and Stewart's dissent soon provided a focus for the Court's critics. Black's more narrowly based opinion, which only countered Douglas's and Stewart's assertions in a short footnote, was soon forgotten. Added to this initial misstatement of the Court's ruling were the adverse reactions of prominent people. For example, the president of the American Bar Association stated that the ruling meant the elimination from coins of the motto "In God We Trust."[47] The chief justice of the Pennsylvania Supreme Court was quoted as saying that the "First Amendment sometimes aids reds and criminals more than other citizens." Professor Mark De Wolfe Howe of the Harvard Law School was reported as saying, "Justice Black's opinion is ridiculous." The chief justice of Indiana was said to have criticized the ruling on the ground that the First Amendment applied only to Congress. Joined to this flurry of adverse reaction from within the legal profession were the strong condemnations by many members of the Roman Catholic and Protestant clergy. All this received extensive media attention. Although a few high governmental and religious leaders spoke in defense of the Court, generally their comments were only published in the locality where their views were offered. In fact, the only defense that received wide and prominent coverage was that made by President John F. Kennedy in his June 27, 1962, press conference three days after the decision was announced.

The *Engel* decision clearly touched many sensitive nerves within the nation. Yet the misstatements and the emphasis on irresponsible criticism that characterized its treatment by the media have occurred on other occasions. Typically, the emphasis is on decisions more concerned with symbols than concrete matters affecting vast numbers of citizens. Major economic cases generally receive only the most cursory coverage by the media. On the same day *Engel* was announced, the Court disposed of 40 other cases (15 by full opinion and 25 by memorandum orders). Many of these had important and wide-ranging policy dimensions, but the only other cases that received significant media attention were one dealing with homosexuals and another striking down a California narcotics law. Among the other cases announced that day was one that set forth a major new step in antitrust policy, but this case was given attention in only the New York and Washington papers. Although judgments in this area are always subjective, one may well question how many life-styles and what vital social interests were substantially affected by *Engel*.

This brings us to a consideration of what role the media actually play as feedback channels to the courts. Certainly in the aftermath of a widely reported decision, editorial writers, columnists, and even reporters behave as if they see themselves as sources of feedback to whom judicial authorities should pay attention. In making an assessment, one should look at who receives the feedback, its content, and how it fits in with the policy views of those receiving it. One suspects that most lower court judges are subjected to different media feedback to Supreme

Court decision making than are members of the Court itself. For the members of the high Court, it is likely that only the prestige papers serving the Washington community—the *New York Times* and *Washington Post* in particular—are seen, read, and perceived of as references. District and circuit court judges, particularly those living outside the Northeast, might be more likely to read the papers serving their local regions. One might speculate that since the Washington and the northeastern press in general tended to be more pro-Court than the press in other regions during the Warren Court years, the effect was to reinforce the Warren Court's liberal activism. At the same time, a more negative press elsewhere in the country, read by the more locally oriented judges at the trial court level as well as by the local law enforcement establishments and the general public, promoted a more negative reception of the liberal Court's output.[48]

It should be remembered, however, that current regional divisions are not nearly as great or divisive as in some earlier historical periods, largely because of improvements in transportation, communications, and economic development. In communications, television network news and the news magazines have served to transmit the type of Court-supporting views typical of the eastern prestige press to all sections of the nation. But local and regional resistance to Supreme Court decisions does occur and is usually supported by regional media. This has been particularly characteristic of the responses to the Court's decisions on civil rights, school prayers, and abortion. In contrast to the problems of compliance and strongly negative attitudes that these decisions produced among the public in certain localities, one might note the generally favorable public opinion response (of those few members of the public with opinions) the Court had and the high rate of compliance that has occurred with regard to the reapportionment decisions. It is probably not unimportant that these decisions were greeted with praise by the big urban dailies throughout the country.

Returning to the example of the *Engel* case, it is of interest to note that the justices of the Supreme Court were not oblivious to the storm of criticism and confusion that greeted that decision. As one scholar who interviewed most of the justices noted,[49] the justices were sufficiently "shaken" by the 1962 feedback so that when the 1963 *Schempp* case concerning Bible reading and the Lord's Prayer was to be decided, steps were taken "to avoid a recurrence of the confusion." These steps included (1) assigning the task of writing the Court's opinion to Justice Clark rather than a recognized civil libertarian activist; (2) "emphasis in the majority opinion on the importance of religion and on historical background for perspective"; (3) lengthy concurring opinions by Justices Brennan and Goldberg that sought to precisely clarify the dimensions of the Court's decision. (Note also that Justices Clark, Brennan, and Goldberg were affiliated with the Protestant, Roman Catholic, and Jewish faiths, respectively—perhaps a conscious attempt to appeal to their coreligionists.) However, despite the best efforts of the justices, the Court's decision in *Abington School District* v. *Schempp,* prohibiting Bible reading and other prayer recitation as part of public school devotional exercises, produced negative reactions that over the years have led to a movement (supported by 81 percent of Americans in a 1983 Gallup poll[50]) for a constitutional amendment overturning *Schempp.* President Ronald Reagan actively supported such an amendment, but it failed to pass the Senate on March 20, 1984. Earlier, opponents of the Court in Congress had mounted a campaign to remove federal court jurisdiction in several areas, including school prayer. Perhaps with these developments in mind, a majority of the justices in the spring of 1983 decided two religion cases in such a way that it is plausible to argue that they were responding to this feedback. In *Marsh* v. *Chambers,* [51] the Court upheld the practice of legislatures hiring and using chaplains, while in *Mueller* v. *Allen,* [52] the Court approved the use of tax credits as applied against the tuition parents paid for parochial (and other private) school education. On March 5, 1984, the day the Senate began debate on a constitutional amendment to overturn *Schempp,* the Supreme Court handed down its decision in *Lynch* v. *Donnelly,* in which the Court upheld the city of Pawtucket, Rhode Island's, sponsorship of nativity displays during the Christmas season as not violating the establishment-of-religion guarantee. Several weeks later, the Court agreed to consider whether a moment of silent meditation in the public schools (permitted by almost half the states [52a]) constituted a violation of the First Amendment. The Court was evidently trying to convey the message (and presumably counting on the media to do the conveying) that it was not antireligion while still standing by the *Schempp* decision itself.

As far as the Supreme Court is concerned, it is likely that occasionally the feedback transmitted and generated by the media has some immediate effect on the substance of controversial Court policies. For example, Justice Felix Frankfurter recorded in his diary that in the fall term after the first Flag Salute case[53] had been decided (the vote was 8–1 against the First Amendment claims of the Jehovah's Witnesses), Justice Douglas remarked to him, "Hugo [Justice Black] would now not go with you in the Flag Salute case." Frankfurter wrote that he replied: "Why, has he reread the Constitution during the summer?" to which Douglas responded, "No, but he has read the papers."[54] When the feedback suggests positive support, it may have the effect of encouraging the justices to do what they were going to do anyway. When negative, the amount of misstatement and distortion inevitably involved may sensitize the justices to problems of communication and public relations.

Media comment is also quite important in an indirect way as it both reflects and shapes public and political authorities' opinion. By support of and opposition to specific outputs and general Court behavior, the media provide vital inputs of information and opinion for politicians, public officials, interest group leaders, and private citizens that help determine their responses to judicial policy-making. In the deep South, for example, the constant drumfire of a negative press attacking the legitimacy of the *Brown* decision tended to isolate those political and judicial authorities who were predisposed to carry out the Court's policy during the 1950s and early 1960s. This rendered the formula of "all deliberate speed" into one of "all determined resistance." With other decisions, such as those concerned with reapportionment, a press generally supportive of the Court was instrumental in achieving fairly rapid compliance. In general, however, the press is neither so monolithic nor so one-sided as the preceding two examples imply. Even in the same newspaper, a Court decision may be praised on the editorial page and condemned by a columnist or ridiculed in a political cartoon. The press thus shares in the process by which judicial decision making is removed from narrow confines and thrust forward as a subject fit for political controversy.

COMPLIANCE BY LOCAL OFFICIALS AND PRIVATE CITIZENS

Constitutional law casebooks as well as many studies of judicial policy-making often imply that a knowledge of the law as it really is can be found merely by looking at the content of judicial (i.e., Supreme Court) opinions and decisions. The obvious implication of such a formulation is that what the law really is, is also a description of how members of the political community behave. Doubtless with some types of judicial policy this is true. For example, when the Court in 1895 ruled an early form of the income tax constitutionally invalid, such tax collections ceased. And, some 57 years later, when the Court declared presidential seizure of the steel mills illegal, management of the mills was immediately returned to their private owners. Or in 1983, when the Court invalidated the legislative veto in immigration matters, Congress ceased utilizing it in that sphere. The outcomes of these decisions thus seem fairly obvious. One of the reasons that the tax and steel decisions' enforcement was so rapid was that they involved well-organized, well-financed, and highly articulate groups who had a substantial self-interest in seeing that enforcement occurred. Moreover, with all three decisions compliance involved the action of only a limited number of highly visible public officials. Yet there are many areas of the law where neither of the above litigant characteristics is true. Sometimes, even though there are those in society with an interest in enforcement, those opposing enforcement hold a monopoly or near monopoly of money, legal skill, and other forms of political and social power. In such cases compliance may become a massive problem as occurred, for example, with the famous *Brown* decision.

After *Brown* v. *Board of Education* was announced, there was no sudden disappearance of racially segregated school systems. In fact, a full decade after *Brown,* less than 3 percent of the black schoolchildren in the South were attending desegregated schools.[55] (By 1972, however, the proportion was about 91 percent, a better integration record than the rest of the nation, but this was achieved after several years of sustained pressure from the federal government, including threats of a cutoff of federal aid. Even so, this figure is misleading as over half the black students attended schools that had a large majority of black students.[56]) By 1972, a large majority of southern school districts had formally eliminated dual school systems (*de jure* segregation). Nevertheless, *de facto* segregation, which occurs as a result of behavior not required by law, particularly in the urban areas of the entire nation, has remained a continuing reality. Indeed, in 1984 at the time of the thirtieth anniversary of the handing down of the *Brown* decision, close to two-thirds of black students nationwide attended schools in which black students constituted the majority of students.

If the intent of the *Brown* policy and subsequent decisions was not just to end legal segregation by race but to achieve a fully integrated society, that policy still has far to go, although progress has been made. In 1970, a Gallup poll found that white southern opinion on the subject of school racial integration had substantially reversed itself. In 1963 in response to the question "Would you, yourself, have any objection to sending your children to a school where a few of the children are Negroes?" 61 percent of the southern white respondents objected to racial integration. By 1970, only 16 percent said they would object (the figure was 6 percent for nonsouthern white parents).[57] Furthermore, the formidable opposition to enforcement by the local authorities appears to have lessened, at least in comparison with previous decades. Whether the South as well as the rest of the nation will achieve full racial integration within education and other areas is still, however, problematic.[58]

If one surveys the whole spectrum of judicial policy, it is not difficult to find other areas where the originally objectionable patterns of behavior long persisted in the face of a Court ruling. Earlier it was mentioned how evasion by lower court judges could yield such a result. It is also relevant to note the activities, backgrounds, and attitudes of local officials and private citizens as they relate to the pattern of compliance to Court policies that run counter to local mores.

To consider this question further, it is of interest to examine the findings of one study by Robert Birkby which was concerned with the responses by Tennessee school boards to the Court's 1963 *Schempp* and *Curlett* decisions forbidding devotional religious activities (Bible reading and the Lord's Prayer) in public schools.[59] Coupled with the earlier Court rulings, these decisions in effect made illegal the use of public school facilities and faculties for religious instruction or devotional purposes. The study of religion, however, including the Bible, was still permissible "when presented objectively as part of a secular program of education."[60] Although the initial national outpouring of negative public criticism was not as great as that which met the *Engel* decision, the Tennessee "Bible belt" did not take kindly to the *Schempp* and *Curlett* decisions.

In the national response to *Schempp,* some school districts that previously had engaged in the forbidden practices ceased having them altogether. In many others, no change occurred at all and religious exercises went on as before. In yet a third category of districts, previous procedures were changed and "voluntary" religious exercises replaced "required" ones, a change that represented a surface attempt at compliance by misreading the Court's decisions.

In Tennessee prior to the *Schempp* decision, devotional Bible reading was required under state law. After *Schempp,* which invalidated such a law, the state commissioner of education was reported as saying that it was permissible to still have Bible readings, but *that* decision was left to local school officials. To analyze compliance, Robert Birkby in late 1964 and early 1965 sent questionnaires to school superintendents and school board members in Tennessee's 152 school districts. Responses from 121 school districts were received. In 70 districts, no change in practices was reported as having occurred following *Schempp;* in 50, devotional exercises were made discretionary, with the decision being left to the classroom teacher; and in 1, all devotional exercises were reported as having been stopped. Thus in Tennessee more than a year after the Court spoke, massive noncompliance and evasion were commonplace, and, moreover, school officials were willing to admit their noncompliance in a questionnaire. There was little doubt that the school officials knew they were violating the Court's *Schempp* policy because that decision had been well (and unfavorably) publicized.

In looking at noncompliance in Tennessee, the question was raised as to why in some districts changes were made in the direction of compliance and in others nothing at all happened. To better understand the dynamics of compliance, Birkby first looked for distinguishing social and economic differences between the 70 districts in which no change occurred and the 51 others where some minor surface change took place, and he found no differences in degree of urbanization, in religious heterogeneity, in whether or not there was articulate local opposition to devotional exercises, and in the socioeconomic backgrounds of school board members.

After obtaining these negative results, Birkby looked more closely at the reasons that school board officials themselves gave for why they changed or did not change procedures, and he found that changes toward compliance generally occurred where board members and superintendents saw the Court as the legitimate arbiter of the school prayer issue. Although some thought the Court's policy "correct" and others disagreed, in general the more important consideration was that as public officials and citizens they believed they were obliged to adhere to "the law" as announced by the Court and to disregard local public demands for the now-forbidden practices. But, of course, the changes they instituted could not in any meaningful sense be considered compliance. Prayers were still recited, only now they were "voluntary" and at the teacher's "discretion." In districts marked by no formal change whatsoever, officials generally felt that the Court in the school prayer and other areas had consistently misinterpreted the Constitution and that its decisions lacked legitimacy. Thus Birkby found that the only essential difference between school districts where officials took some surface steps to comply with the Court's ruling and those in which it was totally disregarded was attitudinal; that is, how the officials saw their roles as public officials and citizens when the Court ruled on a question of law.

Kenneth Dolbeare and Phillip Hammond also studied compliance to the school prayer decisions,[61] and they relied not only on a questionnaire survey but also on intensive interviewing of local educational system officials, teachers, and community notables. Focusing on one midwestern state, they found that, with the exception of the major city in the state and three university towns, there was *no* compliance with the Court's decision. This was true even for communities that reported in the questionnaire that they were complying! Dolbeare and Hammond examined four communities in the state, two that had indicated compliance and two that had reported continuing religious practices. In all four, prayer and Bible reading and other religious activities continued as if the Supreme Court had never spoken. The researchers came to the conclusion that officials at the state and local levels had no motivation to implement the Court's policy. None had strong feelings about the First Amendment violations their school systems were engaging in and they all felt that stirring up controversy over religion in the schools would cost them more politically than they would benefit and would jeopardize their own goals and priorities. Furthermore, local elites wanted to avoid conflict, and they believed that the implementation of the prayer rulings would produce undesirable community cleavage. The Court's policies themselves were incorrectly understood by local school officials, which may have been one way of rationalizing inertia. Finally, there were no routine governmental channels that would force officials to face up to the Court rulings. There remained only the costly and time-consuming, as well as personally stressful, route for individuals to sue their local school board.

Interestingly, in two other studies on the impact of the prayer rulings, it was found that there *was* compliance essentially because of the actions of certain local school officials who assumed leadership roles in obtaining compliance.[62] This points up the crucial role of local officials for compliance to Court decisions, be they in the prayer, school desegregation,[63] or criminal procedures[64] areas. These and other studies suggest that local officials and the citizenry alike engage in some rough cost-benefit calculations when it comes to compliance with Court decisions.[65] A challenging question is, How can the Court make policy in which it is likely that the costs of evasion will outweigh the benefits, and indeed what can the Court do to maximize the costs of evasion.[66] The other side of the coin is to examine what sorts of decisions produce the most and the least compliance and under what circumstances information of noncompliance will be fed back to the Court and what then can the Court do about it. Dolbeare and Hammond have suggested that noncompliance increases as (1) the degree of change required by the Court policy increases; (2) the number of persons who must comply increases (as opposed to relatively few conspicuous public officials); and (3) enforcement depends upon the actions of local courts.[67]

Does law change attitudes? Are attitudes the necessary catalyst for behavioral compliance? These are intriguing questions. One might speculate that, on the basis of their extensive opinion-writing activity and their behavior as judges, most justices assume answers to these questions in the affirmative, at least as far as the long run is concerned. Some of the studies that have been conducted thus far suggest that, even in the short run, attitude change may indeed come about to some extent, although the relationship of attitudes to compliance is, of course, complex.[68]

FEEDBACK FROM THE PRESIDENT AND CONGRESS

Since the spirited battles between FDR and the conservative anti–New Deal Court of the early- and mid-1930s, presidential criticism of the Supreme Court has been infrequent. President Truman did, of course, verbally lash back after the steel seizure decision, but the dust soon settled and he complied. President Eisenhower, although no staunch defender of the Court in its more liberal thrusts at protecting civil rights and liberties, still never openly attacked the Court while in office and in fact enforced the Court's policy on school desegregation by federalizing the troops in Little Rock. Presidents Kennedy and Johnson were open supporters of the Warren Court in the face of rising congressional criticism and falling public approval. President Carter had no quarrel with the Warren Court's civil liberties precedents. Even President Nixon in the first year of his Administration, although he had campaigned for a more conservative judiciary, did not openly and directly attack the Court. No constitutional amendments were called for. No blatantly anti-Court legislation was proposed. In the main, the Nixon Administration's strategy to reshape judicial policies into a more conservative mold involved the following: the nomination of more conservative judges to the federal bench (and forcing Justice Fortas, the most vulnerable liberal, off the Court); a disinclination to vigorously prosecute cases aimed at insuring full implementation of certain Court policies; and last, a failure to act on behalf of the goals underlying the Court's concern for minority rights which was demonstrated by opposing integration-oriented school busing, proposing amendments to the Voting Rights Act that would have had the probable effect of lessening its impact, failing to vigorously defend the legal services component of the poverty program, and supporting public aid to segregated private schools formed to evade the law. This also turned out to be the agenda of the Reagan Administration, which however, pursued this strategy more vigorously and in addition supported constitutional amendments to overturn Court decisions in the abortion and prayer areas.

In contrast to most recent presidents, Congress in the 1950s, 1960s, late 1970s, and early 1980s actively engaged in anti-Court activity and criticism. Perhaps the reason for the contrast is that the presidency, despite the size and extent of the White House staff and official family, is at heart one individual elected through one national election. For much of the period from 1940 until 1968, victorious presidential candidates have had in their winning coalitions groups who have approved of or benefited by Court output. During this same period, most of the major groups who were strongly anti-Court—for example, segregationists, religious fundamentalists, economic reactionaries—found few friends within the White House. Furthermore, presidents during this period for the most part occupied much the same moderate-to-liberal end of the political spectrum as did many members of the Court. All these factors reinforced the normal expectation that the President supports the law of the land as ultimately determined by the Court.[69]

Congress, on the other hand, is an institution of 535 members. When any one of these members attacks the Court, this is viewed as an attack from Congress. Moreover, there are many aspects of Congress that encourage individual members to make such attacks. Members are elected from different constituencies, some of which are far removed both ideologically and geographically from the "liberal establishment centers" whose views are widely considered to have dominated the White House and the Supreme Court until the presidencies of Nixon and Ford. The minorities with whose liberties the Court was concerned —for example, blacks, communists, atheists, women seeking abortions—are either far removed from or, even worse, perceived as a direct threat by the citizens of such constituencies. Furthermore, accepted conceptions of the congressional role leave much room for unrestrained criticism and court-curbing activities when they express constituency and regional interests and cultures.

The most dramatic and visible conflicts between Congress and the Court have concerned cases involving constitutional interpretations.[70] Without the Court overruling itself, many of these decisions can be fully reversed only by constitutional amendment. Managing any piece of controversial legislation through Congress is typically a long, difficult, complicated, and often unfruitful process. With a constitutional amendment, these difficulties are multiplied by the requirement of a two-thirds vote and the fact that the issues typically become highly charged with symbolism. Although the initial contention of those who would overturn a particular decision may be that it was the Court that violated the Constitution, sponsoring an amendment makes the amenders themselves open to the charge that they are tinkering with the handiwork of the Founding Fathers.[71] Even if it clears Congress, the amendment must still win approval of three-fourths of the states. The sum result is that changing a Court decision by amendment is typically a highly unpromising route. Before 1971, the last time it had been done successfully was in 1913, with the passage of the Sixteenth Amendment overturning the Court's anti–income tax decision of some 18 years earlier. In 1970 the Court ruled that congressional legislation enfranchising 18-, 19-, and 20-year-olds was only constitutional as applied to federal (as opposed to state) elections.[72] This decision, had it stood alone, would have created chaos at the polls; thus there was widespread agreement that a constitutional amendment was needed, and the Twenty-Sixth Amendment, giving 18-year-olds and older the right to vote in *all* elections, quickly won approval in Congress and in the state legislatures.

Head-on conflicts between the Court and Congress over constitutional cases concerning federal power have been relatively rare, however. From 1789 through July, 1983, there were only 122 decisions striking down congressional legislation in whole or in part.[73] Court curbs on presidential powers have even been rarer. Since the late 1930s, when a humbled Court overruled its attempts to limit narrowly the national government's power to regulate the economy, the Supreme Court has been quite restrained in setting limits on Congress and the President. In contrast to the conservative Courts of the late nineteenth and early twentieth centuries, which broadly questioned the federal government's power to govern, the modern Court in striking down federal legislation has dealt mostly either with laws that lacked procedural safeguards but could be repaired by remedial legislation, or with fairly marginal civil libertarian areas involving relatively few persons. Even the *Youngstown* case, a potentially stunning defeat to President Truman in his attempt to guard against the military and economic consequences of a stoppage in steel production during the Korean War, was not a denial of power to the federal government, but merely a denial of that power to the President without supporting congressional action. The famous Nixon Tapes case,[74] although it led to Nixon's downfall, was itself a very narrow ruling relating to the integrity of the criminal judicial process. The Court in its unanimous decision left open ample room for the presidency to maintain executive privilege in matters of legitimate national interests. The modern Court's permissive attitude toward federal power, therefore, may well explain much of the amicable relationship that has existed between the President and the Court.[75]

In contrast to the relative infrequency of Court decisions overturning acts of Congress and exercises of presidential power, cases overturning state and local laws either as unconstitutional or as conflicting with federal statutory law or treaties are much more common. From 1789 through the end of the Court's 1983 term, there were over 1000 cases in which this occurred.[76] The rate had accelerated during the years of the Warren Court as attention was focused on state cases. As compared to federal cases, these cases involved an inordinately high number whose principal issue was constitutional. For example, in the Warren Court's 1967 term, of the cases decided with full written opinion, approximately 80 percent of the cases concerning state laws and procedures involved a constitutional question, while only about 30 percent of the federal cases did so. With the subsequent Burger Court, one finds, for example, in the 1982 term, that about 73 percent of the cases concerning state laws and procedures involved a constitutional question as compared to about 23 percent of the federal cases raising constitutional issues.[77] A large number of state cases decided on constitutional grounds, like similar federal cases, can only be reversed by a constitutional amendment. In fact, during the 1960s the two most serious and near-successful attempts at Court-reversing amendments concerned state law cases. These were the so-called Becker Amendment, which would have reversed the *Schempp* decision and thus allowed school prayers, and the Dirksen Amendment, which would have partially reversed the one person–one vote doctrine of *Reynolds* v. *Sims.* Both these proposed amendments died as victims of the complexities and procedural pitfalls of the legislative process in Congress. The Becker Amendment was killed by the determined opposition of the then-chairman of the House Judiciary Committee, Representative Emanuel Celler, who refused to report the bill out of committee; the Dirksen Amendment was killed by a filibuster by Senate liberals. After the Court's 1973 decision in *Roe* v. *Wade* preventing the states from prohibiting abortion during the first two trimesters of pregnancy,[78] constitutional amendments were introduced in Congress but they were stifled in committee. With the election of Ronald Reagan in 1980, a number of anti-Court politicians were elected to the U.S. Senate and the House of Representatives. There were renewed attempts, with the support of President Reagan, to overturn by constitutional amendment *Roe* v. *Wade* as well as *Abington School District* v. *Schempp.* Ultimately these attempts, like earlier ones aimed at the same decisions, failed, but only after provoking heated controversy, intense lobbying by groups on both sides of the issues, and front-page media coverage.

In face of the great difficulties in reversing Court constitutional policy-making by constitutional amendment, Court critics in Congress have turned to other means for modifying and changing this type of Court output. These include such heavy-handed techniques as threats of impeachment and attempts to remove Supreme Court and even total federal jurisdiction from areas where Court policies are disliked. Impeachment, as a political weapon, has always been difficult to administer. Severe scrutiny of judicial nominations has not. It was such scrutiny that provided the vehicle for senatorial critics of the Court's liberal activism to use when thwarting President Lyndon Johnson's efforts to promote Associate Justice Fortas to the chief justiceship. Furthermore, once the Nixon Administration came to power, disclosure of allegations of Fortas's impropriety in financial arrangements with a financier later in trouble with the law was used to force his resignation (amidst the righteous indignation of primarily conservative congressional critics of the Court). However, the symbolism of judicial ethics and considerations of judicial policy proved to be a two-edged sword, which liberals used against conservatives to defeat President Nixon's first nominee for the seat vacated by Fortas, southern conservative Judge Clement Haynsworth. After the defeat of Nixon's second nominee to the Fortas seat, Judge G. Harrold Carswell, also a southern conservative (his alleged mediocrity and racial insensitivity as a jurist were additional issues), the Republican conservatives in Congress allied with anti-Court Democrats to revive the campaign to impeach liberal Justice Douglas. Although then–House Judiciary Committee Chairman Emanuel Celler once again moved to protect the Court in general and Justice Douglas in particular, the depth of anti-Court hostility was prominent.[79] (Note that when Nixon nominated Harry Blackmun, known as a midwestern conservative with impeccable professional credentials, to the Fortas seat, the Senate gave its unanimous consent, thus tacitly acknowledging its relief at being able to approve a jurist with an unblemished record, but also conceding the legitimacy of the President's using his appointment power to change the ideological balance on the Court.)

Attempts at curbing Court policy-making by removal of jurisdiction, a device that succeeded in the aftermath of the Civil War, have failed to get congressional approval in recent years, although there were some near misses with this ploy in several areas, including abortion and school prayers during the fall of 1982.[80]

In sum, most negative congressional feedback to the Court in recent decades toward its constitutional decision making has been merely verbal—in the late 1960s with criminal law and in the 1970s and early 1980s with the so-called social issues of abortion, busing, and school prayer.[81] Statements have been made on the floor, hearings held to establish a forum for the Court's critics, legislation and constitutional amendments proposed, debated, and defeated. This typical (but not total) lack of success on the part of congressional Court opponents rests on the fact that, for most of the recent past, friends of the Court and its policies have been nearly as numerous, though not necessarily as vocal. Thus the Court's friends have been able to keep most feedback by congressional critics directed into relatively harmless channels. In some areas, particularly civil rights during the 1960s, Congress enacted vital legislation aimed at forwarding the implementation of Court-initiated policy. While in the early 1980s the battles became more severe because of an implicit and sometimes explicit alliance of the Court's enemies and the White House, the friends of the Court were nevertheless able to mobilize to protect the Court and its controversial rulings. (The Court itself in 1983 and 1984 took major steps particularly with criminal procedures but also in some other areas including religion that had the effect of blunting the sharp edge of conservative criticism.)

To emphasize only what Congress has not done or cannot do in the face of unwanted constitutional policy-making by the Court is somewhat misleading. As applied to the recent history of Court-congressional relationships, it tends to imply a will in Congress that is perhaps only marginally there. Congress, and particularly the Senate during the 1960s and the early 1980s, contained a sufficient number of backers of the Warren Court's liberal policies as well as believers in the Court's right to make constitutional policy to protect the Court from congressional retaliation.

The second reason that it is misleading to focus on the ineffectualness of congressional responses to constitutional policy-making is that many cases decided by the Court do not rest on constitutional grounds. For example, of the 162 cases deemed important enough by the Court in its 1982 term to warrant disposal by full written opinions, in only 67 (41 percent) was the principal issue constitutional.[82] The remainder primarily concerned judicial interpretations of federal legislation, which, of course, can be overturned by regular congressional legislation. Even among decisions that are normally listed as constitutional, there are a number that also can be changed simply by congressional legislation. For example, such cases occur when the Court, in lieu of any clear congressional policy, is called upon to uphold federal interests under the commerce power in the face of state activities inhibiting the free flow of commerce. A famous instance of congressional reversal of such Supreme Court policy-making concerned a bridge built under a Virginia charter over the Ohio River. The bridge was built in such a way as to obstruct river navigation. Pennsylvania, acting in the interest of its citizens whose rights were "abridged," asked the Court for and was granted an injunction instructing the company to alter the structure as to not obstruct river traffic.[83] Congress then passed a bill declaring the bridge "a lawful structure" and required boats operating on the Ohio to be so regulated as not to interfere with it. The Court subsequently ruled the act a constitutional use of Congress's power over commerce.[84]

Congressional reversal of Court legislative interpretations and constitutional policy-making of the type just discussed has been found to occur with occasional frequency. In a survey of congressional activities from 1945 to 1957, it was found that Congress overruled Court decision 21 times in this period.[85] Although the circumstances under which this occurred varied, in a large number of cases congressional reversals were marked by the common theme of returning the law to the "common understanding" that had existed prior to the Court's action. For example, in *United States* v. *South-Eastern Underwriters Ass'n*,[86] the Court reversed prior doctrine and held that insurance companies in fact operate in interstate commerce and thus are subject to federal antitrust law. Congress, taking into account the pattern of state insurance regulation that had grown up over the years, then reversed the decision. Certain specific restrictive practices were outlawed, and the states were to continue to regulate the industry. In return, the industry was given back its federal antitrust immunity.

FEEDBACK AND COURT POLICY-MAKING

The federal judicial system with the Supreme Court as its highest and most visible policy-making organ, has always received some minimal level of feedback. Law journals and the mass media always have had some reaction to court behavior, even if that reaction is the journalistic equivalent of "good job, well done." Alternatively, judicial authorities inevitably from time to time make errors in their interpretation of congressional legislation. These often occur not because of any great policy disagreement with the legislative branch, but merely because Congress's latent and often unarticulated intent is incorrectly perceived. Sometimes such rulings are allowed to stand. Other times Congress, with its greater fact-finding devices, interest group sensitivity, and mechanisms for complex poli-cy-making, will pass remedial legislation. In these and other ways, a minimal or background level of feedback is maintained.

Over the history of the nation since constitutional government was estab-lished, there have been times when the level of negative feedback to the Court has risen sharply above this background. Thus, presidents normally during their terms in office have considered it as part of the presidential role to back or at least neutrally enforce Court policies as the sole legitimate interpretation of the law. Presidents Jefferson, Jackson, Lincoln, Franklin Roosevelt, and to some extent, Nixon, and Reagan eschewed that role and attacked the shape of Court policy, seeking to change it while in office. Similarly, in Congress there have been some periods marked by attempts to curb the Court and others when the relationship between the two branches was friendly.

Stuart Nagel, in a study of Court-curbing legislation up through 1959,[87] found that 1802–1804, 1823–1831, 1858–1869, 1893–1897, 1922–1924, 1935–1937, and 1955–1959 were periods in which there was a high frequency of Court-curbing attempts through legislation. Also analyzed was whether or not the Court retreated in its policy stands, that is, the overall or "composite success" of the Court-curbing attempts. Nagel suggested that only the following periods achieved "composite success": 1802–1804, 1823–1831, 1858–1869, and 1935–1937 (although he notes that there was a partial judicial retreat in the 1955–1959 period).[88]

As can be readily surmised, these composite success periods fall within the administrations of presidents noted for their particularly hostile attitudes toward the Court. (Of course, the dates of the Nixon and Reagan Administrations are excluded by Nagel since his analysis ended with 1959.) We can note that with the exception of the 1922–1924 period, each high-frequency Court-curbing period falls within a period in which electoral realignment (as identified by critical election theory) produced a new political era.

Briefly, critical election studies have dealt with patterns of voting behavior. These studies have indicated that voters are typically quite stable in their partisan allegiances and such ancillary behavior as turnout and ticket splitting. However, as an empirical phenomenon it has been found that about once every generation-and-a-half this electoral stability breaks down in one or more tightly grouped "critical elections" in which prior partisan allegiances are permanently and mas-sively changed along with ancillary voter behavior. Although there has been some dispute as to which elections in American history have met these criteria, notably with regard to the earlier history of the Republic, in general the elections of 1828, 1864, 1896, 1928–1936, and 1968–1972 have been identified as having critical election characteristics. (Elections prior to 1824 are normally unanalyzed because of a lack of sufficient popular voting data, although the election of 1800 is generally thought to have at least some critical election attributes.)

To understand the phenomenon further, consider the election of 1888. The voting pattern for that election was more or less the same as the voting patterns of every election back to 1876. This was a pattern in which the two parties were very close, ticket splitting was rare, turnout high, and party allegiances very strong. With 1896 and the election of McKinley, voting behavior altered significantly. Partisanship became much more regionally based, turnout fell, major shifts toward a party (landslides) became more common. This pattern stayed more or less undisturbed until the election of 1928. In that election and subsequently the elections of 1932 and 1936, the New Deal Democratic coalition came into being.

Using this theory along with a consideration of public policy outputs and presidential styles, it has been argued elsewhere that American political history can therefore be split into five major periods:[89] the Federalist-Jeffersonian (1789–1828), the Jacksonian (1828–1860), the First Republican (1860–1896), the Second Republican (1896–1932), and the New Deal Era (1932–1968). (As students of American history will recognize, these periods more or less coincide with those suggested by traditional political historians.) These periods can be briefly summarized, although at the risk of oversimplification.

The Federalist-Jeffersonian period, although split into two parts (Federalist dominated from 1789 to 1800, Jeffersonian dominated from 1800 to 1828), still had the overall unity of the federal government under the control of a fairly select elite of merchants and planters concerning itself with the problems of Constitution building, union, and the creation of economic and political stability in the face of intrigues and tensions both foreign and domestic. The Jacksonian period saw the disappearance of the old Federalist and Jeffersonian Republican parties and their replacement by the mass-based Democrats and Whigs. The common man, at least symbolically, took control of government through widespread political participation in the party system and administration. The balance of political power shifted westward, and major party political competition existed everywhere. The major public policy concerns were state-based governmental encouragement of economic development as industrial takeoff proceeded regionally in the North and the drive toward a compromise solution on slavery.

Lincoln's election signaled a start of a new period, although the period's stable electoral alignments did not take shape until 1864, after four years of Lincoln's leadership. By 1860, however, the Whigs had disintegrated and the Democratic party split in two; the Republicans had blossomed forth full grown and victorious. The dominant themes of this period were, of course, the Civil War, the protection of the freed slaves, the reconstruction of the South, and, most emphasized, the protection and promotion of industry and capitalism.

The significant result of the election of 1896 was to propel the Republican party into a position of overwhelming dominance. The party system created was one in which one-party states, both Democratic and Republican, were quite common. Dramatic shifts in public policy and symbolism are somewhat harder to find than with previous realignments. This is perhaps due to the continuing dominance of the Republican party and that party's continuing support of big business. Also this was the first party-system realignment that did not witness the disappearance of one or both of the system's major party components. It should be noted, however, that this period was marked by the almost complete halt to all attempts to protect black Americans, the first serious attempts at economic regulation, and the first major entrance of the United States into imperialism and great-power politics.

With the realignments of 1928–1932, spurred on by the Great Depression, the dominant party once again shifted, and although partisan cleavages were still strongly regional, these began to break down. Economic cleavages became more important in determining one's vote, particularly outside the South. The public policy concerns were the welfare-warfare state and, certainly by the Truman Administration, a growing concern with civil rights (which dominated national politics through the Administration of Lyndon Johnson). It appears that the politics that began with FDR came to an end with the elections of Richard Nixon in 1968 and 1972. Had the Watergate-related scandals not fatally undermined the Nixon Administration, Nixon might well have been able to solidify for the Republican party the moderate-right coalition including a sizable portion of blue-collar workers and lower-middle-class white "ethnic" groups that twice put him in the White House. Had the aftermath of Watergate and the economic recession of the mid-1970s not occurred, President Ford might have been able to put that coalition together again. Even so, Ford narrowly lost to Jimmy Carter. Although Carter's personal difficulty in dealing with congressional leaders in his own party and trouble holding down inflation and coping with the Iranian hostage crisis help explain his defeat to Ronald Reagan, the underlying trend that became noticeable in 1968 worked in Reagan's favor. The Republicans in 1980 were able to reconstruct the Nixon coalition and not only elect a president but gain control of the U.S. Senate. While it is true that the severe recession-depression of 1981–1982 with double-digit unemployment appeared to threaten the stability of the new coalition, the strong economic recovery of 1983–1984 along with low inflation and low unemployment rates seemed to repair the political damage that occurred. Nevertheless, because of uncertainties about the strength and duration of the recovery, it cannot be stated with any assurance how long and how stable the new political era will be.

What, one might well ask, does all this have to do with feedback to the Supreme Court? The answer is perhaps deceptively simple. Negative feedback to the Court has historically shown its greatest increases when old party system periods have come to an end and new ones are in the process of beginning. These are times when critical electoral realignments change the nature of politics and the groups in power. Because of the inevitable lag between when elected authorities of the "new politics" (i.e., electoral realignments) are put into office and sitting judges recruited under the old regime are replaced, the judiciary typically becomes suddenly out of tune with the times. Although retirement, death, and the selection process eventually correct the situation, this takes time.[90] In the interim, criticism, evasion, and Court-curbing attempts by President and Congress increase. This is suggested by the coincidence of Court-curbing periods found by Nagel and the presidential periods just discussed.[91] And this might explain the flurry of Court-curbing activity during the years of the Reagan Administration, particularly in 1982–1984.

Where does this leave us? In the first place, it appears that the observation of popular commentators that the country in 1968 shifted to the right is supported by data that have special relevance for the judicial system. For example, the combined presidential vote of 1968 of Court opponents, Richard M. Nixon and

George C. Wallace was 57 percent of the popular vote; by 1970 a substantial portion of those surveyed considered themselves "conservative" rather than "liberal," a result repeated well into the 1980s[92] by almost 2 to 1; those surveyed in 1970 advocated the appointment of conservatives rather than liberals to the Supreme Court, and similar results, too, have been found in later years although with a somewhat smaller margin favoring conservatives;[93] and negative feedback to the Warren Court's liberal policies, particularly in the realm of criminal procedures, reached a peak in the late 1960s, and conservative attitudes on matters of criminal law and procedures persisted into the 1980s.[94] Even those looking to youth as a source of hope for a liberal future had their faith tested with the results of the Survey Research Center study of the 1968 election, which showed that, outside the South, Wallace had his greatest support (by age group) in the under-30 set.[95] Nixon's overwhelming landslide reelection in 1972 and Reagan's electoral landslide in 1980 further emphasized the shift in party attachments and the electoral shift to the right.

What this all suggests is that the federal judicial system of the Warren Court era, characterized by civil libertarian output, could have been expected to be transformed in accord with the new political era. Indeed, as we have seen earlier, the Court, particularly in the criminal procedures areas but in other areas as well, was so transformed, at first to a right-of-center Court and then, following the 1982–1983 Court-curbing attempts, to a more solidly right-wing Court. This was a source of obvious bitterness for the liberal Warren Court holdovers, who on numerous occasions in the early 1970s lamented that the new composition of the Court was the principal reason for the change in policy.[96]

Response to feedback during the Burger Court era has not necessarily meant a change only from liberal policies to more conservative ones. At the federal district court level, it has been demonstrated by Beverly Cook that the sentencing behavior of judges of selective service law violators during the Vietnam War changed as public opinion (as measured by opinion surveys) concerning the war and the draft changed.[97] As public opinion over the years became more antagonistic to the war and the draft, judges became more lenient in their sentencing, so that by 1972 there was a turnaround in sentencing patterns in that a majority of violators were given probation. Thus it should be emphasized that the courts continually can be found responding to negative feedback.[98] During the transformation of an old to a new party system, however, the judiciary of the old regime is likely to be incapable of adequately responding to the intensified negative feedback and the new demands of the new coalition.

Because of the Watergate scandals and the economic recession of the mid-1970s, the new electoral coalition that had seemed so promising for the Republicans came apart. But the Democrats, with Jimmy Carter in the White House, were unable to keep that coalition from re-forming under Ronald Reagan's leadership and winning electoral success. The Court can be seen to have been transformed by the Nixon and Reagan appointments. To what extent the Court will maintain its right-wing conservative trend will in part be dependent upon the stability and duration of the new party system.

NOTES

1. An extensive consideration of impact and feedback phenomena can be found in Charles A. Johnson and Bradley C. Canon, *Judicial Policies: Implementation and Impact* (Washington, D.C.: C.Q. Press, 1984). Johnson and Canon's theoretical perspective is particularly worthy of attention. See their Chap. 1 for a presentation of their framework and Chap. 6 for an analysis of other theories that seek to explain impact phenomena. Earlier works of importance are discussed in Stephen L. Wasby, *The Impact of the United States Supreme Court: Some Perspectives* (Homewood, Ill.: Dorsey, 1970). Also see James P. Levine, "Methodological Concerns in Studying Judicial Efficacy," *Law and Society Review,* 4 (1970), 583–611; Charles M. Lamb, "Judicial Policy–Making and Information Flow to the Supreme Court," *Vanderbilt Law Review,* 29 (1976), 45–124. Lawrence Baum, "Implementation of Judicial Decisions: An Organizational Analysis," *American Politics Quarterly,* 4 (1976), 86–114; John Brigham and Don W. Brown (eds.), *Policy Implementation* (Beverly Hills, Calif.: Sage, 1980); John Gruhl, "Anticipatory Compliance with Supreme Court Rulings," *Polity,* 14 (1981), 294–313; Lawrence Baum, *The Supreme Court* (Washington, D.C.: C.Q. Press, 1981), pp. 179–222; Henry R. Glick, *Courts, Politics, and Justice* (New York: McGraw-Hill, 1983), pp. 308–347.
2. 2 Dall. 419 (1793).
3. 157 U.S. 429 (1895); 158 U.S. 601 (1895).
4. Baker v. Carr, 369 U.S. 186 at 237, 226 (1962).
5. 377 U.S. 533 (1964).
6. 103 S. Ct. 2653 (1983).
7. 103. S. Ct. 2690 (1983).
8. Miller v. California, 413 U.S. 15 (1973); Paris Adult Theatre I v. Slaton, 413 U.S. 49 (1973).
9. Jenkins v. Georgia, 418 U.S. 153 (1974). Note that the Supreme Court reversed the Georgia Supreme Court and held *Carnal Knowledge* not to be obscene.
10. 458 U.S. 747 (1982).
11. 384 U.S. 436 (1966).
12. Harris v. New York, 401 U.S. 222 (1971). Note that the Court imposed the Harris policy on a state judicial system that had attempted to reject it. See Oregon v. Haas, 420 U.S. 714 (1975).
13. New York v. Quarles, 104 S. Ct. 2626 (1984). In general, see Michael Wald, Richard Ayres, David W. Hess, Mark Schantz, and Charles H. Whitebread, II, "Interrogations in New Haven: The Impact of *Miranda,*" *Yale Law Journal,* 76 (1967), 1519–1648; Richard H. Seeburger and R. Stanton Wettick, Jr., "*Miranda* in Pittsburgh—A Statistical Study," *University of Pittsburgh Law Review,* 29 (1967), 1–26; Richard J. Medalie, Leonard Zeitz, and Paul Alexander, "Custodial Police Interrogation in Our Nation's Capital: The Attempt to Implement Miranda," *Michigan Law Review,* 66 (1968), 1347–1422; Neal A. Milner, "Comparative Analysis of Patterns of Compliance with Supreme Court Decisions: *Miranda* and the Police in Four Communities," *Law and Society Review,* 5 (1970), 119–134; Neal A. Milner, *The Court and Local Law Enforcement: The Political Impact of Miranda* (Beverly Hills, Calif.: Sage, 1971); Otis H. Stephens, Jr., *The Supreme Court and Confessions of Guilt* (Knoxville: University of Tennessee Press, 1973); James W. Witt, "Noncoercive Interrogation and the Administration of Criminal Justice: The Impact of Miranda on Police Effectuality," *Journal of Criminal Law,* 64 (1973), 320–332; David W. Neubauer, *Criminal Justice in Middle America* (Morristown, N.J.: Gen-

eral Learning Press, 1974), pp. 163–188; Richard W. Long, "Miranda and the Police: the Impact of the Miranda Decision in Medium Size Missouri Cities," Ph.D. dissertation, University of Missouri (Columbia), 1973. Also see Liva Baker, *Miranda: Crime, Law and Politics* (New York: Atheneum, 1983).

14. 295 U.S. 495 (1935).

15. *The Public Papers and Addresses of Franklin D. Roosevelt* (1938), Vol. 4, pp. 297–298.

16. 298 U.S. 238 (1936).

17. 301 U.S. 1 (1937).

18. 312 U.S. 100 (1941).

19. Walter F. Murphy, "Lower Court Checks on Supreme Court Power," *American Political Science Review,* 53 (1959), 1019–1020. For a study of the federal courts, see Michael W. Combs, "The Policy-Making Role of the Courts of Appeals in Northern School Desegregation: Ambiguity and Judicial Policy-Making," *Western Political Quarterly,* 35 (1982), 359–375.

20. Conference of State Chief Justices, *Report of the Committee on Federal-State Relationships as Affected by Judicial Decisions,* as reprinted in Robert Scigliano (ed.), *The Courts* (Boston: Little, Brown, 1962), p. 461.

21. See *Congressional Quarterly,* February 6, 1982, p. 211.

22. U.S. ex rel. Ross v. McMann, 409 F.2d 1016 (1969).

23. *Ibid.* at 1026.

24. 354 U.S. 449 (1957). Note that in this case the Court's ruling reversed the conviction of Mallory, a confessed rapist.

25. *New York Times,* "Court Scored by Top Judge Here: A Jurist Nixon May Name Urges Curbs on Liberal Trend," November 10, 1968, sec. 1, p. 73.

26. Note, "Evasion of Supreme Court Mandates in Cases Remanded to State Courts since 1941," *Harvard Law Review,* 67 (1954), 1251–1259.

27. Jerry K. Beatty, "State Court Evasion of United States Supreme Court Mandates during the Last Decade of the Warren Court," *Valparaiso University Law Review,* 6 (1972), 260–285. Also see Ronald Schneider, "State Court Evasion of United States Supreme Court Mandates: A Reconsideration of the Evidence," *Valparaiso University Law Review,* 7 (1973), 191–195, and Jerry Beatty's rejoinder which follows on pp. 197–200.

28. See Bradley C. Canon, "Reactions of State Supreme Courts to a U.S. Supreme Court Civil Liberties Decision," *Law and Society Review,* 8 (1973), 109–134; Donald E. Wilkes, Jr., "New Federalism in Criminal Procedure: State Court Evasion of the Burger Court," *Kentucky Law Journal,* 62 (1973–1974), 421–451; Neil T. Romans, "The Role of State Supreme Courts in Judicial Policy Making: *Escobedo, Miranda,* and the Use of Judicial Impact Analysis," *Western Political Quarterly,* 27 (1974), 38–59. Also see Stephen L. Wasby, "Communication of the Supreme Court's Criminal Procedure Decisions: A Preliminary Mapping," *Villanova Law Review,* 18 (1973), 1086–1118, for a broader view of the place of state courts in the process of transmitting the Supreme Court's criminal procedures policies down to the local law enforcement authorities; and, in general, Charles A. Johnson, "Lower Court Reactions to Supreme Court Decisions: A Quantitative Examination," *American Journal of Political Science,* 23 (1979), 792–804.

29. A classic example of this is Zorach v. Clauson, 343 U.S. 306 (1952), which limited the earlier decision in McCollum v. Board of Education, 333 U.S. 203 (1948). The issue was released time from the public schools for religious education.

30. Minersville School District v. Gobitis, 310 U.S. 586 (1940).

31. West Virginia State Board of Education v. Barnette, 319 U.S. 624 (1943).
32. As quoted in Murphy, "Lower Court Checks," p. 1027.
33. Ross v. Moffitt, 417 U.S. 600 (1974).
34. This section relies heavily on Chester A. Newland, "Legal Periodicals and the United States Supreme Court," *Midwest Journal of Political Science,* 3 (1959), 58–74. The figures for the 1982 term cited in this paragraph were derived from an analysis of the term prepared for this book.
35. *Ibid.*
36. Charles Warren, "New Light on the History of the Federal Judiciary Act of 1789," *Harvard Law Review,* 37 (1923), 49–132, as cited by Newland, "Legal Periodicals and the United States Supreme Court," p. 66, n. 11.
37. 16 Pet. 1 (1842).
38. Warren, "Federal Judiciary Act," p. 85.
39. Black and White T. & T. Co. v. Brown and Yellow T. & T. Co., 276 U.S. 518 at 535 (1928), as cited by Newland, "Legal Periodicals," p. 67, n. 15.
40. 304 U.S. 64 (1938).
41. Newland, "Legal Periodicals," p. 66.
42. For another and more extensive view of the professional critics, including those representing the American Bar Association, see Clifford M. Lytle, *The Warren Court and Its Critics* (Tucson: University of Arizona Press, 1968), pp. 94–107. Also see Johnson and Canon, *Judicial Policies: Implementation and Impact,* Chap. 2.
43. See, for example, Barbara Matusow, *The Evening Stars: The Making of the Network News Anchor* (Boston: Houghton Mifflin, 1983); Austin Ranney, *Channels of Power: The Impact of Television on American Politics* (New York: Basic Books, 1983); David Halberstam, *The Powers That Be* (New York: Knopf, 1979).
44. Escobedo v. Illinois, 378 U.S. 478 (1964); Miranda v. Arizona, 384 U.S. 436 (1966).
45. David L. Grey, *The Supreme Court and the News Media* (Evanston, Ill.: Northwestern University Press, 1968), p. 134, n. 27.
46. 370 U.S. 421 (1962). The discussion of the press and the Engel decision that follows is based on Chester A. Newland, "Press Coverage of the United States Supreme Court," *Western Political Quarterly,* 17 (1964), 15–36; and Grey, *Supreme Court.*
47. This example and those that follow are taken from Newland, "Press Coverage of the United States Supreme Court."
48. These views are given some added weight concerning an area of criminal law by the findings reported by Bradley Canon in "Reactions of State Supreme Courts to a U.S. Supreme Court Civil Liberties Decision," pp. 127–128. Canon found that northeastern state supreme courts were more positive than southern and midwestern courts in their response to the Warren Court's Mapp policy prohibiting illegally obtained evidence from being introduced in state trials, Mapp v. Ohio, 367 U.S. 643 (1961). The western state supreme courts, however, were found to be close to the northeastern courts in terms of favorable response to Mapp.
49. Grey, *Supreme Court and the News Media,* p. 87. The quotations in this paragraph are from *ibid.*
50. As reported in *New York Times,* September 11, 1983, p. 55.
51. 103 S. Ct. 3330 (1983). Justice Brennan noted in dissent: "If the Court had struck down legislative prayer today, it would likely have stimulated a furious reaction." (p. 3351).
52. 103 S. Ct. 3062 (1983).
52a. *The National Law Journal,* Sept. 10, 1984, p. 26.

53. Minersville School District v. Gobitis, 310 U.S. 586 (1940).

54. As cited in S. Sidney Ulmer, "Bricolage and Assorted Thoughts on Working in the Papers of Supreme Court Justices," *Journal of Politics,* 35 (1973), p. 296, n. 26. Note that Justices Douglas and Murphy, who had joined the majority in the Gobitis case, also changed their minds. In 1943, with the additional votes of two new appointees, a new majority overturned Gobitis in West Virginia State Board of Education v. Barnette, 319 U.S. 624 (1943).

55. Charles S. Bullock, III, "Equal Education Opportunity," in Charles S. Bullock, III, and Charles M. Lamb (eds.), *Implementation of Civil Rights Policy* (Monterey, Calif.: Brooks/Cole, 1984), p. 65.

56. *New York Times,* May 12, 1974, p. 42. Also see Harrell R. Rodgers, Jr., and Charles S. Bullock, III, *Law and Social Change: Civil Rights Laws and Their Conse-quences* (New York: McGraw-Hill, 1972), p. 95; Bullock, "Equal Education Oppor-tunity," in Bullock and Lamb (eds.) *Implementation,* p. 72.

57. *New York Times,* May 3, 1970, p. 53. In 1983 a nationwide poll taken by the National Opinion Research Center found that 76 percent of whites responded that they would allow their children to attend a school that had as much as half the student body consisting of black students. *Chicago Sun Times,* August 31, 1983, p. 3.

58. See the discussion in Rodgers and Bullock, *Law and Social Change,* Chap. 4, and their book *Racial Equality in America: In Search of an Unfulfilled Goal* (Pacific Palisades, Calif.: Goodyear, 1975), Chap. 5. Also see Gary Orfield, *Must We Bus? Segregated Schools and National Policy* (Washington, D.C.: Brookings, 1978); Mi-cheal W. Giles and Douglas S. Gatlin, "Mass Level Compliance with Public Policy: The Case of School Desegregation," *Journal of Politics,* 42 (1980), 722–746. See the studies in Bullock and Lamb (eds.), *Implementation.*

59. The following discussion is drawn from Robert H. Birkby, "The Supreme Court and the Bible Belt: Tennessee Reaction to the 'Schempp' Decision," *Midwest Journal of Political Science,* 10 (1966), 304–319.

60. School District of Abington Township v. Schempp, 374 U.S. 203 at 225 (1963). In general, for a discussion of church-state litigation, see Frank J. Sorauf, *The Wall of Separation* (Princeton, N.J.: Princeton University Press, 1976).

61. Kenneth M. Dolbeare and Phillip E. Hammond, *The School Prayer Decisions* (Chicago: University of Chicago Press, 1971).

62. Richard M. Johnson, *The Dynamics of Compliance* (Evanston, Ill.: Northwestern University Press, 1967); and William K. Muir, *Prayer in the Public Schools* (Chi-cago: University of Chicago Press, 1967). For reactions of state supreme courts, see G. Alan Tarr, *Judicial Impact and State Supreme Courts* (Lexington, Mass.: Lex-ington Books, 1977). Also, in general, see the studies in Mary Cornelia Porter and G. Alan Tarr (eds.), *State Supreme Courts: Policymakers in the Federal System* (Westport, Conn.: Greenwood, 1982).

63. In particular see Bullock and Rodgers, "Compliance to Coercion: Southern School Districts and School Desegregation Guidelines."

64. See, for example, Michael M. Ban, "Local Compliance with Mapp v. Ohio: The Power of the Supreme Court," Ph.D. dissertation, Harvard University, 1973; Brad-ley C. Canon, "Is the Exclusionary Rule in Failing Health? Some New Data and a Plea against a Precipitous Conclusion," *Kentucky Law Journal,* 62 (1973–1974), 681–730; Bradley C. Canon, "Testing the Effectiveness of Civil Liberties Policies at the State and Federal Levels: The Case of the Exclusionary Rule," *American Politics Quarterly,* 5 (1977), 57–82. Also see the citations presented earlier in note 13.

65. See Don W. Brown and Robert V. Stover, "Court Directives and Compliance: A Utility Approach," *American Politics Quarterly,* 5 (1977), 465–480; Rodgers and Bullock, *Law and Social Change;* Bullock and Rodgers, "Compliance of Southern School Officials." Also see Frederick M. Wirt, *Politics of Southern Equality: Law and Social Change in a Mississippi County* (Chicago: Aldine, 1970); and Don W. Brown, "Cognitive Development and Willingness to Comply with Law," *American Journal of Political Science,* 18 (1974), 583–594.

66. See the discussion in Brown and Stover, "Court Directives and Compliance," *ibid.*

67. Dolbeare and Hammond, *The School Prayer Decisions, ibid.* Brown and Stover stressed the number of people who must comply and the sanctions available.

68. See Muir, *Prayer in the Public Schools.* Also see Neal Steven Steinert, "The Supreme Court as an Effector of Attitude Change in Mass Publics: A Quasi-Experimental Approach," Ph.D. dissertation, Emory University, 1973; Austin Sarat, "Compliance and the Law: An Attitude Perspective," Ph.D. dissertation, University of Wisconsin (Madison), 1973, and his "Support for the Legal System: An Analysis of Knowledge, Attitudes, and Behavior," *American Politics Quarterly,* 3 (1975), 3–24; Jarol B. Manheim, *The Politics Within: A Primer in Political Attitudes and Behavior* (Englewood Cliffs, N.J.: Prentice-Hall, 1975, pp. 8, 23–24. Attitude change may be a gradual process taking decades. See the discussion in Canon, "Is the Exclusionary Rule in Failing Health?" pp. 727–729. For a more pessimistic view of the ability of law to change attitudes, see the study by Harrell R. Rodgers, Jr., and Roger Hanson, "The Rule of Law and Legal Efficacy: Private Values versus General Standards," *Western Political Quarterly,* 27 (1974), 387–394 and Larry R. Baas and Dan Thomas, "The Supreme Court and Policy Legitimation," *American Politics Quarterly*, 12 (1984), 335–360. Also see Thomas R. Hensley, *The Kent State Incident: Impact of Judicial Process on Public Attitudes* (Westport, Conn.: Greenwood Press, 1981).

69. See, in general, Robert Scigliano, *The Supreme Court and the Presidency* (New York: Free Press, 1971).

70. In general, see C. Herman Pritchett, *Congress versus the Supreme Court* (Minneapolis: University of Minnesota Press, 1961); Walter F. Murphy, *Congress and the Court* (Chicago: University of Chicago Press, 1962); Lytle, *Warren Court and Its Critics,* pp. 10–49; Lucius J. Barker and Twiley W. Barker, Jr., *Freedoms, Courts, Politics: Studies in Civil Liberties,* rev. ed. (Englewood Cliffs, N.J.: Prentice-Hall, 1972); Robert J. Steamer, *The Supreme Court in Crisis* (Amherst: University of Massachusetts Press, 1971). Also see John R. Schmidhauser and Larry L. Berg, *The Supreme Court and Congress: Conflict and Interaction, 1945–1968* (New York: Free Press, 1972).

71. Note, for example, the fate of the so-called Becker Amendment, which was aimed at overturning the Court's rulings on prayers in the public schools. See William M. Beaney and Edward N. Beiser, "Prayer and Politics: The Impact of *Engel* and *Schempp* on the Political Process," *Journal of Public Law,* 13 (1964), 475–503. Twenty years later, a similar amendment had the support of the President but met a similar fate.

72. Oregon v. Mitchell, 400 U.S. 112 (1970).

73. This was derived in part from material presented in Henry J. Abraham, *The Judicial Process,* 4th ed. (New York: Oxford University Press, 1980), pp. 305–310, and from analyses of more recent terms conducted for this book. Also consulted was Congressional Quarterly, *The Supreme Court: Justice and the Law* (Washington, D.C.:

Congressional Quarterly, 1973), pp. 113–118. Also see Edward S. Corwin, *The Constitution of the United States of America: Analysis and Interpretation* (Washington, D.C.: Government Printing Office, 1964), pp. 1387–1402. See, in general, Dean Alfange, Jr., "Congressional Power and Constitutional Limitation," *Journal of Public Law,* 18 (1969), 103–134; Jonathan D. Casper, "The Supreme Court and National Policy Making," *American Political Science Review,* 70 (1976), 50–63.

74. United States v. Nixon, 418 U.S. 683 (1974). For a journalistic account of the behind-the-scenes deliberations on the Court in this case, see Nina Totenberg, "Behind the Marble, Beneath the Robes," *New York Times Magazine,* March 16, 1975, pp. 58, 67; and Bob Woodward and Scott Armstrong, *The Brethren* (New York: Simon & Schuster, 1979), pp. 292–293, 310–347.

75. The Court in Train v. City of New York, 420 U.S. 35 (1975) ruled that funds appropriated by Congress could not be impounded by the executive branch. Although this was a blow at the Nixon Administration, it was administered after Mr. Nixon's departure and was a narrow ruling upholding Congress's constitutional legislative powers. In this respect it was similar to Youngstown Sheet and Tube Co. v. Sawyer (steel seizure case), 343 U.S. 579 (1952).

76. Lawrence Baum, *The Supreme Court* (Washington, D.C.: C.Q. Press, 1981), p. 161 and more recent analyses conducted for this book. Also see Gregory A. Caldeira and Donald J. McCrone, "Of Time and Judicial Activism: A Study of the U.S. Supreme Court, 1800–1973," in Stephen C. Halpern and Charles M. Lamb (eds.), *Supreme Court Activism and Restraint* (Lexington, Mass.: Lexington Books, Heath, 1982), pp. 103–127.

77. *Harvard Law Review,* 97 (1983), 300–302.

78. Roe v. Wade, 410 U.S. 113 (1973). In general, see Judith A. Baer, "Sexual Equality and the Burger Court," *Western Political Quarterly,* 31 (1978), 470–491; Kathleen A. Kemp, Robert A. Carp, and David W. Brady, "The Supreme Court and Social Change: The Case of Abortion," *Western Political Quarterly,* 31 (1978), 19–31; Susan B. Hansen, "State Implementation of Supreme Court Decisions: Abortion Rates Since *Roe* v. *Wade,*" *Journal of Politics,* 42 (1980), 372–395; Jon R. Bond and Charles A. Johnson, "Implementing a Permissive Policy: Hospital Abortion Services After *Roe* v. *Wade,*" *American Journal of Political Science,* 26 (1982), 1–24; Eva R. Rubin, *Abortion, Politics, and the Courts: Roe v. Wade and Its Aftermath* (Westport, Conn.: Greenwood, 1982); Barbara Milbauer and Bert N. Obrentz, *The Law Giveth: Legal Aspects of the Abortion Controversy* (New York: Atheneum, 1983).

79. See *Congressional Quarterly,* April 17, 1970, p. 1045; *New York Times,* June 7, 1970, p. 38; Milton Viorst, "Bill Douglas Has Never Stopped Fighting the Bullies of Yakima," *New York Times Magazine,* June 14, 1970, p. 52.

80. See *New York Times,* September 25, 1982, p. 9, and *Congressional Quarterly,* September 25, 1982, p. 2359.

81. In general, see Schmidhauser and Berg, *The Supreme Court and Congress.*

82. *Harvard Law Review,* 97 (1983), 302.

83. Pennsylvania v. Wheeling and Belmont Bridge Co., 13 How. 518 (1852).

84. Pennsylvania v. Wheeling and Belmont Bridge Co., 18 How. 421 (1856).

85. Note, "Congressional Reversal of Supreme Court Decisions: 1945–1957," *Harvard Law Review,* 71 (1958), 1324–1336. Also see Harry P. Stumpf, "The Political Efficacy of Judicial Symbolism," *Western Political Quarterly,* 19 (1966), pp. 299–300, Table 1. See Schmidhauser and Berg, *The Supreme Court and Congress,* pp. 142–144, 171–176; Justin J. Green, John R. Schmidhauser, and Larry L. Berg,

"Variations in Congressional Responses to the Warren and Burger Courts," *Emory Law Journal,* 23 (1974), 725–743. Beth Henschen found that 9 out of 222 Supreme Court decisions concerning labor or antitrust law were reversed by Congress between 1950 and 1972. See her "Supreme Court–Congressional Interaction in the Interpretation of Statutes," paper delivered at the annual meeting of the Midwest Political Science Association, 1980, pp. 19–35 as cited by Baum, *The Supreme Court,* pp. 199, 221.

86. 322 U.S. 533 (1944).

87. Stuart S. Nagel, *The Legal Process from a Behavioral Perspective* (Homewood, Ill.: Dorsey, 1969), pp. 260–279.

88. *Ibid.,* p. 262, Table 21-2. See the discussion of Court curbing during these periods in David Adamany, "Legitimacy, Realigning Elections, and the Supreme Court," *Wisconsin Law Review* (1973), 825–841. Also see, Richard Funston, "The Supreme Court and Critical Elections," *American Political Science Review,* 69 (1975), 795–811. But cf. Casper, "The Supreme Court and National Policy Making."

89. Thomas P. Jahnige, "Critical Elections and Social Change: Towards a Dynamic Explanation of National Party Competition in the United States," *Polity,* 3 (1971), 465–500. Also see Walter Dean Burnham, *Critical Elections and the Mainsprings of American Politics* (New York: Norton, 1970). Cf. Funston, "The Supreme Court and Critical Elections"; Bruce A. Campbell and Richard J. Trilling (eds.), *Realignment in American Politics: Toward a Theory* (Austin: University of Texas Press, 1980).

90. For a discussion of the time lag between the rise of a new political era and an agreement in judicial policy-making, see Robert A. Dahl, *Pluralist Democracy in the United States: Conflict and Consent* (Skokie, Ill.: Rand McNally, 1967), pp. 154–170. Cf. Casper, "The Supreme Court and National Policy Making," and Funston, "The Supreme Court and Critical Elections."

91. Also see Adamany, "Legitimacy, Realigning Elections and the Supreme Court," pp. 841–846. Cf. Funston, "The Supreme Court and Critical Elections."

92. *New York Times,* April 19, 1970, p. 58. A 1974 Gallup poll reported 38 percent of the national sample consider themselves "conservative," 26 percent consider themselves "liberal," and 36 percent were undecided. *Current Opinion,* 2 (June 1974), 61. A 1980 Gallup poll found 32 percent identifying themselves as "right of center," 19 percent as "left of center," and 49 percent as "middle of the road." *The Gallup Poll Index,* December 1980, Report No. 183, p. 2. A 1982 Gallup survey found 47 percent identifying themselves as "right of center" compared to 32 percent seeing themselves "left of center." Ten percent said they were *at* the "center" and 11 percent could not respond. *The Gallup Report,* September 1982, Report No. 204, p. 18. A 1984 poll conducted by the *New York Times* and CBS News found that 30 percent of the national sample classified themselves as "conservative" and 19 percent as "liberal" (46 percent said they were "moderate"). See *New York Times,* January 29, 1984, p. 16.

93. See *Current Opinion,* 1 (September 1973), 91.

94. See the surveys cited and discussed in Herbert McClosky and Alida Brill, *Dimensions of Tolerance: What Americans Believe About Civil Liberties* (New York: Russell Sage Foundation, 1983), particularly in Chap. 4. Note especially the 1980 survey cited on p. 153 in which 63 percent of those surveyed agreed with the statement "the *rulings* of the Supreme Court in recent years have given *too much* consideration to the rights of people suspected of crimes." Only 26 percent disagreed.

95. Philip E. Converse, Warren E. Miller, Jerrold G. Rusk, and Arthur C. Wolfe,

"Continuity and Change in American Politics: Parties and Issues in the 1968 Election," *American Political Science Review,* 63 (1969), 1103.

96. That the Burger Court was indeed adjusting its output in certain policy areas in response to negative feedback was explicitly recognized by Justice Marshall in his dissent in the Detroit school busing case when he observed: "Today's holding, I fear, is more a reflection of a perceived public mood that we have gone far enough in enforcing the Constitution's guarantee of equal justice than it is the product of neutral principles of law." Milliken v. Bradley 418 U.S. 717 (1974) at 814. In another instance Justice Stewart in a dissent charged the majority with "A basic change in law upon a ground no firmer than a change in our membership. . . ." Mitchell v. W. T. Grant Company 416 U.S. 600 (1974) at 636.

97. See Beverly B. Cook, "Public Opinion and Federal Judicial Policy," *American Journal of Political Science,* 21 (1977), 567–600. Also see, in general, Herbert M. Kritzer, "Political Correlates of the Behavior of Federal District Judges: A 'Best Case' Analysis," *Journal of Politics,* 40 (1978), 25–58.

98. See G. Gregory Fahlund, "Feedback in the Judicial Process: The Warren Court and Criminal Procedure," Ph.D. dissertation, University of Massachusetts, 1971; and his "Retroactivity and the Warren Court: The Strategy of a Revolution," *Journal of Politics,* 35 (1973), 570–593.

chapter 8

Epilogue

The objective of the previous seven chapters has been to illuminate the workings of the federal judicial system, and the focus has been descriptive, not prescriptive. Volumes can, have been, and will continue to be written about reforming different facets of court systems. The state court systems seem to bear the burden of much of the criticism, but the federal courts also have had their share of close attention.

In this epilogue, brief mention of some of the problem areas within the federal judicial system is offered. This is followed by a consideration of the limits and potential of the systems framework as a tool for the analysis of the federal courts.

SOME PROBLEM AREAS IN THE FEDERAL JUDICIAL SYSTEM

The selection and tenure of the key authorities within the federal judicial system is a subject of continuing interest and debate. "Merit" selection of judges by judicial selection commissions is advocated by the organized bar, and the goal is to remove "political" considerations as the primary factor in the selection process. So, too, with U.S. attorneys, whose positions and whose tenure are more openly partisan. For reasons suggested in Chapter 3, removal of partisan considerations in the selection process is unlikely to occur. Far more serious a problem area is that of the removal from office of judges who are corrupt, who are seen as abusing their office as demonstrated by an obvious lack of judicial temperament on the bench, or who might be suffering from the early stages of senility (Alzheimer's disease).[1] Federal judges with lifetime tenure are extraordinarily secure in their posts. Judicial disciplinary and removal proposals have faced hurdles not the least of which is a great reluctance to tamper with lifetime tenure of the federal judiciary, which is seen as a guarantor of judicial independence.

The issue of legal counsel and access to justice is one concerning the quality of legal representation available not only to poor people but also to the middle class. Problems in this area for the poor include inadequate resources available to assigned counsel or the public defender in criminal trials as well as the problem of lawyer competency. In civil cases, the poor must rely on the legal services program that itself has been under political attack by the Reagan Administration and subject to numerous constraints.[2] The middle class, particularly those at the lower end, face financial hurdles in going to court and availing themselves of legal counsel. However, the fact that there are large numbers of lawyers in private practice who compete for business and whose fees are competitive (some lawyers advertise offering low costs for routine services such as drafting of simple wills, title searches, simple divorce proceedings where no children are involved, and even some defense trial work) has meant that the middle class has somewhat greater access than before lawyers were able to advertise and offer price competition. Also the activities of interest groups in sponsoring litigation has meant that certain classes of persons can have their rights adjudicated without having to foot the bill.[3]

The jury system has frequently come under attack. It has been accused of being an anachronism and irrelevant for the overwhelmingly large proportion of cases resolved without trial. In both civil and criminal cases, it has been argued that laypersons lack the technical competence with which to understand the issues in many cases and/or may be unduly swayed by the charismatic qualities of certain lawyers. The Supreme Court has permitted juries with less than 12 persons and juries that have up to 3 dissenters, thus allowing nonunanimous jury verdicts to be returned.[4] This has raised a host of troublesome questions. The grand jury and its uses and possible abuses by overzealous prosecutors is considered another facet of this problem area.

The systems concept of demand input overload is very relevant as a problem area in the federal judicial system. As will be recalled from Chapter 4, overload on the system occurs when there are too many demands that take an excessive amount of time to process or merely too many demands to be able to be efficiently accommodated. Delay in court and court congestion are the result. There has been interest in what types of demands consume an "excessive" amount of time to process and why.[5] For example, to what extent (if at all) are Supreme Court decisions in various legal areas such as criminal procedures related to demand overload? Have Court decisions, in fact, greatly increased the amount of time that both trial and appellate courts spend on such cases? What can be done to reduce the volume of demands made on the federal courts?

Along these lines, it might be recalled from Chapter 4 that proposed reforms include removal of diversity jurisdiction from the federal courts. The Supreme Court itself, as we have seen earlier, has moved to limit federal court supervision over the state courts in certain areas of criminal procedure. In June, 1983, the Court appeared to be taking a further step by penalizing what the majority considered a frivolous appeal.[6] Some have suggested that the "delay in court" phenomenon itself is a systemic mechanism for frustrating the presentation of certain kinds of "frivolous" demands. Elimination of "victimless" crimes from the court system has also been advocated as a way to reduce the volume of cases in the system.

Systems analysis suggests that demand input overload can be affected not only by changes in jurisdiction and justiciability, but also by changes in certain regime rules such as discovery rules, negotiated guilty pleas in criminal cases, and pretrial conferences. The Supreme Court in recent years has revised the Federal Rules of Civil and Criminal Procedure in these realms to enable these processes to work better in the processing of demands.[7]

The criminal justice system has numerous troublesome areas that have been widely recognized.[8] There has been some concern with the definition of crime, particularly when there are no readily identifiable "victims," such as drug possession, use, or transactions, or prostitution. Aside from the issue of clogging the criminal justice component of court systems, it has been argued that "victimless" crimes are a result of a majority imposing its values on a minority with opposing life-styles and values. Class differences within the criminal justice system also crop up with the handling and disposition of "white-collar" crimes and criminals. Once cases have entered the system, the issue of bail looms large as an area of controversy. There is a serious problem of poor people accused of crime who cannot afford to pay the bail bond premium and therefore must remain imprisoned—although legally innocent—until trial. An alternative to money bail is release on one's own recognizance, which means that the suspect is released on his or her pledge to appear for the trial. However, a careful screening process is part of this method for pretrial release, and many suspects are denied such release, particularly when the crime of which they are accused is a serious one. This, of course raises a very troublesome issue of what to do about the suspect who, on the basis of past behavior, the judge has good reason to believe is dangerous and will commit crimes if released. This is the issue of preventive detention, which is simply the refusal to set bail or otherwise release the suspect so that the accused remains incarcerated until trial. Opponents of preventive detention argue that the accused is legally innocent until proven guilty and that preventive detention is therefore an unconstitutional punishment of a legally innocent person for actions that *might* be committed if the suspect were released.[9]

There have been other problem areas with criminal justice, including police practices in the gathering of evidence. One issue has been what to do about evidence inadvertently obtained in violation of the Fourth Amendment (the so-called good faith exception to the exclusionary rule). The Supreme Court finally confronted this issue and in 1984 ruled that evidence secured by use of a defective search warrant issued in "good faith" *is* admissible in a court of law.[10] In so doing, the Court implied that it was demoting the exclusionary rule from being an integral part of the Fourth Amendment to being a helpful judicially constructed rule that is not necessarily the only option available for judges to enforce that constitutional guarantee.

Interpretation of the *Miranda* rules also continues to be a source of controversy in terms of the admissibility of incriminating statements or confessions and the Supreme Court enlarged the controversy by creating a public safety exception to *Miranda* in a case decided in June of 1984. Once trial has been held and a conviction obtained or a plea bargain arranged, the problem area of sentencing emerges. Questions of sentencing disparity among judges and by the same judges were raised and discussed in Chapter 5 and pointed up the contours of this problem area. The issues of sentencing review councils, fixed versus indeterminate sentences, and creative alternatives to incarceration have all emerged in recent years. The unique sentence of death has provided a continuing source of controversy, particularly as the Supreme Court has removed obstacles to the imposition of the death penalty.[11] Prison reform, prisoners' rights, and the use and abuse of parole have also been topics of public discussion.[12]

Some have begun to see problems resulting from technological advances being applied to the court system. Advanced technology in the communication industry makes it feasible for there to be relatively unobtrusive video-recording of confessions as well as trials.[13] The Court ruled that television coverage of trials is not unconstitutional,[14] and in 1980 formulated a First Amendment right of access of the print media as well as the public to trial proceedings—a ruling reinforced by a 1984 decision.[15] But this right is not absolute, and we can expect a continuing tension between the rights of the media and the rights of the accused. Other issues relate to the computerization of court records and the exchange of information nationally within the federal court system and between the federal court system and state court systems. The issues are not so much that of efficiency in data processing, record keeping, or even the exchange of information, but rather the verification of the information that is exchanged, the way it will be used, how it will influence the decision making of the authorities, and the opportunities for the defendant or respondent to have access to this information and have the opportunity to refute it before adverse decisions are made. If arrest records along with conviction records are exchanged, that too creates difficulties because information about arrests that do not result in convictions can nevertheless have prejudicial effects on how law enforcement, prosecutorial, and judicial authorities treat the accused. Technological advances also raise such problems as whether a valid search and seizure can include the installation of hidden cameras and listening devices in the suspect's home (one judge threw out evidence gathered against a terrorist group making bombs because such evidence gathering smacked of Orwellian *1984* tactics and exceeded the scope of permissible searches and seizures[16]).

Mention should be made of the recent and continuing debate over the role of the federal courts in fashioning remedies following findings of constitutional violations. Judicial system critics have found fault with the broad rulings of some lower court judges and the Supreme Court itself, and have accused the courts of exceeding their competence and their capacity to formulate public policy.[17] Judicial decisions concerning school desegregation, affirmative action, religion in the public schools, abortion, and prisoners' rights, among others, have triggered some intense negative feedback, as we noted in Chapter 7. There is a fundamental tension between a notion of the accountability of federal judges with lifetime tenure to the wishes of the majority (or a vocal minority?) and the concept of judicial independence. In the face of evidence, such as that discussed in Chapter 5, that judges have ample opportunity to and consequently do make policy choices, it is difficult to defend controversial judicial decisions simply as the objective application of straightforward legal scientific principles that determine *the law*. But the flip side of this problem area is that presidents have the opportunity (and take advantage of it) to name their kind of people to the federal bench. The evidence is persuasive, as we saw in Chapter 3, that President Reagan for example, has done precisely that.

Other problem areas in the federal judicial system can be identified, but the preceding discussion is not meant to be exhaustive. It should be pointed out, however, that while systems analysis can help us identify some of the problem areas in the workings of systems, the systems perspective is not focused on identifying them and the mode of inquiry is not prescriptive. This leads us to our final topic of consideration, an assessment of systems analysis in terms of its limitations as well as its strengths.

ASSESSMENT OF SYSTEMS ANALYSIS

There are obvious difficulties with political systems analysis as formulated by David Easton. Perhaps most obvious is its essential ambivalence: Is it sets of hypotheses awaiting empirical testing, or is it really a theory grounded on empirical findings? The answer is simply that it is both. Political systems analysis was suggested by numerous empirical studies and thus can be considered descriptive of political reality. Its concepts then serve as organizing concepts. Yet these concepts, within the context of the analytical framework built with them, suggest a wide variety of hypotheses concerning interactions within the system and various systemic mechanisms and processes. However, these hypotheses have been generally, rather than narrowly, formulated.

To be sure, this has left some scholars dissatisfied with systems analysis. As one critic has warned, "Any putative theoretical effort which cannot achieve, to an appreciable extent, the requisite semantic and syntactic precision can remain substantially insulated against empirical test and is consequently devoid, in large part, of explanatory significance."[18] It would appear that the desired semantic precision is lacking with such concepts as "input," "demand," "support," "within-input," "gatekeeping," "output," "feedback," and so forth. However, Eastonian analysis does not preclude the formulation of operational criteria and their concrete application to specific sets of empirical data. Indeed, in previous chapters some possible criteria have been suggested. Nevertheless, this is no substitute for major empirical undertakings, that develop the criteria and test the utility of the concepts.

Another major limitation to the use of political systems analysis is that description is emphasized to the exclusion of prescription. The emphasis is on what *is,* and there is a danger that systems analysis can be used to defend or maintain the status quo. Systems analysis does not facilitate the fundamental questioning of the basic operating premises of the system. Thus, under the guise of empirical theory, systems analysis can potentially, if inadvertently, assume a politically conservative posture. Yet systems analysis is not necessarily incompatible with normative consideration of systemic processes and output. Systems analysts simply try to distinguish between norms (what should be) and facts (what is). Perhaps the best way for the systems analyst to avoid the problem is to explicitly articulate policy preferences and the norms (whatever they may be) against which the system is evaluated. Proposals for reform or fundamental restructuring would then be not simply in the realm of making the system more efficient (which, of course, implicitly reflects a conservative value), but rather shaping the system so that it can better accomplish those ends and produce those outputs that the analyst thinks it should.

How, then, can one assess, on balance, the current and prospective utility of the judicial systems approach? Perhaps the key to such an assessment lies with the criteria suggested by Karl Deutsch for the evaluation of a mode of analysis (or model), that is, the degree to which the model carries out four distinctive functions: the organizing, the heuristic, the predictive, and the mensurative.[19]

The *organizing* function concerns the ability of the model to order and relate disjointed data (and the analyses based on them) into an integrated and meaningful whole. If it is serving this function well, the model should indicate and illuminate heretofore unperceived interconnections and similarities. To a large degree, the evaluation of whether this function is being served or not rests upon the aesthetic experience of the observer. If what was originally murky and disjointed becomes meaningful, clear, and intuitively more simple, then the model is fulfilling the organizing function. Parenthetically, it might be noted that an explanation may be extremely satisfying without making any sort of quantitative predictions. The theory of evolution, for example, seems to be such an explanation.

The *heuristic* function concerns the ability of the model to raise new questions, suggest new relationships, or lead to previously unobserved or unanalyzed data through new lines of empirical research. For example, the theory of evolution both directed its adherents to look for various "missing links" and allowed them to structure previously mysterious and unexplained fossils into a satisfying explanation.

The *predictive* function involves the production of verifiable predictions. As Deutsch noted, there is broad range in the explicitness of the predictions that may be made:

> At one extreme we find simple yes-or-no predictions; at higher degrees of specificity we get qualitative predictions of similarity or matching, where the result is predicted to be of this kind or of that kind, or of this particular delicate shade; and at the other extreme we find completely quantitative predictions that may give us elaborate time series that may answer the questions of "When?" and "How Much?"[20]

When it implies the latter modes of prediction, a model then serves the *mensurative* function. The measurement in which it deals may vary "all the way from simple rank orderings to full-fledged ratio scales."[21]

Although Deutsch noted that they are "distinct," the organizing, heuristic, predictive, and mensurative functions are not unrelated to one another. Rather, they stand in a loose hierarchical arrangement. Thus a model must first present some satisfying organization and explanation for known data before it can make predictions, even if these predictions are only heuristic in nature. As one moves up the hierarchy, the successful fulfillment of each function becomes increasingly difficult. This characteristic of the functional criteria implies that in testing the adequacy of the model against them one gets a relative measure for evaluating the model's power and utility. One should note that the model need not satisfy the more difficult criteria—in particular, prediction and measurement—in order to be judged valuable.

In assessing whether judicial systems analysis has organizational utility, one's judgment must be relative. This necessitates our brief examination of three other frameworks whose scope is sufficiently general as to be competitors to the judicial systems approach. These are (1) the approach offered by traditional jurisprudence; (2) the "bureaucratic" approach;[22] and (3) the "political" or "conventional" approach, which likens court behavior to the behavior of other political institutions, such as Congress or political parties.[23]

It hardly seems necessary to elaborate the reasons why the traditional approach is unacceptable. Although it may well serve as an important delineation of the norms to which judicial system authorities strive to adhere, the model does not adequately explain existing empirical data. A major contribution of legal realism, the sociology of law, and judicial behavior has been to show how great the deviation is between the real behavior of courtroom actors and that posited by the traditional model. Moreover, as an explanation, the traditional model simply cannot explain such crucial events as the "switch" in judicial policy during the Supreme Court's 1936 term[24] or the Burger Court's marked changes of direction, particularly in the criminal procedures area. The killing blow, as Chapter 5 suggested, has been the quantitative work that shows better prediction of judicial behavior than does the traditional model.[25] Thus, although it has important implications for system behavior as a normative injunction, the traditional model cannot be considered an explanatory model. It suggests an extensiveness of activity that does not exist; it leaves untreated and unexplored too much activity; it makes predictions that simply are not borne out in the empirical world.

The bureaucratic model, whose most concise and clear formulation is still that by Max Weber, although more comprehensive in scope than the traditional model, has the disability of leaving untreated and/or unexplained (particularly appellate) court behavior in which creative policy-making rather than more simple conflict resolution through rule application predominates. Like the traditional model, it also leaves unanalyzed activity external to the system that affects its output—activity that, in systems terms, is subsumed under the categories of "support" and "feedback." Thus the bureaucratic model is at best incomplete in scope. It is still, however, highly suggestive. In its post-Weberian form,[26] it has much to offer both conceptually and as a guide to research. Its functional content makes it easily absorbed into a systems approach.

The "political" or "conventional" model is to some extent the mirror image of the bureaucratic model. Its strength lies in its treatment of those areas of behavior where the bureaucratic model is weakest. Conversely, it is weakest in those areas where the bureaucratic model is strongest. Of all the models discussed, it shows the least formalization. To call the courts—like Congress and the presidency—"political" institutions does not take us very far. When a more precise operational content is given the term "political," it seems either too general or too specific. Thus, for example, if by "political" one means Easton's definition of politics as the authoritative allocation of values, then courts are obviously political. But one is then left with the problem of differentiating judicial processes and the processes characteristic of Congress and the presidency. If, on the other hand, one reads into the term "politics" the drive for power, partisan self-interest, and constituent sensitivity normally imputed to more popularly recruited political leaders, much judicial behavior seems unexplained and unexplainable. Thus, the political model suffers from a lack of semantic precision and the almost complete absence of formalization. Finally, there is an obvious neglect in the model toward a phenomenon whose discussion permeates both the traditional and bureaucratic models, that is, the ability of normative considerations as independent variables to affect judicial role playing.

When one turns to the systems model, one finds at least partial elimination of some of the disabilities affecting the other models. Of all the models discussed, systems analysis can integrate and order the broadest range of what intuitively seems to be the significant data. This very comprehensiveness of the approach is one of its most striking merits. It can order and integrate phenomena treated by both the bureaucratic and political models. It can "make sense" out of the normative considerations involved in traditional jurisprudence. At the very minimum, then, judicial systems analysis has greater organizational power than does its competitors. It appears to have the ability to produce greater clarity and to satisfyingly integrate the many, otherwise disjointed, materials found in legal and judicial studies.

The heuristic value of the judicial systems framework—its ability to suggest new lines of judicial system research and its potential for reinterpreting data already collected in previous studies—is, we believe, a striking merit of the approach.

Our assessment is radically and discouragingly different when we turn to the ability of systems analysis to serve the more formally demanding functions of prediction and measurement. The predictive statements found in systems analysis as distinct from its descriptive statements characteristically maintain that systemic processes tend toward certain states: For example, a system strives to prevent "demand overload," maintain a positive input of support, preserve systemic integrity, and so on. These statements, however, and the processes suggested by them are presented in metaphorical rather than linguistically or mathematically precise language. Simply put, the various concepts of systems analysis as presently given in the Eastonian literature are not defined or linked to one another by a calculus (language) having terminological invariance. It is as if one created a physics that stated that mass/energy, angular and linear momentum, electrical charge, and so on were conserved without having a calculus or set of operational definitions for measuring, identifying, or linking the empirical phenomena signaled by the terms mass, energy, momentum, charge, or conserve. Without such a set of operational procedures for identifying phenomena and an invariant calculus linking them, it is difficult to test the correspondence between the putative theory and the empirical world. In short, systems analysis does not, in its present state, make hard, quantitatively testable predictions.

Judicial systems analysis offers researchers a comprehensive set of categories for organizing and relating data, an impressive number of important heuristic insights, and the ability to handle microcosmic studies displaying predictability. However promising this may be, systems analysis has not yielded a theory of judicial system behavior. For it to do so will require the development of operational definitions for precise identification and measurement of systemic parameters and a formalized calculus for relating these parameters to one another. That such precision is possible is suggested in particular by the mathematically sophisticated judicial conversion literature. Nevertheless, systems analysis, in spite of some severe shortcomings, provides a major analytical tool for students of judicial politics. It is widely used and accepted[27] and has and should continue to provide solid analytical payoffs.

NOTES

1. See Joseph C. Goulden, *The Benchwarmers* (New York: Weybright and Talley, 1974) for numerous examples. Sometimes a judge's cantankerousness will become the basis for newspaper stories. For example, Federal District Judge Willis W. Ritter's antics were reported, including his having ordered court officers to arrest plumbers who were making noise while making necessary repairs near his courtroom. See *New York Times,* October 13, 1977, p. A18, and *New York Times,* March 6, 1978, p. D7. Recently Federal District Judge Alcee L. Hastings was tried and acquitted on bribery-related charges, but judicial disciplinary proceedings, challenged by Judge Hastings, continued. See *The National Law Journal,* January 16, 1984, p. 3. Another federal district judge, Harry E. Claiborne, was indicted and tried on bribery and related charges. He was eventually convicted on some of the charges. See the *New York Times,* August 11, 1984, p. 1. Both judges claimed that their prosecutions were politically inspired—which raises still other complexities in this problem area.
2. Recall the discussion of the legal services program in Chapter Three.
3. See, for example, Clement E. Vose, *Caucasions Only* (Berkeley: University of California Press, 1959); Karen O'Connor, *Women's Organizations' Use of the Courts* (Lexington, Mass.: Lexington Books, 1980); and Karen O'Connor and Lee Epstein, "The Rise of Conservative Interest Group Litigation," *Journal of Politics,* 45 (1983), 479–489.
4. The cases are Williams v. Florida, 399 U.S. 78 (1970) (permitting six-person juries) and Johnson v. Louisiana, 406 U.S. 356 (1972) (permitting nonunanimous jury verdicts with up to three jurors in the minority). Recall the discussion of juries in Chapter Three.
5. See, for example, Paul D. Carrington, "Crowded Dockets and the Courts of Appeals: The Threat to the Function of Review and the National Law," *Harvard Law Review,* 82 (1969), 542–617; Gerhard Casper and Richard A. Posner, "A Study of the Supreme Court's Caseload," *Journal of Legal Studies,* 3 (1974), 339–375; Daniel J. Meador, *Appellate Courts: Staff and Process in the Crisis of Volume* (St. Paul, Minn.:

West, 1974); and William P. McLauchlan, *Federal Court Caseloads* (New York: Praeger, 1984). Also see, in general, Malcolm M. Feeley, *The Process Is the Punishment: Handling Cases in a Lower Criminal Court* (New York: Russell Sage Foundation, 1979). Excessive volume stress does not necessarily mean that the United States is more litigious than ever before or in comparison with other countries. See Marc Galanter, "Reading the Landscape of Disputes: What We Know and Don't Know (and Think We Know) about Our Allegedly Contentious and Litigious Society," *UCLA Law Review,* 31 (1983), 4–71.

6. *New York Times,* June 14, 1983, p. 1. The case was Tatum v. Regents of the University of Nebraska—Lincoln, 103 S. Ct. 3084 (1983).

7. In particular, see the Amendments to the Federal Rules of Civil Procedure, 103 S. Ct. June 15, 1983. The Federal Rules of Criminal Procedure as of this writing are in the process of still further revision. See *The National Law Journal,* February 13, 1984, p. 3.

8. See, for example, James Q. Wilson, *Thinking About Crime* (New York: Basic Books, 1975); Charles E. Silberman, *Criminal Violence, Criminal Justice* (New York: Random House, 1978); Malcolm M. Feeley, *Court Reform on Trial: Why Simple Solutions Fail* (New York: Basic Books, 1983); Herbert Jacob, *The Frustration of Policy: Responses to Crime by American Cities* (Boston: Little, Brown, 1984); Stuart A. Scheingold, *The Politics of Law and Order: Street Crime and Public Policy* (New York: Longman, 1984). Cf. Jonathan D. Casper and David Brereton, "Evaluating Criminal Justice Reforms," *Law and Society Review,* 18 (1984), 121–144.

9. See, for example, Ronald L. Goldfarb, *Ransom: A Critique of the American Bail System* (New York: Harper & Row, 1965); Wayne H. Thomas, Jr., *Bail Reform in America* (Berkeley: University of California Press, 1976); John S. Goldkamp, *Two Classes of Accused: A Study of Bail and Detention in America* (Cambridge, Mass.: Ballinger, 1979); and Roy B. Flemming, *Punishment Before Trial* (New York: Longman, 1982). Note that in 1984 Congress enacted preventive detention legislation as part of a package of anticrime measures. See *Congressional Quarterly,* October 20, 1984, pp. 2752–2758, and *New York Times,* October 15, 1984, p. 1.

10. The cases are Massachusetts v. Sheppard, 104 S. Ct. 3424 (1984) and United States v. Leon, 104 S. Ct. 3405 (1984). In yet another important exclusionary rule case, decided during the spring of 1984, the Court ruled that evidence illegally obtained is nevertheless admissible at the trial if it would have been discovered inevitably without any constitutional or statutory violation. This inevitable discovery exception to the exclusionary rule was announced in Nix v. Williams, 104 S. Ct. 2501 (1984). The Court also ruled in Hudson v. Palmer, 104 S. Ct. 3194 (1984) that the Fourth Amendment "does not apply within the confines of a prison cell." This means that a prison inmate is not protected from the search, seizure, and destruction of personal property including family photographs, letters, and other personal belongings.

11. See, for example, Pulley v. Harris, 104 S. Ct. 871 (1984). Cf. William J. Bowers, Glenn L. Pierce, and John F. McDevitt, *Legal Homicide: Death as Punishment in America, 1864–1982* (Boston: Northeastern University Press, 1983).

12. In general, see the discussion in George F. Cole, *The American System of Criminal Justice,* 3rd ed. (Monterey, Calif.: Brooks/Cole, 1983), Chaps. 14–16; and James B. Jacobs, *New Perspectives on Prisons and Imprisonment* (Ithaca, N.Y.: Cornell University Press, 1983). Also see Ronald L. Goldfarb and Linda R. Singer, *After Conviction* (New York: Simon & Schuster, 1973).

13. In New York City, confessions have been videotaped since the mid- to late-1970s and

have been completely successful in securing trial convictions or plea bargains. The Bronx district attorney was quoted as observing that videotaped confessions made "obsolete" the defense that the confession was coerced. *New York Times*, June 5, 1983, p. 30.

14. Chandler v. Florida, 449 U.S. 560 (1981).

15. See Richmond Newspapers, Inc. v. Virginia, 488 U.S. 555 (1980) and Press Enterprise Co. v. Superior Court of California, Riverside County, 104 S. Ct. 819 (1984).

16. See *New York Times,* January 29, 1984, p. 22.

17. See, for example, Gary L. McDowell, *Equity and the Constitution* (Chicago: University of Chicago Press, 1982). Also see Jeremy A. Rabkin, *Forcing the Enforcers: Judicial Activism and the Politics of Regulatory Enforcement.* Ph.D. dissertation, Harvard University, 1982 and his "The Judiciary in the Administrative State," *The Public Interest,* 71 (1983), 62–84. And see, Richard E. Morgan, *Disabling America: The "Rights Industry" in Our Time* (New York; Basic Books, 1984). Cf. Ralph Cavanaugh and Austin Sarat, "Thinking About Courts: Toward and Beyond a Jurisprudence of Judicial Competence," *Law and Society Review,* 14 (1980), 372–420.

18. A. James Gregor, "Political Science and the Uses of Functional Analysis," *American Political Science Review,* 62 (1968), 462. For another critique, see J. S. Sorzano, "David Easton and the Invisible Hand," *American Political Science Review,* 69 (1975), 91–106. Cf. Edward N. Muller, Thomas O. Jackam, and Mitchell A. Seligson, "Diffuse Political Support and Antisystem Political Behavior: A Comparative Analysis," *American Journal of Political Science,* 26 (1982), 240–263.

19. Karl Deutsch, *The Nerves of Government* (New York: Free Press, 1963), pp. 8–10.

20. *Ibid.,* p. 9.

21. *Ibid.*

22. The original and still one of the best articulations of this approach is to be found in Max Weber, *The Theory of Social and Economic Organization* (New York: Free Press, 1964), pp. 329–341. Modern students of court behavior who have used various components of this model include Frank J. Sorauf, "*Zorach* v. *Clauson:* The Impact of a Supreme Court Decision," *American Political Science Review,* 53 (1959), 777–791; Martin Shapiro, *The Supreme Court and Administrative Agencies* (New York: Free Press, 1968); James Eisenstein and Herbert Jacob, *Felony Justice: An Organizational Analysis of Criminal Courts* (Boston: Little, Brown, 1977).

23. The classic of this genre is Jack W. Peltason, *Federal Courts in the Political Process* (New York: Random House, 1955).

24. Cf. Felix Frankfurter, "Mr. Justice Roberts," *University of Pennsylvania Law Review,* 104 (1955), 313–316.

25. Also see S. Sidney Ulmer, "Mathematical Models for Predicting Judicial Behavior," in Joseph L. Bernd and Archer Jones (eds.), *Mathematical Applications in Political Science, III* (Charlottesville: University of Virginia Press, 1967), pp. 67–95; and Fred Kort, *A Special and a General Multivariate Theory of Judicial Decisions,* Sage Professional Papers in American Politics (Beverly Hills, Calif.: Sage, 1977).

26. Weber emphasized formal considerations—rules, norms, and authority patterns—almost exclusively. Later students of bureaucracy, among them Peter Blau and Robert K. Merton, built on Weber's work, particularly in their emphasis on informal organization and the dysfunctional aspects of formal rules and authority relationships.

27. Glendon Schubert correctly predicted in 1968 that "tomorrow systems analysis will be the conventional mode of discourse in the field." See his "Behavioral Jurisprudence," *Law and Society Review,* 2 (1968), 426.

Index

WITHDRAWN FROM
JUNIATA COLLEGE LIBRARY